FOUR MODERN PHILOSOPHERS

FOUR MODERN PHILOSOPHERS

CARNAP
WITTGENSTEIN
HEIDEGGER
SARTRE

ARNE NAESS

Translated by Alastair Hannay

PHOENIX BOOKS
THE UNIVERSITY OF CHICAGO PRESS
CHICAGO & LONDON

Translated from the Norwegian Moderne filosofer
© *1965 by Arne Naess. Published by Almqvist & Wiksell/Gebers
Förlag AB, Stockholm, Sweden*

Library of Congress Catalog Card Number: 68-14011

THE UNIVERSITY OF CHICAGO PRESS
CHICAGO 60637
THE UNIVERSITY OF CHICAGO PRESS, LTD.
LONDON W.C. I

Introduction

This book is intended as an introduction to the basic viewpoints of four outstanding contemporary philosophers. Each has been singled out as a main contributor to the intellectual life of our time, and their collective influence will be recorded in future histories of philosophy. Yet, although historians of ideas will set the names of these four very different thinkers side by side, it is unlikely that professional philosophers themselves will view their work as a collective *philosophical* achievement. This fact reflects something in the nature of philosophy and philosophizing which deserves comment in itself and also explains an underlying purpose of this introductory work.

To stand apart from philosophy, to look at it from a distance, through literature, theology, or the history of contemporary culture, is to see primarily discord and disunity. The picture of philosophical activity that filters through is one of division and faction; from this perspective philosophy appears mainly as a collection of schools and movements. But as a picture of philosophical *activity* this is certainly misleading. It is true that philosophy derives its sense of purpose and direction from many sources, and that its diversity naturally gives rise to differences in viewpoint and opinion. Yet very little of a philosopher's time is devoted to these differences. Indeed talk of schools and movements scarcely plays any part at all in the active discussion of specific philosophical problems. If philosophical polemics are a topic of the philosopher's conversation, they are not part of his day's business.

Nevertheless, the working philosopher's perspective, too, tends to be distorted. He often seems to identify the aims and procedures of philosophy with those that he himself adopts. There would be nothing wrong in this if he did so consciously and rationally. But in ignoring the controversies he loses sight of the differences; and in losing sight of the differences he is denied the opportunity to understand other ways of thinking. Thus he is led to believe without sufficient justification that there are no other ways of thinking, or at least none of any value.

Narrowness and bias are perhaps necessary ingredients in all productive activity; in philosophy, too, they may have their merits. Indeed, one would suppose that, at least in the short run, their effect upon a philosophical environment is generally stimulating. A framework that is taken as self-evident and absolute fosters confidence, and the clarity it brings to the issues offers a strong inducement to positive achievement. By any standards the result is often outstanding work, and far from narrowing the field of potential contributions, bias probably helps to consolidate and enrich the various traditions —perhaps even to generate them, since if the issues were less circumscribed or the methods adopted more self-consciously, the different traditions might never have taken root at all.

Despite these advantages, however, it is doubtful whether progress in philosophy is ever the product of a one-sided acceptance of prevailing ideas. Great thinkers—Kierkegaard, for example—have retained a sense of direction and purpose even when they have been acutely conscious of the questionableness of all accepted methods; and the same applies within typically eclectic settings where opposing philosophical positions are all duly noted and their respective merits acknowledged. Even when he is strongly influenced by his background, a philosopher's positive contributions—as in the case of Karl Popper—often reflect his own originality rather than his allegiance to a particular school.

An unfortunate effect of the creation of schools or movements in philosophy is the restriction they bring to philosophical education. A glance at the textbooks and historical surveys published within a school's sphere of influence often reveals a very narrow and biased conception of "present-day philosophy." In one, for example, we read: "If one takes a look at the philosophical scene today, it bears decisively if not exclusively the stamp of Wittgenstein's philosophy."[1] But the philosophical horizon stretches far beyond the scene as it appears to those enraptured by the "syncopated pipings of Herr Wittgenstein's flute."[2] And in another, entitled *The Revolution in Philosophy*, though lacking a subtitle referring to its special interest in what, from a broad view, are local trends, we read that "the philosophy of the twentieth century is very largely the history of the notion of sense or meaning."[3] The notions referred to derive from Frege and Bradley, and even though the context is later explicitly narrowed to the English-speaking world, the survey still cannot be said to cover more than the most influential trends;[4] and perhaps 'influence' is a concept best left to the historians.

English-speaking philosophers, for their part, are totally ignored in Ludwig Landgrebe's *Philosophie der Gegenwart*, as

---

[1] Justus Hartnack, *Wittgenstein and Modern Philosophy*, translated by M. Cranston (London: Methuen and Co., 1965), p. 112.
[2] C. D. Broad, *The Mind and its Place in Nature* (London: Routledge & Kegan Paul, 1925), p. vii.
[3] Gilbert Ryle in *The Revolution in Philosophy* (London: Macmillan & Co., 1955), p. 8.
[4] Hermann Wein's short introduction to European and American philosophy of language, *Sprachephilosophie der Gegenwart* (The Hague: Martinus Nijhoff, 1963), gives an idea of the multitude of concepts of meaning and indicates also the existence of other central discussions of philosophy of language than those focussing on concepts of meaning.

are many living continental trends.[5] Landgrebe's bibliography of contemporary philosophy, numbering two hundred and twenty-seven works, contains mainly French and German literature, the only Anglo-Saxons represented being a physicist (Sir James Jeans) and a historian (Arnold J. Toynbee). Surveys from the Soviet Union and Eastern Europe mention English-speaking as well as continental philosophers, but the references are neither detailed nor objective.

The student of philosophy must begin somewhere. But he must not be misled into identifying philosophical life with the local philosophical scene. It seems to me especially important that while he still lacks sufficient reserves of knowledge and personality to withstand the influence of those who have already reached definite conclusions on fundamental matters, he should be provided with every opportunity for serious philosophizing of all kinds. His own appraisal of the truth or falsity of philosophical thoughts is what matters most, and this is surely something that should be made to depend as little as possible on the accident of environment.

My purpose, therefore, in bringing together these four very different philosophers is not to present the reader with a collection of views which I expect him to find equally valuable; rather, I hope to have provided him with an opportunity to begin to assess their value for himself. And whatever his eventual preferences in philosophy, he may derive enjoyment as well as enlightenment from acquaintance with viewpoints which, although perhaps fundamentally distinct from the one he adopts, nevertheless have a living meaning for many of his fellows.

Rudolf Carnap, Ludwig Wittgenstein, and Martin Heidegger all became major influences in philosophy at about the same time, Carnap at the center of the logical positivist movement which emerged from Vienna in the 1930's, Wittgenstein

[5]Ludwig Landgrebe, *Philosophie der Gegenwart* (Frankfurt am Main: Ullstein Bücher, 1957).

in Cambridge as the moving spirit in so-called linguistic philosophy, and Heidegger in Germany as a revolutionary figure in a philosophical climate particularly unaccustomed to change. Sartre, roughly fifteen years younger than the other three, came into his own during the occupation of France in World War II, first as a leading existentialist, novelist, and playwright, and later as a central figure in literary and political controversy in France.

Despite the fact that all four thinkers are acknowledged leaders of contemporary trends in philosophy, they appear here in their own right and not as outstanding representatives or initiators of particular movements. Nor is any special significance to be attached to the inclusion of these particular philosophers. Although the choice seems a natural one to me, this is perhaps due as much as anything to my own contact with their works. As far as movements are concerned, I think that from a purely philosophical point of view such classifications are unreal. The real centers of philosophy are individual philosophers, perhaps their individual works. The more one understands them, the less easy it is to apply a label or specify the lineage; and however diverse the basic viewpoints, one can usually detect some common origin far back in the thought of classical Greek or Indian antiquity. This is as true of current Anglo-American and continental European philosophizing as of any. Despite the schism that has grown up between the analytically educated and those brought up in existentialist metaphysics, analytical philosophy and existentialism are not two clearly demarcated fields of activity.

Because this book is an introduction to basic viewpoints I have had to leave out matters that many readers might have found interesting but which do not directly affect the viewpoints as such. On the other hand, I have gone into a number of points in some depth, where this seemed necessary, although I have presupposed throughout only a very bare acquaintance with philosophical concepts and procedures. Finally, since I have tried to present these viewpoints individually and with a minimum of cross-reference and comparison, the chapters stand on their own and can be read in any order.

I would like to thank those younger philosophers whose interest and co-operation have made the preparation of this book so much easier. I am especially grateful to Guttorm Flöistad, Ingemund Gullvåg, Alastair Hannay and Bernt Vestre.

Oslo, Norway   ARNE NÆSS

Acknowledgments

For permission to quote from the following works, acknowledgment and thanks are due to their publishers:

E. Stenius, *Wittgenstein's 'Tractatus'*, Basil Blackwell & Mott, Ltd., Oxford; L. Wittgenstein, *Philosophical Investigations*, Basil Blackwell & Mott, Ltd., Oxford; L. Wittgenstein, *The Blue and Brown Books*, Basil Blackwell & Mott, Ltd., Oxford; L. Wittgenstein, *Notebooks 1914-1916*, Basil Blackwell & Mott, Ltd., Oxford; J.-P. Sartre, *Saint Genet: Actor and Martyr*, George Braziller, Inc., New York, and Éditions Gallimard, Paris; J.-P. Sartre, *Situations* II and III, Éditions Gallimard, Paris; M. Heidegger, *Über den Humanismus*, Francke Verlag, Bern-Munich; J.-P. Sartre, *Lucifer and the Lord*, translated by Kitty Black, Hamish Hamilton Ltd., London; M. Heidegger, *Being and Time*, Harper & Row, Publishers, Inc., New York, and Max Niemeyer Verlag, Tübingen; M. Heidegger, *Lectures and Addresses*, Harper & Row, Publishers, Inc., New York; M. Heidegger, *Nietzsche*, Harper & Row, Publishers, Inc., New York; M. Warnock, *The Philosophy of Sartre*, Hutchinson Publishing Group, Ltd., London; G. E. M. Anscombe, *An Introduction to Wittgenstein's 'Tractatus'*, Hutchinson Publishing Group, Ltd., London; M. Heidegger, *Kant und das Problem der Metaphysik*, Vittorio Klostermann, Frankfurt am Main; M. Heidegger, *Was ist Metaphysik?*, Vittorio Klostermann, Frankfurt am Main; J.-P.

Acknowledgments

Sartre, *Critique de la raison dialectique*, translated by Hazel Barnes, Alfred A. Knopf, Inc., New York, and Methuen & Co., Ltd., London; J.-P. Sartre, *The Devil and the Good Lord*, translated by Kitty Black, Alfred A. Knopf, Inc., New York; A. J. Ayer, *Logical Positivism*, The Macmillan Company, New York; J.-P. Sartre, *Existentialism and Humanism*, translated by Philip Mairet, Methuen & Co., Ltd., London; M. Cranston, *Sartre*, Oliver & Boyd, Ltd., Edinburgh; P. A. Schilpp, *The Philosophy of Rudolf Carnap*, now published by The Open Court Publishing Company, La Salle, Illinois; N. Malcolm, *Ludwig Wittgenstein: A Memoir*, Oxford University Press, London; H. Feigl, "Logical Empiricism," in D. D. Runes (ed.), *Twentieth Century Philosophy*, The Philosophical Library, Inc., New York; J.-P. Sartre, *Being and Nothingness*, The Philosophical Library, Inc., New York; R. Carnap, *The Logical Syntax of Language*, Routledge & Kegan Paul, Ltd., London; L. Wittgenstein, *Tractatus Logico-Philosophicus*, Routledge & Kegan Paul, Ltd., London; H. Nohl, *Character und Schicksal*, Verlag G. Schulte-Bulmke, Frankfurt am Main; W. Dilthey, *Gesammelte Schriften*, B. G. Teubner, Stuttgart; R. Carnap, *The Logical Structure of the World*, The University of California Press, Berkeley; A. Maslow, *A Study in Wittgenstein's 'Tractatus'*, The University of California Press, Berkeley; M. Heidegger, *An Introduction to Metaphysics*, Yale University Press, New Haven.

For permission to quote from the following articles, acknowledgment and thanks are due to the authors and to the editors of the journals and anthologies in which they appear: G. Ryle, "Ludwig Wittgenstein," *Analysis*; R. Carnap, "The Elimination of Metaphysics through Logical Analysis of Language," A. J. Ayer (ed.), *Logical Positivism*; K. Rahner, "Introduction au concept de philosophie existentiale chez Heidegger," *Recherches de Science religieuse*; R. Carnap, "Empiricism, Semantics and Ontology," *Revue Internationale de*

Acknowledgments
Philosophie; M. Gandillac and A. de Towarnicki, "Deux documents sur Heidegger," *Les Temps modernes.*

Thanks are due in particular to Professor Rudolf Carnap, Dr. Martin Heidegger, and M. Jean-Paul Sartre for consent to reprint extensive passages from their works.

Contents

Martin Heidegger

Jean-Paul Sartre

FOUR MODERN PHILOSOPHERS

Rudolf Carnap

Life

The years from 1891 to 1928

Rudolf Carnap was born in 1891 in Ronsdorf, near Barmen, in
northwest Germany. His mother and father were deeply religious, though without any trace of dogmatic ardor. Carnap
says that his mother insisted that what was essential in religion
was "not so much the acceptance of a creed, but the living of
the good life."[1] The emphasis on integrity was what underlay
her tolerance toward those who held other beliefs, and it is
certainly tempting to see a parallel here with Carnap's own
"principle of tolerance" and his evaluation of the time-
honored standpoints of traditional philosophy on the basis of
what they enable one to do.

Carnap gradually, and without inner crises, freed himself
from his parents' religion. Belief in a personal God gave way
first to a kind of pantheism, though he felt himself impelled
more by its poetic Goethean strain than by its discursive manifestations as an explicit philosophical system in the style of
Spinoza. The key word in his growing intellectual renunciation of religion, theology, and metaphysics was always the

[1]As a source for Carnap's life I have drawn mostly on his autobiog-
raphy in *The Philosophy of Rudolf Carnap*, Vol. XI of the *Library of
Living Philosophers*, ed. P. A. Schilpp. (La Salle, Ill.: The Open Court
Publishing Co., 1963).

same: their "irreconcilability" with the results of modern science and with the scientific attitude. Ludwig Büchner and the zoologist Ernst Häckel, both professed materialists, were great names to him. The young Carnap's enthusiasm for, and faith in, the scientific had a strong ethical motive: in it he saw a guarantee of seriousness, genuineness, and integrity in human thought and affairs.

In the years before 1914 Carnap studied at Jena and at Freiburg im Breisgau. The philosophical environment was a rich one. Neo-Kantianism was the main trend, but others were also represented. Among his contemporaries in Freiburg we find one Martin Heidegger, student of theology.

Carnap acquainted himself with all philosophical disciplines, and also experimental psychology, but soon came to prefer theory of knowledge and philosophy of science. Kant became one of his favorites among the philosophical classics. On the other hand, what the universities had to offer in logic he found dull and old fashioned. But this was due to the fact that "the new logic" was so far generally unknown, what was given in university courses being a dusty and somewhat jaded Aristotelian logic bearing the stamp of centuries of neglect. Indeed, it was typical that even several years after the war the library of the University of Freiburg contained no copy of the basic work in the New Logic, Russell and Whitehead's *Principia Mathematica*, although the first volume had been published in 1910. Russell helped Carnap by sending him "a long list containing all the most important definitions of *Principia*" in thirty-five handwritten pages ("a priceless possession," says Carnap in his autobiography).[2] Carnap first heard of Cantor's theory of sets, a new mathematical discipline of great importance to problems of logic, from a retired major, one of Carnap's two fellow students in Frege's course at the University of Jena.

Carnap's attitude to logic changed slowly but fundamen-

[2] *Ibid.*, p. 14.

tally once he had come upon Gottlob Frege's lectures. His early encounter with the New Logic, and its development in the hands of a man of outstanding mathematical and philosophical talent, proved decisive both for the future course of Carnap's life and for his achievements; in the New Logic he found an inexhaustible source of intellectual satisfaction.

It was not after any intense agonizing over the metaphysics of his time that Carnap acquired his negative attitude. Although later he was to be well known as a leading antimetaphysician, Carnap had both respect and admiration for a number of the works of "metaphysicians" and in many ways saw his own work as a development of theirs.

Besides Bruno Bauch, who gave him his taste for Kant, there was also Herman Nohl, who gave him an understanding of philosophers on the basis of their respective cultural backgrounds and attitudes to life *(Lebensgefühl)* and aroused his interest in works as remote from his main preoccupations as Hegel's *Rechtsphilosophie.*

For Carnap the outbreak of war in 1914 was an "incomprehensible catastrophe."[3] His attempt to understand it led to the full realization of his latent cosmopolitanism and pacifism. Nevertheless, though military service was altogether repugnant to him, he accepted it as his duty, believing it to be necessary in order to save his country. Of his life at the front he says nothing apart from mentioning quieter periods, and in these we notice that his reading matter included poetry and Einstein's theory of relativity. The war and the terrible postwar years in Germany had no noticeable affect upon his philosophy. For his contemporary, Martin Heidegger, things were different.

After the war Carnap lived in Jena where he took his Doctor's degree with a dissertation entitled *Der Raum* (University of Jena, 1921), a piece of neo-Kantian theory of science strongly leavened with the New Logic—a component which

[3]*Ibid.,* p. 9.

gradually came to supplant nearly all traces of "traditional philosophy" in Carnap's thinking.

In 1926 Carnap went to Vienna and joined the philosophical circle that became known as the Vienna Circle. From that time to this, his basic attitude to any philosophical question has remained unchanged. In the years before 1926 there had been a transition in his viewpoint from a positivistic attitude, adopted not without misgivings, with regard to the main philosophical traditions, to a rejection of them in a dramatically elaborated antimetaphysics. This transition was characterized not by polemic or any detailed critical study, but by a positive contribution of the kind he thought must take the place of metaphysics. Being wholly absorbed in the new, Carnap to all intents and purposes omits to give any detailed criticism of the old that he is rejecting. This fact is important for understanding the powerful impact of his thought, which lies in what he helped to create, rather than in any especially penetrating or compelling criticism of the tradition he was turning his back upon. His explicit analyses of "metaphysics" are quite few, short, and philosophically slight, and it is hardly on the basis of these that people have been led to align themselves with Carnap in their philosophical researches.

Even as late as 1928, when Carnap, already thirty-nine years old, published his first major philosophical work, *Der logische Aufbau der Welt* (*The Logical Structure of the World*), the link with the metaphysical philosophers was far from broken. Carnap sees "the new philosophy" as a step by step development of the old, though the decisive steps are for him those that are made possible by the use of modern logic. Consequently, it is not strange that the *Aufbau* contains radical antimetaphysical remarks, while at the same time not only referring to, but directly building upon a large number of the works of "the metaphysicians."[4] Carnap is far from being a revolution-

[4]Carnap refers both specifically and positively—sometimes as precursors and guiding spirits—to the following "metaphysicians" (in his terminology): Richard Avenarius, Bruno Bauch, Franz Brentano, Ernst

ary; his aims are rather those of one who looks for harmony and continued development, who sees his work as a fruition of the work of his predecessors and not as a break with it.

Yet, despite this, in the comparatively brief, crusading and expanding period of the Vienna Circle's influence, between 1928 and 1936, Carnap became something of a revolutionary figure. Indeed, these years in his life might justifiably be referred to as Carnap's militant antimetaphysical period. At this time there was a tendency in his hypotheses toward system formation and extreme generality. (But, of course, it is difficult to be consciously anti-something without sharing some fundamental principles with whatever one is opposing.) But otherwise, both before 1928 and after 1936, Carnap's thinking should perhaps be described as ametaphysical rather than antimetaphysical.

The most influential factor in drawing Carnap away temporarily from a more ametaphysical attitude was his contact with Bertrand Russell (b. 1872) and Ludwig Wittgenstein (1889-1951), both very stimulating personalities. Carnap felt as if Russell's messianic call for a logically anchored scientific philosophy was directed at him personally: "All this supposed knowledge in the traditional systems must be swept away, and a new beginning must be made. . . ." And Russell induced in him the dream of "a future achievement surpassing all that has hitherto been accomplished by philosophers."[5] But Carnap did not see himself in this dream as the great hero and con-

---

Cassirer, Hans Cornelius, Wilhelm Dilthey, Hugo Dingler, Hans Driesch, Benno and K. O. Erdmann, M. Frischeisen-Köhler, Heinrich Gomperz, Edmund Husserl, Günther Jacoby, Oswald Külpe, Alexius Meinong, Paul Natorp, Friedrich Nietzsche, Joseph Petzold, Max Scheler, Richard von Schubert-Soldern, Wilhelm Schuppe, Paul Tillich, Hans Vaihinger, Johannes Volkelt, Hermann Weyl, Wilhelm Windelband, Wilhelm Wundt, and Theodor Ziehen, among others. Few creative philosophers have made so many detailed and itemized *positive* references to thinkers in their own and previous generations.
[5]From *Our Knowledge of the External World as a Field for Scientific Method in Philosophy* (Chicago: The Open Court Publishing Co., 1914), quoted in Carnap's autobiography, p. 13.

queror; rather as one who would work jointly with others in an intimate and loyal co-operative enterprise in order to reach the measure of scientific knowledge necessary to found any human knowledge worthy of the name.

The influence of Wittgenstein was mainly indirect, through those members of the Vienna Circle who were engrossed in what they understood of Wittgenstein's philosophy and enthusiastically campaigned for it. Wittgenstein expressed his views—especially those about the *meaninglessness* of all metaphysics—in uncompromising, almost dramatic terms. And under his influence Carnap's cautious, well-tempered statements gave way to something altogether more provocative and extreme.

In Vienna, Carnap was an instructor in philosophy from 1926 to 1931, a feverishly active period of constant discussions with kindred spirits. His publications from this time have an urgent, prophetic character, not least in the article "Überwindung der Metaphysik durch logische Analyse der Sprache" ("The Elimination of Metaphysics through Logical Analysis of Language"), printed in the Circle's own periodical, *Erkenntnis*[6] *(Erkenntnis* first appeared in 1930; the last volume was that for 1938/39). We shall later expound some of the contents of this article.

Largely on account of its opposition to nationalistic and particularly National-Socialist forces, the Vienna Circle, in the mid-thirties, came into contact with scientists and philosophers all over the world, as most of its leading members took refuge abroad. Its viewpoint now became more flexible, less marked by the specific cultural struggle in Austria. Philipp Frank echoed the expectations of the Circle's members as it emerged on the wider, international scene, when at the international congress the Circle arranged in Copenhagen

---

[6]*Erkenntnis,* Vol. II (1932), No. 4. An English translation by Arthur Pap ("The Elimination of Metaphysics through Logical Analysis of Language") is included in A. J. Ayer (ed.), *Logical Positivism* (Glencoe, Ill.: The Free Press, 1959).

in 1936, he expressed the hope that their thinking would be as much an improvement on what it had been as the so-called *wienerbröd* in Copenhagen was on the bread in Vienna.

From 1931 to 1935 Carnap worked in Prague, where he occupied a newly established chair in Natural Philosophy, but the political atmosphere finally became "intolerable" and he left at the end of 1935 for the United States where he became attached first to the University of Chicago. At present he is Professor of Philosophy at the University of California at Los Angeles. Since 1941 he has been an American citizen.

In the German-speaking world, Carnap was surrounded by powerful philosophical opponents who completely dominated university life. He was recognized as an antimetaphysician, but little notice was taken of the constructive content of his philosophy.[7] In the United States the situation was just the reverse. There empiricism and viewpoints committed to rigorous logical methods had their respected place, even if "the metaphysicians" (in Carnap's terminology) remained in the ascendancy until the 1950's.

From the very beginning one finds in Carnap's work the tendency to look for new conquests for *scientific*, for *exact* research. This accounts for the technical and scientific character of his non-popular writings. Carnap rightly asks to be judged according to the technically most well-considered formulations he has made of his views, not according to any of the more or less popularized versions. However, we shall have to ignore material in many of the writings he himself finds central, since they lose a disproportionate amount of their precision if expounded without use of the symbolic-logical apparatus.

Carnap's work in the development of the new branches of science has concentrated on two main fields: semantics and inductive logic. The object of *semantic analysis* is "the analy-

---

[7]Concerning this, see the Preface to Victor Kraft's *Der Wiener Kreis* (Vienna: Springer Verlag, 1950).

sis, interpretation, clarification or construction of languages of communication, especially languages of science."[8] Carnap sees himself here as continuing the work begun by Plato and Aristotle and carried on in a more technical manner with the aid of symbolic logic by Frege (1848-1925) and, among American philosophers, C. S. Peirce (1839-1914).

Carnap's *Studies in Semantics*, his *Meaning and Necessity*, and his other semantical works bear clearly the stamp of his remarkable formal talent. Emphasis on the formal introduces, inevitably, an element of specialization, and if, as some believe, semantics as a science should have a comprehensive, all-round structure, then Carnap must be considered one-sided. However, it is often by burrowing down deep in their material that outstanding researchers have founded new branches of science, that is, precisely by adopting definite, strictly delimited perspectives and "methods." An all-embracing, general theory of the phenomena of linguistic meaning is of course no mean thing to aspire to. Nor is Carnap's semantics the only branch of the science; others are needed to complement it.

Carnap's appeal is to the constructive researcher in us, his point of departure Aristotle's first sentence in *The Metaphysics:* "All men by nature desire to know."

The task of building up another, and partly new, branch of science, inductive logic, has claimed most of Carnap's energies in recent years, and it appears that he intends to devote his

---

[8]"Empiricism, Semantics and Ontology," *Revue internationale de philosophie*, IV, No. 11 (January, 1950), 39. Reprinted in L. Linsky (ed.), *Semantics and the Philosophy of Language* (Glencoe, Ill.: The Free Press, 1952), and in Carnap's *Meaning and Necessity* (2d ed.; Chicago: The University of Chicago Press, 1958), p. 221. Carnap began a series of books, *Studies in Semantics*, in 1942 with the publication of *Introduction to Semantics* (Cambridge, Mass.: Harvard University Press). In 1943 came *Formalization of Logic* (Cambridge, Mass.: Harvard University Press). The first edition of *Meaning and Necessity* (also published by The University of Chicago Press) came out in 1947.

remaining years of active research to this. The ambitiously conceived *Logical Foundations of Probability*[9] came out in 1950, but was intended only as the first volume in a work whose determining insights were to be presented in a further volume. Carnap's revisions of many points in the thinking of the first volume, however, have led him to plan to publish the new inductive logic in the form of a series of smaller publications.

Carnap's writing on both semantics and inductive logic has a strong technical stamp. However, for the interested reader with only a modest knowledge of symbolic logic there are fairly easily understandable presentations of the main points.[10]

The Vienna Circle

Since the middle of the nineteenth century Vienna had been a center of liberalism in politics and political philosophy. Ties with Western Europe were strong and lively, and it was natural that British empiricism should be extended a welcome there which was otherwise denied it in the German-speaking world. Ernst Mach (1838-1916), for a long time a leading figure within the empiricist movement, was characteristically enough a creative physicist as well as a philosopher. Indeed, the combination of philosophical training and active scientific

---

[9] *Logical Foundations of Probability* (Chicago: The University of Chicago Press, 1950).

[10] In Carnap's own books one always finds short elementary summaries of the main points. A fairly detailed presentation of Carnap's views is given in Wolfgang Stegmüller's *Haupströmungen der Gegenwartsphilosophie* (2d ed.; Stuttgart: Alfred Kröner Verlag, 1960), chaps. 9 and 10. It may be remarked that the idea of philosophy as a *kind* of scientific research is now widely discredited, especially in empiricist and analytical circles. But all the same, the idea that all philosophy, or an essential part of professional philosophy, must have, should have, or in fact does have the character of a scientific enterprise is one of the most fundamental and, to my mind, valuable in the entire philosophical tradition from the time of Plato and Aristotle.

Rudolf Carnap

research seems to have been a qualification for the type of bridge-building work the Vienna Circle carried out:[11] all of its members were both philosophically and scientifically active. As a political philosopher himself Ernst Mach was by no means an independent thinker, but his liberal and social attitude was influential enough to provoke Lenin into writing an immense work attacking Mach's "empirio-criticism."[12] Intimate co-operation within the Vienna Circle itself was partly made possible by the fact that most of those concerned with political philosophy were of a liberalist and socialist bent, and thus not bound to any philosophical system such as dialectical materialism.

In 1922 the physicist and philosopher Moritz Schlick (1882-1936) acceded to the chair of Philosophy of the Inductive Sciences which had been established for Ernst Mach. Around Schlick there gathered a group of men who, like Ernst Mach, fell between two stools; pure philosophers classified their work as mathematics, physics, or social science, while the pure scientists dismissed them as "philosophers." In the beginning, co-operation was confined to only a few of those who attended Schlick's seminar, but it soon spread, and Schlick's Philosophical Circle became the Vienna Circle, though membership was not at all dependent on actual physical presence

[11]There are some interesting accounts of the Vienna Circle's philosophy written by its own members: Otto Neurath, *Wissenschaftliche Weltauffassung der Wiener Kreis* (Vienna: Verlag v. Julius Springer, 1929). This scarce book *was* in fact written by Neurath even though no author's name appears on it. It gives an extremely vivid account of the Circle's historical background seen through Neurath's Austro-Marxist eyes. See also Jörgen Jörgensen, "The Development of Logical Empiricism," *International Encyclopedia of Unified Science*, Vol. II, No. 9 (Chicago: The University of Chicago Press, 1951) (a very good survey); and Victor Kraft, *Der Wiener Kreis. Der Ursprung des Neupositivismus* (Vienna: Springer Verlag, 1950) (written after the war, but thoroughly in the spirit of the thirties).

[12]V. I. Lenin, *Materialismus und Empiriokritizismus*, 1908 ("*Materialism and Empirio-Criticism: Critical Comments on a Reactionary Philosophy*") (Moscow: F.L.P.H.: 1947). English translation by A. Fineberg (London: Lawrence & Wishart, 1948).

in Vienna. The organizing genius was Schlick, but the leading thinker and precise formulator of the Circle's views was Rudolf Carnap.

Among those who played a special part through important publications were Friedrich Waismann (1896-1959, mathematics, philosophy), Otto Neurath (1882-1945, social economy, sociology, philosophy), and Philipp Frank (b. 1884, physics, mathematics, philosophy), Einstein's successor as professor in Prague.

In the same category must be mentioned Hans Reichenbach (1891-1953), although he was seldom in Vienna and had his own circle in Berlin. Reichenbach's competence embraced mathematics, physics, and philosophy. Several of the members of the Circle were or still are prominent teachers and "circle formers" in their own right, such as Herbert Feigl, whose work in the United States continues in the spirit of the Vienna Circle.

The circle of active sympathizers was already wide in the beginning of the thirites and included many outstanding people within the exact sciences, for example, the gifted young logician and mathematician, Kurt Gödel, and the mathematicians Hans Hahn and Karl Menger. Bertrand Russell and Karl Popper were close to the Circle, but dissented on a number of points which they, but not the leading figures of the Circle, considered central. Neurath, in particular, but also to some extent Carnap and others, had some difficulty in comprehending the extent of the differences between their own point of view and that of their sympathizers.[13] A "close affinity" often

[13]K. R. Popper (b. 1902) was especially unfortunate in being stamped as a thinker whose ideas differed in no essentials from those of the Circle. In fact, by 1934 Popper was already a bold and original thinker on his own account. My own experience was rather similar to Popper's, though I was never able to formulate my own standpoints with sufficient clarity. (The polemic in my *Wie fördert man heute die empirische Bewegung? Eine Auseinandersetzung mit dem Empirismus von Otto Neurath und Rudolf Carnap*, written in final form between 1937 and 1939, was *intended* to be directed against *fundamental* theses and trends in the Circle, but was understood by Neurath as a proposal

existed only in a common rejection of the German *Geistes-wissenschaft* (not the neo-Kantian) philosophy, and a common respect for modern science as a model for all exact thinking. We will touch later on the special case of Wittgenstein's relationship to the Circle.[14]

Through international congresses, in which the inner circle manifested its strong belief that any thinker who rejected German *Geisteswissenschaft* metaphysics really belonged to the Circle, the influence of the movement became worldwide. Within Scandinavia, Jörgen Jörgensen (b. 1894) collaborated with the Circle's leading men, and can be considered to have been a "member"—if this word can be permitted among philosophers. The Finnish philosopher, Eino Kaila (1890-1958), though not so close, was an active as well as critical participant. That his influence was less than it might have been is due to the fact that his main works were not translated into any of the world languages. In Britain the Circle's work burst upon philosophers and the public alike in the form of A. J. Ayer's brilliant and provocative *Language, Truth and Logic*.[15]

The increasing influence of Nazism in Austria, and later the *Anschluss* itself, drove the Circle from Vienna, Prague, and Germany. In terms of Nazi ideology, the Circle's views were considered "Kulturbolschewist." Its members scattered over the English- (and the Turkish-)[16] speaking world.

---

for modifications which were already accepted in principle and were to be made official in future publications. Upon this assurance I gave up plans to publish the work.)

[14]The most judicious account, in my view, of the various philosophers closely or remotely tied, geographically or intellectually, to the Vienna Circle is to be found in Herbert Feigl's "Logical Empiricism," in D. D. Runes (ed.), *Twentieth Century Philosophy* (New York: Philosophical Library, 1947). The survey on pp. 408-9 is particularly good regarding the more remote connections.

[15]*Language, Truth and Logic* (London: Gollancz, 1936; 2d ed. with new introduction, 1946).

[16]Reichenbach left Berlin for Istanbul (1933-38) and from there went to Los Angeles. Popper was for many years in New Zealand, afterwards in London (from 1948). Neurath went to The Hague, could not

So much for the Vienna Circle's history and outer framework. From about 1936 the Circle, in effect, no longer existed. From then on one should speak rather of logical empiricism or neo-positivism, terms covering the direction in which the Circle's work evolved, though not following in detail the positions of the original participants. From about 1950 the number of creative philosophers professing to be logical empiricists began to dwindle, and today although influential and widely supported views owe a great deal to the Circle's work, they have acquired from their proponents a rather different stamp. Here we may refer to the work of such philosophers as Ernest Nagel, Carl G. Hempel, P. W. Bridgman, S. S. Stevens, Willard V. O. Quine, Nelson Goodman, Alonzo Church, members of the Minnesota circle around Herbert Feigl, and Paul K. Feyerabend.

Carnap and Wittgenstein

The intense interest aroused in Ludwig Wittgenstein's person and writings after World War II had the effect of pushing Carnap and his cultivation of the scientific aspects of philosophy somewhat into the background. But there was perhaps another factor too. The war's revival of questions about last or final things, "thought's disquiet," this may have worked against Carnap's initial conception which in some sense presupposes a state of clarity and peace of mind in the researching philosopher.

In this respect and others the relationship between Wittgenstein and Carnap is itself extremely informative and deserves its own discussion.[17] It is safe to say that the two men represent fundamentally different kinds of personality. In the

---

get permission to enter Norway, and finally escaped to England in 1941.

[17]The following is based partly on Carnap's autobiography and partly on discussions with members of the Vienna Circle between 1933 and 1939.

Vienna Circle, a large (probably not including the mystical) part of Wittgenstein's *Tractatus Logico-Philosophicus* was read aloud and discussed sentence by sentence.[18] Some things seem to have been understood, others not, according to Carnap's own frank account.

Carnap was influenced most of all by Wittgenstein's conception "that the truth of logical statements is based only on their logical structure and on the meaning of the terms. Logical statements are true under all conceivable circumstances; thus their truth is independent of the contingent facts of the world." Logical validity rates very highly therefore, but the cost is considerable: "On the other hand, it follows that these statements do not say anything about the world and thus have no factual content."[19] Logic is meaningless.

Wittgenstein's antimetaphysical ideas were nothing novel to Carnap. Already in the first draft of *Der logische Aufbau der Welt* (which he concluded in 1925; the book was published in 1928) Carnap was entertaining similar ideas, and by the time he completed the work, his attitude toward most of traditional philosophy, perhaps especially ontologically stamped metaphysics, was very critical. On this point Wittgenstein's influence, mostly through the mediation of his admirers in the Circle, made itself felt in Carnap's new antimetaphysical predilection for pointed, general slogans, among them the famous "Metaphysics is meaningless."[20]

[18]Autobiography, in Schilpp, *The Philosophy of Rudolf Carnap*, p. 24.
[19]*Ibid.*, p. 25.
[20]Carnap has said that in the first years of the Vienna Circle no distinction was made between different kinds of meaning. Yet in 1957 (see *Logical Positivism*, p. 81) he says that "meaning" in "The Elimination of Metaphysics" is always to be understood in the sense of "cognitive meaning," and that in the section of that work entitled "Metaphysics as Expression of an Attitude to Life" he does not deny that the sentences of metaphysics can have expressive meaning. (Cf. *Logical Positivism*, p. 78: ". . . metaphysics does indeed have a content; only it is not theoretical content. The (pseudo) statements of metaphysics . . . serve for the *expression of the general attitude of a person towards life . . .* ('Lebenseinstellung, Lebensgefühl')." (Italics in the original.)

This change in approach on the part of Carnap, even though it lasted only from 1929 until 1935, is all the more remarkable in one whose usual quietly constructive style of thought seems so foreign to revolutionary grandiloquence. Looking back over the years in which Carnap has become an acknowledged leader in the field of strict thought, universally respected for his persistent, painstaking and single-minded approach to complex problems, it seems in retrospect that pioneering and prophecy were not his true forte, and that the *sturm und drang* period can be considered a temporary lapse.

Moritz Schlick, who had become personally acquainted with Wittgenstein, asked him on behalf of the Circle to come to one of their meetings to explain and discuss some puzzling points in his *Tractatus*. Wittgenstein was at first unwilling but finally agreed to have meetings (in the summer of 1927) with Schlick, Waismann, and Carnap. Schlick impressed upon his two fellow members that they should not begin a discussion in the brisk give-and-take style they were accustomed to. They were not to ask Wittgenstein direct questions. "The best approach . . . would be to let Wittgenstein talk and then ask only very cautiously for the necessary elucidations."[21] Neurath had compared the Circle's activity to that of the encyclopedists of the Enlightenment, and their meetings were modeled on the frank, straightforward and constructive discussions of scientists. With Wittgenstein a quite different spirit prevailed:

> When I met Wittgenstein I saw that Schlick's warnings were fully justified. But his behavior was not caused by any arrogance. In general, he was of a sympathetic temperament and very kind; but he was hypersensitive and easily irritated. Whatever he said was always interesting and stimulating, and the way in which he expressed it was often fascinating. His point of view and his attitude toward people and problems, even theoretical problems, were much more similar to those of a creative artist than

[21]Autobiography, in Schilpp, *The Philosophy of Rudolf Carnap*, p. 25.

17

to those of a scientist; one might almost say, similar to those of a religious prophet or a seer. When he started to formulate his view on some specific philosophical problem, we often felt the internal struggle that occurred in him that very moment, a struggle by which he tried to penetrate from darkness to light under an intense and painful strain, which was even visible on his most expressive face. When finally, often after a prolonged arduous effort, his answer came forth, his statement stood before us like a newly created piece of art or a divine revelation. Not that he asserted his views dogmatically. Although some of the formulations of the *Tractatus* sound as if there could not be any possibility of a doubt, he often expressed the feeling that his statements were inadequate. But the impression he made on us was as if insight came to him as through divine inspiration, so that we could not help feeling that any sober rational comment or analysis of it would be a profanation.[22]

The reader may be wondering how this passage can add appreciably to our historical understanding of Rudolf Carnap and *his* philosophy. I think that it does, for the quotation reveals how deeply affected Carnap was by the magnetic power which Wittgenstein radiated. We may hardly doubt that in turning against Wittgenstein's ideas he had first to undergo an inner struggle, in order to break the spell, and that after the spell was broken his intellectual integrity would force him to undertake a careful evaluation. And of course Carnap did in fact turn against certain basic Wittgensteinian ideas in the *Tractatus* as also, more generally, against the assumed consequences for philosophical research which, at Oxford and elsewhere, were read into Wittgenstein's second main work, *Philosophical Investigations*. Thus also with regard to our appreciation of subsequent philosophy, the very fact of personal contact between Carnap and Wittgenstein

[22]*Ibid.*, pp. 25-26.

lends significance to the contrast, especially in the 1950's, between the work inspired by the two men.

To return to the meetings which began in the summer of 1927:

> From the beginning of 1929 on, Wittgenstein wished to meet only with Schlick and Waismann, no longer with me or Feigl, who had also become acquainted with him in the meantime, let alone the Circle. Although the difference in our attitudes and personalities expressed itself only on certain occasions, I understood very well that Wittgenstein felt it all the time and, unlike me, was disturbed by it. He said to Schlick that he could talk only with someone who "holds his hand."[23]

Schlick and Waismann continued their meetings with Wittgenstein, and his influence on them grew stronger. Correspondingly, the distance between them and Carnap increased. After a meeting with Wittgenstein they would return to their colleagues and elatedly announce that this or that problem was now solved. But after hearing the solution, Carnap would remind them that the Circle had long ago considered just the same solution and after careful evaluation rejected it. What new arguments had Wittgenstein brought forward? The answer to this was difficult. The effect of Wittgenstein's pronouncements seems to have been that of a kind of revelation. Arguments were not necessary.[24]

---

[23]*Ibid.*, p. 27.

[24]Justus Hartnack in *Wittgenstein and Modern Philosophy*, translated from the Danish by M. Cranston (London: Methuen & Co., 1965), pp. 51 ff., gives a good elementary survey of the differences between the positions expressed in the *Tractatus* and those of the logical empiricists. One of his concluding remarks (p. 63) is as follows: "Although logical positivism has removed itself considerably from the *Tractatus*, it is no less clear that without that work, without its penetrating grasp of the nature of language and logic, logical empiricism would not have had the logical foundation and the logical sharpness and strength that in spite of everything it did have." One wonders whether the comment might not have been more apt if "logical" had been replaced by "metaphysical."

Rudolf Carnap

A glance at Carnap and philosophy today

In their explicit views Wittgenstein and Carnap came gradually to an almost complete divergence. At a deeper level there was a profound contrast in basic personal attitude and understanding. Carnap's direction was toward a scientifically oriented philosophy, while Wittgenstein's was toward a personal, almost aesthetic, grasp of the problems of philosophy. Both stood for seriousness in philosophy, and turned against what they took to be superficiality, lack of concern for accuracy and perseverance, and an undue deference to tradition. For Carnap this meant that philosophizing should consist in the scientific, detailed working out of a thought. But Wittgenstein saw philosophical troubles as personal matters, even of life and death, and for him, seriousness consisted in their elimination by individual effort where no remedy could be expected to apply twice.

The break between logical empiricism and philosophizing inspired by Wittgenstein was especially marked in the United States in the 1950's. In Britain the two sides were less equal; there Wittgenstein had an intense philosophical influence which persisted and spread, while capable representatives of logical empiricist viewpoints could provide no real opposition, at least in terms of numerical support. A change has recently come about, though perhaps not to the advantage of specifically logical empiricist positions, in that the basic problems of the scientist and the philosopher of science are now viewed with increased interest. One thinker in particular who was close to the Vienna Circle, Karl R. Popper, has been largely

---

Wittgenstein stimulated Carnap chiefly in the field of antimetaphysics. Besides, the logical and metalogical views expressed in the *Tractatus* could be combined with rather different philosophical and metaphysical positions. In Wittgenstein, extensional viewpoints and the theory of tautology were combined with statements on logical form, the unsayable and other "antipositivistic" notions that had a definite metaphysical stress.

influential in working for the rehabilitation of a scientifically oriented philosophy.

In comparing Carnap's thinking with that of Wittgenstein, Heidegger, or Sartre, it is natural to ask whether Carnap has really allowed himself to be at all deeply affected by the crises of his time. Have the darkest moments made any profound and lasting impression on him; has he battled with their possible philosophical consequences or presumptions? Or in pursuing his own thought has he had to put such problems aside?

Carnap is able to say with Nietzsche, "Gott ist tot," and with Wittgenstein and the later Heidegger, "Die Metaphysik ist tot." But for him there appears to have been nothing particularly harrowing about this; he can say these things with equanimity. Indeed, having no love for metaphysics Carnap should hardly be expected to suffer deeply, as Wittgenstein did, at the thought of its meaninglessness, or to look away from thinking and up toward thinking-about-Being (*Denken des Seins*) as Heidegger did.

Carnap has an unformulated but quite clearly implied intellectual creed; it might be called "the gospel of clarity and exactitude," and it harks back to an ethical creed. The unformulated intellectual creed reveals itself even in quite simple questions about the criteria of clarity and exactitude. For Carnap, the established exact sciences provide the only form of clarity and exactitude which can be relevant in the case of knowledge.

It is interesting to note that Husserl's ideas on exactitude and his completely different program for philosophy as an exact science were known to Carnap. He mentions Husserl's aim of "a mathesis of experience" and sees in it points of contact with his own aim of "the rational reconstruction of the real world."

Carnap again refers to Husserl when dealing with the constitution of the field of vision. Husserl has been mistaken, as he himself was earlier, in assuming that the field of vision is given for us originally as two-dimensional. In its original form it has neither two nor three dimensions. Therefore a theory of constitution must be capable of reducing dimensionality to something more basic. As far as his own intentions go, Carnap claims to stand closer to Jacoby, in the latter's *Allgemeine Ontologie der Wirklichkeit*,[25] than to Husserl. However, nowhere does Carnap show himself as in principle opposed to Husserl, a fact that poses historians of philosophy with a basic problem. In what does the difference between a Husserlian and a Carnapian ideal of clarity and exactitude consist? Carnap has certainly not found his model in Husserl, or indeed in any other philosopher who has set a high price on these ideals. Instead, he has found it in the established exact sciences—but, be it noted, as these have been cultivated by certain *outstanding* representatives. (Gottlob Frege was full of scorn and ridicule for the *normal* level of exactitude in mathematics.)

Carnap was recently asked to put his ethical creed into words. The directness and simplicity of the answer, its simple candor, is a challenge to the modern in modern philosophy. The style might seem more natural for someone still on the threshold of his adult life, still unacquainted with the compromises and frustrations that tend to foster a complex, indirect, professional way of talking. But in his main strivings, Carnap has *lived* in a way that admirably suits the simplicity and directness of his answer.

> The main task of an individual seems to me the development of his personality and the creation of fruitful and healthy relations among human beings. This aim implies the task of co-operation in the development of society and ultimately of the whole of mankind towards a community in which every individual has the possibility of leading a satisfying life and of participating in cultural goods. The fact that everybody knows that he will eventually die, need not make his life meaningless or aimless. He himself gives meaning to his life if he sets tasks for

[25]G. Jacoby, *Allgemeine Ontologie der Wirklichkeit*, Vol. I, (Halle: Kommision Verlag v. V.E.B. Max-Niemeyer-Verlag Halle, 1925).

himself, struggles to fulfill them to the best of his ability, and regards all the specific tasks of all individuals as parts of the great task of humanity, whose aim goes far beyond the limited span of each individual life.[26]

"Der logische Aufbau der Welt"

Genetic and rational reconstruction

Today there is a major field of research known as genetic epistemology, the theory of the causal factors involved in the origin and growth of the knowledge implicit in the normal adult's way of grasping the world and himself. Among the most important questions raised in it are those concerning the evolution of our concept of material things, that is, of three-dimensional entities with visual, tactile, etc., properties and with a continuous existence independent of the constant variation in their visual, tactile, etc., components. From empirical studies with small children it is clear that the concept, or rather concepts, of things have very long and complex origins. One important factor is that things that are quite evident to older children or adults are ambiguous and uncertain to the very young. Genetic epistemology encompasses the subject matter of ordinary and social psychology, but it also borders on, and has consequences for, philosophy, and especially, as one would expect, for theory of knowledge.[27] For centuries, on the basis of more or less pure speculation, philosophers have advanced their theories about the origins of three-dimensionality on the premise that the field of vision, analogous to the retina, is a kind of surface and thus two dimensional. Among the questions of a genetic type that philoso-

[26]Autobiography, in Schilpp, *The Philosophy of Rudolf Carnap*, p. 9.
[27]Reference should be made here particularly to the extensive investigations undertaken by Jean Piaget and his collaborators at the Centre d'Épistémologie Genetique in Geneva.

phers have taken up are: How have human beings come to "see in space," that is, to have a direct perception of distance in space; and how have they come to apprehend, say, an apple which turns and moves backward and forward as a "thing" of constant size and shape?

But even if it were possible for genetic epistemology, sometime, to give the immensely varied account necessary for a complete presentation of the steps toward the normal adult's conception of the world (within dissimilar cultures), this major achievement would still not solve a large epistemological problem, at any rate not in the only conceivable way: the problem of *justifying* our most elementary knowledge or our acquaintance (mostly in implicit form) with the world and ourselves. The *justification* of beliefs about the constant size, weight, and shape of particular things through (moderate) periods under (moderate) changes in distance and light conditions need not, according to most concepts of 'justification' and 'knowledge,' coincide with the demonstration that we have actually developed conceptions to the effect that such constants obtain. The belief that an apple has three dimensions while the words on a printed page have only two cannot be justified by stating that this is how adults have come to conceive matters. The *origin* of an idea is not the same thing as its *validity*.

The question of the justification of our common sense picture of the world was one that occupied empirical philosophers a great deal in the last part of the nineteenth century and in the first part of the twentieth, among them Bertrand Russell. Russell's penetrating epistemological analysis in *Our Knowledge of the External World as a Field for Scientific Method in Philosophy* (1914) made a strong impression on Carnap. Inspired by Russell's example he set himself the immensely ambitious and demanding task of creating a *rational reconstruction* of the world as we conceive it. What this meant was that all concepts used in our knowledge of the world should be reduced to more fundamental concepts,

24

which in turn should be reduced to the most fundamental. Several of Russell's own works can be considered as forerunners of such a project.[28] In agreement not only with positivism, but also with Husserl's phenomenology and other theories within the Cartesian tradition as well, Carnap assumes that there is something which is *directly given*, something completely original and therefore also *certain*, from which all knowledge can be derived or constructed. But while the Cartesian tradition seeks the derivation of all assertions from absolutely certain basic statements, Carnap confines himself to *types* of statements defined by the type of concepts which occur in them. The task he set himself was to provide a system of concepts in which all concepts, and thereby all objects in the widest sense, should be placed in definite stages or levels above the foundation. In this way all types of knowledge could be ordered in a hierarchy according to their priority in the chain of justification, with knowledge of the directly given as the final link.

Carnap's presentation of the problem and his precious tool—the logic of relations

The project that Carnap embarks upon in the *Aufbau* is hardly less ambitious than what Aristotle, Aquinas, Descartes, or Spinoza had earlier attempted. Its dimensions can best be judged by bearing in mind that the objects concerned encompass all that is real, and even more than that, unreal things—things, for example, which we conceive of only in imagination. The point of departure is not unlike that of Aristotle in his *Metaphysics:* the aim is to form a science of "that which is," in complete generality, to arrive at a classification that gives maximum comprehensiveness together with minimum

---

[28]*Principia Mathematica* (Cambridge: Cambridge University Press, 1910-13) is a reconstruction of mathematics on the basis of logic; *Analysis of Mind* (New York: The Macmillan Co., 1921) and *Analysis of Matter* (New York: Harcourt, Brace & Co., 1927) are reconstructions of, respectively, psychology and physics.

arbitrariness, in fact, a rational classification of our concepts about that which is. Using the root in the Greek word for "to be," or more properly, for "being," *ont*, we obtain a term "ontologic" which very aptly conveys what Carnap aims to create: a science about that which is—in complete generality. The principle of classification he adopts is how we can *know* something about the individual objects: the cognitive priority of the concepts of them. If, in order for a thing *a* to be made an *object of knowledge*, one must first have knowledge about another thing *b*, then *b* is primary in relation to *a*. However, there is no single order that is definitive in all respects; hence there is a certain flexibility in the carrying out of the project.

Carnap is opposed to previous ontological endeavors, "traditional metaphysics" as he often referred to them later, and aims at establishing the closest possible contact with the individual special sciences. He refuses, therefore, to refer to his work as a combination of ontology and epistemology. The word "ontology" he finds has too many associations with vague speculation and an unscientific attitude.

Since among the objects of discourse there are those that do not exist, for example, a golden mountain, it is understandable that Carnap makes use of a terminology in which "concept" and "object" stand for the same: *x* is an object or a concept if and only if *something can be said about x*. It is understood here that the expression "saying something about" is meant in the sense of "assert something," that is, "saying something which can be true or false about *x*." As for the reduction of one concept to one or more others, Carnap thinks here of a special type of definition of one concept by one or more others, a "constitutional definition."

By means of this special terminology Carnap is able to formulate his aim as the creation of a genealogy or system of constitution of all concepts.

The significance of the *Aufbau* lies essentially in Carnap's discovery of a powerful logical tool with which to carry out the gigantic task.[29] We must therefore look more closely at this instrument, and here we can follow Carnap's own clear instructions.

Briefly, Carnap uses that part of modern logic which is concerned with expressing *relationships*. His aim is to explain reality as a network of relations, that is, as *structure*, not as "content." It is characteristic of science that it apprehends only structure. The logic of relations goes back to Leibniz (1646-1716), to whom also is due the idea of a kind of genealogy of concepts and a logical universal language *(characteristica universalis)* which can state explicitly and unequivocally the mutual relationships that all things bear to one another. Among those who had most recently anticipated him in his use of the logic of relations in ontology were Bertrand Russell (b. 1872) and Alfred North Whitehead (1861-1947).

The special logical methods which Carnap's system of constitution made use of are fairly complicated. However, it is easy enough to grasp what the logic of relations is about. The relations 'has the same father as,' 'is married to,' 'is as kind as,' for example, have in common the feature that if a thing x stands in one of these relationships *(R)* to another thing y, then y stands in the same relation to x. The relations are *symmetrical*. By using symbols, the property of symmetry can be expressed as: "for all x and y, it is the case that if xRy then yRx." *Asymmetrical* relations are those where the contrary applies: "for all x and y, it is the case that if xRy then not yRx." Examples are 'is to the left of,' 'is father of,' 'is west of.' There are other relations, *non-symmetrical* relations, which are such that simply in virtue of themselves

---

[29]It is worth noting that the distinction between the contribution of logic and that of the logician is not at all easy to make, i.e., between what is owing to the exceptional character of the instrument or the exceptional ability of the man who uses it. It would be of great historical and methodological interest to discover what difficulties a researcher unversed in symbolic logic would have if he tried to follow the same path as Carnap in the development of his work.

neither the first formulation nor the second can be applied to x and y, as, for example, in the case of 'is philosophically influenced by,' 'loves,' 'attacks.' Another simple classification of relations is into *reflexive*, *irreflexive* and *non-reflexive*. A relation which x always bears to itself is called reflexive, one in which x cannot stand to itself irreflexive, and others non-reflexive. 'Is a compatriot of' and 'is as old as' are reflexive, while 'is a cause of' is, for many philosophers, irreflexive, though for Spinoza it is non-reflexive, in that according to him there is an x such that x is a cause of x: namely substance. The logic of relations consists in a classification of kinds of relation and an account of what can be logically inferred from a proposition about relations.

The constitution of concepts and objects

In the following will be presented some relatively simple examples of what Carnap takes to be the constitution of a concept. We shall take an elementary mathematical example, the constitution of the fraction $3/7$ by the natural numbers 3 and 7 and of the fraction $2/5$ by 2 and 5. But why an example from mathematics? Well, it is simply a fact that nearly all of Carnap's elementary, and convincing, examples are drawn from mathematics or symbolic logic; this is something one has to get used to.

A sentence in which "$3/7$" and "$2/5$" appear can be transformed into a sentence in which they do not appear, and in which the numerals "2," "3," "5," and "7" appear instead. The sentence "$3/7$ is greater than $2/5$" can be given the alternative form "for all natural numbers x and y, it is the case that $3x$ is greater than $2y$, when $7x$ is equal to $5y$." More briefly: "$3/7$ $2/5$" can be rendered "for all natural numbers x and y: $3x$ $2y$ if $7x = 5y$." As can be seen, the reformulation may not be immediately recognizable as such. However, if the formulator of the original sentence were to consider this an objection, Carnap would ask him: is there anything you have said, in the

sense of *stated,* in your own sentence which is not also expressed in the new version? And is there anything expressed
in the new version which was not expressed in your original
formulation? Can you, in general, distinguish between two
states of affairs, one of which is that whose existence you are
asserting, and the other of which is said to exist according to
the rephrased sentence? It may not be easy to see the cognitive equivalence (Carnap: "logical" equivalence) between
these two formulations, but the constitutionalist does not
claim that it should be so.

The fraction example suggests how the concept of fraction
can be reduced to the concept of natural number in the sense
that for all sentences in which fractions occur there is a *rule*
("constitution rule") which says how such sentences can be
transformed into sentences in which natural numerals but not
fractions, appear. Carnap points out that the concept of fraction in this way can be reduced to that of natural number,
and that of irrational number to that of fraction. In this way
we get a kind of chain; it is clear, moreover, that the relation
of 'being constituted by' is a "transitive" one: if *a* can be
reduced to *b* and *b* to *c, a* can be reduced to *c.* On the other
hand, the relation is neither symmetrical nor reflexive.

In tracing back the links of various chains of reduction, do
we ever reach a point where the same link keeps on coming
up in each? In other words, are there certain concepts which
indirectly constitute a great number of others, so that the
respective chains can be joined together? If this is *not* the
case, it seems clear that a constitution system will be able to
provide no more than a catalogue of disconnected chains of
reduction (with two or more links): the last link of each
chain will not be able to stand in any mutually clarificatory
relationship to any others. If, on the other hand, there *are*
concepts capable of generating a number of chains, we can
arrive at a (cognitive) genealogy of concepts and hence also
of objects. It is, of course, the fond dream of metaphysical
system builders to explain all things in terms of one. For

Carnap such wishful thinking would be unbecoming; we should not be surprised, then, that for him the dream appears in the form of a scientific hypothesis! His intention is to indicate just how a reduction to one single concept is possible. Instead of a forest of family trees, we should then have a single giant tree, rich in branches, but with one trunk. There is a further system-builder's hypothesis that Carnap assumes to be verified: that every kind of object is in the last instance reducible to first-person experiences ("methodological solipsism"). Physical objects can be reduced to first-person experiences; third-person experiences and mental processes (other minds) can be reduced to the physical.

It is not, of course, Carnap's view that any one man, let alone he himself, could actually adduce all the rules of constitution needed to carry out the program. Yet he did think that in broad outline he had shown the possibility of completing such a system.

In regard to his analysis of individual objects, however, Carnap proceeds with a degree of logical consistency and explicitness unparalleled in the history of epistemology and ontology. The "message" of Carnap the epistemologist comes through clearly, though implicitly, for the *Aufbau* by its very example stresses the duty to carry an idea through, not just to throw it off airily and continue on one's way. This is what, by implication, he accuses the earlier empiricists of doing when they asserted that all knowledge was reducible to sense-experiences, or the positivists when they spoke about the given, the positive, which all knowledge proceeds from. It seems to be Carnap's view that in this respect the ontologist and biologist Hans Driesch and the creator of phenomenology, Edmund Husserl, have taken their scientific responsibilities more seriously.

The basic concept in Carnap's system of constitution is not one of sense data or of simple qualities (for example, olive green of a certain degree of saturation, lightness, and so on), but of total moments of experience. Though simple qualities do in some way come into these, they are not immediately given in them. Those experiences which cannot be further analyzed Carnap calls *Elementarerlebnisse*, or elementary experiences. Between these there obtain relations of similarity and from these we arrive at concepts of that in virtue of which one experience resembles or does not resemble another. By comparing and abstracting we then come, indirectly, to concepts like 'olive green.' Carnap calls this process "quasianalysis"—a *kind* of analysis which is not "real" analysis since it does not divide a whole into its parts. The parts here are not immediately given, like the whole, and one and the same experience in the flow of experience can contain sense experiences or, more generally, perceptions of the most widely differing kinds.

Compared with empiricist philosophers from Locke through Berkeley and Hume to Mach, it is striking how complex, conceptually, Carnap makes the first, or most basic, step in his system of constitution. His procedure reflects a perhaps rather surprising homage to the work of psychologists, more specifically to that of the Gestalt school. Carnap states that he "recognized, under the influence of the Gestalt psychology of Wertheimer and Köhler that the customary method of analyzing material things into separate sense-data was inadequate—that an instantaneous visual field and perhaps even an instantaneous total experience is given as a unit, while the allegedly simple sense-data are the result of a process of abstraction."[30]

As for the flow of experience itself, Carnap did not assume that it lent itself to division into discrete "slices," but he allowed that one could at least make statements about points along its course.

There is only one basic relation among experiences: 'memory that *x* resembles *y*,' 'memory of similarity.' *(Ähnlichkeitserrinerung)* Given such memory it is possible to compare different *loci* in the flow of experience. On the basis of the

---

[30]Autobiography, in Schilpp, *The Philosophy of Rudolf Carnap*, p. 16.

class concept of 'experience' and the relational concept of 'memory of similarity' it is possible to construct the concepts belonging to the "sense class"—visual qualities, auditory qualities, and so forth. The concepts of visual field, positions in the visual field, three-dimensionality, and so forth, come later.

So much for the step-by-step reduction of concepts. Corresponding to it is the step-by-step reduction of *objects* in the wide sense that the word must be given for a cognitive reconstruction of the whole world, ourselves included. Naturally, an important point in the system is the constitution of such things as tables, chairs, and so forth, on the basis of sense qualities. But this would take us too far into Carnap's complex presentation. The rule of constitution for the concept of sense class alone takes up three lines of symbolic logic.[31] The rule or "definition" contains, apart from a symbol ("Rs") for the one primitive relation of 'remembered similarity,' only purely logical signs, especially those of the logic of relations. Even the one empirical relation, 'Rs', is eliminated with the help of purely logical formulae in order to show that the constitution system as such—all its propositions and objects—can be expressed in pure logic: "all scientific propositions are propositions about structure." In the final instance—when everything derivable has been eliminated and the purely cognitive import is all that remains, one sees that science speaks only about *relationships*.

The fact that all relations are reducible to one alone shows, in Carnap's view, that all earlier attempts to adduce *categories*, from Aristotle to Driesch, have led to far too prolix lists. And this has been because there were no adequate logical-methodological means to help in the work of construction. Future generations, however, will be able to contribute with

---

[31]*Der logische Aufbau der Welt* (2d ed.; Hamburg: Felix Meiner Verlag, 1961), p. 159. English translation by Rolf A. George, *The Logical Structure of the World* (Berkeley: University of California Press; London: Routledge & Kegan Paul, 1967), p. 187. References to the English edition will appear in parentheses.

increasing precision and scope to the logical reconstruction of the world with modern logic as their most valuable instrument.

The *Aufbau* is a work which compels admiration and respect; yet only a few years after its publication serious objections were raised both to details of the work and to the project as a whole.[32] In the vanguard of the critics has been Carnap himself.

Logical Empiricism

Basic theses

Toward the end of the 1930's and well into the 1940's, it was possible for a large number of philosophers and scientists to consider their own views on the basic questions within the individual sciences as "logical empiricism," or at least as closer to logical empiricism than to other positions. Many of them have made independent contributions to the actual shaping of logical empiricism. Historians of philosophy, however, as historians are wont, simplify and condense, and they have contributed, in their turn, to the tendency today to equate logical empiricism with Carnap, a suggestion which he himself would be the last person to accept.

Most of the theses of logical empiricism, as Carnap understands them, can be arrived at by various more precise and elaborate interpretations of the following initial formulations.

---

[32]Criticism has been especially strong from the linguistic philosophers (cf. pp. 156 ff.), and has been directed at the very bases of Carnap's work. In linguistic quarters all system philosophy has at times been looked upon as moribund, if not actually dead. But in the last ten years there has been a trend in the opposite direction, and now there seems to be a renewal of interest in the system builders. In the long run such general trends and reactions are of little interest compared to the positions of individual thinkers, whether they move with or against the tide.

1. All necessary truths are analytic. There are no synthetic a priori truths.

2. Scientific and thus also cognitive meaning in general is a property only of statements that can be tested, directly or indirectly, by means of observation. Metaphysics does not satisfy this condition.

3. Science, and thereby all knowledge, can be expressed in concepts whose meaning is due to their occurrence in directly testable statements or can be reduced to concepts which acquire their meaning in this way.

4. The testability of statements presupposes a set of rules of language. In our choice of these we are free (the Principle of Tolerance). The rules themselves, however, are not knowledge, and attempts to talk as if they were result in metaphysics.

5. Philosophy is an activity through which the consequences of the above four theses are drawn within the various existing areas of scientific research and which helps to incorporate new areas under such research. But philosophy itself cannot be an area of knowledge, alongside or beyond the sciences.

The meaninglessness of all metaphysics

In "The Elimination of Metaphysics through Logical Analysis of Language" Carnap's antimetaphysical attitude is given its most unequivocal and vivid expression. Wittgenstein's prophetic personality and the crusading spirit among the members of the Vienna Circle had the effect of eliciting from the normally critical Carnap expressions which he himself soon saw would not stand up to close analysis. On the other hand, their extreme simplicity and dogmatic character were largely responsible for the attention the Vienna Circle drew upon itself from the outside world. Among scientists and philosophers with practical experience in science there was wide mistrust, even scorn and contempt, for German metaphysics, and Carnap's words found a ready and general response. It will be illuminating, therefore, as well as a matter of historical interest, to recount some of the main points.

With the help of modern logic, says Carnap, it is now possible, on the one hand, to clarify the concepts in the individual sciences, and on the other, to expose the meaninglessness of metaphysics (including any science of values or norms).[33] The so-called statements of metaphysics are strings of words which provide no statements in any definite language; they are *pseudo-statements*. When they appear with a question mark suffixed, they do not express questions. The "problems" of metaphysics are *pseudo-problems*.

Attempts to disprove or, indeed, in any way to bring arguments against metaphysical "theses" have, therefore, been a result of misunderstanding: it has been erroneously assumed that they have meaning. The refutation of metaphysical theses needs to be replaced by analysis of the metaphysician's "language."

> A language consists of a vocabulary and a syntax, i.e. a set of words which have meanings and rules of sentence formation. . . . Accordingly, there are two kinds of pseudo-statements: either they contain a word which is erroneously believed to have meaning, or the constituent words are meaningful, yet are put together in a counter-

[33]Carnap has found it hard to hit upon any one definite concept of metaphysics. Scattered remarks occur in the most widely differing writings. A note from 1957 to the English translation of "Überwindung der Metaphysik" goes as follows: "['Metaphysics'] is used in this paper, as usually in Europe, for the field of alleged knowledge of the essence of things which transcends the realm of empirically founded, inductive science. Metaphysics in this sense includes systems like those of Fichte, Schelling, Hegel, Bergson, Heidegger. But it does not include endeavors towards a synthesis and generalization of the results of the various sciences." In A. J. Ayer (ed.), *Logical Positivism*, p. 80. Cf. note 20 above and note 34 following.

syntactical way, so that they do not yield a meaningful statement.[34]

Metaphysics contains pseudo-statements of both kinds. As examples of words which have no meaning in *metaphysics*, Carnap mentions, among others, "principle" (Latin: *principium;* Greek: ἀρχή), "God," "primordial basis," "the Idea," "the Absolute," "the Unconditioned," "the Infinite," "the being of being," "non-being," "thing in itself," "objective spirit," "essence," "the Ego," "the non-Ego." It is not, of course, Carnap's thesis that these words never have meaning, only that they lack meaning when they occur in metaphysical texts. (The word "Metaphysics," on the other hand, is only defined in terms of the occurrence of meaningless words which are implicitly claimed to have meaning. At any rate Carnap provides no other kind of definition. The thesis about the meaninglessness of metaphysics is thus analytic.)

Let us examine Carnap's arguments as they are put into actual antimetaphysical practice. For this purpose we can take his logical analysis of some statements from the text of Martin Heidegger's *Was ist Metaphysik?* ("What is Metaphysics?"). They are assembled by Carnap in the following series.

> What is to be investigated is being only and—*nothing* else; being alone and further—*nothing;* solely being, and beyond being—*nothing. What about this Nothing?* . . . *Does the Nothing exist only because the Not, i.e. the Negation, exists?* Or is it the other way around? *Does Negation and the Not exist only because the Nothing exists?* . . . We assert: *the Nothing is prior to the Not and the Negation.* . . . Where do we seek the Nothing? How do we find the Nothing. . . . We know the Nothing. . . . *Anxiety reveals the Nothing.* . . . That for which and

---

[34]"The Elimination of Metaphysics through Logical Analysis of Language," English translation by Arthur Pap of "Überwindung der Metaphysik durch Logische Analyse der Sprache" (cf. note 6 above), in A. J. Ayer (ed.), *Logical Positivism*, p. 61.

because of which we were anxious, was 'really'—nothing.
Indeed: the Nothing itself—as such—was present. . . .
What about this Nothing?—The Nothing itself nothings.[35]

The three statements, "We seek the Nothing," "We find
the Nothing," and "We know the Nothing" are pseudo-
statements because "Nothing" does not have a meaning as a
noun. Although in the ordinary use of language "nothing"
does appear in sentences as if it were a substantive, in a correct language the same sense is expressed, not by a name but
by a special logical form (that of a negative existential statement): "There is not anything which we seek," or, adapted
to the language of logical formulae: "There is nothing such
that it may be truthfully said of it: it is sought by us."[36] The
formula may be written: $\sim (\exists x). S(x)$. Here "S" stands for a
logical predicate: "sought by us."

The statement "The Nothing itself nothings" is in even
worse case. Not only is "Nothing" used as a noun without
there being anything it could possibly designate, but another
meaningless word appears along with it. "Does the Nothing
exist only because . . .?" is a pseudo-question, because any
direct answer of the type "The Nothing exists only because
. . ." must itself be a pseudo-statement. Even if it were appropriate to use "nothing" as a name or description of something, it could only be of something whose existence was
denied in its very definition. Consequently, "The Nothing
exists only because . . ." would be contradictory: something
would be said both to exist and not to exist.

Thus Carnap discovers "gross logical errors" in Heidegger's
text which render it meaningless. There is no language in
which the quoted word sequences could comprise statements;
and so the question of whether what Heidegger says is true or

---

[35]The quotations are taken from *Was ist Metaphysik?* (Frankfurt am
Main: V. Klostermann, 1955), pp. 9-10, 12-13, 16-17, and 18. Quoted
here from "The Elimination of Metaphysics" in A. J. Ayer (ed.),
Logical Positivism, p. 69.
[36]This formulation is not Carnap's.

false naturally falls by the wayside. If one has not succeeded in saying anything, one has not succeeded even in uttering a falsehood. (It must be remembered that Carnap is all along taking "meaning" in the sense of "cognitive meaning," or, in his own terminology, "theoretical content.")

Carnap of course admits that his conclusion is based on a hypothetical interpretation of Heidegger's text. In particular he assumes that "Nothing" in "What about this Nothing?" is intended to have the same reference as "nothing" in "What is to be investigated is being only and—*nothing* else." Thus Carnap assumes it is the old "nothing" that suddenly crops up as a noun, not a new "nothing," not the word "nothing" used in another sense. In this way the ground is already cut from under those who might make sympathetic attempts to attach to the word a meaning which avoids pseudo-statements and contradiction. But Carnap's interpretation of Heidegger goes further still: Heidegger quite simply does not want to be saved from contradictions. Thus Carnap takes Heidegger's view to be that if a contradiction occurs, so much the worse for the law of contradiction.

And indeed Heidegger does say that although the law of contradiction "destroys" questions regarding the Nothing and Being, all the same, the questions are somehow able to strike forcefully back.

> If thus the power of the *understanding* in the field of questions concerning Nothing and Being is broken, then the fate of the sovereignty of 'logic' within philosophy is thereby decided as well. The very idea of 'logic' dissolves in the whirl of a more basic questioning.

And Heidegger warns the servants of science: "The alleged sobriety and superiority of science becomes ridiculous if it does not take the Nothing seriously."[37]

---

[37]The two passages from, respectively, pp. 21 and 25 of *Was ist Metaphysik?* are quoted in "The Elimination of Metaphysics," pp. 71-72.

Carnap is not slow to draw his conclusions from this. The metaphysician admits—even exults in the claim—that metaphysical questions and answers are irreconcilable with logic and the scientific way of thinking. Certainly the examples of metaphysical "statements" that he, Carnap, has analyzed come only from one work, but, he claims, his results apply "with equal validity, in part even in verbally identical ways, to other metaphysical systems."[38]

It would not be wholly unreasonable to say that Carnap reads Heidegger much as the Devil would read the Bible; both, certainly, on the basis of special knowledge, but at the same time each adopting presuppositions which are only a selection of those possible. A reading of Heidegger's text, in fact, makes it quite plausible to deny that "the Nothing" *(das Nichts)* is meant as a noun, and also—despite Carnap's cogent counterargument (the occurrence of the word "this" in "this Nothing")—to deny that "the Nothing" *(das Nichts)* is a substantivization of "nothing" *(nichts)* in the quoted sentences. Moreover, there is nothing in Heidegger's text which *requires* us to assume that any incompatibility of the kind Carnap mentions is either stated or insinuated. No matter what object science investigates, logic and the scientific attitude are appropriate and indeed necessary. But science investigates the world, the things that exist in it, all conceivable objects—and beyond that, *nothing*. The metaphysician tries to grasp this very delimitation, and a hint of it ultimately conditions the scientist's own wonderment and all his cognitive endeavors—according to Heidegger.

So much for a possible defense of Heidegger. But even if a defense was successful, a vital question remains. To what extent can the use of language exemplified in Heidegger's *Was ist Metaphysik?* be in any way related to discursive argumentational thinking? If it has some connection, what rules of formation and transformation can be applied to Heidegger's

[38]"The Elimination of Metaphysics," p. 73.

concepts and statements? It is clear that Heidegger would not take Carnapian rules to hold for his text, for example, the rule implied by Carnap's criticism that substantivization is only to be undertaken in the form of a transition to terms designating *objects*.

Following its violently antimetaphysical phase, Carnap's thinking entered upon a period of greater calm and stability. It no longer occurred to him, without further ado, to stamp metaphysical texts as (cognitively) meaningless. Rather, his position was: (1) that on the basis of certain, far from self-evident, criteria of meaning the statements of metaphysics are meaningless; and (2) that if a metaphysician has *other* criteria, the onus is on him to formulate them in such a way as to make the difference clear and to render the criterion amenable to debate.

Carnap appreciates that his special strength lies in abstract and formal thought; it is there that he has found his vocation. But this by no means implies that he has only a limited concern with concrete states of affairs. Indeed, far from lacking examples, as one might expect, his work is extraordinarily rich in illustrations—constant sources of danger in the opportunity they provide for critical readers to pick holes in a philosopher's theory. But Carnap is always anxious to make his meaning quite clear. The Heidegger example serves as an illustration of what he means by logical analysis of a metaphysical text, and it shows precisely the line of attack he adopts in his attempted elimination of metaphysics. But there are a great many other examples of historical as well as systematic interest. We can cite, again from "The Elimination of Metaphysics," his quite brief criticism of a not unfamiliar metaphysical pseudo-statement: *cogito ergo sum*.

> We notice . . . two essential logical mistakes. The first lies in the conclusion "I am." The verb "to be" is undoubtedly meant in the sense of existence here; for a copula cannot be used without predicate. . . . But in that

case this sentence violates the . . . logical rule that existence can be predicated only in conjunction with a predicate, not in conjunction with a name (subject, proper
name).

The term "copula" here refers to "am," "is," or "are," for
example, in "I am hungry." It is written symbolically: P(a),
and read "*a* has the property P"; thus, "I have the property of
being (hungry)." Carnap continues:

An existential statement does not have the form "*a* exists"
(as in "I am," i.e. "I exist"), but "there exists something
of such and such a kind." The second error lies in the
transition from "I think" to "I exist." If from the statement "P(a)" ("*a* has the property P") an existential is to
be deduced, then the latter can assert existence only with
respect to the predicate P, not with respect to the subject
a of the premise. What follows from "I am a European"
is not "I exist," but "a European exists." What follows
from "I think" is not "I am" but "there exists something
that thinks."[39]

Though one may deplore Carnap's tendency to elevate
rules of symbolic logic to the status of general rules for all
meaningful language, there can be no doubt that the acute
analyses he and other logical empiricists have provided have
helped us to see the problem more clearly. Has everything in
the classical literature of philosophy meaning; if so, what kind
of meaning?

Metaphysics as the expression of an attitude to life
Dilthey, Nohl and Carnap

Even if one accepts the arguments for the meaninglessness of
metaphysics, one is still, Carnap says, liable to a feeling of
perplexity. How is it that such highly gifted men in the most
diverse cultures and epochs have spent so much time and

[39]*Ibid.*, p. 74.

energy on nonsensical juxtapositions of words? What is the explanation of the considerable historical influence of the great metaphysicians? Carnap replies that metaphysics does after all have some content—but not theoretical (cognitive) content. Its "statements" serve for the expression of an attitude to life.[40] Indeed, it is precisely because it passes itself off as something it is not that the days of metaphysics are numbered. "The metaphysician believes that he travels in territory in which truth and falsehood are at stake. In reality, however, he has not asserted anything, but only expressed something, like an artist."[41]

When it comes to giving expression to an attitude toward life, however, the metaphysician is an inferior artist.

> Perhaps music is the purest means of expression of the basic attitude because it is entirely free from any reference to objects. The harmonious feeling or attitude, which the metaphysician tries to express in a monistic system, is more clearly expressed in the music of Mozart. And when a metaphysician gives verbal expression to his dualistic-heroic attitude towards life in a dualistic system, is it not perhaps because he lacks the ability of a Beethoven to express this attitude in an adequate medium? Metaphysicians are musicians without musical ability.[42]

Carnap goes into no further details about what kind of substantial research might tend to confirm his very general theses about the character of metaphysics. But he does refer to the investigations on world views of Wilhelm Dilthey (1833-1911) and of Dilthey's students. The reference is very welcome: it gives us an opportunity to say a little about an important trend in German philosophy, and one that exerts a strong influence in contemporary continental philosophy.

[40]*Ibid.*, p. 78.
[41]*Ibid.*, p. 79.
[42]*Ibid.*, p. 80.

Herman Nohl (1879-1958), Carnap's gratefully remembered teacher at Jena, later especially known for his philosophy of education, had stressed the non-theoretical component in a person's "metaphysical view of life" (little suspecting, no doubt, to what effect this would be put by one of his pupils). The famous German philosopher Fichte (1762-1814) had already said something about this non-theoretical component when he wrote:

> Which philosophy one chooses depends on what kind of man one is, for a philosophical system is not some inanimate piece of furniture; it is infused with the soul of the man who has it. To put it in another way: a world view is but the theoretical elucidation of the experience of one's own existence. But at the same time it shapes this existence, because it consciously draws the consequences. Here, then, is disclosed the high heaven of the spiritual molders, their solemn procession through the millennia. What power to influence does not devolve upon their followers![43]

And Herman Nohl, himself a pupil of Wilhelm Dilthey, the philosopher to whom the clarification of the non-theoretical component in metaphysics is particularly due, wrote:

> What ultimately determines man's spiritual reality is how far one places the absolute in a transcendence, or knows it in oneself, or how far one exists godless. What Hegel presents in a still manifestly one-sided interpretation, has been given its freedom in Dilthey's typology of systems. Dilthey realized that the whole manifold of metaphysical standpoints, this seeming chaos in which, down through the centuries, one view always opposes the other, only

[43]Quoted in Herman Nohl, *Charakter und Schicksal: Eine pädagogische Menschenkunde* (6th ed.; Frankfurt am Main: Verlag Gerhard Schulte-Bulmke, 1963), p. 181. Cf. J. G. Fichte, *Über das Wesen des Gelehrten und seine Erscheinungen im Gebiete der Freiheit, Erste Vorlesung, Fichtes Werke*, Vol. 5 (Leipzig: Felix Meiner, 1910), e.g., p. 11.

lends itself to any organization when one examines the structure of the systems and, what is related to these, the distinctive consciousnesses of their creators.[44]

Nohl's remarks reveal that he himself is very far from anti-metaphysics. Only if metaphysical systems were *not* inspired by their creator's souls would they be like so much furniture. Not that Dilthey's speculations in life philosophy provide on that account any less fertile soil for a rejection of metaphysics: for Carnap all that was needed was a slight adjustment in perspective. To see more clearly the point on which this adjustment pivots we may profitably take a brief look at some of the substance of Dilthey's "theory of world views." Dilthey writes:

> I will show that the philosophical systems, too, as much as religions and works of art, contain an understanding of life and the world which is based, not in conceptual thought, but in the living persons who produced them. . . .
>
> In the first place, every system contains unprovable presuppositions. This extends to bare connections between established statements. Even positivism contains more than just scientific cognitions and their relations to our knowledge of psychical phenomena. In that philosophical systems aim at giving a totality to a world view, they inevitably give rise to antinomies. . . .[45]

How are we to explain the fact that system builders, in direct opposition to the procedures prescribed by the empirical scientist and heedless of antinomies, continue to build? The fact would be quite unintelligible, Dilthey believes, unless they were driven on by a strong *will* to give verbal expression to some sort of disposition. And this, he claims, is

[44]Nohl, *Charakter und Schicksal*, p. 181.
[45]Wilhelm Dilthey, *Das Geschichtliche Bewusstsein und die Weltanschauungen*, in *Gesammelte Schriften* (Stuttgart: B. G. Teubner, Verlagsgesellschaft, 1962), Vol. 8, p. 30.

indeed generally the case. A definite state of feeling (*Gefühlsvorhalten*) is expressed even in philosophical thinking.

If, as we might suppose, Carnap was interested in justifying positivism, these remarks of Dilthey's about the antinomies which any view gives rise to if presented as a philosophical system would seem to be of direct relevance. However, they are little more than historically relevant, since it was quite clear to Carnap—even as early as in his work on the *Aufbau*—that it was not *his* aim to give anything resembling a general, systematic statement of positivism, and that his concern was to proceed not from axioms in the form of propositional presuppositions, but from such bases as rules, decisions about language, or *proposals* about ways of talking about things. Thus, even if Carnap were to succeed in his aim, there would be nothing to prevent him from subscribing to Dilthey's characterization of positivism (with regard, for example, to the views of Comte, Mill, and Mach).

Basic philosophical positions are expressions for basic dispositional attitudes, but their claim to be generally valid conceptually is not to any extent diminished on that account. The claim to general validity is, so to speak, a universal component in all basic dispositional attitudes. According to Dilthey:

> All higher consciousness . . . expresses itself in the fact that all one undergoes and experiences in its parts and in their relation to one another is made clear. Therefore logical energy is absolutely indispensable in the philosopher's work.[46]

From the requirements of this consciousness proceeds the intention to *justify* the activity of life autonomously by understanding and reason—to make it generally valid. A philosophical system claims to be true and accurate. Consequently, the differences between systems are not things that will gradually be settled. To each main type of cognition of reality,

[46]*Ibid.*, p. 31.

evaluation of life and purpose, there belongs a type of philosophical system.[47]

Understood in this way, the task of the metaphysician cannot in principle be satisfactorily carried out. A world view just cannot be made generally valid. A peculiarity of metaphysics is the fact that it looks in two directions: on one side it faces poetry and religion, on the other it addresses itself to the individual sciences. But the creative metaphysician is unable to reach scientific knowledge in any of the departments in which he seems to claim competence:—either in regard to his understanding of nature, in his appraisal of life, or in the determining of practical goals. Metaphysics contains "a secret, inner contradiction."[48]

Dilthey, Nohl, and many other *geisteswissenschaftlich* and historically oriented philosophers in Carnap's environment venerated metaphysics as an expression of human genius. Far from considering it a bad substitute for poetry and music, it seemed to them to have its own intrinsic worth. For these historicizing philosophers the theoretical value—or lack of value—of metaphysics was a secondary consideration. For Carnap, however, it was the other way round: theoretical knowledge, that is, insight within the limits of what can be conceptualized was just what he valued most highly. It was natural, therefore, that his model should be that of the exact sciences.

The "proof" of the "personalism" of metaphysics offered by these philosophers became Carnap's point of departure for an

---

[47]Cf. *ibid.*, p. 32, and *Das Wesen der Philosophie* (1907), in *Gesammelte Schriften*, Vol. 5, First Part, pp. 404 ff.

[48]Carnap's view was that empiricism, suitably interpreted, does not have the character of a metaphysical system. Here he found a resting place, as Dilthey did in his *geisteswissenschaftlich* historicism. Thus far and no farther are the tools which dismiss systems as acognitive effective. But as far as I can see, the tools are equally effective against the positions of Carnap and Dilthey. The final links in their chains of justification seem to me no different from those of metaphysical systems. They are "totalizing" views of reality, in Dilthey's sense; they "set" certain values and represent decisions.

attempt to demarcate the boundary between science and metaphysics. For this purpose he found the criteria of cognitive meaning the most suitable means. In keeping with the insight that naturalism, materialism, and positivism, as negations of supernaturalism and idealism, are still metaphysics, he made it his aim to eliminate all remnants of such "antimetaphysical" metaphysics in his own and the Vienna Circle's thinking. Should he succeed in delimiting science from metaphysics, all the different branches of science would acquire a unity simply in their common distinction from metaphysics. It was this idea that underlay the slogan of "the unity of science" and the idea of an encyclopedia of the unified sciences. This encyclopedia was regarded by its chief organizer, Otto Neurath, as a twentieth-century counterpart to the encyclopedia of the Enlightenment in the eighteenth century.[49]

The preface to *Der logische Aufbau der Welt* concludes with remarks that show very clearly both what Carnap grants the philosophers of life in their conception of philosophy and just how he would put a stop to their tendency to place feeling or intuition above reason. Speaking here of what he would "render unto Caesar and what unto God," Carnap says:

> The practical handling of philosophical problems and the discovery of their solutions does not have to be purely intellectual, but will always contain emotional elements and intuitive methods. The *justification*, however, has to take place before the forum of the understanding; here we must not refer to our intuition or emotional needs. We too have "emotional needs" in philosophy, but they are filled by clarity of concepts, precision of methods, responsible theses, achievement through coöperation. . . .[50]

[49]The war and Neurath's death soon after it put an end to systematic work on the *Encyclopedia of Unified Science*, and naturally enough, more recent contributions to it have not followed the pattern Neurath laid down.

[50]*Der logische Aufbau der Welt*, pp. ix-x (xvii).

47

So heartfelt have been these needs in Carnap himself that he has been led to concern himself far more with the foundations of science and other problems on the borderline between philosophy and science than with those less tractable regions where philosophy itself borders on the theoretically meaningless.

Philosophy as logical syntax

In his work, *The Logical Syntax of Language*, Carnap aims at showing, among other things, that the living substance of philosophy is the logic of science, and that the latter consists in the syntax of scientific language. "All philosophical problems which have any meaning belong to syntax."[51] It is only by a kind of linguistic illusion that philosophy is taken to have its own exclusive subject matter. According to Kronecker, "God created the natural numbers (integers); fractions and real numbers on the other hand are the work of man." Carnap, instead, says, "The natural-number symbols are primitive symbols; the fractional expressions and real-number expressions are introduced by definition."[52] And where Wittgenstein says, "The world is the totality of facts, not of things," Carnap says, "Science is a system of sentences, not of names." Carnap aims to replace the "material" way of speaking with a "formal" way, so as to prevent the formulation of "pseudo-sentences." Instead of talking of the Given, as he had done in the *Aufbau*, he now talks of primitive symbols of description; instead of saying that "time is continuous," he says that "real-number expressions are used as time co-ordinates." The use of the material mode of speech conceals "the relativity to language of philosophical sentences."[53] For every philosophical

[51]*The Logical Syntax of Language*, trans. Amethe Smeaton, Countess von Zeppelin (London: Kegan Paul, Trench, Trubner & Co., 1937), p. 280.
[52]The examples are from *Logical Syntax*, pp. 303-7.
[53]*Ibid.*, p. 299. The original is italicized.

sentence one formulates, one must state which language, or what kind of language, it belongs to.

Among the most distinctive features of the philosophy of Wittgenstein is his thesis about what cannot be said, about there being something which cannot be talked about. Carnap opposes both this and another "negative thesis" of Wittgenstein's. First, Wittgenstein's assertion that propositions cannot convey logical form, and that it is nonsense to assert or deny that a proposition has a certain formal property, etc., is condensed by Carnap into the following theses: "There are no sentences about the forms of sentences; there is no expressible syntax."[54] If this reformulation does cover Wittgenstein's meaning (which indeed seems unlikely), Carnap's contrary conclusion can hardly be objected to; his own construction of syntax in *The Logical Syntax of Language* has clearly demonstrated that syntax can indeed be formulated correctly and that therefore there are syntactical sentences, sentences which state formal properties, the forms of sentences. An example can be taken from Carnap's "physical syntax": " 'Nu(x)' is to be taken as true when and only when a written character having the figure of an upright ellipse ('O') is to be found at the position x." Among valid, descriptive, analytic, syntactical sentences we find, for example, "A zero symbol (physical character in ink) is a numeral." Carnap concludes: "Thus syntax is exactly formulable in the same way as geometry is."[55]

Looking at the matter now, forty years after Carnap's meetings with Wittgenstein, it is hard to understand how Carnap could believe that Wittgenstein's statements about logical form could be easily and straightforwardly translated into the framework of Carnap's own theory of language. The conclusion Carnap might have drawn, had his position with regard to Wittgenstein been rather more neutral at the time of

[54]*Ibid.*, p. 282.
[55]*Ibid.*, p. 283. The original is italicized. The two immediately preceding examples are from p. 80.

writing *Logical Syntax*, is that Wittgenstein's sentences were metaphysical (in intention), and thus pseudo-sentences. Their "translation" into a (false) thesis about syntax can only prove anti-Wittgensteinian in all essentials.[56]

The second negative thesis Carnap opposed is in Wittgenstein's statement: "Philosophy is not a body of doctrine but an activity. A philosophical work consists essentially of elucidations. Philosophy does not result in 'philosophical propositions', but rather in the clarification of propositions." (*Tractatus*, 4.112.) Carnap takes this to imply that the logic of science (and thus also logical syntax, in Carnap's interpretation of the logic of science) "contains no sentences, but merely more or less vague explanations which the reader must subsequently recognize as pseudo-sentences and abandon."[57] But far from being disposed to construct a syntax which, once used, would have to be kicked away—like Wittgenstein's ladder[58]—Carnap, in his own view, has established that logical syntax is not nonsense but a scientific discipline. He would agree that its sentences are not of a special, "philosophical" character, but for him this is because they belong to physics (for example, talk about elliptical figures, such as the numeral "O"), and to arithmetic, and not because they have no genuine function as propositions.

Any question can in principle be answered

The claim elaborated by Carnap that if anything is a question it can be answered, is not new. Carnap himself refers to the statement of the phenomenologist Becker (from 1923): "According to the principle of transcendental idealism, a question which is in principle (in essence) undecidable does not have any meaning at all. No state of affairs corresponds to it,

---

[56]See, e.g., G. E. M. Anscombe, *An Introduction to Wittgenstein's Tractatus* (London: Hutchinson University Library, 1959), pp. 82 ff.
[57]*Logical Syntax*, p. 283.
[58]See p. 102 below.

which could provide an answer for it. For there are no states of affairs which are in principle inaccessible to consciousness."[59] That all questions are in principle decidable and essentially soluble is not a tenet peculiar to positivism. But what is a question? "In the strictly logical sense," says Carnap, "to pose a question is to give a statement together with the task of deciding whether this statement or its negation is true."[60]

Accordingly the "problems" and "riddles" of life are ruled out: they are not questions in Carnap's sense and he has not taken any position with regard to them.

> The "riddles of life" are not questions, but are practical situations. The "riddle of death" consists in the shock through the death of a fellow man or in the fear of one's own death. It has nothing to do with questions which can be asked about death, even if some men, deceiving themselves, occasionally believe that they have formulated this riddle by pronouncing such questions. In principle, these questions can be answered by biology (though presently only to a very small extent), but these answers are of no help to a grieved person, which shows that it is a self-deception to regard them as formulations of the riddle of death. Rather, the riddle consists in the task of "getting over" this life situation, of overcoming the shock, and perhaps even making it fruitful for one's later life.[61]

[59]*Der logische Aufbau der Welt*, p. 256 (292).

[60]*Ibid.*, p. 254 (290).

[61]Ibid., pp. 260-61 (297). (Carnap's italics.) Wittgenstein's attitude to life's problems and mysteries is more ambiguous. On the one hand he declares that mysteries do not exist, and that if a question can be posed then it can be answered *(Tractatus*, 6.5), but on the other he says that what is mystical is that the world exists (6.44), and he remarks upon many other things traditionally associated with life's problems and mysteries. One reasonable interpretation of Wittgenstein's *Tractatus Logico-Philosophicus* is that none of its statements (except perhaps the last two) are meant to be meaningful, thus not even 6.5.

Even though Carnap talks of what it is, in a strict logical sense, to ask a question, it is clear that he means this sense to apply to all of science, indeed to all thinking whatsoever.

As for the requirements of solubility in principle, these are exceedingly modest: that there be no established facts which themselves establish the inconceivability of finding a solution. This account of the matter is consistent with Carnap's own theory of constitution: either the concepts employed in a question are locatable within the system or definable by concepts which can be so located, or the question has no cognitive meaning. If the former, then the question ultimately concerns relationships between elementary experiences. Carnap "presupposes"[62] that propositions concerning such relationships are decidable. Therefore the original question is also decidable and soluble. A critic of Carnap's philosophy, however, will try to establish that in his definition of questionability Carnap excludes the possibility of there being any scientific or, more generally, theoretically meaningful questions about the adequacy of the definition.

Scientific knowledge has no limits. There are in principle no obstacles in the path of science, no objects that lie outside the range of scientific knowledge, so Carnap says. Of course pronouncements like these are provocative, and are perhaps intended to be so. However, if one waits for Carnap's more precise formulations of them, they lose something of their pungency: Scientific knowledge is like an unending surface in space; it does not fill space, and yet, unlike, for example, a triangle, it has no boundaries. Life has many dimensions, of course, and science is only one. Certainly it is possible to "grasp" something by faith or by intuition without conceptual thought; nevertheless, what one can achieve in this way are only certain attitudes or outlooks, perhaps *favorable* for

---

[62]Carnap uses this word on p. 255 (292) in the *Aufbau*. But what status can such a presupposition have, according to Carnap? Can he take it to express a true proposition, a piece of knowledge? If not, what of the whole system of constitution? Carnap does not take up these questions. Perhaps he would later have talked, not of presuppositions, but of choice of linguistic forms, or framework. (Cf. the following section on internal and external questions, especially pages 59 f.)

52

knowledge, but not themselves knowledge.[63] The word "knowledge" as Carnap defines it designates something that is formulated in propositions actually asserted. We are, then, already inside the framework of conceptual knowledge and within the scope of systems of constitution.

Despite the fact that Carnap's system builds upon a set of definitions, it is an open question whether one can insist that "questions" about these definitions, and arguments for or against them, should have meaning for him. Would not such insistence be in effect a request for him to abandon his own system in favor of another? To proceed *jenseits des Letzten?* If, as seems reasonable, the critic's own utterances are anchored in other definitions, then he too must start somewhere. Carnap has himself had something to say on these matters.

Questions inside and "questions" outside a framework
Settlement with empiricist and nominalistic metaphysics

Within contemporary philosophy we find many empiricist and positivist trends. Bacon, Locke, Berkeley, Hume, Mill, Comte, Mach—these and many others continue to live in the attitudes and philosophical positions of present-day thinkers. Carnap has sought to define his place in relation to them, often in a way that has caused some astonishment. The key to an understanding of his distinctive place in this context lies in his own peculiar relationship to the philosophical tradition, marked on the one hand by a wide and many-sided acquaintance with it, and on the other by a certain detachment toward the controversies that have been its lifeblood.

The realization of his own neutrality toward the traditional philosophical positions came to Carnap at the time he was working on the *Aufbau*. On being questioned about his own position he found himself unable to answer, almost as if he had no part in the tradition himself. If one considers his thoroughgoing study of both German and British philosophers,

[63]*Der logische Aufbau der Welt*, p. 256 (293).

this is certainly surprising. The same situation arose in the 1950's, when, as we shall see, Carnap again appeared as an "outsider" in connection with, among other things, Quine's resuscitation of certain ontological positions. Perhaps crucial questions for the history of philosophy are to be uncovered here. Carnap's own words may help us to grasp the point more thoroughly.

> Since my student years, I have liked to talk with friends about general problems in science and in practical life, and these discussions often led to philosophical questions. My friends were philosophically interested, yet most of them were not professional philosophers, but worked either in the natural sciences or in the humanities. Only much later, when I was working on the *Logischer Aufbau*, did I become aware that in talks with my various friends I had used different philosophical languages, adapting myself to their ways of thinking and speaking. With one friend I might talk in a language that could be characterized as realistic or even as materialistic; here we looked at the world as consisting of bodies, bodies as consisting of atoms; sensations, thoughts, emotions, and the like were conceived as physiological processes in the nervous system and ultimately as physical processes. Not that the friend maintained or even considered the thesis of materialism; we just used a way of speaking which might be called materialistic. In a talk with another friend, I might adapt myself to his idealistic kind of language.[64]

The same attitude marked Carnap's relationship to Platonic and anti-Platonic, or "realist" and nominalist theses, and in fact to all main positions relevant, especially ontologically, to the philosophical disputes of his time.

I was surprised to find that this variety in my way of

[64]Autobiography, in Schilpp, *The Philosophy of Rudolf Carnap*, p. 17.

speaking appeared to some objectionable and even inconsistent. I had acquired insights valuable for my thinking from philosophers and scientists of a great variety of philosophical creeds. When asked which philosophical positions I myself held, I was unable to answer.[65]

How is it that Carnap can come to understand what have traditionally been understood to be major philosophical positions as "merely modes of speech"? A partial explanation is that in his philosophizing Carnap has never been absorbed in the last and deepest questions. The problems he has tackled are those which one might, not unjustifiably, call the next last, the next deepest—the penultimate rather than the ultimate.

In the *Aufbau* Carnap asks what is epistemologically primary and what derived, or more exactly, how one chain of derivations can be constructed for all objects *of thought*. That the objects are objects *for thought*, for scientifically informed thinking, altogether overshadows any other features they may have; the ontological aspect is pale and remote compared with the epistemological. But then the final ontological questions about possible characterizations of all that exists, and the main kinds of that which exists, are not even raised—questions which, perhaps, must be solved before one asks about the relative status of different types of object in chains of derivation, or constitution. The objects for Carnap's main preoccupations are already at hand, clearly demarcated. It is the world's *logical structure* that excites his wonder, not the world.

Against this it could be objected that, in fact, Carnap does go a step deeper when he considers the suitability of different kinds of language for different purposes. Because intersubjectivity is important for the scientist, the realist language, or thing language, is more appropriate than the phenomenological language which is based on the individual's experiences. Under Neurath's influence, Carnap developed a physi-

[65]*Ibid.*, p. 17.

calistic "attitude"—not, of course, a "belief," since the question of the type of language was a "practical question of preferences, not a theoretical question about the truth", the considerations are themselves of a linguistic nature, though involving also some purely technical arguments about objects of various kinds which are thus already ontologically and linguistically determined. But then, the choice of language is not made in a pre-linguistic state, so the questions raised are penultimate, not ultimate questions, since it is certainly meaningful to ask, for example, about the properties of the language they are posed in and about the basis on which the objects in question are delimited in relation to one another.

The question of introducing languages and of judging them on grounds of their suitability was taken up by Carnap once again in 1950 in a short but cogent article, "Empiricism, Semantics, and Ontology."[66] Here he gives a more refined account of his theory of the limits of theoretical (cognitive) meaningfulness, at the same time offering his latest views on the relationship to metaphysics and scientific research (or "work").

Carnap reminds us that Berkeley, Hume, and other British empiricists denied the existence of abstract entities on the grounds that immediate experience presents us only with particulars, not with universals. This or that red patch is part of what we experience, but not Redness or Color-in-General. Some contemporary philosophers, followers of Bertrand Russell especially, adopt a similar view, emphasizing a distinction between data and constructs based on the data.[67] The latter do not exist; at least not in reality. Thus we have to exclude all references to space-time points, the electro-magnetic field, the unconscious complexes which psychoanalysts use in their explanations and diagnoses, inflationary trends in economics, complex numbers—indeed all the kinds of numbers that math-

---

[66]"Empiricism, Semantics and Ontology." See note 8.
[67]*Ibid.*, pp. 36-37 (in *Meaning and Necessity* [2d ed.], pp. 219-20).

ematics deals with—and such abstract entities as meanings and propositional content, the stock in trade of the semanticist.

Carnap complains that contemporary nominalists accuse him of subscribing to "Platonic metaphysics" and of "hypostatizing." Gilbert Ryle describes him as an adherent of the " 'Fido'=Fido principle." Others simply ask him to show his true colors: is he *for or against* the view that numbers really exist? What is his *ontology*? What kind of entities does he take to be real? The reason for the commotion is that Carnap, who does after all belong to the empiricist and positivist tradition, makes no bones about introducing and making references to all kinds of abstract entities in his theories, moreover in a way that suggests he finds nothing in the least problematic in this. But surely any empiricist with a grain of conscience would at least look very carefully first to see whether or not some of these entities could be eliminated from his language.

Carnap sees in these accusations the results of a deep misunderstanding. This concerns the interpretation of statements such as "The word 'red' designates a property of things," "The word 'five' designates a number," etc., statements in which apparently an assertion is being made to the effect that properties, numbers, and other abstract entities belong to or are parts of reality. The mention of properties and numbers in these statements is misinterpreted in such a way that it seems quite clear that they imply a "populating" of the world with these and an infinite number of similar mysterious entities. Belief in abstract entities is thus put on an equal footing with belief in centaurs and demons.

Take the statement "Five is a number." Carnap considers that a statement of this kind has acquired its meaning as the result of a conscious decision to talk in a certain way: the word "number" has been *introduced* for the individual numbers one, two, three . . ., in general, and the acceptability of statements such as "Five is a number" resides in no further fact than this. The use of the term "five" is a function of the conscious acceptance of statements like "There are five books on this table." To have already introduced the word in this way to designate an abstract entity makes any answer to the question "Are there numbers?" trivial: "five" has already been introduced (by definition) as a legitimate substitution for the blank in the first part of the statement schema ". . . is a number." But acceptance of statements of this form and the use of them within mathematics does not imply any answer to the "question" of whether numbers exist independently of the introduced mode of speech, unrelated to the "linguistic form," or "the language framework." To accept or reject a linguistic form implies neither a Yes nor a No to "questions" of whether words and statements designate anything that *really* exists. The person who first grants that if a certain linguistic-mathematical system is given, then there "are" numbers and there "are" properties of numbers in the sense that "Five is a number" and "Five has the property of being prime" are correct ways of speaking, but then goes on to ask whether the numbers and properties existed before or subsist independently of the linguistic framework, must explain what he means by his question, what he will take to confirm or disconfirm the claim that numbers or properties have the metaphysical and ontological status of "being real." In the absence of scientifically acceptable information about the meaning of such an "ontological" question, Carnap finds himself compelled to classify it as a *pseudo*-question.

We can see, therefore, the outline of his defense of his own use of abstract terms such as "proposition," "property," and so forth. He will neither attribute to abstract entities any kind of Platonic ideal existence, nor, with the nominalists, *deny* that they exist independently of the language in which the words are introduced. The number five is neither a *flatus vocis* nor a real non-material entity. All meaningful questions about the number five can be answered on the basis of the rules introduced for the use of the word "five," and from these rules nothing at all follows about ontological status.

By *internal questions* Carnap understands questions of the existence of certain new entities within an introduced framework. ("Are there prime numbers greater than 100?" is an *internal* question in that the rule for the use of the expression "prime number" is already introduced.) By *external questions* he understands questions concerning the existence or reality of the framework.[68] These have a problematic character—everything indicates that they are pseudo-questions.

An example of a framework is the spatio-temporally ordered system of the ordinary familiar things and events that we observe and which are referred to in everyday language. Another is the system of sense data and other "phenomenal" entities. Whether we are to talk within the one framework or the other is something we are to make up our own minds about. Whichever choice we make, however, our decision is not itself of a cognitive character; it is not something that is true or false. On the other hand, it can appear more or less suitable for our purposes. If we decide to adopt the first framework, to use the language of a spatio-temporally ordered system of things and events, then it will be a wholly trivial matter that there are things and events. If we decide on the language of sense data, it will be equally trivial that there are sense data. In adopting the first framework, however, a person does not thereby subscribe to a belief in the *real* existence of the world of things and events. Once the framework has been introduced and adopted, the statement that there are things and events will say no more than that things and events are elements in the framework. The suitability of the "thing

[68] *Ibid.*, pp. 21-22 (in *Meaning and Necessity*, pp. 205-6). "The existence of a framework" seems to mean nothing more than "the existence of a system of new modes of speech," if the formulations on p. 21 (p. 205) are taken literally. But the existence of the latter is trivial and it can hardly be a pseudo-inquiry to ask about this or that rule or this or that set of expressions. On the page following it looks as if a framework is not so much a way of speaking as the entities that are spoken about. And, of course, systems of events and things can indeed constitute a framework. I am not yet clear about what Carnap's more precise account of "framework" would be.

language" is a generally acknowledged fact, but this in no way supports a thesis about the reality of the world of things. Nor does it mean that there can be no cases where this language may be found to be unsuitable. It merely confers upon it a certain qualified commendability.[69]

External questions are not posed in everyday life or in science. In fact, only philosophers have asked them, and they have done so because they have misunderstood what it means to choose a framework.

What, then, about the "Fido"-Fido principle? This, according to Ryle, assumes that just as the name "Fido" designates an entity well known to the happy owner of the dog in question, so for every meaningful expression there must be a particular entity to which it stands in the same relation. But "red," "redness," "five," and so forth, are not names, and consequently the possibility of their having meaning does not depend on the naming relation. The "Fido"-Fido principle is a false theory, a "grotesque" one, according to Ryle. But, says Carnap, it is not a theory at all; rather, it is the practical decision to accept certain modes of speech, certain frameworks. To use a linguistic framework as if it were a theory is to raise all the old metaphysical confusions once again. As for the decision to adopt the "Fido"-Fido principle, it so happens that it is not one that he, Carnap, has made.

During the 1950's there was little co-operation or understanding between the linguistic philosophers in Oxford and Carnap and his collaborators. Now that the more serious oversimplifications of the standpoints of both sides have been eliminated, there is some indication of peaceful co-existence. An example of fruitful and illuminating discussion can be found in P. F. Strawson's contribution on behalf of "linguistic naturalism" against "linguistic constructionism" in the volume devoted to Carnap in the Library of Living Philosophers, and

[69]*Ibid.*, p. 24 (p. 208).

Carnap's own reply in the same volume.[70] By "linguistic naturalists" Strawson means those who attempt to clarify philosophical questions by describing the complex patterns of the everyday use of language; by "linguistic constructionists" he means those who aim at clarification through the construction of formal languages which introduce their terms according to exact rules. For Strawson, because it seems "evident that the concepts used in non-scientific kinds of discourse could not literally be *replaced* by scientific concepts serving just the same purposes," then at least in most cases "it seems to require no argument"[71] to show that the operation would either be unfeasible or fail to fulfil its purpose.

To Carnap, however, what is evident is just the feasibility and effectiveness of this method. And just because it is only after extensive practice with the method that he has come to this conclusion about it, he finds arguments on either side not at all superfluous. Again, while Strawson thinks that philosophical questions are raised by people "who know very well how to use the expressions concerned,"[72] Carnap believes that although people usually believe they know this, they often deceive themselves and use expressions in such a way as to involve confusion or even inconsistency.[73] Frege, for example, showed that mathematicians were not completely clear about the meaning of numerical words, like "one," "two," and so forth. His explication of this is "one of the greatest philosophical achievements of the last century."[74] For this he made use of symbolic logic, everyday language not being sufficient for the purpose. Zeno's paradoxes ("motion is impossi-

[70]P. F. Strawson, "Carnap's Views on Constructed Systems versus Natural Languages in Analytic Philosophy," *The Philosophy of Rudolf Carnap*, pp. 503-18; and "Rudolf Carnap, Replies and Systematic Expositions," *ibid.*, pp. 933-40.
[71]*Ibid.*, p. 505.
[72]*Ibid.*, pp. 508-9.
[73]*Ibid.*, p. 935.
[74]*Ibid.*, p. 935.

ble") and the celebrated antinomy of the liar have also been grist to the mill of constructionism, which has devised a formal language in which the paradoxes cannot arise.

According to Carnap, such clarification of philosophical issues has been attained by an operation in two phases, the second of which has included the construction of languages. The first phase is the clarification within the framework of everyday language of a term that has philosophical relevance (the explicandum). The second phase consists in the proposal of one or more "explications." These are exact concepts, in most cases from a definite science, which are used in place of the vague everyday words within those discussions where greater precision is called for. It is in this way that problems in philosophy become clarified, according to Carnap—by the two steps of the method of explication.

But, objects Strawson, the physicist's quantitative concept of temperature—an explication of the everyday term "warm" —does not help in solving the philosophical question, "Does it follow from the fact that the same object can feel warm to one man and cold to another that the object really is neither cold or warm nor cool nor has any such property?"[75] Carnap's reply seems to be that we should not necessarily expect the physicist's concept of temperature to help here—it is only in relation to certain aims that an explication may be expected to work, not all aims. The clarification of Strawson's question will consist first in a clarification formulated within the framework of everyday language of the distinction between "the thing x feels warm to person y" and "the thing x is warm." But then by gradually increasing the requirements for precision in these clarifications one reaches a stage where scientific explications, possibly in an artificial language, are the only ones able to satisfy these demands. Explications of "the thing x feels warm to person y" lead to psychology, of "the

[75]*Ibid.*, p. 506.

thing *x* is warm," to physics. Carnap might also have pointed out that, according to his program, the expression "really is" in Strawson's question makes it an "external question" (cf. p. 59) or else one reducible to a question about syntax and semantics.

As for the familiar argument against putting natural and artificial languages on an equal footing which states that the latter can only be introduced by means of the former, Carnap says this view is certainly wrong: an artificial language can be learned by children in just the same way as natural languages —as in the Berlitz method. Constructed languages are autonomous, not parasitic upon natural languages. "A natural language is like a crude, primitive pocketknife, very useful for a hundred different purposes. But for certain specific purposes, special tools are more efficient, e.g. chisels, cutting-machines, and finally the microtome."[76] And it is not inconceivable, surely, that the microtome should have preceded the pocket-knife.

In conclusion, we shall briefly examine the relevance of this account of Carnap's distinction between internal and external questions for our speculations on the ultimate and the penultimate.

Decisions to adopt specific linguistic frameworks, conceptual structures, and the like, occur not only with regard to subordinate frames within particular disciplines, but also with regard to enormously comprehensive structures: Carnap mentions the spatio-temporal system of things and events. And yet decisions are made on the basis of comparisons between frameworks, with regard to their relative fruitfulness, suitability, aptness with regard to the purpose the language was chosen to serve, and so forth.[77] Now, although these decisions themselves are not of a cognitive sort, the justifications for

[76]*Ibid.*, pp. 938-39.
[77]"Empiricism, Semantics and Ontology," p. 31 (p. 214).

them, arguments for and against hypotheses concerning the relative fruitfulness, appropriateness, and so forth, of different frameworks do have a cognitive status. They can be formulated, tested, altered, counted; consequences can be drawn from them, and so on.

Carnap says nothing about the kind of languages used in all these stages preparatory to a judicious choice of framework, nor about the frameworks of such languages. Neither are we told anything about the choice of language forms which might be thought to influence the way in which differences between distinct frameworks are formulated. In short, it looks as though Carnap had little interest in the more basic moves in thinking, the stages before the conscious adopting of particular, or perhaps all, frameworks. From the point of view of bringing a high level of exactitude to scientific research this is of course understandable: whatever precedes the adopting of a linguistic framework for mathematics, logic, and physics can hardly be considered to be scientific in character.

However, according to Carnap's own account of what precedes the choice of framework, it is clear that there are indeed questions involved on which, consciously or not, one takes a position; and that these questions are not pseudo-questions. But then neither are they *internal* questions. It seems, therefore, that there are non-internal questions which do not coincide with what Carnap calls external questions. If this is so, it is reasonable to suppose that philosophical questions are non-internal questions of this kind, and that they are not necessarily affected by criticisms which apply to questions that are external in Carnap's sense.

These reflections suggest that Carnap's preference for internal to external questions is perhaps due to his concentration on the penultimate rather than the ultimate. By focusing on the penultimate, the different answers to the ultimate questions are examined and judged on the basis of their consequences for the penultimate. It is because of this that Carnap can say: Away with taboos on any particular linguistic forms or frameworks.[78] Carnap's final words in his piece on internal and external questions are in fact precisely an appeal for tolerance.

> To decree dogmatic prohibitions of certain linguistic forms instead of testing them by their success or failure in practical use, is worse than futile; it is positively harmful because it may obstruct scientific progress . . . *let us be cautious in making assertions and critical in examining them, but tolerant in permitting linguistic forms.*[79]

The aim of logical empiricism has been brilliantly expressed by Herbert Feigl, one of its pioneers. "The future of empiricism will depend on its ability to avoid both the *reductive* fallacies of a narrowminded positivism . . . as well as the *seductive* fallacies of metaphysics."[80]

The pet phrase of the reductivist, as Feigl remarks, is "nothing but": organisms are nothing but machines, mind nothing but matter, ideas are only epiphenomena of economic (or physiological) processes. This is the way of the reductive materialist. There are other sects too: matter is nothing but clusters of sensations (reductive phenomenalism), universals are only words (reductive nominalism). Good and evil are no more than projections of our likes and dislikes (ethical scepticism), and so forth. These reductions are destructive, they make our world poorer.

---

[78]"Everyone is at liberty to build up his own logic, i.e. his own form of language, as he wishes." (*Logical Syntax*, p. 52.) On many reasonable interpretations this statement is absurd. In order to arrive at tenable interpretations the statement should be formulated in exact connection to the special prohibitions, "negative requirements," which Carnap takes to be dispensable. Definite or indefinite languages can be *chosen*, and with or without the law of excluded middle, etc. But Carnap's own institution of a general theory of language forms *(Syntax beliebiger Sprachen)* seems to imply that the various forms have a good deal in common. He can hardly mean that one can choose to deny *all* these.
[79]"Empiricism, Semantics and Ontology," p. 40 (p. 221). (Carnap's italics.)
[80]Herbert Feigl, "Logical Empiricism," p. 375. (See note 14.)

In the opposite camp we have the exponents of "something more," speculative minds who *seduce* men to accept the existence of all kinds of fantastic entities, who try to make man more than he has reason to believe that he is.

> Full maturity of thought will be attained when neither aggressive destruction nor fantastic construction, both equally infantile, characterize the philosophic intellect. The alternative left between a philosophy of the "Nothing But" and a philosophy of the "Something More" is a philosophy of the "What is What." Thus an attitude of *reconstruction* is emerging: an attitude which recognizes that analysis is vastly different from destruction or reduction to absurdity. . . .[81]

[81]*Ibid.* (Feigl's italics.)

Ludwig Wittgenstein

His life from 1889 to 1929

Ludwig Wittgenstein's thoughts, as we have them in his writings, are concentrated upon a fairly small number of questions which are at once specialized and remote from everyday life. It is natural for the reader absorbed in Wittgenstein's discussion of some technical issue to pause and wonder what bearing this has on philosophy in general, and why it meant so much to Wittgenstein himself. His influence on Anglo-American philosophy is both widespread and deep, and in many respects it is a particularly personal one. Like Socrates, though in another way, Wittgenstein has come to affect profoundly the style and even the character of his listeners and readers. No doubt this is due in part to his own manner of philosophizing, which was proof itself of the vital importance to him of these abstract topics. Indeed Wittgenstein himself was living confirmation of the view that philosophic reflection must be a personal thing, engaging all one's powers and encompassing all one's experience. Mainly for this reason we have given a fairly full account of the events of Wittgenstein's life. The reader may thus catch a glimpse of the intense personality behind the works and thereby grasp more fully their underlying significance.

Wittgenstein was born in Vienna in 1889, the youngest of a family of eight. His father was a prominent businessman and distinguished engineer, a Protestant, though the family was of mostly Jewish extraction. His mother, a woman of keen artistic sensibility and extremely musical, was a Roman Catholic. The family's cultural attainments generally were of a very high level, and the Wittgenstein home was well known in Viennese musical circles.

Wittgenstein was educated at home until he was fourteen. Then for three years he went to school at Linz in Upper Austria, his interests and talents at that time being in physics and engineering—when still a boy he made a sewing machine which aroused much admiration.[1] From 1906 to 1908 he attended the Technische Hochschule in Berlin-Charlottenberg. This early developed interest in machines did not, however, mean that the young Ludwig was unacquainted with the philosophical classics; philosophy was read at school as an important part of the national literature, and it was philosophy and art rather than science and engineering that characterized the prevailing atmosphere in which he grew up.

A leading authority on Wittgenstein paints a picture of the philosopher's childhood and youth. "His father . . . was a man of forcible character who was generally both much feared and much respected. The children were brought up in an atmosphere of extreme contempt for most kinds of low

[1]The expression is taken from G. H. von Wright's biographical sketch in the *Philosophical Review*, LXIV, No. 4 (1955), 529. Most of my biographical material is from this valuable source and from Norman Malcolm's *Ludwig Wittgenstein: A Memoir* (London: Oxford University Press, 1958), in which a slightly revised version of von Wright's sketch is included. I have also drawn on passages in the writings of Bertrand Russell, e.g., *My Philosophical Development* (London: George Allen & Unwin, Ltd.; New York: Simon & Schuster, Inc., 1959) and the memorial article in *Mind*, LX (1951), 297-98. George Pitcher's chapter on Wittgenstein's life and character in *The Philosophy of Wittgenstein* (Englewood Cliffs, N. J.: Prentice-Hall, Inc., 1964) contains some interesting additional information.

standard. The whole generation had an unusual fire about them. All were aesthetically and, in particular, musically talented to a high degree; the father, however, though sharing such interests up to a point, regarded them as suited only to be a side-line for his sons: the only fit career for them was civil engineering. (It had to be concealed from him that one of them as a child played the violin in St. Peter's Church in Vienna.) The combination of family temperament and the attitude of the parents—who could not conceive that their children might suffer miseries worth taking account of—led to at least one suicide among the sons. Of himself, Ludwig said: 'I had an unhappy childhood and a most miserable youth'; but again, in connection with the work that a man was content to publish: 'I had luck: I was very well brought up'—i.e. as far as concerned critical standards."[2] As early as 1908, when he was still less than twenty, Wittgenstein went for the first time to England. He studied engineering at the University of Manchester and became deeply engrossed in experiments with kites and later with important developments in aeronautics. But during this time of restless activity it became increasingly clear to him that he was not really at home in the practical sciences. His thoughts moved first to pure mathematics and then, on becoming acquainted with the works of Frege and Russell, to questions of the foundations of mathematics.

From the fall of 1911 until that of 1913, from his twenty-second to his twenty-fourth year, Wittgenstein was at Cambridge. Within an amazingly short time he was entering into advanced discussions with three important English philosophers, Bertrand Russell (b. 1872), George Edward Moore (1873-1959), and Alfred North Whitehead (1861-1947). With Russell, especially, who was thirty-nine years old in 1911, he came to be on close terms. The immediate influence

[2]G. E. M. Anscombe in the introduction to her *An Introduction to Wittgenstein's Tractatus* (London: Hutchinson University Library; New York: Hillary House Publishers, Ltd., 1959), p. 11.

of the two men on one another was profound, though by the 1920's they had begun to grow apart, understanding each other's viewpoint less and less.

It was apparently on the advice of Gottlob Frege (1848-1925), the gray eminence of analytical philosophy, whom he visited in Germany, that Wittgenstein went to Cambridge to study with Russell. There was an exceptionally creative and brilliant atmosphere at Cambridge in the years preceding World War I, and it was there more than anywhere that Frege's own life work was developed and brought to fruition.

Once engaged in philosophy, Wittgenstein quickly plunged into investigations, though of a somewhat, even, dare one say, dangerously limited and specialized kind, in the distinctive Fregean-Russellian genre. Yet Wittgenstein himself was anything but one-sided. Apart from philosophy he carried out experiments in rhythm in music, played the clarinet, and was also occupied with problems of aesthetics. It was in philosophy that he was, at this time, intensely selective.

In the fall of 1913 he went with a friend to Norway, and shortly after returned there alone, staying on, first at a farm and later at his own hut at Skjolden in the innermost reaches of Sognefjord, northeast of Bergen. There he found the peace he had long sought and began writing down the notes which were to evolve into the only work (except for an article) to be published in his lifetime, the "Logisch-philosophische Abhandlung" better known by the title given to its English translation, *Tractatus Logico-Philosophicus*. The outbreak of World War I brought Wittgenstein's stay in Norway to an end. Though exempt on medical grounds, he volunteered for duty in the Austrian army. Neither his service nor the war, however, prevented him from working on the *Tractatus*. He continued to write down his thoughts in a notebook as they came to him. Some of the notes are preserved, and those from 1914 to 1916 are now published and serve as a considerable aid to our understanding of the *Tractatus*.

Late in 1918 Wittgenstein was captured by the Italians and

for nine months was in a prison camp near Monte Cassino in southern Italy. During this time he corresponded with Russell. On his release Wittgenstein returned neither to Cambridge nor to philosophy. Instead he took a teacher's training course in Vienna and from 1920 to 1926 was a village schoolteacher in various places in Lower Austria. For a time he worked as a gardener and at one time planned to enter a monastery.

However, in 1926 he undertook to design a house for one of his sisters in Vienna, a project which occupied him for two years. The result was a building of impressive architectural originality. During this time he had some contact with philosophers—with Moritz Schlick, professor in the philosophy of inductive science and originator of the so-called Vienna Circle,[3] and with some of the Circle's members. A lecture given by Brouwer, the great Dutch mathematician, in March, 1928, seems to have been a decisive event in his life. During his schoolteacher days, Wittgenstein's friends in Cambridge had been urging him to return there, and early in the spring of 1929, feeling once more capable of creative work, he returned to Cambridge. He was registered as a research student. In June of the same year, with the *Tractatus* as his thesis and Russell and Moore as his examiners, he was awarded his Doctorate. The next year he was made a Fellow of Trinity College.

From about 1930, Wittgenstein's thoughts were turning in a new direction; at this point, therefore, it will be convenient to break off our chronicle of the events of his life.

In these years of crisis, Wittgenstein had been much taken up with the writings of Tolstoy. These, together with the philosophical works of Schopenhauer and Lichtenberg, may provide us with a key to Wittgenstein's own deeply serious

---

[3]According to Carnap, Schlick first met Wittgenstein in 1927. See Carnap's autobiography in *The Philosophy of Rudolf Carnap*, ed. P. A. Schilpp (Library of Living Philosophers [Evanston, Ill.: The Open Court Publishing Co., 1963]).

and pessimistic outlook. What exactly this outlook was we do not know—Wittgenstein seems to have given no systematic or fundamental account of it either verbally or in writing. And from an examination of his views on language it will become apparent that a factual account (Kierkegaard's "sheer information") in the usual sense would not be sufficient in any case. We can only resort to conjectures based on premises he himself could not acknowledge—a peculiar situation that has, understandably, done little to undermine interest in him.

When his father died in 1912, Wittgenstein inherited a large fortune, but shortly after the war he gave it away. Some say he refrained from giving his fortune to the poor because he considered poverty valuable (Tolstoy!), and gave it to his family instead because they were so rich already that a little more could hardly hurt.[4] Even before that, Wittgenstein had shown his contempt for money, as well as his taste for literature, when (anonymously) he established a fund for writers. Among the beneficiaries were Georg Trakl and Rainer Maria Rilke.[5]

The "Tractatus" philosophy up to 1929

Frege

As we have already mentioned, it took Wittgenstein barely three years of study to make his mark in philosophy and to identify for himself the questions that he felt must be answered. Although there was not the same strict systematizing to be found in British philosophy as in German, the logical

[4]M. Cranston, "Bildnis eines Philosophen," in *Ludwig Wittgenstein, Schriften, Beiheft* (Frankfurt am Main: Suhrkamp Verlag, 1960), p. 18.
[5]The fact that Rilke, in particular, was one of the beneficiaries has been seen as proof of Wittgenstein's good taste in literature, especially in modern writing. But it appears that he had nothing to do with the allocation of the funds.

writings of Russell nevertheless expressed, despite their technical nature, a way of thinking that assumed definite positions on a number of fundamental questions. This was less true of Frege, since much that came later to be said in his name was only hinted at in his writings. Nevertheless, Frege may be said to have supplied the charge that Russell and Wittgenstein buried deep into the solid edifice of traditional Anglo-Saxon philosophy.

What kind of questions did Russell take up, what was Frege's contribution, and what precisely was the importance of both these men for Wittgenstein?

A significant fact is that both Wittgenstein and Russell came to philosophy from a study of mathematical logic and the philosophy of mathematics. From his early study of Frege, Russell, together with Whitehead, had developed a rich logic from which all of mathematics seemed to be derivable. It was not unnatural, then, to expect an even wider application of this logic to the solving of vexed and intractable questions in philosophy.

There are a number of assumptions underlying the plausibility of such a project, and we cannot do justice to them here. But one assumption appears crucial, and that is the view that language and the world share a common logical "form." If language has the same form as the world, to clarify philosophical questions concerning the nature of "what is" it seems one need only be clear about the form that it has in common with reality—an idea that Russell was much taken up with.[6]

But, of course, the form of language is not something that is directly obvious from actual grammatical forms. These vary from one natural language to another, and even where there is a correspondence, many expressions in a natural language which share the same grammatical forms really have quite different logical forms. This fact can then be seen as a

[6]See "My Mental Development" in *The Philosophy of Bertrand Russell*, ed. P. A. Schilpp (Library of Living Philosophers [Evanston, Ill.: The Open Court Publishing Co., 1946]), p. 45.

source of much confusion, especially in philosophy, where many perplexing problems and unwanted conclusions seem to be due precisely to taking the grammatical forms of statements at their face value. To solve these problems and reach satisfactory conclusions we must first appreciate that if language is a mirror of reality, it is at best a distorting mirror, and we need some method, perhaps even a closer look at the mirror itself, to transform its misleading images into adequate representations of the real thing. In his famous theory of descriptions[7] Russell shows how sentences including designating expressions of the form "the so-and-so," can be analyzed into sentences in which such expressions do not occur. Such sentences, instead of naming one definite object corresponding to the definite description they contain, "really" say something more complex, to the effect that one and only one object possesses a certain property. Thus awkward philosophical problems about what "The King of France" or "the golden mountain" designate are resolved by showing that they, along with all expressions of the same type, including, therefore, "The President of the United States," do not designate anything. The existence or non-existence of something answering to a certain description is accounted for in language simply by the truth or falsity of that part of the complex sentence which says that there is something that possesses the property in question.

The kind of analysis given by Russell's theory of descriptions assumes some degree of structural identity between language and the facts. What Russell showed was the kind of structure underlying sentences which include expressions of one certain type. But what about the structure of different kinds

---

[7] See "On Denoting" (1905) in Bertrand Russell, *Logic and Knowledge*, ed. Robert C. Marsh (London: George Allen & Unwin, Ltd.; New York: The Macmillan Co., 1956), pp. 39-56. The first full statement of the theory of descriptions comes in the first volume of *Principia Mathematica* (1910).

of sentences themselves? In fact, what about the structure of all language? If language as a whole can be considered a complex structure, what are the basic elements out of which it is built? (In the Introduction to *Principia Mathematica*, Russell had already propounded a theory of elementary propositions.) Furthermore, in what does the correspondence between language and reality ultimately consist? It seems reasonable to assume that language manages to be "about" reality by designating or naming things, events, and so on. However, if the theory of descriptions is correct, and phrases of the form "the so-and-so" do not name definite objects in the world, what are the *real* names that make descriptive language possible? And how do they function in language?

Russell's own early philosophical background adds a special point to his analysis of language. Formerly he had been a sympathizer of the view of the English idealist F. H. Bradley (1846-1924) that reality must be conceived of as an indivisible whole and not as an aggregate of self-contained facts. A very significant consequence of Bradley's monism, in our context, was that language, that is, any proposition, was incapable of adequately representing a fact. Language and thought, in order to relate things to one another, must abstract terms and relations from the whole; but according to monism there just are no self-contained facts for the logical form of a proposition to mirror, apart from the whole of reality. A corollary to this is that any structured view of the universe is an abstraction and hence a distortion of the real. Thus not only is the world, or reality, not mirrored by language, it cannot even be grasped by thought.

In his essay "Logic as the Essence of Philosophy" (1914) Russell declared, however, that the philosopher's task is to "give an account of the world of science and daily life," but that philosophers had rendered themselves incapable of this task "because they were less anxious to understand the world of science and daily life than to convict it of unreality in the

interests of a supra-sensible real world."[8] For the logical analysis of language to have philosophical point two assumptions
seem to be necessary: language must be capable of representing experience, and the world as we experience it must be real
enough.

Although Wittgenstein's viewpoints did not coincide altogether with those of Russell, it was within the general outlook
typified by these assumptions that he sought answers to the
problems that absorbed him. The problems themselves were
framed in a terminology derived from Frege, and we should
begin by a brief introduction of some of Frege's logical concepts, two of which proved to have a decisive effect upon
the development of philosophy, less through Frege's own use
of them than through their extensive employment by many
later philosophers. These were the concepts of 'function' and
'quantification.'

By analogy with the notion of mathematical functions (for
example "square root of x"), Frege introduced the notion of
propositional functions, for example, "x is mortal," and "the
father of x is blind." Just as with the substitution of a specific
numeral, say "9," for x in "square root of x" we get the name
of a specific number, in this case "3," so with the substitution
of "John" or "the Archbishop of Canterbury," we get specific propositions such as "John is mortal," "the Archbishop
of Canterbury is mortal," "John's father is blind," and "the
Archbishop of Canterbury's father is blind."

Frege also introduced the concept of logical quantification,
as a standardized way of introducing the words "all" or
"some." In order to bring out a sentence's logical structure
one writes "For all x, (it is the case that) x has extension"
instead of "Everything has extension," and "For some x, (it is
the case that) x has extension" instead of "Some things have
extension." In Wittgenstein's own symbolization, "fx" represents propositions with the structure "x has the property f,"
and "fa" represents a specific proposition with such a structure,

[8]Quoted by D. F. Pears in *The Revolution in Philosophy* (London: Macmillan & Co., Ltd., 1956), p. 45.

for example, "The table has extension." The symbol "$(x)fx$" stands for "For all x, (it is the case that) x has the property f."

Especially associated with Frege is the distinction between a linguistic expression's 'Sinn' and its 'Bedeutung,' or between its 'sense' and 'reference.' By the "Bedeutung" of an expression Frege means that in the world about which the expression says something; by its "Sinn" he means the expression's meaning. Thus, to use Frege's classic example, "the Morning Star" and "the Evening Star" have the same *Bedeutung*, namely the planet Venus, but each expression has a different *Sinn*. Here we shall translate "Bedeutung" by "that which is referred to" or "reference." The two expressions, "the Morning Star" and "the Evening Star," have different meanings insofar as the former is an expression for the star visible in the morning, and the latter for that visible in the evening. Naturally, it may take time for us to discover that both expressions refer to the very same thing, that is, that they have the same reference.

Some descriptions have meaning but no reference, for example, "the Emperor of Iceland," and "the least rapidly convergent series."

By means of this distinction and a number of others Frege made effective criticism of much in the mathematical philosophy of his time.[9] The work he initiated was mainly carried on by Russell, who extended it far beyond the realms of the foundations of mathematics and logic to which Frege's investigations had been chiefly devoted.

Probably it would be misleading to emphasize too much the importance of technical aids, especially symbolic logic, of the kind which give to the works of Frege, Russell (until World War I), and Wittgenstein (until World War II) their characteristic stamp. The achievements of these thinkers may be just as much due to their exceptional acuteness, their intense concentration on basic problems, and also their incorruptible seriousness.

[9] Cf. Miss Anscombe's examples on pp. 15-16 in *An Introduction*.

The "Tractatus": the text in broad outline

Wittgenstein developed his philosophical ideas partly in sympathy with, partly in criticism of, both Frege and Russell. His technique was to write down his thoughts as they came. The manuscript he was preparing was completed in August, 1918, and first appeared in the Austrian journal, *Annalen der Naturphilosophie* (1921), under the title "Logisch-philosophische Abhandlung." A year later the first combined German and English edition came out under the title *Tractatus Logico-Philosophicus*, with an introduction by Bertrand Russell, the accuracy of whose interpretation of Wittgenstein has been much discussed.

The *Tractatus*, as it is more familiarly known, has no chapter divisions; instead it is divided up in accordance with the main topics of thought, which are numbered from 1 to 7. These main ideas are refined and commented upon in subparagraphs numbered 1.1, 1.2, 2.1, 2.2, and so on. Further refinements and comments are numbered similarly, 1.11, 1.12, and so on. This system helps the reader considerably in picking up and following the threads of the argument.[10]

Not very much is conveyed by isolating the seven main thoughts from their context, but it will be a useful introduction to present them here if only to give an idea of the ground they cover. In two cases, for the sake of clarity, subordinate remarks are included.[11]

[10]Wittgenstein's own words of guidance: "The decimal numbers assigned to the individual propositions indicate the logical importance of the propositions, the stress laid on them in my exposition. The propositions $n.1$, $n.2$, $n.3$, etc. are comments on proposition no. n; the propositions $n.m.1$, $n.m.2$, etc. are comments on proposition no. $n.m$; and so on." The consistency of Wittgenstein's use of this system of classification has been questioned. See, e.g., David Favrholdt, *An Interpretation and Critique of Wittgenstein's Tractatus* (Copenhagen: Munksgaard, 1964), pp. 220 ff.; and Erik Stenius, *Wittgenstein's 'Tractatus'* (Oxford: Basil Blackwell; New York: Cornell University Press, 1960), chap. 1.

[11]All quotations from the *Tractatus* are from the translation by D. F. Pears and B. F. McGuinness, *Tractatus Logico-Philosophicus* (London: Routledge & Kegan Paul, Ltd.; New York: Humanities Press, Inc.,

1 *The world is all that is the case.*

This becomes a little clearer when taken in conjunction with the statement following.

1.1 The world is the totality of facts, not of things.

2 *What is the case—a fact—is the existence of states of affairs.*

3 *A logical picture of facts is a thought.*

3.001 "A state of affairs is thinkable"—this means that we can picture it to ourselves.

4 *A thought is a proposition with a sense.*[12]

5 *A proposition is a truth-function of elementary propositions. . . .*

1961). This is a parallel German-English edition, as in the case of the 1922 translation by C. K. Ogden, and includes the original introduction by Bertrand Russell. The Pears-McGuinness translation of some of the key terms is as follows:

Sachverhalt	—	State of affairs
Sachlage	—	Situation
Tatsache	—	Fact
Sinn	—	Sense
Bedeutung	—	Meaning
Sinnlos	—	Without sense
Unsinnig	—	Nonsensical

The distinction between *Sachverhalt* and *Sachlage* is a technical one. The former means something simple (elementary), the latter something complex.

As for "Bedeutung," this is not always used in the technical sense of "reference"—see, for instance, 6.53—and, besides, there is some dispute as to what exactly Wittgenstein did mean by "Bedeutung." The English translation as "meaning" perhaps simplifies the issue by obscuring it.

The distinction between "Sinnlos" and "Unsinnig" is an important one in the *Tractatus*. Tautologies are *sinnlos*, i.e., without sense, while sentences that arise from a failure to understand the "logic of our language," as in the case of philosophy, are *unsinnig*, i.e., nonsensical.

[12] If the definition of "thought" in 3 is put in at 4, we get the following important thesis: "A logical picture of facts is a proposition with a sense." By combining 4 with 4.01 we get: "A thought is a picture of reality." In these cases it is safe to make the substitutions, but the procedure is not always to be relied upon.

6 *The general form of a truth-function is* [$\bar{p}$, $\bar{\xi}$, N ($\bar{\xi}$)]. . . .

7 *What we cannot speak about we must consign to silence.*

Although there is no lack of instructive comment on the two logically flavored thoughts 5 and 6, nevertheless, many points remain extremely obscure, and one feels that much more remains to be said. To his last main thought, Wittgenstein provides no comment at all. He lets it stand as his final word.

How are we to understand the train of thought and its separate items? This is a vexed question upon which many views are held, and we cannot here take into account all that has been written on it.[13] Instead we shall select some of the ideas for mention and brief comment. The Finnish philosopher, Erik Stenius, points out a reasonable procedure. In the introduction to his very thorough exposition of the *Tractatus*, he finds that for him the statements in the work fall into four distinct categories.

---

[13]A useful survey of the *Tractatus* literature is to be found in G. K. Plochmann and J. B. Lawson, *Terms in their Propositional Contexts in Wittgenstein's Tractatus: An Index* (Carbondale: Southern Illinois University Press, 1962). According to these authors the most basic and thorough commentary on the *Tractatus* is that of D. S. Shwayder (*Wittgenstein's Tractatus: A Historical and Critical Commentary*). This commentary is unpublished, but is available at the Bodleian Library in Oxford. Among the published commentaries are A. Maslow, *A Study in Wittgenstein's Tractatus* (Berkeley: University of California Press, 1961); G. E. M. Anscombe, *An Introduction to Wittgenstein's Tractatus* (cf. note 2); Erik Stenius, *Wittgenstein's 'Tractatus'* (cf. note 10); James Griffin, *Wittgenstein's Logical Atomism* (Oxford: Clarendon Press, 1964); Max Black, *A Companion to Wittgenstein's Tractatus* (New York: Cornell University Press, 1964); George Pitcher, *The Philosophy of Wittgenstein* (cf. note 1); and David Favrholdt, *An Interpretation and Critique of Wittgenstein's Tractatus* (cf. note 10). An extensive bibliography is to be found in Irving M. Copi and Robert W. Beard (eds.), *Readings on Wittgenstein's Tractatus* (New York: The Macmillan Co.; London: Routledge & Kegan Paul, Ltd., 1966).

First, there are statements which I believe I understand and which I think are clarifying, stimulating and important. . . . Secondly come statements which I believe I understand and with some certainty think are essentially false or misleading. . . . Thirdly, there are those which I do not understand and the value of which I am therefore unable to estimate. And fourthly, there are a number which seem on the one hand to be understandable, but on the other to be so in such a way as to give an indeterminate and obscure impression, hence they become impossible either to accept or reject.[14]

Anyone wanting to grasp the ideas of the *Tractatus* must naturally concentrate on statements in the first and second categories. And this will be our procedure in what follows.

Wittgenstein's picture theory

Wittgenstein invites us to ask the question, "What makes a picture a picture?" and an understanding of the *Tractatus* depends in great measure on our ability to pose this question with sufficient depth and concentration.

2.12   A picture is a model of reality.

2.13   In a picture objects have the elements of the picture corresponding to them.

2.131   In a picture the elements of the picture are the representatives of objects.

2.141   A picture is a fact.

2.15   The fact that the elements of a picture are related to one another in a determinate way represents that things are related to one another in the same way.

         Let us call this connexion of its elements the structure of the picture, and let us call the possi-

[14]Erik Stenius, *Wittgenstein's 'Tractatus,'* p. vii.

bility of this structure the pictorial form of the
picture.

2.1512 It is laid against reality like a ruler.

2.15121 Only the end-points of the graduating lines
actually *touch* the object that is to be measured.

2.1513 So a picture, conceived in this way, also includes the pictorial relationship, which makes it
into a picture.

2.1514 The pictorial relation consists of the correlations of the picture's elements with things.

2.1515 These correlations are, as it were, the feelers
of the picture's elements, with which the picture
touches reality.

2.16 If a fact is to be a picture, it must have something in common with what it depicts.

2.161 There must be something identical in a picture
and what it depicts, to enable the one to be a
picture of the other at all.

2.173 A picture represents its subject from a position
outside it. (Its standpoint is its representational
form.) That is why a picture represents its subject correctly or incorrectly.

2.201 A picture depicts reality by representing a
possibility of existence and non-existence of states
of affairs.

2.221 What a picture represents is its sense.

2.222 The agreement or disagreement of its sense
with reality constitutes its truth or falsity.

It is worth noting that in not one of these sixteen statements is there any mention of language. They are all concerned with pictures and the relation of a picture to what it
depicts.

So much for Wittgenstein's statements on pictures as such.
The next two main topics relate to the application of the
picture theory to the limits of language and to what cannot

be said. The theme of the application of the picture theory to language can be seen as a central thread running through all the theses of the *Tractatus*. Briefly and in broad outline the picture theory is applied to language as follows.

Language is the totality of propositions. Propositions are pictures of that to which they refer. If we analyze complex propositions we eventually come down to the smallest units of language, elementary propositions. These are to be rendered as functions of names: $f(x)$, or more briefly, fx. The relations between the names, of which the units of language exclusively consist, correspond to the relations between objects in states of affairs.

An example may show what is meant here. The proposition "The dog's father is lying on the carpet" refers to the state of affairs (situation) *that* the dog's father is lying on the carpet, and by changing the relative positions of the elements in the proposition we generate other propositions which picture different states of affairs. "The father's dog is lying on the carpet," "The father's carpet is lying on the dog," and so on.

Some, indeed most, propositions refer to and hence depict complex states of affairs, or situations *(Sachlage)*. Others, the elementary propositions, refer to states of affairs *(Sachverhalte)* that cannot be further analyzed.

For example, "Father's carpet is lying on the dog" is a picture of a complex state of affairs; "The carpet is lying on the dog" is a picture of a slightly less complex state of affairs; and "Father is lying" of an even less complex state of affairs. A *Sachverhalt* is a state of affairs that is not complex, in that it is not composed of other states of affairs.

Between the parts of a proposition there are therefore relations to which one can point or at least refer, and corresponding to these relations are the relations between the objects in a possible state of affairs.

Needless to say, many questions arise from this outline presentation of the picture theory. For instance, one would like to know something more about what a state of affairs *(Sach-*

verhalt) is. Shouldn't we ask Wittgenstein for an example? No, it seems not, for in Wittgenstein's view philosophy has nothing to do with finding examples and illustrations. That is an empirical matter. The philosopher's task is to solve the problem of conceiving how states of affairs can be composed of elements. Again, what would be an example of an elementary proposition? Here too, Wittgenstein provides no instances, considering the question to be an empirical one, and hence outside his competence as a philosopher. But nevertheless, the existence of these, as of irreducible, non-analyzable "atomic situations," is a *requirement* of Wittgenstein's picture theory. The theory implies that these entities exist.

We would also like to know what it is that enables propositions to be understood as pictures. On this point Wittgenstein gives us rather more to go on. Von Wright recounts (see note 1) Wittgenstein's explanation of how he came to conceive of a proposition as being a picture. The idea occurred to him while he was serving in the army during World War I. He was reading a magazine which, with the help of diagrams, showed how a certain motor accident had taken place. It struck Wittgenstein that the diagrams were propositions: they were pictures saying *this* is what happened. In other words, the diagram revealed the essential feature of a proposition: that it is a picture of reality. Possibly to begin with Wittgenstein saw propositions as pictures of reality in some quite concrete way, just as maps are pictures of the lie of the land, with specific features on the terrain corresponding to features on the map, and vice versa. Later, however, Wittgenstein seems to have thought that the character of the picturing function of language must be somewhat different from that of the map.

But what exactly is this character? And what precisely hinges on our grasping it, whatever it is? No clear answers to these questions are given in the *Tractatus*, though some points seem to be easier to interpret than others. For example, it is at least clear that Wittgenstein's pictures are not (or not just) spatial pictures like maps or photographs; he calls his pictures "logical" pictures. The resemblance between a picture and what it describes is not visual but formal, or structural. The constituents in a picture need only correspond numerically with those in the situation it depicts, and it is the structural features of the latter that must be mirrored in the picture. However, these two conditions are not enough for one thing to be a picture of another; there must also be "rules of projection," and the disparity between a Wittgensteinian picture and an ordinary picture can be measured by noting what Wittgenstein takes to be examples of what he means here. He instances the "general rule by means of which the musician can obtain the symphony from the score, and which makes it possible to derive the symphony from the groove on the gramophone record . . ." (4.0141).

Because a *Tractatus* picture is, therefore, apparently at least, a much wider concept than that of a picture in the ordinary sense, there is a problem about how far the analogy with ordinary pictures holds. An ordinary picture can be put in a frame and hung on the wall; and it can be stored away where no one can see it. And the same sort of thing would seem to be applicable in the case of musical scores and grooves on gramophone records. Perhaps a Wittgensteinian picture is therefore also something that can be recognized, pointed to, stored away, in fact something with a continuous and independent existence of its own.

However, a musical score can only give rise to a performance of a symphony (in imagination or the concert hall) by having certain rules applied to it. It is these rules that enable the musical notation to picture a particular piece of music. By using other rules, different pictures and different performances are produced. It seems, therefore, that for A to be a musical picture of B the rules must be, if not actually included in the picture, at least presupposed by it. So if a musical score is a picture, it is only insofar as we think of it in conjunction with a specific set of rules of projection.

But can we conceive the picture as something that exists independently of the actual applications of the rules that are needed to give it its definite sense? Or should we not rather conceive it as really only occurring when a definite sense is being given it by the actual application of the rules? In the first case we think of the picture rather as the musical man might look upon his collection of musical scores. Because he only needs to read them or play from them in order to project the appropriate patterns of sound, he comes to think of them much as we think of ordinary pictures, that is, as containing their sense whether they are looked at or not. In the second case we think of the picture as playing the part of the musical score in an actual performance by the musician, even if the performance is only one that goes on in his head.

That the latter is the correct interpretation is suggested both contextually and by specific statements (for example, 2.15, 2.153, and 4.022). On the other hand, because Wittgenstein at one time or another equates the picture with the thought (3), the thought with the proposition (4), and also says that the proposition can be set out on the printed page (4.011), the matter is by no means clear. If, in line with our first interpretation, the picture is regarded as the publicly manifested proposition or as the propositional sign *(Satzzeichen)*, the concept of thought will have to be suitably depsychologized. If "thought" is taken psychologically, on the other hand, there is the problem of its being also the publicly manifestable proposition or the propositional sign. It may be, of course, that Wittgenstein tended to adopt both views, or as has been plausibly suggested, that he moved from the first to the second in the light of factors that had not at first occurred to him.[15]

If we do regard the *Tractatus* pictures as having mental

[15]See David Favrholdt, *An Interpretation and Critique of Wittgenstein's Tractatus,* pp. 77 ff. Favrholdt proposes that the correct interpretation of the picture theory is obtained by systematically replacing "elementary proposition" with "thought," at all places in the text, the latter concept being more fundamental than that of a proposition in the *Tractatus*. If so, the detailed explanation of propositions which precedes the few statements about thought can be seen as an explanation of *thought* in terms of propositions. (See Favrholdt, p. 80.)

rather than simply physical components, the question of the analogy with ordinary pictures can still be pressed. If we think of pictures as mental complexes we may, of course, still tend to think of them on the analogy of real pictures, namely as *mental* pictures, a kind of mental (or not simply physical) object. However, maybe the analogy with *things* is wrong altogether. Thus if we take the picture to be "the *thought* which *may* be expressed by hanging the picture upon the wall," rather than as the picture actually hanging on the wall, and agree therefore that "every picture is a presentation that such and such is the case," and that "every presentation that such and such is the case is a picture," we might conclude that "a presentation that such and such is the case is an act of thinking that such and such is the case."[16] But then if we think of a *Tractatus* picture as an *act*, the analogy with real pictures (as ordinarily conceived) must seem on the whole misleading. The better analogue would be an ordinary picture insofar as it actually represents something for someone, and perhaps we should then regard the picture theory as a picturing theory.

In whatever way one interprets the picture, it seems that one must at least accept some element of activity or interpretation. The picturing relation connecting a proposition with reality cannot be interpreted simply (as 2.1514, for example, might suggest) in terms of a one-to-one correspondence be-

---

[16]D. S. Shwayder in his critical notice of Stenius' book in *Mind*, LXXII (1963), 281. Shwayder interprets Wittgenstein's picture as an assertion (see p. 286). He also claims: "You cannot form a *Tractatus*-picture except by making it picture, and the elements of a picturing fact cannot be identified for what they are except insofar as they contribute to a pictorial representation of fact, viz. insofar as they function semantically." ("Gegenstände and Other Matters," a critical discussion of James Griffin's *Wittgenstein's Logical Atomism*, in *Inquiry*, IV [1964], No. 4, 394.) Pitcher, however, talks of "a mental act . . . of intending [the elements of a picture] to stand for [the elements of reality]" (*The Philosophy of Wittgenstein*, p. 88) as if the elements were identifiable outside their function of meaning, and this function was conferred upon them by some act.

tween the elements of the picture, understood as a fact, and elements in the reality that it pictures, and vice versa (complete isomorphism)—at least not without serious difficulties arising.[17] In the first place, one can just as well use what is pictured to depict the picture as the other way round: for example, a small piece of terrain can be used to depict a large scale map of it. But then what is it that ensures that the one means the other and not vice versa? The relation has a direction. If A is a picture of B, it is not automatically the case that B is a picture of A. Secondly, since for any two facts, A and B, with the same number of elements there is more than one possible way of correlating them, we cannot even ensure a one-to-one correspondence between A and B unless we *interpret* the elements in A in a way that excludes all the other possibilities.

The sixteen statements we have quoted by way of introduction provide a basis for an understanding of Wittgenstein's theory of pictures and picturing. They amount to an expression of his picture theory. But now, from the quotations that follow one can see how the theory is applied to language. It is significant that Wittgenstein begins his discussion of language very late on in his account; first he speaks at length and in detail about the picture, as if our understanding of that was a prerequisite of our understanding of language.

> 4.011 At first sight a proposition—one set out on the printed page, for example—does not seem to be a

[17]For a discussion of the question of isomorphism, see G. E. M. Anscombe, *An Introduction*, p. 67; E. Stenius, *Wittgenstein's 'Tractatus'*, chap. 6; H. R. G. Schwyzer, "Wittgenstein's Picture-Theory of Language," *Inquiry*, V (1962), No. 1, reprinted in Copi and Beard, *Essays on Wittgenstein's Tractatus;* Stenius, "Wittgenstein's Picture-Theory: A reply to Mr. H. R. G. Schwyzer," *Inquiry*, VI (1963), No. 2, reprinted in Copi and Beard; and D. Favrholdt, *An Interpretation and Critique of Wittgenstein's Tractatus*, pp. 73ff. H. Wein says: "Wittgensteins kardinale Aporie betrifft die 'logische Mannigfaltigkeit' welche dieselbe sein muss im Abbildenden (Gedanke, Sprache, Satz) und im Abgebildeten (Welt, Wirklichkeit, Sachlage)." See Wein's *Sprachphilosophie der Gegenwart* (The Hague: Martinus Nijhoff, 1963), p. 66.

picture of the reality with which it is concerned. But no more does musical notation at first sight seem to be a picture of music, nor our phonetic notation (the alphabet) to be a picture of our speech.

And yet these sign-languages prove to be pictures, even in the ordinary sense, of what they represent.

4.012 It is obvious that a proposition of the form '*aRb*' strikes us as a picture. In this case the sign is obviously a likeness of what is signified.

(The form "*aRb*" expresses that something, *a*, stands in relation *R* to another thing, *b*; for example, *a* is to the left of *b*, or *a* is larger than *b*.)

4.014 A gramophone record, the musical idea, the written notes, and the sound waves, all stand to one another in the same internal relation of depicting that holds between language and the world.

They are all constructed according to a common logical plan.

(Like the two youths in the fairy-tale, their two horses, and their lilies. They are all in a certain sense one.)

4.0141 There is a general rule by means of which the musician can obtain the symphony from the score, and which makes it possible to derive the symphony from the groove on the gramophone record, and, using the first rule, to derive the score again. That is what constitutes the inner similarity between these things which seem to be constructed in such entirely different ways. And the rule is the law of projection which projects the symphony into the language of musical notation. It is the rule for translating this language into the language of gramophone records.

4.016   In order to understand the essential nature of a proposition, we should consider hieroglyphic script, which depicts the facts that it describes.

        And alphabetic script developed out of it without losing what was essential to depiction.

4.021   A proposition is a picture of reality: for if I understand a proposition, I know the situation that it represents. And I understand the proposition without having had its sense explained to me.

We should note that although the English translation uses the term "proposition," the original German has "Satz." However, this German word could just as well be translated by the English "sentence." Perhaps the adoption of the word "proposition" tends to obscure a latent ambiguity in Wittgenstein's use of "Satz" as to whether he means the items of language we call sentences or the more logical items which we call propositions. Furthermore, looked at as sentences, Wittgenstein's *Sätze* are an extremely special case of what we generally mean by a sentence; he excludes, for example, imperative, optative, interrogative, and evaluative sentences. Accordingly, what Wittgenstein means by "language" when he identifies language with the totality of *Sätze* is in fact a very small part of what most of us mean by "language." From a conventional point of view Wittgenstein's terminology is decidedly idiosyncratic, although much less so within the philosophical tradition to which he then belonged. We also note, however, that in other statements in the *Tractatus* there is mention of a wider concept of language, as, for example, in 4.0141, quoted above.

As is evident from these quotations, written and spoken language is to be set alongside a whole range of other kinds of language. What all these kinds of language have in common is the picturing function. Perhaps the best way of understanding Wittgenstein's application of the picture theory of language is simply to see it as a general theory about picturing. And from this general theory he derives a theory about the picturing function of sentences (propositions) that assert that something or other is the case. Then from this in turn he derives his theory about what can and what cannot be said.

The consequences of the picture theory
The sayable and the unsayable: "the cardinal problem of philosophy"

We shall now turn to the uses to which Wittgenstein put his picture theory. First and foremost he used it to clear up problems in the foundations of logic. These we unfortunately must leave aside, though we should note in passing that for Wittgenstein himself they were of the greatest importance. While in Norway (1913) he wrote to Russell, "Identity is the very Devil and *immensely important; very* much more so than I thought." And later: "It is the *dualism*, positive and negative facts, that gives me no peace. For such a dualism can't exist. But how to get away from it?"[18]

We must first try to throw as much light as possible on the connection between thinking, logic, and picturing. The question is certainly a very difficult one, and once again a solution depends on our ability to concentrate as deeply as possible on the question of what makes a picture a picture. The best procedure is to compare the following eleven statements with the sixteen already quoted.

2.15   The fact that the elements of a picture are related to one another in a determinate way represents that things are related to one another in the same way.

Let us call this connexion of its elements the structure of the picture, and let us call the possibil-

[18]Ludwig Wittgenstein, *Notebooks 1914-1916*, ed. G. H. von Wright and G. E. M. Anscombe; English translation by G. E. M. Anscombe (Oxford: Basil Blackwell, 1961), first passage from p. 122; second from p. 33.

2.15   ity of this structure the pictorial form of the picture.

2.151   Pictorial form is the possibility that things are related to one another in the same way as the elements of the picture.

2.1511 *That* is how the picture is attached to reality; it reaches right out to it.

2.17   What a picture must have in common with reality, in order to be able to depict it—correctly or incorrectly—in the way it does, is its pictorial form.

2.171   A picture can depict any reality whose form it has.

A spatial picture can depict anything spatial, a coloured one anything coloured, etc.

2.18   What any picture, of whatever form, must have in common with reality, in order to be able to depict it—correctly or incorrectly—in any way at all, is logical form, i.e. the form of reality.

2.181   A picture whose pictorial form is logical form is called a logical picture.

2.182   Every picture is *at the same time* a logical one. (On the other hand, not every picture is, for example, a spatial one.)

2.2   A picture has logico-pictorial form in common with what it depicts.

3   A logical picture of facts is a thought.

3.01   The totality of true thoughts is a picture of the world.

Perhaps it is not necessary to grasp the concept of pictorial form in all its details in order to understand the principal features of Wittgenstein's ideas here. The important point is that the concept refers to something underlying the manifest features of language when it gives us pictures of reality. On the other hand, we may well wonder just how deep and inaccessible the pictorial form of a picturing fact is. It seems that it is more than the *mere* possibility of one thing (or rather, fact) depicting another: we are told that this possibility consists in the elements in each of the facts being related to one another in the same way (2.151); moreover, a picture of spatial colored reality has a different pictorial form from a picture of a spatial but not colored reality (2.171). Insofar as these two features of pictorial form can be detected, the concept of pictorial form seems not so very recondite. And perhaps this is also true even of what *any* picturing fact must possess in order to depict reality, namely logical form, or the form of reality (2.18).

This should suffice as a preliminary to understanding how Wittgenstein looked for—and believed he had found—the definitive solution to "the cardinal problem of philosophy," namely, "what can be expressed *(gesagt)* by propositions—i.e. by language (and, what comes to the same, what can be *thought*) and what cannot be expressed by propositions, but only shown *(gezeigt)*. . . ."[19]

4.022   A proposition *shows* its sense.

A proposition shows how things stand *if* it is true. And it *says that* they do so stand.

4.024   To understand a proposition means to know what is the case if it is true.

(One can understand it, therefore, without knowing whether it is true.)

It is understood by anyone who understands its constituents.

4.03   A proposition must use old expressions to communicate a new sense.

A proposition communicates a situation to us, and so it must be *essentially* connected with the situation.

---

[19]Taken from a letter written to Russell while Wittgenstein was in a prison camp in Italy just after World War I. Quoted in Anscombe, *An Introduction*, p. 161.

And the connexion is precisely that it is its logical picture.

A proposition states something only in so far as it is a picture.

4.032 It is only in so far as a proposition is logically segmented that it is a picture of a situation.

(Even the proposition, *Ambulo*, is composite: for its stem with a different ending yields a different sense, and so does its ending with a different stem.)

4.12 Propositions can represent the whole of reality, but they cannot represent what they must have in common with reality in order to be able to represent it—logical form.

In order to be able to represent logical form, we should have to be able to station ourselves with propositions somewhere outside logic, that is to say outside the world.

4.121 Propositions cannot represent logical form: it is mirrored in them.

What finds its reflection in language, language cannot represent.

What expresses *itself* in language, *we* cannot express by means of language.

Propositions *show* the logical form of reality.

They display it.

4.1211 Thus one proposition '*fa*' shows that the object *a* occurs in its sense, two propositions '*fa*' and '*ga*' show that the same object is mentioned in both of them.

If two propositions contradict one another, then their structure shows it; the same is true if one of them follows from the other. And so on.

4.1212 What *can* be shown, *cannot* be said.

5.6 *The limits of my language* mean the limits of my world.

The important distinction here is between what can be said in language and what can only be shown. In making the distinction, Wittgenstein intends to give an exhaustive classification of the possible content of language. This content divides into what *we* can express in language (the sayable) and what only language *itself* can express; we might say into what can be *re*presented by language and what can only be presented *in* language.

Logical form cannot be represented in propositions, it can only be, as Wittgenstein says, mirrored, reflected, shown (4.121). The force of these expressions is not quite clear. If we took logical (and pictorial) form to be the *mere* possibility of structure, a proposition might be said to reflect or mirror its form in the sense that any actual state of affairs reflects its own possibility. But it would be a little forced or misleading to say that the possibility was also represented. If, on the other hand, pictorial form is not simply the picture's possibility of being a picture but also something the picture can be seen to have insofar as it is a picture, the notions of reflection, mirroring, and showing can be understood in a fairly straightforward way: the form of a picture is directly intuitable. But being shown, it cannot be said; even if I can make another picture of that picture, this other picture could never be a picture of the logical form of the first. Thus form cannot be represented at all.

Wittgenstein's account of language in terms of picturing appears to have paradoxical consequences. It might seem that these were also awkward and frustrating consequences. Gilbert Ryle puts the matter as follows.

> For a statement, map or diagram to be true or false, there must be a plurality of words or marks; but, more, these bits must be put together in certain ways. And underlying the fact that the truth or falsity of the statement or map partly depends upon the particular way in which its bits are arranged, there lies the fact that whether a signifi-

cant statement or map results at all, depends wholly on the general way in which the bits are put together. Some ways of jumbling them together are ruled out. What rules rule them out?

In the *Tractatus* Wittgenstein came to the frustrating conclusion that these principles of arrangement inevitably baffle significant statement. To try to tell what makes the difference between significant and nonsensical talk is itself to cross the divide between significant and nonsensical talk.[20]

The consequences are frustrating for anyone who wants to formulate propositions (say anything) about the conditions of meaningful discourse. They are awkward because the *Tractatus* is itself an attempt to make clear what those conditions are. By making picturability a condition of meaningful discourse Wittgenstein is forced to accept that his own statements about the conditions of meaningfulness have no meaning. Presumably then, what is wrong is precisely the picture theory of meaning. Ryle considers that Wittgenstein was "over-influenced by his own analogies between saying things and making maps, diagrams and scale-models." He continues:

Certainly, for marks on paper to constitute a temperature-chart, or for spoken words to constitute a significant statement, the dots and the words must be arranged according to rules and conventions. Only if the zigzag of dots on the nurse's graph-paper is systematically correlated with the thermometer-readings taken at successive moments of a day, can it represent or even misrepresent the alterations in the patient's temperature. Only if words are organized according to a number of complex general rules does a true or false statement result.

Suppose we now ask the nurse to depict on a second

---

[20]"Ludwig Wittgenstein," *Analysis*, XII (1951), reprinted in Copi and Beard, *Essays on Wittgenstein's Tractatus*, p. 5.

sheet of paper, not the course of the patient's temperature, but the rules for representing his temperature by dots on graph-paper, she would be baffled. Nor can the rules and conventions of map-making themselves be mapped. So Wittgenstein argued in the *Tractatus* that the philosopher or logician is debarred from saying what it is that makes things said significant or nonsensical.[21]

Wittgenstein accepted that "In order that you should have a language which can express or *say* everything that *can* be said, this language must have certain properties; and when this is the case, *that* it has them can no longer be said in that language or *any* language."[22] However, too literal an interpretation of Ryle's analogy may be misleading. There is nothing to prevent the fact that a proposition and the state of affairs have the same structure being *shown*. Thus even if the nurse would be rightly baffled on being asked to produce a representation of the rules for representing the patient's temperature, she could still point to the structural identity between the changes in temperature and the graphic representation of them. She could point to their "common logical plan" (4.014). And even if one could not *say* that this is what made the representation possible, the fact might still be said to express *itself* in language. If so, then it is not quite so frustrating that we cannot express it ourselves.[23]

When we express something in language, it is of course not the state of affairs depicted that we express, but *that* something is so and so. The sentence "It is raining" expresses *that* it rains, it does not express rain. (Rain is condensed in

---

[21]*Ibid.*, pp. 5-6.
[22]"Notes Dictated to G. E. Moore in Norway" (1914) in *Notebooks*, p. 107.
[23]Perhaps Ryle, like Carnap, assumes that Wittgenstein fails to distinguish between logical *form* and geometrical or other kinds of *structure*. Certainly there is some difficulty in determining the degree to which Wittgenstein did distinguish between the two. See 2.032, 2.033, 2.15, 2.151.

the sky and falls down on us; it may be made artificially, blessed, predicted, but it cannot be expressed. Indicative sentences do not express reality, but express something about reality, namely, precisely what we understand when we hear or read a meaningful configuration of words. Sentences expressing propositions can say a lot *about* rain, and what they say about it is what we understand when we understand the propositions. In Wittgenstein's terminology, what a sentence expressing a proposition says is identical in content with the proposition's *meaning*, not with a state of affairs, or, in Frege's terminology (cf. p. 77 above), its reference. To comprehend everything that can be said is therefore to comprehend all possible meanings, and, corresponding to these are all possible (meaningful) propositions. Thus Wittgenstein says (4) that the thought is the meaningful proposition. To comprehend a possible meaning is also to comprehend a possible thought. The transition from meaning to reference or possible state of affairs is *possible* because the proposition has a "logical form" which is apparent in its structure and which is also the form of reality.

Logical form, as we say, is something that a proposition can show but not say (4.12, 4.121). Propositions with the structure "*x* has the property *f*" or "*xRy*" ("*x* stands in relation *R* to *y*") *show* or *mirror* a logical form, yet they do not *represent* this form. Propositions *say that* it is in reality as it is *shown* by their form. It is up to us to see logical form mirrored in the proposition.

In terms of the model of picturing we can put it thus: Propositions are pictures of reality; they do not express pictures, but reveal themselves as such; what they say is that reality is as the picture shows. If in fact reality is as the picture shows, then the proposition is true; if not, then it is false. However, even when a proposition is false, we know what it expresses, thanks to its meaning, for its meaning is independent of its truth-value.

The vital philosophical consideration here is the thesis that logical form is also the form of reality; the concept of logical form is thus taken to belong to ontology as well as to logic.

Central, too, is the notion of there being something that cannot be said, the notion, that is, of a limit to what it is possible to say. This limit is at the same time the limit of meaningful utterance, and constitutes, by the same token, the boundaries both of language and thought.

The role of philosophy—to make it clear that there is no such thing

The door now stands open for a direct treatment of the most profound questions of all. As a key to their solution, Wittgenstein uses the thesis about the logical form of the proposition being the same[24] as the inner structure of reality, and about this being something that *shows* itself, cannot be expressed, hence cannot be object for *discussion*.

Meaningful propositions fall into one of two classes: the class of true propositions and the class of false propositions. Those propositions are true which state that which is the case, that is, which describe existing states of affairs, and false propositions are those that state what is not the case but what nevertheless, logically speaking, *might have been* the case—insofar as they are not self-contradictory. Wittgenstein calls "science" all speculation directed toward the identifying of true propositions[25]—certainly an unconventional usage, and one suggesting that he had a particular philosophy of science in mind. But of this he says nothing more.

Such sentences as "Life is beautiful," "It is a sin to steal," "Beethoven's Fifth Symphony is a valuable work of art," and "God is eternal and unknowable," cannot be said to describe possible states of affairs, for nothing can count as their being either true or false.[26] Now philosophers, moralists, aestheticians, and preachers have certainly always been thought to be

---

[24]It is an open question what Wittgenstein means by "same" here. Of the same kind? Absolutely identical? Numerically distinct but otherwise identical?

[25]Cf. Spinoza's distinction between *natura naturata (Sachverhalt)* and *natura naturans* ("logical form," "essence").

[26]The examples are not Wittgenstein's.

99

propounding truths, or if not, at least falsehoods—that is propositions. On the other hand, they have also been claiming to propound something other than science. But if, once science has had its say, there is nothing more to be said, then there are no further propositions for philosophers or anyone else to concern themselves with.

Still, there is something for philosophers to *do*. They can undermine belief in there being something beyond reality which can be the subject of meaningful propositions—that is, propositions which picture possible states of affairs.

The sole function of philosophy, then, is to clarify, and if, in the process of clarifying, the philosopher is compelled, for didactic purposes, to make statements, once clarity is achieved there will be no philosophical propositions left over. Or, in Wittgenstein's own words:

4.11 The totality of true propositions is the whole of natural science (or the whole corpus of natural science).

4.111 Philosophy is not one of the natural sciences.

(The word 'philosophy' must mean something whose place is above or below the natural sciences, but not beside them.)

4.112 Philosophy aims at the logical clarification of thoughts.

Philosophy is not a body of doctrine but an activity.

A philosophical work consists essentially of elucidations.

Philosophy does not result in "philosophical propositions," but rather in the clarification of propositions.

Without philosophy thoughts are, as it were, cloudy and indistinct: its task is to make them clear and to give them sharp boundaries.

4.114 It must set limits to what can be thought; and, in doing so, to what cannot be thought.

It must set limits to what cannot be thought by working outwards through what can be thought.

6.5 When the answer cannot be put into words, neither can the question be put into words. . . .

6.52 We feel that even when *all possible* scientific questions have been answered, the problems of life remain completely untouched. Of course there are then no questions left, and this itself is the answer.

6.521 The solution of the problem of life is seen in the vanishing of the problem.

(Is this not the reason why those who have found after a long period of doubt that the sense of life became clear to them have been unable to say what constituted that sense?)

6.53 The correct method in philosophy would really be the following: to say nothing except what can be said, i.e. propositions of natural science—i.e. something that has nothing to do with philosophy—and then, whenever someone else wanted to say something metaphysical, to demonstrate to him that he had failed to give a meaning[27] to certain signs in his propositions. Although it would not be satisfying to the other person—he would not have the feeling that we were teaching him philosophy—*this* method would be the only strictly correct one.

After this come the last two passages, retrospective and summing up:

6.54 My propositions serve as elucidations in the following way: anyone who understands me eventually

[27]Here the non-technical sense of "meaning" is in place; that is, the sense in which it does not mean 'reference.' One cannot give a sign a reference, but one can give it, or fail to give it, a (clear) meaning. (Propositions or signs do not need to have references.) When a sign has no meaning the result is nonsense (in Wittgenstein's terminology: *Unsinn*). If all the signs in a proposition have meaning but nevertheless say nothing, as in the case of tautologies, the proposition fails to have a sense (in Wittgenstein's terminology: *Sinnlosigkeit*).

recognizes them as nonsensical, when he has used them—as steps—to climb up beyond them. (He must, so to speak, throw away the ladder after he has climbed up it.)

He must transcend these propositions, and then he will see the world aright.

7 What we cannot speak about we must consign to silence.

With this analogy of the ladder, also to be found in Sextus Empiricus,[28] who used it to eliminate commitment to any truth claim whatsoever, the *Tractatus* comes to an end.

However, there are still some questions to be discussed, even in our brief exposition, and we shall devote a little space to them.

Have philosophers kept strictly to their proper path? Although Wittgenstein does make some comments on the subject of philosophy in its historical perspective, he goes into no details and provides no examples.

4.003 Most of the propositions and questions to be found in philosophical works are not false but nonsensical. Consequently we cannot give any answers to questions of this kind, but can only establish that they are nonsensical. Most of the propositions and questions of philosophers arise from our failure to understand the logic of our language.

(They belong to the same class as the question whether the good is more or less identical than the beautiful.)

And it is not surprising that the deepest problems are in fact *not* problems at all.

These conclusions, both about the strictly correct philosophical method and about philosopher's having gone astray, are anticipated in Wittgenstein's Preface to the *Tractatus*.

[28]See Sextus Empiricus, *Against the Logicians*, trans. R. G. Bury, Book II, sec. 481 (Cambridge, Mass.: Harvard University Press; London: W. Heinemann, 1935), p. 489.

The book deals with the problems of philosophy, and shows, I believe, that the reason why these problems are posed is that the logic of our language is misunderstood. The whole sense of the book might be summed up in the following words: what can be said at all can be said clearly, and what we cannot talk about we must consign to silence.

Reflections on ultimate things

Still, it can hardly be claimed that the *Tractatus* discusses philosophical problems purely from an outside point of view: it also contains direct commitment to familiar metaphysical standpoints. A question that naturally arises then is how far these reflections, in the form of numbered propositions, are consistent with the book's conclusion about the role of philosophy. We shall elaborate a little on this question.

Wittgenstein says:

1 and
1.1 The world is all that is the case, the totality of facts, not of things.
6.4 All propositions are of equal value.
6.41 The sense of the world must lie outside the world. In the world everything is as it is, and everything happens as it does happen: *in* it no value exists—and if it did, it would have no value.

If there is any value that does have value, it must lie outside the whole sphere of what happens and is the case. For all that happens and is the case is accidental.[29]

---

[29]Regarding the accidental nature of the world: If the world consisted of two facts—it is raining and it is night—everything could have been otherwise. Thus we get four possible worlds (i.e., conceivable, i.e., non-contradictory worlds). (1) The real one, (2) It is raining and it is not night, (3) It is not raining and it is night, (4) It is neither raining nor is it night. The *accident* that (1) should obtain consists simply in that it is not logically necessary.

What makes it non-accidental cannot lie *within* the world, since if it did it would itself be accidental.

It must lie outside the world.

One way of deciding whether these reflections are in any way affected by Wittgenstein's conclusions, is to ask in respect of each such statement: Is there a picture that it represents such that, following 2.201, one can say that it presents the possibility of the existence *or the non-existence* of a state of affairs?

Applying this procedure to the first paragraph of 6.41, we should be able to envisage the possibility of the meaning of the world as *not* lying outside the world. What 6.41 says should then be compared with reality so that we might decide whether what it says is or is not the case. But *has* the sentence "In the world everything is *not* as it is" any meaning? In general, it appears that only insofar as Wittgenstein's thinking can be true or false can it be incorporated into his "system" in the form of propositions.

Wittgenstein distinguishes between the contingent and the necessary, and the only necessity he accepts is logical necessity, that is, necessity due to logical form and hence inexpressible. A proposition such as "One and the same area in one's field of vision cannot have two different colors" has a necessity which is due to the inner *logical* structure of colors, not to anything *in* the world. (Wittgenstein says that logic pervades the world [5.61].) Strictly speaking, then, no proposition about the world is able to express it.

There are propositions that *cannot* be false. To this category belongs all of logic. Logical propositions cannot be false because they are without meaning. That they are meaningless is obvious from their structure, as for example in the case of propositions which consist of two meaningful but mutually contradictory propositions linked by "or," such as 'It is raining or it is not raining'. Here the impossibility of the proposition being false is quite evident, but the proposition does not *say* anything about the world. In fact all logical propositions are tautologies, empty propositions that have neither meaning nor reference.

The kind of pictures that propositions give are descriptive, not normative. We should perhaps bear this in mind when proceeding to the next reflection.

> 6.42 And so it is impossible for there to be propositions of ethics.
>
> Propositions can express nothing of what is higher.
>
> 6.421 It is clear that ethics cannot be put into words.
>
> Ethics is transcendental.
>
> (Ethics and aesthetics are one and the same.)

In the Notebooks from 1916 we find the following.[30]

> The work of art is the object seen *sub specie aeternitatis;* and the good life is the world seen *sub specie aeternitatis.* This is the connexion between art and ethics.

> 6.422 When an ethical law of the form, 'Thou shalt . . .', is laid down, one's first thought is, 'And what if I do not do it?' It is clear, however, that ethics has nothing to do with punishment and reward in the usual sense of the terms. So our question about the *consequences* of an action must be unimportant. . . .
>
> 6.423 It is impossible to speak about the will in so far as it is the subject of ethical attributes.
>
> And the will as a phenomenon is of interest only to psychology.
>
> 6.43 If good or bad acts of will do alter the world, it can only be the limits of the world that they alter, not the facts, not what can be expressed by means of language.

---

[30]*Notebooks*, p. 83.

In short their effect must be that it becomes an altogether different world. It must, so to speak, wax and wane as a whole.

The world of the happy man is a different one from that of the unhappy man.

6.431 So too at death the world does not alter, but comes to an end.

This last will be more intelligible after reading some of Wittgenstein's remarks on 'I.'

5.63 I am my world. (The microcosm.)

5.631 There is no such thing as the subject that thinks or entertains ideas. . . .

5.632 The subject does not belong to the world: rather, it is a limit of the world.

5.64 Here it can be seen that solipsism, when its implications are followed out strictly, coincides with pure realism. The self of solipsism shrinks to a point without extension, and there remains the reality co-ordinated with it.

Finally, some thoughts which form a continuation of Wittgenstein's reflections on ethics:

6.432 *How* things are in the world is a matter of complete indifference for what is higher. God does not reveal himself *in* the world.

6.4321 The facts all contribute only to setting the problem, not to its solution.

Which seems to mean: From an ethical point of view I must will to do this or that within the world of facts, and consequently my tasks are posed for me in a way defined by the way things are. But whether it is possible for me later to say that I have solved a task cannot depend on factual conditions since my will has only a factual, contingent, relation to the world. It cannot change anything.

G. E. M. Anscombe has some inside information on this:

'Aufgabe,' which I translate 'task set,' is the German for a child's school exercise, or piece of homework. Life is like a boy doing sums. (At the end of his life he used the analogy still.) Now the reason why the solution cannot bring in any facts is that it is concerned with good and evil; and the good and evil character of what is good or evil is non-accidental; it therefore cannot consist in this happening rather than that, for that is accidental.[31]

What could be the basis for understanding the good or bad in an action as being non-accidental, whereas its actual course, motivation and everything else to do with states of affairs are accidental? The question becomes crucial if Miss Anscombe's statement is to be accepted.

> 6.44 It is not *how* things are in the world that is mystical, but *that* it exists.
>
> 6.45 To view the world *sub specie aeterni* is to view it as a whole—a limited whole.
>
>   Feeling the world as a limited whole—it is this that is mystical.

Following the remark in 6.521 about the ineffability of life's meaning, we come to a well-known statement concerning the *existence* of something ineffable.

> 6.522 There are, indeed, things that cannot be put into words. They *make themselves manifest*. They are what is mystical.

Following upon these reflections the book ends with the passages already quoted, in which Wittgenstein declares what are the proper methods of philosophy, speaks of the non-sensicalness of his own propositions, and finally enjoins silence concerning that of which we cannot speak.[32]

---

[31]G. E. M. Anscombe, *An Introduction*, p. 171.

[32]The topics that have not been included in this presentation are mainly logical matters: truth-functions, tautology, logic as outside the world, the general form of a proposition, and so on. Those who want

The second to last statement (6.54) takes *his own propositions ("meine Sätze")* to be clarificatory insofar as anyone who *understands* them *eventually* recognizes their nonsensicalness. The three underlined expressions allow interpretations of crucial philosophical interest. The propositions Wittgenstein refers to as "his" cannot be all the propositions in the *Tractatus* up until 6.54. Certainly a great number of his propositions must be considered blameless: for example, such statements as "Suppose I know the meaning of an English word and of a German word that means the same: then it is impossible for me to be unaware that they do mean the same" (from 4.243). It seems then that we must go into the question of how much of the *Tractatus* is nonsensical according to Wittgenstein's own criteria.[33]

According to the answer one gives, one arrives at one's own interpretation of the division in Wittgenstein's thoughts. By excluding very little one will assign to the author of the *Tractatus* meaningful opinions of the following kind: "Questions about God, morality, and the meaning of life cannot be formulated in meaningful sentences in language," "Ethics and aesthetics are the same," "It isn't *how* the world is that is the mystical, but *that* it is."

To grant that such propositions, in the normal sense of the word, can be accepted as propositions in the Wittgensteinian sense, is to let in a great number of the normal metaphysical

---

to go into these and other things more deeply must consult the original and the relevant commentaries. (See note 13.)

[33]Anders Wedberg's distinction between "lower" and "higher" nonsense is helpful here. An example of the former is "Socrates is identical," where no property has been attached to the word "identical." "Higher" nonsense arises from attempts to say the unsayable, attempts to give words meanings that cannot be expressed in language. Traditional philosophy, in Wittgenstein's view, is largely comprised of low nonsense, while his own statements can be regarded as high nonsense. See *Filosofins Historia*, Vol. 3 *(Fran Bolzano till Wittgenstein)* (Stockholm: Bonniers, 1966), pp. 205 ff. An English translation is forthcoming (New York: The Bedminster Press).

terms, and the antimetaphysical strain then becomes very tenuous.

To exclude more than this, as one should according to any reasonable interpretation of the text, may still be to allow meanings to such expressions, and questions formed with them, but then only as expressions of emotion, or perhaps, more favorably, as expressions of experiences or intuitions which do not lend themselves to being pictured. One might also consider introducing a special metaphysical terminology parallel to that of language "proper," a way of talking that is not properly linguistic. Thus when Wittgenstein discusses metaphysical questions he often uses the term "problem" *(Problem)* rather than "question" *(Frage)*. Metaphysical problems could then be understood, though scarcely *thought*, as something corresponding to, without actually being, questions expressed in language.

However, such a half-acceptance of "metaphysical" propositions would surely obliterate the very distinction that Wittgenstein saw it as his task to uncover. And it would be patently illogical to fail to apply it rigorously precisely in the case of his own propositions.

The most radical interpretation of the *Tractatus* is that nearly all its propositions must be classified as nonsense. This is perhaps the most influential interpretation. It is also the oldest, and is formulated by Bertrand Russell in his introduction to the first German-English edition.

His life and influence from 1929

The influence of the "Tractatus"

As we noted, Wittgenstein declined to give any more specific account of his monads, the elementary propositions. What information he does provide, however, is enough to arouse keen curiosity. Elementary propositions are the simplest kind of proposition, and they assert the existence of states of affairs (4.21). If an elementary proposition is true, the state of affairs obtains; if it is false the state of affairs does not obtain (4.25). Elementary propositions are what we come to in the analysis of propositions (4.221). They can be written as functions (fx, etc.) of names. Introducing elementary propositions provides the basis for understanding all other kinds of proposition (4.411). And from one elementary proposition no other can be deduced (5.134).

Because propositions are to be thought of here as pictures of reality, and the proposition's logical form as being also the logical form of the world, these statements acquire a strong ontological flavor. It is, of course, an assumption of the greatest philosophical importance that we can say of the world in general that it has a logical form. The fact remains, however, that Wittgenstein gives no clear indication of what is meant by "logical form" as a property of the world or reality.

Within the philosophical atmosphere of Cambridge, just as in the trend-setting circles of his home town, Vienna, it was more or less taken for granted that elementary propositions were to be interpreted within the framework of empiricism, in particular according to its sense datum versions. In his own theory of logical atomism, which was much influenced by his early discussions with Wittgenstein, Russell tended to regard simple colored patches in the visual field as examples of the particulars that occurred in "atomic facts."[34] But there seems no compelling reason why a logical atomist should be committed to identifying basic units with names of elements of direct experience. The empiricist tradition and the existing sense data terminology was no doubt a main factor here, both in Russell's conception of logical atomism and in the way in which Wittgenstein's *Tractatus* was understood.

The *Tractatus'* "Sachverhalt" was translated into English as

[34]"The Philosophy of Logical Atomism" (1918) in Robert C. Marsh (ed.), *Logic and Knowledge*, e.g., p. 198. See note 7.

"atomic fact." Indeed there has been a general predisposition to use the word "fact"; it was also used in translating "Tatsache." Thus logical atomism came to be considered the thesis that facts not reducible to other facts are sense data, observation data, or immediate sensory experiences, that such items are mutually independent and that all knowledge should in principle be either expressible in terms of them or derivable from them.

Such interpretations came to mind all the more readily in the vacuum left by Wittgenstein's insistence that it was an empirical matter to identify states of affairs. On the other hand, this insistence itself seems to suggest that the interpretation is distinctly arbitrary, and that it is just as likely that for Wittgenstein elements were significant only, or primarily, as *consequences* of his picture theory, and hence as forming a necessary part of his solution to questions of logic and language.[35] Interpreted in this way, Wittgenstein's basic concepts, and perhaps also his basic project, may be seen to differ significantly from Russell's.[36]

In the Vienna Circle the influence of the *Tractatus* was much more marked and immediate than in England. Wittgenstein seemed to its members to have provided a compendious and systematic exposition of their own views about the limits of meaning in language. But in Vienna too the *Tractatus* was interpreted in the light of local interests. Being concerned with the task of distinguishing the meaningfulness of scientific language from the meaninglessness of metaphysics, the Vienna Circle was inclined to interpret Wittgenstein's *Sachverhalte* as

[35]See Paul Wienpahl, "Wittgenstein and the Naming Relation," *Inquiry*, VII (1964), No. 4, 329-47. Wienpahl says that the *Tractatus* is primarily an attempt to avoid the conceptual realism of Frege and Russell with respect to propositions. The picture theory develops out of a solution that assumes the units of language to be names of simple objects.

[36]See, e.g., Dudley Shapere, "Philosophy and the Analysis of Language," *Inquiry*, III (1960), No. 1, 29-48, reprinted in Richard Rorty (ed.), *The Linguistic Turn: Recent Essays in Philosophical Method* (Chicago: The University of Chicago Press, 1967).

observable states of affairs. Thus the appeal of the *Tractatus* to the Circle's members lay in its apparent systematization of the view that the meaning of any statement, however complex, is ultimately to be expressed in terms of the observation statements upon which acceptance of the statement's truth or falsity is based.[37]

Even though Wittgenstein says nothing about verification in the *Tractatus*, it does seem plausible to attach to his concept of truth-conditions a theory of verification through sense experience. According to Wittgenstein a proposition must be so analyzed as to specify under what conditions of observation it is true. And it is said that in the years between 1929 and 1933 Wittgenstein sometimes expressed himself in ways which indicated support of the Vienna Circle brand of empiricism.[38]

We can at least recognize in Wittgenstein's equating all meaningful discourse with science, in his "antimetaphysics," and in his detailed and extremely acute logical investigations, the extent to which his own thought could accommodate the high value that the Vienna philosophers placed on scientific research.

There was much of the prophetic in Wittgenstein's personality (we shall return later to this aspect), and it became increasingly a point of honor and prestige among serious-minded philosophers and philosopher scientists to have Wittgenstein's opinion on their side. Now, seventeen years after his death, it is easy to understand how Wittgenstein's distinctive and very personal style made it impossible or at least extremely difficult to come to any fixed agreement about his views on certain philosophical questions. Indeed, the ideas of

[37]Cf. J. O. Urmson, *Philosophical Analysis* (Oxford: The Clarendon Press, 1956), e.g., p. 99, and Pitcher, *The Philosophy of Wittgenstein*, pp. 164 ff.
[38]Cf. von Wright's discussion (in Malcolm's *A Memoir*, p. 13) of two unpublished typescripts of Wittgenstein from this period.

the *Tractatus* remind one more of Spinoza (the harmony of thought and reality), Leibniz (theory of monads, logic of universals), and rationalism of the kind typified by Russell up to the time of World War I, than of any empiricist philosopher.[39] In some ways, if one looks at the main exponents of empiricism from Locke onwards, Wittgenstein's thoughts and theirs seem to be poles apart. Consider, for example, the concept of 'world.' If Wittgenstein's concept of the world really had an empiricist slant, we would find this expressed in statements claiming that everything in the world can be experienced, or that empirical, as opposed, say, to intuitive methods are the only methods that can lead to positive results. But we find nothing of this kind in the *Tractatus*. The term "empirical" appears once, when Wittgenstein says "Empirical reality is limited by the totality of objects" (5.5561), but even here we are not warranted in interpreting him as saying that all objects are objects of experience or that they are to be explored only by means of observation.[40] The *Tractatus*, in fact, says little about experience, and then only in a negative way, as for example when Wittgenstein says that logic is outside all experience.

This, of course, is not to say that we can find in the *Tractatus* anything directly opposing the idea that the world is a totality of things that can be experienced, or the idea that observation and sense experience are in principle the only

[39] Of Wittgenstein's position with regard to theory of knowledge Wedberg says that there is one point on which it is in essential agreement with that of the empiricist philosopher David Hume: "Every truth . . . according to the *Tractatus* must be either a logical tautology or an empirical statement of fact." (*Filosofins Historia*, Vol. 3, p. 191). Miss Anscombe and others seem to have established that Wittgenstein had no intention of taking up questions about theory of knowledge in the *Tractatus*.

[40] A (suspiciously) straightforward empiricist interpretation of the *Tractatus* can be found in Karl R. Popper, "Philosophy of Science: A Personal Report," in *British Philosophy in the Mid-Century*, ed. C. A. Mace (London: George Allen & Unwin, Ltd., 1957), pp. 163-64.

ways of finding out which states of affairs obtain. The question just is not raised.

When Moritz Schlick (cf. page 12) in 1922 founded the discussion group that became known as the Vienna Circle he sought out Wittgenstein as a man whose philosophical ideas were of decisive importance. Friedrich Waismann, mathematician and philosopher, associated his own ideas even more closely with those of Wittgenstein. Waismann completed a manuscript entitled *Logic, Language, Philosophy: a Critique of Philosophy through Logic*, intended as the first volume in a series of monographs entitled *Writings in the Scientific Understanding of the World*, in which the common points of the Vienna Circle philosophers were to be developed and supported. But the first volume never appeared, because Waismann would not publish the manuscript without Wittgenstein's approval of the main ideas and Wittgenstein never gave the work his imprimatur. From 1930 onward Wittgenstein was immersed in a personal philosophical revolution, turning, at times passionately, against his own *Tractatus* and its disciples.

Rudolf Carnap (b. 1891) did much to divert the current of the influence of Wittgenstein's ideas within the Vienna Circle. Carnap's respect for and confidence in scientific research went too deep for him to be dissuaded from his attempt to form a scientifically based theory of language and of language's relation to reality, an impossible project according to the *Tractatus*. Carnap's views found support from, among others, the Polish mathematician and logician Alfred Tarski (b. 1901), who devoted himself to a more exact working out of the notion of a metalanguage, that is, a language in which it is possible to talk meaningfully about language. In the view of Carnap and his supporters, logical form could be talked about as much as any topic.

Although during this time Wittgenstein's name became increasingly known, he published nothing and did all he could

114

to restrict his contacts with other philosophers, a fact that should not, however, lead one to believe that his philosophical ideas evolved independently of other philosophers, or that they cannot be compared with similar ideas of other thinkers.

Hints of the "Tractatus" in other philosophers

The immediate and very emphatic influence of Frege and Russell has already been mentioned—though not enlarged upon in any detail. In fact the *Tractatus* gives one the impression of being Wittgenstein's own attempt to put their ideas to the test of a comprehensive systematic exposition. But other influences are to be detected, more especially in the wider terms of philosophy of life. The influence of Schopenhauer and Tolstoy, both of whom had a special place in Wittgenstein's thoughts, is particularly noticeable.[41]

When we think of Wittgenstein's attempt to locate the boundaries of thought and his conclusion that they coincide with the possibility of forming meaningful propositions, we are reminded of Kant's attempt to draw the boundaries of theoretical reason. And to Kant's "judgments of practical reason" there correspond in Wittgenstein propositions about ethics in which, as with Kant, we have the idea of a kind of necessity that is not of this world, but is somehow brought in from the outside. The connection with Kant is unmistakable even if no direct influence can be shown. Stenius in his "Critical Exposition" believes that the *Tractatus* exemplifies a new

---

[41]Von Wright mentions the notebook from 1916 as illuminating those parts of the *Tractatus* dealing with the ego, the freedom of the will, the meaning of life, and death. Beside the influence of Schopenhauer on Wittgenstein's thinking, "An occasional Spinozistic flavour is also recognizable." (In Malcolm, *A Memoir*, p. 9.) Thus Wittgenstein terms that which is indestructible in the world—and in opposition to states of affairs—"substance." Note the singular form—there is only one substance, and it "subsists independently of what is the case" (2.024). The expression "sub specie aeternitatis" occurs quite frequently in Wittgenstein.

kind of Kantianism, an interpretation that he develops in some detail.[42]

The connection between the Socratic method and the logical analysis of statements is a point stressed in one of the first thorough commentaries on the *Tractatus*, Maslow's *A Study in Wittgenstein's Tractatus*. But according to Maslow, Socrates failed to observe certain important distinctions. The comparison is certainly instructive, since it provides a good example of how those who see philosophy as a kind of analysis of language, and without any special domain of its own, contrive to incorporate the history of philosophy into their own framework.

> Socrates' method was not to give any information, but to make clear what was meant by certain questions concerning human nature and conduct. It is not the subject matter dealt with by Socrates, namely, ethical problems, that is important here, but the method he used to investigate this subject matter, because, according to Wittgenstein, this method is the right method of philosophy when dealing with any subject matter whatsoever. The method consists in the attempts to make clear the sense of the propositions under consideration. Socrates, of course, went farther, and claimed that by the persistent application of this method, and only by this method, we can arrive at least at some ethical truths. The rationalistic metaphysics of Socrates is due to his confusion of the activity of clarification of language with the investigation of the world. Wittgenstein accepts Socratic practice as sound philosophy, but he rejects his metaphysical theory. . . . The trouble with Socrates was that he was not sufficiently Socratic![43]

[42]E. Stenius, *Wittgenstein's 'Tractatus'*, chap. 9.

[43]Alexander Maslow, *Wittgenstein's Tractatus* (Berkeley: University of California Press, 1961), p. 139. The book was prepared for publication as early as 1933.

Underlying this characterization is the confident assumption that we can safely disregard the fact that Socrates was using his method to investigate the nature of things, that his definitions are a kind of "essential" definition. Though we can see in the *Tractatus*, too, this attempt to reach the essence of things, at the time that Maslow wrote (1933) this aspect of Wittgenstein's thought was generally not acknowledged. The result in this case is a distorted impression, both of the similarity with Socrates and of the dissimilarity with empirically oriented philosophy.[44]

There are parallels to Wittgenstein's rejection of philosophy as anything except a critique of language. Thus Georg Christoph Lichtenberg (1742-99) wrote, "Our entire philosophy is the rectifying of language."[45] (The words remind one of the Chinese doctrine of "rectification of names.")

There are numerous points of similarity, too, between the *Tractatus* and the views of the language philosopher Fritz Mauthner (1848-1923). Wittgenstein was acquainted with Mauthner's work, although he says that what is needed is another kind of critique of language (see 4.0031). According to Mauthner philosophy is "critical attention to language" as that in which all thought must be expressed.

> Critique of language . . . is the last attempt, it is the last word, and because it cannot be the solution of the riddle of the sphinx, so it is at least the redeeming act that

[44]On the basis of the texts of the *Tractatus* and the Socratic dialogues, one would be hard pressed to find reasonable interpretations of Socrates' "midwife procedure" that accorded with what Wittgenstein envisages as the correct philosophical method: namely, "whenever someone else wanted to say something metaphysical, to demonstrate to him that he had failed to give a meaning to certain signs in his propositions" (6.53).

[45]Quoted from G. H. von Wright's article, "Georg Christoph Lichtenberg als Philosoph," *Theoria*, VIII (1942), 215. Von Wright thinks that Lichtenberg anticipated Wittgenstein's view of philosophy but did not influence it.

forces the sphinx into silence, because it destroys the sphinx.[46]

Mauthner's understanding of language is generally closer to that of the later Wittgenstein.

It is far from clear that there is in Fritz Mauthner any anticipation of Wittgenstein's main ideas. Mauthner's work is somewhat rhapsodic in approach, and though occasional passages give one the impression that he is saying the same things as Wittgenstein, there is a marked absence of the latter's inner coherence and intensity. The difference between the two philosophers' depths of intention is very marked.

His life from 1929 to 1951

From about 1929 Wittgenstein's thoughts moved in new directions. Some of those who followed his development from close at hand and were influenced by him consider the new directions to have been not merely relatively but altogether new. "Wittgenstein's new philosophy," says G. H. von Wright, "is, so far as I can see, entirely outside any philosophical tradition and without literary sources of influence."[47]

Though the new was undoubtedly to a very great extent of Wittgenstein's own making, his faith in some of the standpoints of the *Tractatus* had been effectively undermined by one or two of his own friends, especially F. P. Ramsey and P. Sraffa at Cambridge. About his discussions with the latter Wittgenstein said that they "made him feel like a tree from which all branches had been cut."[48] As before, Wittgenstein

---

[46]Fritz Mauthner, *Beiträge zu einer Kritik der Sprache* (3d ed.; Leipzig: Verlag v. Felix Meiner, 1923), Vol. 3, p. 634. Quoted in G. Weiler, "On Mauthner's Critique of Language," *Mind*, LXVII (1958), 85.

[47]In Malcolm, *A Memoir*, p. 15. "A whole new way of philosophizing" is the expression used by D. A. T. G[asking] and A. C. J[ackson] in their obituary notice in the *Australasian Journal of Philosophy*, XXIX (1951), No. 2, 73.

[48]*A Memoir*, p. 16.

found difficulty in giving adequate expression to his thoughts. During an extended stay abroad (1935-36), living in his hut in western Norway, he began to write the first draft of his famous posthumous work, *Philosophical Investigations*. In 1939 Wittgenstein succeeded G. E. Moore as professor in Cambridge.

Wittgenstein's lectures deserve comment. Through them he not only exercised a radical influence on his listeners, he also instituted a new "oral" tradition in philosophy, a new style and technique in impromptu philosophizing.

It is perhaps difficult for a Continental philosopher to gauge the effect and depth of Wittgenstein's influence. Writings and systematic presentations, the usual source of one's knowledge of such things, are not part of the *modus operandi*. Moreover, it appears that much of Wittgenstein's influence lay in the emphasis he placed on various questions of language, and although his ideas can be traced in the written works of philosophers who were not at all directly influenced by him, and who affected none of his personal style, it is not clear how much of this was due to Wittgenstein himself, and how much to existing trends which he simply gave impetus to. Wittgenstein's lectures were open to anyone who was seriously interested in the questions taken up for discussion. Students who meant to attend and actively participate in the discussions over a number of semesters were welcomed. Not so, however, visitors, even distinguished ones, who just came "to find out what sort of thing Wittgenstein is doing."[49] He disliked academic "tourists" or anybody who was not seriously interested in learning to philosophize.

In his lectures Wittgenstein thought with an intense and strenuous concentration. Often there were long silences. It was as though the thoughts were coming to light for the first time, as if one was witnessing the act of philosophical creation itself. Some of his former students hold, however, that each

[49]This point and the following one about the lectures are taken from Gasking and Jackson's obituary notice, pp. 74 ff.

lecture was thoroughly prepared and planned, not only in general outline but also in detail, including the examples that he produced to illustrate his points.[50] Whether or not they were prepared, these examples could be remarkable, although their relevance to philosophical questions was often hard to discern. What, for example, would one make of this story about some imaginary savage tribe?

> Suppose the members of the tribe decorate the walls of their houses by writing on them rows of Arabic numerals—and suppose that what they write is exactly what would be written by someone doing arithmetical calculations. They do it *exactly* right every time, but they never use it except for internal decoration—never use it in computing how much wood they need to build a hut or how much food they need for a feast, and so on. Would you say they were doing mathematics?[51]

The matter discussed was nearly always something commonplace and concrete, with an avoidance of technical terms. Indeed it is sometimes possible to identify those who have been influenced by Wittgenstein through their preference for ordinary, everyday expressions, their avoidance of a "philosophical" vocabulary. One hears of "jobs" rather than "functions" of language, of conceptual "muddles," "puzzlement," and so on. It was natural enough, too, for his manner as well as his way of thinking to be, consciously or unconsciously, imitated. Even highly gifted people with independent minds, for whom the repeating of catch-phrases and any kind of affectation would be anathema, acquired Wittgensteinian traits. In a moment of deep gloom Wittgenstein once said that the only thing he would bequeath would be "a certain

---

[50]*Ibid.*, p. 76. Malcolm's account is a more convincing one, however, when he says that the lectures were given "without preparation," provided, of course, that the choice of topic is not included in the preparation.

[51]*Ibid.*, p. 75.

jargon." Be that as it may, the intensity of his inner life and the impressive power of his words left none who came close to him quite the same. One is reminded of Alcibiades' testimony to another famous philosopher.

> . . . when we hear any other person—quite an excellent orator, perhaps—pronouncing one of the usual discourses, no one, I venture to say, cares a jot; but so soon as we hear you, or your discourses in the mouth of another,—though such person be ever so poor a speaker, and whether the hearer be a woman or a man or a youngster—we are all astonished and entranced.[52]

However, with its deadly seriousness, the atmosphere in Wittgenstein's discussions differed markedly from that of the Socratic debate. The tension was not even broken by Wittgenstein's many amusing examples. It is clear that Wittgenstein himself did not lack humor—one need only read some of the (few) published letters to realize that—yet in his philosophical seances, not a moment's lapse was tolerated.

It was one of Bertrand Russell's main objections to the philosophy that followed from Wittgenstein that it had become too easy, it evaded the issues. But this criticism is not leveled at Wittgenstein himself. Wittgenstein's own students record how the right solutions to apparently quite simple questions seemed terribly difficult to come by, and how they needed to employ all their powers unremittingly in the attempt to solve them.

There are moments when one suddenly feels that one has a clear and obvious solution to a question that has long been vexing one. One gets, sometimes very strongly, what Bühler called an "Aha!" experience. But an attempt to express the simple and obvious solution to others who have not participated may be quite useless. This was true for those who took

[52]Plato, *Symposium,* 215D. W. R. M. Lamb's translation, Loeb Classical Library (London: W. Heinemann; Cambridge, Mass.: Harvard University Press, 1953), pp. 219-21.

part in the discussions with Wittgenstein, and of course it is entirely in keeping with his own view—that philosophy can *show* something but not culminate in explicit statements of the solutions to its problems.

Wittgenstein disliked philosophical attitudes that were not expressions of deep personal involvement, and he particularly disliked sheer cleverness. "Don't try to be intelligent!" he told his students. The philosopher with problems to solve is someone who feels profound wonder about something. Unable to find his way, and confused, he gropes about in "deep puzzlement." It was those who were seriously concerned in the unraveling of problems, in finding the way, whom Wittgenstein sought out, and not the intellectually brilliant.

Wittgenstein's antipathy toward imitators was natural, not least on account of his own view that a philosophical problem should develop from within a person's own personal situation, and the solution be arrived at in the same individual context. We can think here of his own deep concern over his reputation; he did not wish posterity to think of him as a man who imitated others or who indulged in wild or foolish thoughts. His reflections on his own influence were painful and he constantly saw confirmation of his fear that he would be, must be, misunderstood.

Knowledge of Wittgenstein's new ways of thought was not confined to those who were able to hear him personally. Some of his thoughts he had dictated to his students in 1933-34, and more to two pupils in 1934-35. These notes were published in 1958 as *The Blue and Brown Books, Preliminary Studies for the Philosophical Investigations*. The titles "Blue Book" and "Brown Book" derive from the color of the covers in which the two sets of notes were bound.

These preliminary studies are a great help in understanding parts of the *Philosophical Investigations*. They are very clearly written, with less emphasis on style and less consideration for the Wittgensteinian principle that as little as possible be said, as much as possible shown or suggested. However, one must also bear in mind that the preliminary studies contain material from a transitional period in Wittgenstein's thinking, material that perhaps he would have rejected in light of his later views.

He sent a stenciled copy of the Blue Book to Russell. In the covering note he said:

> . . . I don't wish to suggest that you should read the lectures; but *if* you should have nothing better to do and *if* you should get some mild enjoyment out of them I should be very pleased indeed. . . . As I say, if you don't read them *it doesn't matter at all.*[53]

According to some who followed Wittgenstein's lectures, they had something of a negative character. What was important was to be rid of one's confusion—though certainly having first become aware that one was far more confused than one suspected. Yet when clarity follows upon confusion, to express what one sees with one's clear vision has no purpose, and indeed is impossible. It is no use trying to convey one's vision to others, for they must go through the same agonizing if they are to arrive at the same kind of clarity.

The important consideration here is that philosophy is not really able to be expressed or expounded in words at all. His own *Investigations* are no exception: Wittgenstein himself never came to the point where he could say of his manuscript, "Now, that's what I want to say to people!" It seems that the "new way" of philosophizing did not lend itself to elucidation in the normal discursive manner, and it is unlikely that it was only ill-health and weakness in his last years that forced him to leave the manuscript uncompleted.

To have to produce thoughts to schedule, and generally to *be* a professor was for Wittgenstein something of a nightmare, "a living death" he called it.[54] Perhaps what he feared

---

[53]*The Blue and Brown Books* (Oxford: Basil Blackwell, 1958), quoted in the Preface, p. v.
[54]Malcolm, *A Memoir*, p. 43.

most was the inevitable loss of spontaneity and freshness, even of sincerity, in his thoughts. When his friend Norman Malcolm became a lecturer at Princeton, Wittgenstein wrote:

> I wish you good luck; in particular with your work at the university. The temptation for you to cheat yourself will be *overwhelming* (though I don't mean more for you than for anyone else in your position). *Only by a miracle* will you be able to do decent work in teaching philosophy. Please remember these words, even if you forget everything I've ever said to you; &, if you can help it, don't think that I'm a crank because nobody else will say this to you.[55]

Wittgenstein warned against *being* a philosopher. Philosophizing is something that one cannot help doing; one never does it for amusement. Perhaps this is why he came to approve less and less of the highly productive Bertrand Russell; everything indicated that Russell actually *enjoyed* philosophizing, that he wrote books easily, with pleasure and satisfaction. Wittgenstein once remarked with a smile, "Russell isn't going to kill himself doing philosophy now."[56]

In this light we can understand Wittgenstein's ambivalent attitude toward the institutions of professional philosophy, for example philosophical journals. Though quoting a passage out of context can make it appear unduly portentous, it would be a pity to omit the following from a letter to Malcolm:

> Your mags are wonderful. How people can read Mind if they could read Street & Smith beats me. If philosophy has anything to do with wisdom there's certainly not a grain of that in Mind, & quite often a grain in the detective stories.[57]

[55]*Ibid.*, p. 37.
[56]*Ibid.*, p. 68. This was in 1946.
[57]*Ibid.*, p. 36.

In his later years Wittgenstein was in more or less constant depression. He was plagued not only by philosophical "troubles." When, in 1945, he invited Malcolm to read his book, he wrote:

> It'll probably disappoint you. And the truth is: it's pretty lousy. (Not that I could improve on it essentially if I tried for another 100 years.) This, however, doesn't worry me. What I hear about Germany and Austria does. . . .[58]

In 1947 Wittgenstein gave up his chair. Since he had given up his work during the war to become a porter in Guy's Hospital, London, and later to work in a medical laboratory in Newcastle, his effective tenure had been comparatively short. In the years until his death in 1951, he sought peace to complete his work. Frequently, however, he lacked the strength, and his last years were scarcely any happier. "When a person has only one thing in the world—namely, a certain talent—what is he to do when he begins to lose that talent?"[59] In April, 1951, he fell mortally ill. Among his last words were, "Tell them [his nearest friends] I've had a wonderful life!"

The later Wittgenstein: The "Philosophical Investigations"

The book

That Wittgenstein's main posthumous work is far from easy to approach one gathers from its Preface (written in 1945).

> The thoughts which I publish in what follows are the precipitate of philosophical investigations which have occupied me for the last sixteen years. They concern many

[58]*Ibid.*, p. 43.
[59]*Ibid.*, p. 94.

subjects: the concepts of meaning, of understanding, of a proposition, of logic, the foundations of mathematics, states of consciousness, and other things. I have written down all these thoughts as *remarks*, short paragraphs, of which there is sometimes a fairly long chain about the same subject, while I sometimes make a sudden change, jumping from one topic to another. . . .[60]

Wittgenstein goes on to explain that he would like to have produced a well-constructed book in which the thoughts should "proceed from one subject to another in a natural order and without breaks." But despite several attempts this design eluded him. The thoughts did not lend themselves to arrangement in any one way; instead they went "criss-cross in every direction." "The philosophical remarks in this book are, as it were, a number of sketches of landscapes which were made in the course of these long and involved journeyings . . . Thus the book is really only an album."

The Preface concludes with memorable words.

I make them [his remarks] public with doubtful feelings. It is not impossible that it should fall to the lot of this work, in its poverty and in the darkness of this time, to bring light into one brain or another—but, of course, it is not likely. I should not like my writing to spare other people the trouble of thinking. But, if possible, to stimulate someone to thoughts of his own.

I should have liked to produce a good book. This has not come about, but the time is past in which I could improve it.[61]

The *Philosophical Investigations* falls into two parts, the first a series of remarks numbered from 1 to 693. This is the

[60]*Philosophical Investigations (Philosophische Untersuchungen)*, English translation by G. E. M. Anscombe (Oxford: Basil Blackwell, 1958), p. ix. Hereafter cited as *PI*.
[61]*PI*, p. x.

part that the Preface refers to. The second part consists of fourteen remarks, some of them of considerable length.

We will present the main topics, or rather areas, in the following order: first, some remarks directed against fundamental ideas and assumptions in the *Tractatus*—Wittgenstein's settlement with his own earlier thoughts; then, some new thoughts which are to resolve the old and in some ways provide polar opposites to them. These thoughts all concern language, so that when occasionally he speaks as if the *Tractatus* was full of mistakes, we must take him to be referring to certain assumptions about language which lay at the basis of the earlier work. Then, finally, we will present some of Wittgenstein's reflections about philosophy generally and also about a few key philosophical terms.

The reaction against the "Tractatus" and against language as exact naming

There are pictures of what human language really is, says Wittgenstein. One of them is this:

> ... the individual words in language name objects— sentences are combinations of such names.—In this picture of language we find the roots of the following idea: Every word has a meaning. This meaning is correlated with the word. It is the object for which the word stands.[62]

Wittgenstein thinks that Augustine's *Confessions* (I.8) contains such an understanding of language. Augustine writes:

> When they (my elders) named some object, and accordingly moved towards something, I saw this and I grasped that the thing was called by the sound they uttered when

---

[62]*PI*, 1. (i.e., *Philosophical Investigations*, first note in Part I. Unless stated otherwise, references are to Part I). The following translation of Augustine is unattributed and from *PI*. The passage may also be found in R. S. Pine-Coffin's translation, *Saint Augustine: Confessions* (London: Penguin Books, 1961), p. 29.

they meant to point it out. . . . Thus, as I heard words repeatedly used in their proper places in various sentences, I gradually learnt to understand what objects they signified; and after I had trained my mouth to form these signs, I used them to express my own desires. . . .

"If you describe the learning of language in this way," says Wittgenstein, "you are, I believe, thinking primarily of nouns like 'table', 'chair', 'bread', and of people's names, . . ."[63] Augustine thinks that as soon as we have given names to things we can talk about them, and that this is all that occurs with the introduction of language.

> As if there were only one thing called "talking about a thing." Whereas in fact we do the most various things with our sentences. Think of exclamations alone, with their completely different functions.
>
> > Water!
> > Away!
> > Ow!
> > Help!
> > Fine!
> > No!
>
> Are you inclined still to call these words "names of objects"?[64]

What Wittgenstein objects to in Augustine's (and the *Tractatus'*) picture of the nature of language is expressed in the following remark:

> Augustine, we might say, does describe a system of communication; only not everything that we call language is this system. And one has to say this in many cases where the question arises "Is this an appropriate description or not?" The answer is: "Yes, it is appropriate, but

only for this narrowly circumscribed region, not for the whole of what you were claiming to describe."

It is as if someone were to say: "A game consists in moving objects about on the surface according to certain rules . . ."—and we replied: You seem to be thinking of board games, but there are others. You can make your definition correct by expressly restricting it to those games.[65]

Language as we know it is many-sided and complicated; certainly we cannot take it all in at one glance. Hence one of Wittgenstein's main devices is to invite us to consider extremely simple kinds of language, or uses of language. Usually we are asked to consider an imaginary language of some primitive tribe that is invented for the occasion. Or we are put among simple people engaged in simple operations. In such contexts we can more easily survey the purposes and functions of words.[66]

What, then, is a word's *meaning (Bedeutung)?* "The meaning of a word is its use in the language."[67] This is true for a *"large* class of cases . . . in which we employ the word 'meaning'." If I give an adequate description of the use of a word and someone asks, "Yes, but what is the *meaning* of the word here?" he is asking about something that does not exist.

Words occur in sentences, and what is it that these are used for? Can one say that, in general, sentences say that something is the case, something which is either true or false? Can the *Tractatus'* most general statements be accepted? No! and again, No! Wittgenstein turns strenuously, even indignantly, against his own work on this point. Perhaps one can find sentences that fit the *Tractatus* theory, but

. . . how many kinds of sentence are there? Say assertion, question, and command?—There are *countless* kinds:

[65]*PI*, 3.
[66]See *PI*, 5.
[67]*PI*, 43.

countless different kinds of use of what we call "symbols", "words", "sentences". And this multiplicity is not something fixed, given once for all; but new types of language, new language-games, as we may say, come into existence, and others become obsolete and get forgotten. . . .

Here the term "language-*game*" is meant to bring into prominence the fact that the *speaking* of language is part of an activity, or of a form of life. . . .[68]

And the processes of naming the stones and of repeating words after someone might also be called language-games. Think of much of the use of words in games like ring-a-ring-a-roses.

I shall also call the whole, consisting of language and the actions into which it is woven, the "language-game".[69]

Our willingness to accompany Wittgenstein on his journey through language depends on our willingness, at least experimentally, to accept what he says here. And his meaning comes out first and foremost through emphasizing sufficiently the word "kinds" in the quotation: there are innumerable *kinds* of uses. One cannot safely assume that what one finds to be true of one *kind* of language applies automatically to another. Even where *kinds* of language seem fairly much alike, we cannot disregard the possibility of a difference in *kind*.

Whether or not Wittgenstein was entirely happy in his choice of the word "game" in "language-game" is a matter of opinion, but the main point is that we are to consider speech as part of a way of life, or as part of our total biological and social existence, along with eating, and building, and innumerable other activities. If we are building something and say "Here with the hammer!" the sentence itself, the nail, and the hammer are none of them pictures of the situation, or reality.

[68]*PI*, 23.
[69]*PI*, 7.

Language is no more a picture, let alone a mirror-image, of reality than are activities that do not involve words at all.

> Review the multiplicity of language-games in the
> following examples, and in others:
> Giving orders, obeying them—
> Describing the appearance of an object, or giving
> its measurements—
> Constructing an object from a description (a drawing)—
> Reporting an event—
> Speculating about an event— . . .
> Play-acting—
> Singing catches—
> Making a joke; telling it— . . .[70]

Compare this multiplicity, says Wittgenstein, with what "logicians have said about the structure of language. (Including the author of the *Tractatus Logico-Philosophicus*.)"

The functions of language are so various that there is no warrant for believing that there is some feature common to them all: something that makes language language. (Recall the questions asked in the *Tractatus* about what makes a picture a picture, etc.)

> We see that what we call "sentence" and "language" has
> not the formal unity that I imagined, but is the family of
> structures more or less related to one another. . . .[71]

The family resemblance between a group of persons, as we know, need not consist in there being at least one characteristic, for example an upturned nose, that all members of the family have. No such common feature is required.

Similarly, there is no basis for assuming, thinks Wittgenstein, that there is a specific feature common to all kinds of use of language. But might it not be fruitful to *suppose* that

[70]Extract from *PI*, 23.
[71]*PI*, 108.

there is in fact some common feature, to *try to find* something in common? Now Carnap, in the spirit of the nomothetic sciences, would certainly answer yes to this question. Indeed, Carnap has even attempted to construct a special branch of science to determine a universal syntax, a syntax that is meant to apply to all of language, and its field of operations, pure pragmatics, which is supposed to cover every application of language. However, Wittgenstein is concerned less with the possibilities for research than with dealing with the legacies of traditional philosophy. For the purposes of winding up philosophy's affairs there is no need to research into or make capital out of any part of philosophy's effects. Thus there is no motivation for a search into language to see if there is something common to all its various applications. What could we do with such a thing?

The illusion that for each word there is a crystal-clear, sharply defined meaning creates the further illusion that because everyday language employs words that lack this crystal clarity, it must be inadequate, or somehow insufficient, that language in its ordinary use must in some way be impure.[72] One who succumbs to this illusion about language is easily led to believe that it is possible to construct a "perfect language," a language altogether different from that we use every day. However, attempts to bring about fundamental changes in our language merely betray fundamental confusions on the part of those who are dissatisfied with the ordinary uses of terms.

Failure to locate crystal-clear meanings in the observable uses of language in daily life, or even in science, encourages one to look for this clarity elsewhere. One begins to look for it, or to posit it, in the mind or in consciousness. And then we get theories of meaning in the form of theories about mental processes or consciousness, a Cartesian cul-de-sac with untold confusing consequences.

[72]*PI*, 426.

But what does language actually *show* itself to be when one takes simple examples of it?

Language-games, rules, family resemblance

The simplest, most primitive language or language-game that Wittgenstein constructs is that used by two persons, *A* and *B*, when they are building something. *A* calls out "Brick!," "Slab!," "Column!," "Beam!," to *B*, and *B* brings to *A* what he has learned to bring with those calls. Perhaps for a language like this Augustine's description would be apt. (But perhaps not altogether, since "brick" does not stand simply and absolutely for one thing, but for a thing associated in certain ways with fetching and carrying.)[73]

Starting from the simple builder's language, we can introduce *other* language-games: a person learning a language can learn to point at specific things when certain words are uttered by his teacher. "Slab," the teacher says, and his pupil points at a slab (*or* at a specific slab), or the pupil repeats the word, or sings it, and so on. All these are, for Wittgenstein, potential self-contained languages or language-games.

The family likeness between different languages can be illustrated by the family likeness between games: between such different kinds of games as board games, card games, ball games, Olympic games, and so on.

> Don't say: "There *must* be something common, or they would not be called 'games' "—but *look and see* whether there is any thing common to all.—For if you look at

---

[73]Questions that naturally arise on this point have been taken up by Wittgenstein in *The Blue and Brown Books*, pp. 77-78. Answering the objections that in the extremely simple language the word "brick" does not have the meaning which it has in *our* language, he says that this is certainly true if it means that in our language there are usages of the word "brick" different from our uses of it in the simple language. ". . . But don't we sometimes use the word 'brick!' in just this way? Or should we say that when we use it, it is an elliptical sentence, a shorthand for 'Bring me a brick'? . . ."

them you will not see something that is common to *all*,[74] but similarities, relationships, and a whole series of them at that. To repeat: don't think, but look!—Look for example at board-games, with their multifarious relationships. Now pass to card-games; here you find many correspondences with the first group, but many common features drop out, and others appear. . . . In ball games there is winning and losing; but when a child throws his ball at the wall and catches it again, this feature has disappeared. Look at the parts played by skill and luck; and at the difference between skill in chess and skill in tennis.[75]

The games constitute a family; subclasses have something in common, but not the whole class. Similarly with languages.

Language *follows* rules, but the use of a word is not in every case *bounded* by rules.[76] A rule is like a signpost.[77] There is room for doubt about where the sign is directing us. And, just as in games, we can make up rules as we go along. In actual fact, language is not a game, but it is in some ways analogous to games. Certainly it does not follow rules in some more slavish way than people do when they play games (in the wide Wittgensteinian sense of "players of games").

We can easily imagine people amusing themselves in a field by playing with a ball so as to start various existing games, but playing many without finishing them and in between throwing the ball aimlessly into the air, chasing one another with the ball and bombarding one another for a joke and so on. And now someone says: The whole time they are playing a ball-game and following definite rules at every throw.[78]

[74]It seems that Wittgenstein doesn't mean to ask about common characteristics, but about characteristics that are common *and also* specific to the class.
[75]*PI*, 66.
[76]*PI*, 84.
[77]*PI*, 85.
[78]*PI*, 83.

To follow a rule is not at all the same as to interpret it, rather it is to *practice* it. What we do when we interpret a rule is simply to substitute one expression of it for another.[79]

We are now in a position to indicate in more general terms the direction in which Wittgenstein's conception of language lies.

Instrumentalism and contextualism

A language is not something that can be understood and characterized independently of specific activities, objectives, circumstances, or "forms of life" in which words and sentences are used.

> When someone says "I hope he'll come"—is this a *report* about his state of mind, or a *manifestation* of his hope?— I can, for example, say it to myself. And surely I am not giving myself a report. It may be a sigh; but it need not. If I tell someone "I can't keep my mind on my work today; I keep on thinking of his coming"—*this* will be called a description of my state of mind.[80]

Only by an exact analysis of the situation in which an utterance occurs, an exact analysis of the occasion, of the intention, and also of the practical consequences of making the utterance, can the kind of use it has in a given case be shown. And then all that can be said about "meaning" has been said.

We recall that Wittgenstein says that "for a *large* class of cases" of the employment of the word "meaning" we can say that a word's meaning is its *use* in the language.[81] But now it appears that he uncovers a whole multitude of features of a word's use which most of us have never been clearly aware of at all. If we are asked what a particular word means, then,

[79]*PI*, 201, 202.
[80]*PI*, 585.
[81]*PI*, 43.

should our correct answer be one that gives a fairly complete, yet general, account of the way the word is used? Perhaps such general accounts of a word's use should be considered unsuitable replies to questions about meaning—the customary kind of answer that provides an alternative expression or definition being considered more appropriate. In that case we could distinguish between answers to questions about meaning and answers to questions about use, in Wittgenstein's terminology.[82] In the latter sense, "meaning" stands for something which such words as "function," "purpose," "aim," "role," "application," sometimes stand for. Wittgenstein's program of clarification may therefore more aptly be described as a broad program for the clarification of the functions, roles, purposes, and so forth, of words than a program for stating the meanings of words.

The way a word's role comes into an account of its use can be illustrated by the way we use the word "gift", and similar words.

> Why can't my right hand give my left hand money?— My right hand can put it into my left hand. My right hand can write a deed of gift and my left hand a receipt. —But the further practical consequences would not be those of a gift. When the left hand has taken the money from the right, etc., we shall ask: "Well, and what of it?" . . .[83]

So the right hand cannot give money to the left hand; the very idea is nonsensical. The example appears in the course of an extremely comprehensive discussion about the part played by inner occurrences such as experiences, feelings, and images in the clarification of the meaning of mental terms. The gist of the discussion is that references to such occurrences cannot

[82]An occurrence analysis might be appropriate—except that to undertake one would be to fall for scientific ways: *we* cannot exhibit matters of law and rule.
[83]*PI*, 268.

provide adequate accounts, or even coherent accounts, of the use of such terms. To *understand*, for example, cannot *only* be to feel something, to have an inner experience, an experience of understanding. Understanding is something that must show itself in practice and actual behavior. If one referred only to inner occurrences or experiences one would be justified in saying, "Well, and what of it?"

In *The Blue and Brown Books* we find the following examples to illuminate the boundaries between *nonsense* and *non-nonsense*. These somewhat uncompromising terms will be recalled from the *Tractatus*, where they occurred frequently. In the *Investigations* they appear much more rarely; generally Wittgenstein makes use here of more qualified terms such as "purposelessness," "pointlessness," "emptiness," and the like.

> Suppose we ask, "Is it possible for a machine to think?"
> . . . the trouble which is expressed in this question is not really that we don't yet know a machine which could do the job. The question is not analogous to that which someone might have asked a hundred years ago: "Can a machine liquefy a gas?" The trouble is rather that the sentence, "A machine thinks (perceives, wishes)": seems somehow nonsensical. It is as though we had asked "Has the number 3 a colour?"[84]

The second example relates to a question that was fiercely debated in the thirties. "Can we have unconscious thoughts, unconscious feelings, etc.?" Both the psychoanalysts who said yes and their opponents who said no were, according to Wittgenstein, beguiled by language. The objectors could have voiced their objection by saying, "We don't wish to use the phrase 'unconscious thoughts'; we wish to reserve the word 'thought' for what you call 'conscious thoughts.'" Wittgenstein says that they state their case wrongly when they say, "There can only be conscious thoughts and no unconscious

[84]*The Blue and Brown Books*, p. 47.

ones." If they do not want to talk of "unconscious thought" they should not use the phrase "conscious thought" either.[85]

Is it possible for thoughts to be other than conscious? Or is the adjective quite pointless? Can it have no purpose or function? As I understand him, Wittgenstein is saying that when the objectors used the expression "conscious thoughts" they said something absurd. Generalizing, we get an absurdity rule which says that qualifying adjectives generate linguistic absurdity when the opposite qualification cannot be employed.[86]

A third example: "When we ask, 'Has this room a length?', and someone answers: 'Of course it has'. He might have answered, 'Don't ask nonsense'. On the other hand 'The room has length' can be used as a grammatical statement. It then says that a sentence of the form 'The room is — feet long' makes sense."[87]

So much for reflections bearing upon the problem of meaning. The next main topic is one that Wittgenstein has already announced, the subject of *understanding*.

Wittgenstein argues characteristically against the view that to understand a word is a mental state. A mental state can either last without a break or be interrupted. "Except for a short time this morning, he has been in bad humour for almost a week," "He has been in continuous pain since yesterday," "He was very upset the whole time" are all perfectly intelligible statements. But not so "He has understood the word continuously since yesterday morning." Certainly, understanding can be interrupted, but not in the same way as mental states. It is even possible to demonstrate that understanding is not a

---

[85] *Ibid.*, p. 57.

[86] The rule leads to the rejection of what one may call conceptually analytic utterances, e.g., "Thoughts are conscious," "Bodies are extended," "Space has length," etc.

[87] *The Blue and Brown Books,* p. 30. The parallel with Carnap's views about the subject matter and recommendations of formal ways of speaking is striking. Cf. *The Logical Syntax of Language* (London: Kegan Paul, Trench, Trubner & Co., 1937), pp. 302 ff.

mental state by going through examples of the way the word "understand" is used and comparing these with examples of the use of expressions for mental states such as "depressed," "excited," and so on. One carries out what Wittgenstein calls a "grammatical investigation."

> "Understanding a word": a state. But a *mental* state?— Depression, excitement, pain, are called mental states. Carry out a grammatical investigation as follows: we say "He was depressed the whole day".
> "He was in great excitement the whole day".
> "He has been in continuous pain since yesterday".— We also say "Since yesterday I have understood this word". "Continuously", though?—To be sure, one can speak of an interruption of understanding. But in what cases? Compare: "When did your pains get less?" and "When did you stop understanding that word?"[88]

Practical situations and activities within our form of life are complicated, and so, therefore, are the *criteria* for the use of the words—far more complex than appears at first glance. And perhaps the roles of the words are quite different from what we tend to believe they are. In order to solve philosophical paradoxes it is generally the roles of the words that we must understand, in most cases "definitions" will not suffice.[89]

In this way Wittgenstein argues against what he takes to be the unwarranted tendency to delegate things and processes to the mind—a tendency sometimes referred to as "mentalism." Mentalism is based, among other things, on a false theory of meaning; it is precisely in order to save this false theory that one resorts to mental states of understanding.

An expression in language has a service to perform; it has a purpose. Insofar as language is an instrument, its concepts are tools adapted to our interests.[90] When these interests change,

[88]Note to *PI*, 151.
[89]*PI*, 182.
[90]*PI*, 569, 570.

and with·them our form of life, words that are retained change their meaning.

Wittgenstein tries to draw the consequences of this for an understanding of the key words in the philosophy of language. The important consideration here is that these words originate in everyday language, and that instead of measuring their failure in terms of some abstract philosophical standard, we take a sober look at the ways in which they are actually used in everyday situations.

> . . . We are under the illusion that what is peculiar, profound, essential, in our investigation, resides in its trying to grasp the incomparable essence of language. That is, the order existing between the concepts of proposition, word, proof, truth, experience, and so on. This order is a *super*-order between—so to speak—*super*-concepts. Whereas, of course, if the words "language", "experience", "world", have a use, it must be as humble a one as that of the words "table", "lamp", "door".[91]

The aim here seems to be unequivocably expressed: an instrumental, context-dependent description of the everyday use of the terms in the "philosophical" vocabulary, and the ruthless removal of all tendencies to create problems over and above those which arise from the ordinary everyday use of the words in question.

> When philosophers use a word—"knowledge", "being", "object", "I", "proposition", "name"—and try to grasp the *essence* of the thing, one must always ask oneself: is the word ever actually used in this way in the language-game which is its original home?—
>
> What *we* do is to bring words back from their metaphysical to their everyday use.[92]

As a further extension of Wittgenstein's undermining of

[91]*PI*, 97.
[92]*PI*, 116.

the traditional concepts of philosophy, there presumably goes the undermining of all, or most, of the general terms he himself uses. Such words as "logical," "grammatical," "use," "function," "everyday," "form of life," and so on. If one applies the family likeness principle—the principle that a group of people can have a family likeness without their all having at least one feature (e.g., protruding ears) in common —what Wittgenstein calls "use" has no definite feature common to all cases, so we cannot say that there is a unitary concept of 'use.' All we have are occurrences of the word which bear a family resemblance to one another.

What is philosophy?
Analysis of the words in the philosopher's vocabulary

In the Blue Book Wittgenstein raises the question of what knowledge is. In doing so he touches on the very heart of the problem of scepticism and solipsism.

> Again, when you say, "I grant you that you can't *know* when A has pain, you can only conjecture it", you don't see the difficulty which lies in the different uses of the words "conjecturing" and "knowing". What sort of impossibility were you referring to when you said you *couldn't* know? Weren't you thinking of a case analogous to that when one couldn't know whether the other man had a gold tooth in his mouth because he had his mouth shut? Here what you didn't know you could nevertheless imagine knowing; it made sense to say that you saw that tooth although you didn't see it; or rather, it makes sense to say that you don't see his tooth and therefore it also makes sense to say that you do. When on the other hand, you granted me that a man can't *know* whether the other person has pain, you do not wish to say that as a matter of fact people didn't know, but that it made no sense to say they knew (and therefore no sense to say they don't know). If therefore in

141

this case you use the term "conjecture" or "believe", you don't use it as opposed to "know". That is, you did not state that knowing was a goal which you could not reach, and that you have to be content with conjecturing; rather, there is no goal in this game.[93]

This passage from the Blue Book is quoted at length because here Wittgenstein's argument is unusually explicit. Its steps are clear, and the statements comprising it can be seen to derive from a general position. It is no accident that we find fewer such clear-cut and articulated arguments in the *Investigations*. A central thesis of the later work is that generalizations in the form of hypotheses, theories, and chains of argument, are altogether unnecessary and inappropriate. What is necessary is that one be brought to the awareness of something, of that which *shows itself*. We find in the Blue Book what appears to be an easily understood reference to how a philosophical problem is to be got rid of, *dissolved*. The problem in question is the relation between mind and body.[94]

We have a tendency to assume that substantives are names of things. Now, when we speak about our own personal experiences we use a whole range of substantives. The experiences that we refer to are clearly independent of any of the physical and physiological objects and processes we are able to observe. The grammar of the words shows that they are not the names of material things. Surely then they must be names of *immaterial* things, "ethereal" objects, mental entities. But now we get into trouble. We are led to raise problems such as "How are the two totally different kinds of thing connected to one another?" However, the problems are to be resolved by seeing that the substantives in question need not stand for things, indeed that they do not function as *names* at all. So we see that there is no good basis for instituting a distinction between material and mental *things*.

[93]*The Blue and Brown Books,* pp. 53-54.
[94]*Ibid.,* p. 47.

This is a relatively simple and rather free account of the remarks in the Blue Book, in fact an interpretation. A more faithful rendering must inevitably be more complicated. In what follows I shall mainly quote Wittgenstein himself, drawing from what seem to me particularly illuminating passages in the *Investigations*. The topic here is "knowing."

Wittgenstein explains himself by means of examples of number series: 1, 2, 3, 4 . . .; 1, 3, 5, 7 . . .; and formulae which give the rule for the steps in such series. The series 1, 4, 9, 16, for example, is built up from 1^2, 2^2, 3^2, 4^2 . . . The "rule" here is $a_n = n^2$. The criterion of whether someone has understood a formula lies, according to Wittgenstein, in his *use* of the formula, not in the existence of some special mental state. Wittgenstein then voices the kind of objection that an opponent of such a view might make.

> "But how can it be? When *I* say I understand the rule of a series, I am surely not saying so because I have *found out* that up to now I have applied the algebraic formula in such-and-such a way! In my own case at all events I surely know that I mean such-and-such a series; it doesn't matter how far I have actually developed it.". . .[95]

But what does this *knowledge* consist in? Does he know it day and night? If knowledge is a state of consciousness, does it disappear when one state is succeeded by another? Does he know it in the same way as he knows his ABC? To know the rule for the series has to do with being able to go on with the series, with actually developing it.

> The grammar of the word "knows" is evidently closely related to that of "can", "is able to". But also closely related to that of "understands". ('Mastery' of a technique.)[96]

The question of what knowledge really is, of what lies at

[95]*PI*, 147.
[96]*PI*, 150.

the basis of, and warrants, our saying "Now I know that . . ." is wrongly posed. In certain circumstances—characteristic of a form of life—it *is* in order to use the expression, but in others it is not.

It seems clear that Wittgenstein admits the possibility of our being in error when we are said quite correctly to know something. That is, he admits we are right, or that it is in order, to use the expression "I know that . . .," even though our claim to know may be wrong. The correctness of the use does not exclude the possibility of a retrospective "I thought I knew that . . ., but it seems that I was wrong. I didn't know it." Thus the cases where we *are* mistaken will be a subclass of cases of the "grammatically justified," or linguistically justified use of the expression "I know that . . .," that is, of cases where we are right in *saying* that we know, even if what we say is wrong. Wittgenstein focuses on the linguistic, and not, as is more usual among philosophers, on the "epistemic" aspects of the question.[97]

> In what sense are my sensations *private?*—Well, only I can know whether I am really in pain; another person can only surmise it.—In one way this is wrong, and in another nonsense. If we are using the word "to know" as it is normally used (and how else are we to use it?), then other people very often know when I am in pain.—Yes, but all the same not with the certainty with which I know it myself!—It can't be said of me at all (except perhaps as a joke) that I *know* I am in pain. What is it supposed to mean—except perhaps that I *am* in pain?[98]

Thus Wittgenstein does not assert that possibly I do *not* know *that* I have, or *whether* I have, certain *sensations*. In the way words for feelings are normally used it is implied that

[97]The paragraph about "knows" is an extrapolation. I have brought in something that Wittgenstein states explicitly in connection with "understanding."
[98]*PI*, 246.

one quite simply *has* them. The word "know," whether one is denying or asserting that one knows, is used about things less immediate than one's own feelings, about things one cannot be certain of in this way, simply because of some experience we *have*. Therefore we should say also, "it makes sense to say about other people that they doubt whether I am in pain; but not to say it about myself."[99] Insofar as it is not "linguistically" correct to *say* this, neither will it be correct to *say* "I am not in doubt."

These brief elucidatory comments must be taken with a grain of salt. It may be that Wittgenstein's failure to provide fuller or more exact explanations is due more often than not to a desire to avoid inconsistency. Every explanation must be an explanation in terms of something—maybe a principle, a hypothesis, or a theory. It is to quite obvious things, things that are plain to see and hence stand in no need of explanation, that Wittgenstein wishes to draw our attention. In short, if something needs to be explained, it is not something Wittgenstein has meant to draw our attention to.

But is there absolutely nothing that one knows oneself and which only oneself knows? An established, quite normal expression goes: "Only *you* can know if you had that intention." But under what conditions and for what purposes can one say such a thing?

If what one speaks about is something one could meaningfully say one was ignorant of, one should avoid using the word "intention" in regard to it. The established expression is thus really only of use in explaining the word "intention" to someone. But it would be a very special use of the word "know."[100]

Behavioral psychology has not a little to learn from Wittgenstein's suggestions about how words referring to the most private, inner, mental aspects of consciousness are used accord-

[99]*PI*, 246.
[100]*PI*, 247.

ing to criteria which refer to a public, observable environment of behavior, action, utterance, and so on—in fact to matters and things which everyone is able to inspect and identify. A great deal of reflection lies behind that brief remark of Wittgenstein's: "An 'inner process' stands in need of outward criteria."[101]

There is very little that, strictly speaking, one can identify in the way of elements or objects within one's consciousness at any particular moment.

> What is a *deep* feeling? Could someone have a feeling of ardent love or hope for the space of one second—*no matter what* preceded or followed this second?—What is happening now has significance—in these surroundings.[102]

Returning to the question of whether my sensations are private (and thereby also to the philosophical discussion about whether it is in principle possible to know that other people have inner lives), Wittgenstein says that the sentence "Sensations are private" can be compared with "One plays patience by oneself."[103] That is, it elucidates the rules of a game. In other words the sentence "Sensations are private" says something about the language-game of sensations.

> I can know what someone else is thinking, not what I am thinking.
>
> It is correct to say "I know what you are thinking", and wrong to say "I know what I am thinking."
>
> (A whole cloud of philosophy condensed into a drop of grammar.)[104]

To explain: when Wittgenstein says "I know what someone else is thinking, not what I am thinking," the function of the sentence is to refer to something obvious about the use of the words "I," "think," and so on. What he means to convey

[101]*PI*, 580.
[102]*PI*, 583.
[103]*PI*, 248.
[104]*PI*, II, 222.

could also be put by writing "It is (linguistically) correct to say 'I know what you are thinking,' and wrong to say 'I know what I am thinking.'" If I say "I cannot know what I am thinking," another person may be led to some odd conclusion: "There is something which is more or less uncertain for you: namely, what it is you are thinking about!" I can be led to think that either I know or do not know what I am thinking. In *this* case, however, the word "knowledge" will not do. What we have, then, is a method for bringing out a point which is not at first obvious, but can be made so—a method that Wittgenstein makes frequent use of in other examples too.

In one's imagination one can make up all kinds of special situations where the expressions "I know what I am thinking" and "I know that I am thinking" would find a quite natural place. For example, someone may be remonstrating against the charge that he parrots other people's views and doesn't think *for himself*. Under continued conversation on the same topic, the expression "for himself" ceases to function if the qualification is no longer being raised. It is characteristic of philosophical discussion, for example in the manner of Descartes, that words continue to be used when the conditions for their meaningful employment no longer exist. This happens when a term is taken from its "home" in everyday usage and made to play some spurious part in a philosopher's system.

Exactly which of the many philosophical clouds does Wittgenstein hope to disperse? This is something he says nothing about. However, we may reasonably assume that the problems in question stem from the philosophy of Descartes and attempt to counter scepticism by constructing absolutely secure systems based upon absolutely certain knowledge; hence, ultimately upon our own private sensations and thoughts. Perhaps the unsuccessfulness of these attempts consists in their having led not to mistaken views or conclusions, but to linguistic nonsense, for example by putting words like "know" and "sensation" in places where there is no function for them to perform. Strictly speaking, it is not that words are being used in *new* ways in these philosophical contexts, but rather that they are being misused, wrongly placed, mistreated. Philosophical profundities about knowledge arise from the failure of the words to do anything. Language in philosophy is empty. Philosophical problems are confusions arising when "language is like an engine idling," when it is not doing anything.[105]

When a philosophical cloud condenses into a drop of grammar, naturally it is not a drop of *philosophy* we are left with. And yet only someone well versed in the philosophical tradition is capable of distilling such drops. Such a person becomes, in a sense, the philosopher's heir. Why should we not then transfer to him the *title* of philosopher too? The answer, of course, is that in the case of Wittgenstein this is just what we have done. It is in this way that the language theorist, or rather the guide to language, has acquired the name "philosopher" and his activity come to be called "philosophy."[106]

A genuine problem, that is a scientifically or otherwise cognitively defined question, cannot be solved by subjecting the questioner to psychiatric or any other kind of treatment. One cannot dispose of such problems simply by removing them from the questioner's mind. But in philosophy it is otherwise: the expressions "problem" and "solution" must, in philosophical terms, be compared with (we should avoid using the technically-loaded "defined by") "to be in difficulties, in trouble, or bewildered." And here therapy is clearly in order. Treatment can bring you out of one state into another; it is something you undergo personally, not like the resolution of a theoretical or technical difficulty. *You* come out of *your* puzzlement, *you* grow out of *your* difficulties.

[105]*PI*, 132.
[106]One can retain one's professorship with equanimity even if one "goes over to Wittgenstein." See Ernest Gellner's application of the existentialist slogan, "Existence precedes essence": "Irrespective of whether it is true of things in general, it is clearly true of the philosophic profession, which *exists* well before it defines its own essence." *Words and Things* (London: Gollancz, 1959), p. 259.

About his own procedure Wittgenstein says that he makes us see so-called concepts in ways we had never thought of, and shows us ways of using expressions that we were never previously aware of. "In philosophy one feels *forced* to look at a concept in a certain way." Wittgenstein leads us to see other ways; and thus our "mental cramp is relieved."[107]

Apparently, when philosophical "problems" are all made to disappear in this way, "everything interesting, that is, all that is great and important" is destroyed. So how can philosophical investigation itself be considered important, if all that it does is to destroy what *is* important? "What we are destroying," says Wittgenstein, "is nothing but houses of cards and we are clearing up the ground of language on which they stand."[108] "The results of philosophy are the uncovering of one or another piece of plain nonsense and of bumps that the understanding has got by running its head up against the limits of language. These bumps make us see the value of the discovery."[109] "Philosophy is a battle against the bewitchment of our intelligence by means of language."[110] "The philosopher's treatment of a question is like the treatment of an illness."[111] But the method of dealing with philosophical questions through examples of how people normally speak is not the only method. "There is not *a* philosophical method, though there are indeed methods, like different therapies."[112] And in this way philosophy becomes language therapy.

Everyday speech and general language usage

Wittgenstein tries to show, through examples, how language functions. Every example has as its aim the uncovering of some misuse; it is not support for any more or less general theory of language. This freedom from theory is both an aim

---

[107]Remarks from a lecture quoted in Malcolm, *A Memoir*, p. 50.
[108]*PI*, 118.
[109]*PI*, 119.
[110]*PI*, 109.
[111]*PI*, 255.
[112]*PI*, 133.

and a program for Wittgenstein, though there are, as a matter of fact, a number of general statements to be found in the *Investigations*. It is not impossible that he would have removed these had he worked longer on his material.

Theories of the function of language will at best be false, owing to the multiplicity and unhomogeneity of language, at worst they will be meaningless. ". . . we may not advance any kind of theory. There must not be anything hypothetical in our considerations. We must do away with all *explanation*, and description alone must take its place."[113]

Accordingly it is not a question of finding or showing the nature of language, at least not in any usual philosophical sense. Language could only have a "nature" in such a sense if there was some definite feature common to all language-games and this common feature was hidden, not open to inspection. Within the philosophical tradition it is not "something that already lies open to view and that becomes surveyable by a rearrangement" that has been seen in the nature of language, "but something that lies *beneath* the surface. Something that lies within, which we see when we look *into* the thing, and which an analysis digs out."[114]

Therapeutic philosophy, we see, seeks nothing in the occult.

> Philosophy simply puts everything before us, and neither explains nor deduces anything. —Since everything lies open to view there is nothing to explain. For what is hidden, for example, is of no interest to us.
>
> One might also give the name "philosophy" to what is possible *before* all new discoveries and inventions.[115]

An analogy can perhaps illustrate the extent to which Wittgenstein took everyday ways of speaking to be immediately and unanalyzably given: Ryle's analogy between the way Witt-

[113]*PI*, 109.
[114]*PI*, 92.
[115]*PI*, 126.

genstein refers to specimens of language and tea-tasting (which is not tea *analysis*).

> One favourite procedure of [Wittgenstein's] might be called the "tea-tasting method". Tea-tasters do not lump their samples into two or three comprehensive types. Rather they savour each sample and try to place it next door to its closest neighbours, and this not in respect of just one discriminable quality, but along the lengths of various lines of qualities. So Wittgenstein would exhibit the characteristic manner of working of a particular expression, by matching it against example after example of expressions progressively diverging from it in various respects and directions.[116]

Thus one does not *describe* what is specific to each expression, one *shows* it by contrasting it with other, also undescribed, expressions. One ends by pointing, not by providing a description. "I shan't say anything that you won't all immediately agree with; and if you do dispute something I'll drop it and go on to something else."[117] So said Wittgenstein to his students. Not, of course, that he avoids controversial questions; the point is that he does not conclude his treatment of them by saying anything about them—he only presents the question, or the set of questions, in a new light. The continuity between the *Tractatus* and the *Philosophical Investigations* is here, as elsewhere, unmistakable.

The vital significance of the idea that the functioning of language can be suggested or shown, namely that it is not *necessary* to give a description in words, arises from the consideration that if verbal descriptions *were* needed, a special technical vocabulary would be required. The descriptions would then be examples of scientific data and would figure as entries in observation journals. Philosophy would smack of

[116]"Ludwig Wittgenstein," p. 7.
[117]Gasking and Jackson's obituary notice (see note 47), p. 75.

science, it would be expressible in terms of hypotheses and theories. Observation journals are, of course, not philosophically neutral; they are subject to standards of correctness based on more or less well grounded rules and assumptions. The idea that the functions of language can be described, therefore, leads to the undermining of the whole idea that the philosopher's use of everyday terms should be measured directly against their actual everyday use.[118]

Wittgenstein was not opposed to the introduction of technical terms within individual sciences. Nor indeed was it specifically the technical terms to be found in philosophical literature that he attacked—words like "transcendental," "a priori," and "hypothetico-deductive." He was concerned with the simplest and most common expressions of everyday language, such as "understand," "know," "teach," "play," "think," "sense," "I," and "this," insofar as technical philosophical meanings and concepts were attached to them. It is the misuse of such terms as these that he comes to grips with; and it is their ordinary use that he points to in his examples.

A general objection to philosophers' treatment of ordinary language is that they have misunderstood its vagueness. For even vague expressions can be subject to rules. It is all right in certain cases, and for special limited practical purposes, to try to use everyday expressions in a clearer, less ambiguous and more precise way.[119] But for ordinary purposes nothing can

[118]A criticism of linguistic philosophy could probably be based on this point: "The difficulty about LP [linguistic philosophy] is the extent to which it *assumes* ordinary language, ordinary word-usage, and ordinary communication." (Nathan Isaacs, "What do Linguistic Philosophers Assume?" in *Proceedings of the Aristotelian Society*, LX [1960], 214.) Isaacs, who himself repeatedly pays homage to LP, says that the basis for the decisions made in the name of "pre-philosophical clarification" about what "jobs" particular words in daily usage have should be made explicit. It is clear that Isaacs has not seen his way to the view that it is *enough to present* the jobs. In his program the next step should be to demand principles for occurrence analysis. See Isaacs, p. 218.

[119]*PI*, 132.

replace everyday usage. Indeed to seek such help in *special* circumstances presupposes that there are normal ones in which no improvements are called for. Consequently there can be no logically complete language, for example, symbolic logic, and it is absurd to think of philosophical language *replacing* everyday speech.

Carnap related that Wittgenstein indignantly rejected attempts to produce ideal languages (Esperanto, Ido). He also objected to the title "ideal language" as misleading. It suggested that these languages were better, more complete, than ordinary conversational language, and that we should call upon the logician to show us what a proper sentence looks like.[120]

> On the one hand it is clear that every sentence in our language 'is in order as it is'. That is to say, we are not *striving after* an ideal, as if our ordinary vague sentences had not yet got a quite unexceptionable sense, and a perfect language awaited construction by us.—On the other hand it seems clear that where there is sense there must be perfect order.—So there must be perfect order even in the vaguest sentence.[121]

One can see this by considering just how appropriate vague expressions can be, for example in drawing up a common program for different factions within a political party, or in attempts to reconcile speakers in an acrimonious debate. To be able to find expressions with just the *right* amount of vagueness in such cases is one of the most difficult, and also most important, tasks for experts in the art of language.

> When I talk about language (words, sentences, etc.) I must speak the language of every day. Is this language somehow too coarse and material for what we want to say? *Then how is another one to be constructed?*—And

[120]*PI*, 81.
[121]*PI*, 98.

how strange that we should be able to do anything at all with the one we have!

In giving explanations I already have to use language full-blown (not some sort of preparatory, provisional one); this by itself shews that I can adduce only exterior facts about language.

Yes, but then how can these explanations satisfy us? —Well, your very questions were framed in this language; they had to be expressed in this language, if there was anything to ask!

And your scruples are misunderstandings. . . .[122]

There is no escape: he who objects must justify the expressions in which his objection is phrased. If he says "everyday language is too vague," what purpose has this conjunction of words? Does he take them to constitute an exception? Either they themselves betray the alleged misuse of language and so fail to provide any clear sense, or they have a clear meaning, the ordinary one, and so express a falsehood.

Philosophy may in no way interfere with the actual use of language; it can in the end only describe itself.

For it cannot give it any foundation either.

It leaves everything as it is. . . .[123]

With these words we conclude our presentation.

His influence
Linguistic philosophy

Wittgenstein's originality

There can hardly be any questioning Wittgenstein's originality as a philosopher. But in judging the extent of a philoso-

[122]*PI*, 120.
[123]*PI*, 124.

pher's originality one should perhaps bear in mind that "new" philosophies are constantly being advanced without attracting much, or any, support. If Wilhelm Ostwald's collection of sermons on energy had received wide support as philosophy they would no doubt, and quite rightly, have been accepted as extremely original. However, that they cannot be recognized as philosophically original is surely not due simply to a shortage of followers. Nor is it due to his background. It is rather that his thoughts are not delivered in the customary philosophical package. But on what criteria can posterity judge the way in which a philosopher's thoughts are presented?

Have Wittgenstein's investigations any far-reaching consequences for philosophy outside the Fregean and Russellian tradition? What is his significance, for example, for phenomenologically inclined thinkers, or for neo-Thomists? And what about those numerous thinkers whose thoughts are comparatively unaffected by the influence of particular schools of thought? These questions, only seventeen years after Wittgenstein's death, are still not decided.

A leading Oxford philosopher, P. F. Strawson, concludes his review of the *Investigations* by saying that the value of the book as a model of philosophic method is greater even than the value of its special doctrines, and "it will consolidate the philosophical revolution for which the author more than any other person was responsible."[124] But it seems clear that it

---

[124]*Mind*, LXIII (1954), 99. To state my own views at this point, I should say (not without feelings of inadequacy) that I fail to see anything very revolutionary in English linguistic philosophy.

In the first place it is difficult to feel that Wittgenstein's *Investigations* and works with a similar orientation constitute a violent break with earlier philosophy, particularly for someone who has already felt the powerful impact of the pragmatic, *Lebensform*-theoretical positions of William James, Bergson, and Georg Simmel. (Around the turn of the century, Simmel had a strong antimetaphysical and instrumentalist-biological phase which is little known.) Furthermore, there is little new in the opposition to the mirroring theory of language, and generally to the transferring of concepts such as proposition and

is within the school of thought dominated by Frege and Russell that Wittgenstein's novelty and originality are most marked, and that it is to this tradition that his later philosophy stands out in most striking contrast.[125]

Linguistic philosophy

Some philosophers have been accused of knowing too little of their contemporaries. Wittgenstein, or rather his followers, can perhaps be faced with a quite different charge, that so widespread was his fame among his contemporaries that he became exposed to the insistent embraces of many who did not really understand him. Gilbert Ryle writes:

> . . . from his jealously preserved little pond, there have spread waves over the philosophical thinking of much of the English speaking world. Philosophers who never met him—and few of us did meet him—can be heard talking philosophy in his tones of voice; and students who can barely spell his name now wrinkle up their noses at things which had a bad smell for him.[126]

Philosophical views and discussion inspired by the later Wittgenstein are often termed "linguistic philosophy," linguistic in the sense of the *Investigations'* concept of language

---

rule from formal logic to daily language, among those who have had the pleasure of reading William James and F. C. S. Schiller in their amusing criticisms of Russell's intellectualistic prewar philosophy. (Russell, on his part, ridiculed William James' "transatlantic truth.") There was little sympathetic study of pragmatism within the circles dominated by Russell, Moore, and Frege.

[125]"Why then do we in philosophizing constantly compare our use of words with one following exact rules?" (*The Blue and Brown Books*, p. 25.) This expression and many others indicate that Wittgenstein was thinking of the Frege/Russell tradition, above all, when he spoke of philosophizing. In other traditions the comparison between the use of words and the following of exact rules has not played anything like such a central part.

[126]"Ludwig Wittgenstein," pp. 1-2.

rather than that of the *Tractatus*. Among linguistic philosophers the terms "philosophical analysis" or "logical analysis" are generally in disrepute: "analysis" is too easily associated with discursive argument and the establishing of unobvious results, a method and program more befitting the logical empiricists (Carnap among others), and to some extent G. E. Moore. The reaction against both has been sharp.

However, despite the fact that linguistic philosophy followed Wittgenstein in rejecting the logical atomist theory of language as a structure built up from simple units, another essential feature of the earlier type of analysis persisted: the idea that reality possesses a certain logical structure, and that the failure of grammatical and syntactical forms in ordinary language to correspond with this structure is a main source of philosophical problems and "confusion." According to Gilbert Ryle (b. 1900) "there is, after all, a sense in which we can properly inquire and even say 'what it really means to say so and so'. For we can ask what is the real form of the fact recorded when this is concealed or disguised and not duly exhibited by the expression in question."[127]

If the grammatical or syntactical form of expression is not appropriate to the kind of fact it describes, we can presumably hold it up to comparison with the form of the fact in question and then recast the expression in its more appropriate, less misleading, form. Characteristic, therefore, of this method of clearing up philosophical problems is an appeal to the "facts," and the assumption that the facts can be adequately represented in the grammatical forms of (ordinary) language. This is exemplified in Ryle's arguments for his behavioristic concept of mind. Everyday ways of talking

[127]Gilbert Ryle, "Systematically Misleading Expressions," in A. G. N. Flew (ed.), *Essays in Logic and Language* (1st ser.; Oxford: Basil Blackwell, 1952), p. 36. The article first appeared in the *Proceedings of the Aristotelian Society*, 1931-32. For discussion of the point see, e.g., J. O. Urmson, *Philosophical Analysis* (Oxford: The Clarendon Press, 1956), especially p. 165; and Dudley Shapere, "Philosophy and the Analysis of Language" (see note 36).

about our experiences and mental states can mislead us into believing in the existence of all sorts of *things* or *processes* that do not exist. For example, just because we have an expression "mental image," we are led to believe that there are special mental objects that correspond to physical replicas and pictures, and that these mental copies inhabit a special mental space parallel to the physical space in which physical objects occur. When we visualize something and, as we say, "see it in the mind's eye," the language we use to express this leads philosophers into postulating mental resemblances of whatever it is we imagine. We talk as if there were inner things and outer things, a tree-copy in our consciousness and a tree in the garden. But by appealing to the facts, Ryle proposes that it would be more accurate to say when we imagine a tree, not that we are "a spectator of a resemblance" of a tree, but that we "are resembling a spectator" of a tree.[128] It is less misleading, it accords more with the facts, to say that we do something which resembles seeing than to say that we see a resemblance. Not being misled, we spare ourselves the spurious task of trying to account for something denoted by the expression "the mind's eye" and for some mental analogue of the real pictures we see with the real eye.

Ryle's discussion of the concept of mind contains another Wittgensteinian feature, but in this case one that is more characteristic of the *Investigations*, namely, the appeal to particular cases. By looking at particular examples of imagining, knowing, willing, feeling, perceiving, and so forth, we find that inner mental events and processes, which dualistic views of mental activity assume to be necessary concomitants of all mental activity, are simply not general features of mental activity and that therefore the dualistic view must be wrong.

Although it seems plausible to assume that Ryle has been influenced here by Wittgenstein, especially since the latter's appeal to particular cases occurs also in a discussion of mental

[128]Gilbert Ryle, *The Concept of Mind* (London: Hutchinson, 1949), p. 248.

entities, it would be rash to assume that Ryle was directly influenced by Wittgenstein. It could equally well have been that certain attitudes and changes were in the air, and that many thinkers happened to express the new viewpoints at about the same time though largely independently of one another.

Among linguistic philosophers in Oxford, John L. Austin (1911-60) is generally recognized as the leading exponent of a style of philosophizing that to some appears to have developed into an exercise in sheer virtuosity. The style spread from England to the United States when Austin himself payed a visit there shortly before his untimely death.

Austin evolved his special brand of linguistic philosophy in the years preceding World War II—and essentially in independence of Wittgenstein.[129] This may seem all the more remarkable in that not only do their statements frequently correspond in detail, but they are sometimes couched in almost similar terms. This strengthens the impression that a great deal of what we attribute to "the later Wittgenstein" was in fact an attitude or approach—a reaction perhaps—that hung in the philosophical air over the British Isles.

About the significance of detailed analysis of language and about the future of philosophy itself, Austin was extremely guarded. His main objection to traditional philosophy was that philosophers had been too prone to generalize and were overambitious. The result was that systems were built up much too early in the game. Hence the everlasting swing of the pendulum from one system to another. The trouble is that there is never a basis solid enough to withstand unprejudiced criticism. What is needed first is patiently to gather together the facts. And for this it is not enough to exercise a private initiative: what is really needed is a large and centrally directed project in which many philosophers work together in

---

[129]Many philosophers, including Austin himself, have postulated this view of their relationship with Wittgenstein, and so far as I can judge there is little reason to doubt it.

forming a common stock of examples, an inventory of usage for all expressions of relevance to philosophy.[130] In this way scientific method can gradually be adopted, though with great caution, because it is precisely the uncritical and sweeping use of a small number of procedures that has caused so much mischief in the past.

Austin set respect for honest patient work, for accuracy, and for facts, as the aim of the philosophical education to which he so intensively dedicated himself. Such a philosophical training he considered the best bulwark against fanaticism and blind faith in social or political doctrines. And to those who have proposed the sociological thesis that linguistic philosophy adopts and enforces a conservative attitude, a passivity in the face of the *status quo*, it should be of interest to note that Austin, like many other linguistic philosophers, was not himself a conservative and was indeed fervently interested in social and political reforms.

Among the most effective philosophical contributions Austin made was his calling attention, through numerous examples, to the *performative* functions of language. When someone says "I name you Queen Elizabeth," for example, on the launching of a ship, these words are not so much a description of a state of affairs as an action founded on special authority. The importance of the performative aspect of language for philosophy comes out especially in connection with the use of the expression "I know." In saying "I know," one "is *not* saying 'I have performed a specially striking feat of cognition, superior, in the same scale as believing and being sure, even to being merely quite sure. . . .' When I say 'I know', I *give others my word: I give others my authority* for saying that 'S is P.' "[131] Here again a source of confusion is

---

[130]This and other points are taken from Stuart Hampshire's memorial article on Austin, *Proceedings of the Aristotelian Society*, LX (1960), i-xiv.

[131]"Other Minds," *Proceedings of the Aristotelian Society*, Supplementary Vol. XX (1946), reprinted in Austin's *Philosophical Papers*, ed. J.

located, and discovered not by just looking more closely at, or into, language *itself*, as the *Tractatus* account of language assumes, but, in accordance with the procedures of the *Investigations*, by looking at the *uses* of language.

As for the future of philosophy, Austin seems to have considered two possibilities. Either, the analysis of language usage is to be regarded as a preliminary investigation: once sufficient material is at hand and a certain degree of caution has become the rule, the time will be opportune for theorizing. Or, the producing of philosophical theories will never be in order, for the analysis of language usage will leave no basis for such theorizing.

These alternatives correspond to two possible interpretations of the *Investigations*, particularly those parts of it that deal with the winding up of the affairs of traditional philosophy. Was it Wittgenstein's view that nothing in the tradition would survive? Or was his settlement more in the nature of a chastening of the tradition in the way of making it linguistically more cautious and self-critical? It is interesting to note the parallel between these questions and those that arose in the interpretation of the antimetaphysics of the *Tractatus* (cf. pp. 108 f.).

Perhaps difficulties in interpreting the later Wittgenstein are responsible for the failure of both apologists and opponents to commit themselves one way or the other. For even those whom one might consider most likely to venture an opinion protest their distance from Wittgenstein. "What I offer," says Ryle in his memorial article on Wittgenstein, "is a set of impressions, interpretations, partly, of mere echoes of echoes."[132]

Representatives of linguistic philosophy claim that the movement contains marked differences of opinion and approach, and that one must therefore be extremely cautious in

O. Urmson and G. J. Warnock (Oxford: The Clarendon Press, 1961), p. 67.
[132]"Ludwig Wittgenstein," *Analysis*, XII (1951), 2.

positing any characteristics common to all its proponents. There is at best a "family resemblance"! To outsiders, at any rate, the most characteristic feature of linguistic philosophy, at least during the 1950's, was that certain jargon, that characteristic style of delivery and discussion.

It is not easy, therefore, to pinpoint specific arguments of Wittgenstein's that were taken up by the proponents of linguistic philosophy, but we may nevertheless briefly mention some definite views and arguments which have repeatedly been voiced and for which Wittgenstein's support has often been claimed. In the following pages, therefore, we give a few characteristic samples of such views and arguments.

1. The theory of language-games and the thesis of polymorphism

To talk is to take part in a game, in a wide sense of the word, and there are countless different sorts of games. Corresponding to these there are countless *kinds* of use of words. It is never to the point to generalize about the use of a particular word; there is nothing common to them all, and new uses are constantly arising. To break the rules of a game is to break off the game, or to begin some new game. Every game has a point.

2. The Paradigm-Case Argument

Traditional problems in philosophy can frequently be solved by showing that the key words are used by philosophers in ways that differ altogether from the way in which they are used in the standard cases—the paradigm cases. A word is introduced, or comes to be used, in standard cases, and to remove it from these is (except where one is introducing scientific terms) pointless. The philosopher breaks off the game in which the word is used in a standard way.

For example, for quite small children the expressions "I know that . . .," "It is certain that . . .," and so forth, have no meaning. They acquire their meaning in certain actual situations. These situations are what give the expressions meaning, and they thus constitute the standard, or paradigm cases for the use of the expressions, the cases where it is proper, or in order, to use them. Then if there can be found at least one paradigm situation for the expression "I know that . . .," it will be the case that there is at least one thing that I know. If someone claims that the expression cannot be correctly applied in the case we take to be its paradigm, we should ask in what situations it would be correct to use it. A philosopher who denied that, strictly speaking, we can be said to know anything at all, would be saying that there was no paradigm, that there was no proper use for the expression. But this is tantamount to saying that the expression has no meaning. Yet it is plain that it does have a meaning, and therefore there must be a paradigm case for its use. Thus Descartes' *"de omnium dubitandum"* is a false doctrine stemming from a misunderstanding of the functioning of language.

That, very briefly, is one version of the argument from paradigm cases,[133] a type of argument that has typified epistemological discussions inspired or influenced by the later Wittgenstein. The argument itself has even earned an abbreviation—PCA. It became customary, using the PCA, to "refute" scepticism quite simply by pointing out that there *must* be situations in which one can *rightly* say "I know that . . .," "It is certain that . . .," "It cannot be doubted that . . .," and so on.

Other formulations of the PCA have expressed a weaker thesis. Thus it is claimed, not that the argument enables us to prove the existence of something, for example, knowledge,

---

[133]Antony Flew has summarized the argument thus: ". . . if there is any word the meaning of which can be taught by reference to paradigm cases, then no argument whatever could ever prove that there are no cases whatever of whatever it is." A. G. N. Flew (ed.), *Essays in Conceptual Analysis* (London: Macmillan & Co., Ltd., 1956), p. 19. Good short surveys of the controversies that raged around the PCA are given by L. D. Houlgate in his article "The Paradigm-Case Argument and Possible Doubt," *Inquiry*, V (1962), No. 4, 318 ff., and by J. W. N. Watkins in "Farewell to the Paradigm-Case Argument," *Analysis*, XVIII (1959), 25-33.

only that it indicates the logical connection between the characteristics of a situation and the words, or the concepts, in terms of which it is correct to describe it. That there are paradigm cases for the use of the expression "I know that . . ." does not prove that what I claim to know must be the case when I use the expression in the standard kind of case; rather it shows that there are cases, like this one, in which it is quite right for me to say that "I know" something, even though there is a possibility that I may be wrong, and, if so, could *not* be said to know it.

3. The contrast theory

There is no point in giving a word a meaning such that there could never be an occasion to use it. But if a word could not be said to express any possible contrast, this is just what would happen; there would be nothing that it managed to say. Thus if as sceptics we set conditions for the use of "know" which cannot be satisfied, we will never be justified in using such expressions as "We know that . . .," "It is known that . . .," and so on. But in that case the sentence "We *cannot* know anything" becomes completely pointless. The word "know," however, is used to express a contrast that occurs in standard everyday situations, and it is in these that it gets its meaning. The contrast necessary for the meaning is therefore provided. If it is claimed that we can never "know," no contrast is provided, so there is nothing that we can know and hence nothing that we can be said to fail to know.

Similarly, to say that everything can in principle be perceived is to use the word "perceive" in such a way as to express no contrast. What, then, is the point in saying that this or that is in principle perceivable? The argument applies generally to all-embracing philosophical concepts and theories.

4. Against the neologism

There is no point in changing daily language habits. The proposals by philosophers to do so ignore the fact that the meanings of our words are embedded in the distinctions expressed by the words of everyday language. Philosophers who make definitions designed to establish a usage that has no basis in ordinary language habits are wasting their time. To think that everyday language can be emended, its inner structure more clearly represented, for example, by symbolism, is fallacious, as is the ideal upon which the notion is based. After all, "our common stock of words embodies all the distinctions men have found worth drawing. . . ." (J. L. Austin)[134]

5. In support of casuistry

Philosophy is not, and never can become, something resembling science. As an activity philosophy does not culminate in hypotheses or theories. Generalization in philosophy is "unclarification" (Gilbert Ryle).[135] It is not general truths that the philosopher is to concern himself with, but close and accurate description of the particular case. And particular cases are to be described not in terms of philosophical theories or distinctions, but according to the place we find for them in the complex of definitions and descriptions to which our *ordinary* expressions belong in our *actual* language habits.

The above outlines are, of course, extremely bare and merely represent the gist of some of the more basic philosophical arguments to be found in linguistic philosophy. What is remarkable is that none of these views or arguments, so current in post-Wittgensteinian discussion, is to be found

---

[134]J. L. Austin, "A Plea for Excuses," *Proceedings of the Aristotelian Society*, LVII (1956-57), 8, in *Philosophical Papers*, p. 130.

[135]G. H. von Wright lays great weight on this point. "Wittgenstein's perhaps most important task—not only in the *Tractatus* but also later—was to show how *different* from one another positive (empirical) science and philosophy are." The philosopher's task is to clarify the limits of science and its investigation of objective truth. ("Wittgenstein's *Tractatus*," *Dagens Nyheter* [Stockholm], March 16, 1957.) This aim is very near to that of Kant. Ryle attaches the greatest weight for the future of philosophy precisely on the negative aspect of Wittgenstein's thought, that philosophy is *not* a kind of science. This idea, according to Ryle, Wittgenstein has "demolished."

actually *expressed* in Wittgenstein's own text. It could be said indeed that insofar as they are views, they are all contrary to the injunction "don't think, but look!" On the other hand, you would think that even this piece of advice expressed a view of some kind, something that could be formulated as a general rule.

Some of the difficulty lies in Wittgenstein's style. This is strongly dialogic in character, with but rare occurrences of straightforward assertions. Instead of conclusions which may bring our thinking to a close, we get trains of thought, and hints, and suggestions about where to think from here. And when an assertion *is* made, it is often heavily qualified.

Accordingly, we find two distinct trends in the literature: one which tries to formulate and establish definite insights thought to be expressed in the *Investigations*, or at least to be implicit in them, and another which mainly refrains from expressions of this kind and tries to comply with Wittgenstein's insights more indirectly by adopting his style of discussion.[136]

If one is a representative of the indirect approach and yet wants to say something positive about it, the qualifications one must add are so strong that one's statement almost ceases to bear any resemblance to what we ordinarily think of as a contribution to discussion. All that we can be offered, as one such representative put it, are "these hints of echoes of shadows of Wittgenstein's 'intention,'"[137] not a straightforward thesis about his intention being this or that.

As might be expected, discussion in post-Wittgensteinian circles was marked by its own very special character. Indeed, its idiosyncracies became something of a rule, or at least a pattern, a way of looking at problems, especially a way of

---

[136]Ernest Gellner's distinction in *Words and Things* between "low church" and "high church" is useful in this connection, although perhaps not altogether apt. (See note 106.)

[137]Stanley Cavell, "The Availability of Wittgenstein's Later Philosophy," *Philosophical Review*, LXXI (1962), No. 1, 73.

looking at traditional philosophical problems. This latter point is significant, for it shows that in these circles, too, the classics, especially Plato, were diligently read and studied, the tie with the past thus not altogether broken.

Was Wittgenstein a metaphysician?

It is not completely surprising that within his "home" circles the literature on Wittgenstein as a metaphysician is extremely meager.[138] That the earlier Wittgenstein can be seen to have an affinity with the philosophical mystics is clear enough, however, and deserves further discussion.

According to the *Tractatus* there *is* something that is unsayable. "The things that cannot be put into words," says Wittgenstein, *"make themselves manifest.* They are what is mystical" (6.522). However, despite the fact that the unsayable also figures in negative theology and related metaphysical viewpoints, it is certainly not possible to make any documented and detailed comparison between these and Wittgenstein's statements in the *Tractatus*. There have been attempts to make such comparisons, but with so little to go on progress has been modest.[139]

The same is true of any comparison between phenomenologists, Husserl in particular, and Wittgenstein. From the point of view of the history of ideas, there are indeed resemblances, but they fail to stand up to a closer inspection of the actual ideas of the two philosophers.

A much more convincing comparison for the sayings of the earlier Wittgenstein is to be found in certain thoughts of Martin Heidegger. Here a number of parallels appear.[140] One

---

[138]The word "metaphysics" is used here in a sense close to Aristotle's "first philosophy," about basic principles, basic categories, and so on. (Aristotle *Metaphysics*, Book 4.)

[139]See, for example, R. Freundlich, "Logik und Mystik," *Zeitschrift für philos. Forschung*, VII (1953), 554-70.

[140]See Ingvar Horgby, "The Double Awareness in Heidegger and Wittgenstein," *Inquiry*, II (1959), No. 4, 235-64.

interesting possibility is that an understanding of Wittgenstein's vision of the world as a colorless, accidental, value-alien collection of states of affairs can be illuminated by an acquaintance with gnosticism and the views of Heidegger. This vision seems to depend on another, a vision of man's double nature. Man is able to stand outside the world as though a stranger to it, surveying all that is factual, and yet at the same time be part of it, just one assemblage of states of affairs among all the others.

Corresponding to the *Tractatus* vision of the world, we find in Heidegger the notion of "the things that are" or "entities" *(Seiendes)*. We recall that for Wittgenstein it is only possible to talk about what is in the world; in this he does not completely resemble Heidegger, for Heidegger thinks it is possible to talk about something besides. Yet he does set up conceptual requirements for what it is possible to "discuss" which make it clear that only what is in the world can be *discussed*, and this is clearly Tractarian in character.

When Wittgenstein first mentions the mystical in the *Tractatus* (cf. p. 107) it is to say that what is mystical is *that* the world exists. Since the world, for Wittgenstein, is not an organic whole, but a collection of obtaining states of affairs, it is possible to extend the notion of what is mystical and equate it with the fact that *anything exists*. The mystical itself is not a state of affairs, it is not anything in the world; it is, for Wittgenstein, *that* states of affairs obtain, that there is a world.

Now a central topic in Heidegger is precisely the distinction between *what* is and *that* it (anything) is. We find this distinction playing an important part in *Being and Time* and also in *Was ist Metaphysik?* ("What is Metaphysics?") In both works 'Being' *(Sein)* can perhaps be taken as equivalent to '*that* something is,' that is, to '*there being* things *(Seiendes),*' rather than to plain existence conceived apart from its relation to *that* it exists.[141] "Why is there anything at all, and not rather nothing?" asks Heidegger.

[141]The more cautious and vague, "can perhaps be taken as equivalent," is preferred to Horgby's "is equivalent."

We know that Wittgenstein continually, and significantly for his philosophical views, wondered at there being *anything*. In a lecture[142] he gave in Cambridge in 1929 he remarked that he sometimes had an experience which could best be described by saying that "when I have it *I wonder at the existence of the world*. And I am then inclined to use such phrases as 'How extraordinary that anything should exist!' or 'How extraordinary that the world should exist!' "

Experimentally, then, we can put an equation sign between Wittgenstein's "the mystical" and Heidegger's "Being," based on textual support for the parallel between the latter and "that anything exists."

According to the *Tractatus*, any question that can be decided by logic is independent of the world, independent of the way things actually are. Nothing existing *in* experience is needed to understand logic, but to understand it we do need the "experience" *that* something exists. (These are not Wittgenstein's exact words but interpretation.) But he says that *that* something *is* "is itself *not* an experience. Logic is prior to every experience of something *being so*. It is prior to the question 'How?,' not prior to the question 'What?' "[143] Experience is experience *about something*, but logical insight is not about something, it is that something. And, for Heidegger, *that* something exists, "that something or other is as it is," cannot be found in any perception. (Again interpretation, not exposition.)

Heidegger's formulation includes the term "facticity," a term which it would be hard to rephrase in terms of *Tractatus* terminology. "Facticity" does not refer to the factual occurrence of a thing; rather, it is a characteristic of being which, even if usually not "visible," nevertheless determines the existence of being.[144] We may now quote Heidegger

---

[142]Published in the *Philosophical Review*, LXXIV (1965), 8.
[143]Cf. *Tractatus* 5.551 and 5.552.
[144]Paraphrased from *Sein und Zeit* (7th ed.; Tübingen: Max Niemeyer, 1953), p. 135.

directly: "Facticity's That is never to be encountered in any perception."

The parallel between what Wittgenstein says about logic—the notion *that* anything exists—and experience, on the one hand, and Heidegger's 'facticity' and 'perception,' on the other, is certainly remarkable. However, it would be pure speculation to say that the resemblance ran deep.

It has already been mentioned that Wittgenstein identified natural science with the totality of true propositions about the world. The view implied is that the only unity we can talk about is the unity of each element that combines with other elements to make up each existing state of affairs; the world itself is not a unity, it is only a collection. Closely relevant to this point are the following statements about philosophy.

> 4.113 Philosophy settles controversies about the limits of natural science.
> 4.114 It must set limits to what can be thought; and, in doing so, to what cannot be thought.
>
> It must set limits to what cannot be thought by working outwards through what can be thought.
> 4.115 It will signify what cannot be said, by presenting clearly what can be said.

Interpretation of 4.115 is by no means easy, not least because of Wittgenstein's unusual use of "Bedeutung." (The original reads: *Sie wird das Unsagbare bedeuten, indem sie das Sagbare klar darstellt.*) We should note, too, that "to show" *(zeigen)* is not used here.

It is just when philosophy delimits the unthinkable and at the same time alludes to the unsayable that the view *(Anschauung)* of the world *sub specie aeternitatis* presents itself—as Wittgenstein himself suddenly remarks after declaring that what is mystical is *that* the world exists.

> To view the world *sub specie aeterni* is to view it as a whole—a limited whole.

Feeling the world as a limited whole—it is this that is mystical.

Heidegger says that consciousness *that* the world exists is at the same time consciousness of a unity. What is only a collection can thus be conceived as a whole in that-consciousness. The parallel here between Wittgenstein and Heidegger may seem less close, but when taken in conjunction with the two previous points of similarity, the comparison seems not insignificant.

It is tempting to see a connection between Wittgenstein's gloomy outlook on the world and the absence of all consoling features in his concept of the world. In Heidegger's case, however, the homeless man, cast into the world, is protected by the guardian angel of science. "What happens to us essentially in the basis of our being now that science has become our passion?" asks Heidegger. We do not ask ourselves what the nothing is that limits knowledge, but we let it work upon us in such a way as to arouse wonder, and wonder brings its own source of scientific satisfaction. In this way the world itself, as an existent, becomes an object worthy of man's thought.

Martin Heidegger

Life from 1889 until the present day

If the demand for information about Wittgenstein's life has been greater than the supply, the same can equally be said of Martin Heidegger. Heidegger has shown great reluctance to talk about himself, and attempts to provoke him into doing so have generally been in vain. Following a period of intensive writing in the 1950's, Heidegger is presently engaged in re-working the manuscripts of his lectures from the thirties. It is unlikely that any autobiography will be forthcoming.

The whole orientation of Heidegger's thinking is toward strongly objective, impersonal insights. His main works show a complete lack of direct pronouncement or evaluation, and any hints in this direction are accompanied by clear disclaimers. For Heidegger, the pathos and grandeur of a visionary "philosophy of life" are anathema, though it has to be re-marked that access to his own philosophy depends on an ability to relive, with sufficient intensity, certain "basic states of mind" or "attitudes toward life and the world." His system is sustained by these, and even if it can be considered in separation from them, they provide the only adequate means of really grasping it.

By way of introduction, then, it may be apt to quote the opening words of one of Heidegger's lectures.

University philosophers will never understand what Novalis said: "Philosophy [and all philosophy, for Heidegger, is metaphysics] is strictly speaking a homesickness."[1]

It is not a discipline that can be learned. The sciences are only servants in relation to it. But art and religion are its sisters. He who does not know what homesickness is, cannot philosophize. It is only possible for us to philosophize if, and because, we do not feel at home anywhere, because we are unceasingly being pushed up against Being, against that in Being which is total and essential, because we feel at home nowhere except on the way to the total and essential. We are without a native land and are restlessness itself, living restlessness: it is because of *this* that it is necessary for us to philosophize. And this restlessness is *our* confinement, in us who are finitude itself. And we are not allowed to let it pass away, to comfort ourselves in an illusion about totality and a satisfactory infinitude. We must not only bear [this restlessness] in us, but accentuate it, and when we are not only confined but entirely isolated, only then do we strive more to incite ourselves to be important, civilized; only then are we in a position to be "gripped." And when we thus make ourselves grippable, by handing ourselves over to reality, our homesickness makes us into human beings.[2]

---

[1]Novalis, *Fragmente, Philosophie*, in *Auswahl aus den Schriften* (Hamburg: Fischer-bücherei, 1956), p. 153. The full quotation goes: "Die Philosophie ist eigentlich Heimweh-Trieb überall zu Hause zu sein."

[2]Translated from the French. Karl Rahner, "Introduction au concept de philosophie existentiale chez Heidegger," *Recherches de science religieuse* (1940), pp. 152-71. I have omitted Rahner's emphasis on "on the way to the total and essential" as it seems to be due to his special perspective: he wants, as he himself says, to show that Heidegger's existential philosophy can prepare us for divine revelation, lay us open to "the God of Abraham, Isaac, and Jacob."

In these words of Heidegger we hear the echo of Nietzsche's "God is dead," and Christ's "My God, why have You forsaken me?" Man today has been abandoned in the midst of things[3] and is afflicted by a forgetfulness of Being.[4] So goes Heidegger's version. But not only does Heidegger deny himself the idea of man's relation to a God, to a world beyond *(jenseits)*, something "absolute," or a Spinozistic substance, he also repudiates that source of mental repose which resides in the naturalistic idea of man's total absorption in "this" world. Man can be understood neither in terms of God nor of the world.[5]

Martin Heidegger was born on the twenty-sixth of September, 1889, in the small town of Messkirch in Baden, in southwest Germany. The family was Catholic, his father a verger. The young Martin was himself taken up with religion and joined the Jesuits as a novice after he had finished his studies at the high school. Then for a number of semesters he studied Catholic theology at the University of Freiburg im Breisgau, though gradually purely philosophical questions came to occupy his interest. It is clear from Heidegger's later works that his familiarity with theology and medieval Christian theology have influenced him throughout his life and have left deep marks on his philosophy.

In 1914 the promising young philosopher and theologian submitted a doctoral thesis entitled *The Theory of Judgment in Psychologism*. The work bears the stamp of Husserl's criticism of psychological strains in contemporary formal logic, and Heidegger's characteristic style is already apparent: he refers to psychologism as an "un-philosophy" *(Unphiloso-*

---

[3]"Die Selbsthauptung der deutschen Universität," *Freiburger Universitätsreden*, 11-20 (Freiburg, 1934-35), p. 12. See also note 4.

[4]For instance, in *Was ist Metaphysik?* (3d ed.; Frankfurt am Main: V. Klostermann, 1954), p. 12. Henceforth this work will be referred to as *WM*.

[5]The latter aspect of *Dasein* receives one of its clearest formulations in *Sein und Zeit* (henceforth referred to as *SuZ*), p. 15; pp. 36-37 in the English edition. (See note 6.)

phie). In the following year he qualified as a university lecturer with his work *The Theory of Categories and Meaning in Duns Scotus,* which he dedicated to the neo-Kantian philosopher, Heinrich Rickert (1863-1936). It could be said of Heidegger that it was Scotus, together with Kant and Brentano, who aroused him from his theological slumbers. He acclaimed Scotus (*ca.* 1266-1308, "doctor subtilis") as the most penetrating of the scholastics and greater even in significance for the philosophy of the Middle Ages than Thomas Aquinas (1225-74). Yet Heidegger considered that neither Kant, Brentano, nor Duns Scotus had provided a complete or correct list of categories. Twelve years later Heidegger himself was to confront the astonished philosophical world with his "existentials"—or categories of being—"care," "state of mind," "understanding," "thrownness," and many others.

In 1917, after being passed over for an appointment, Heidegger associated himself with Edmund Husserl (1859-1938). For five years he functioned as leader of Husserl's philosophy seminar, and then in 1923, at the age of thirty-four, he was appointed professor ordinarius at Marburg, the neo-Kantian center. In 1928, one year after the publication of his main work, *Sein und Zeit*[6] *(Being and Time),* he was called back to Freiburg to succeed Husserl. It is primarily this work that we shall try to acquaint ourselves with in the following pages, this and his inaugural lecture, *Was ist Metaphysik?* ("What is Metaphysics?"), notorious for its obscure doctrine of the Nothing *(das Nichts).* In 1929 he published another major work, *Kant und das Problem der Metaphysik (Kant and the Problem of Metaphysics),* but after that came an interval of almost fifteen years before his

---

[6]*SuZ* (8th ed.; Tübingen: Max Niemeyer, 1957); English translation by John Macquarrie and Edward Robinson, *Being and Time* (New York: Harper & Row, 1962). Page references to the English translation of *Sein und Zeit* will be given in parentheses following page references to the German text.

next work appeared. Then it was to demonstrate that in the intervening period he had undergone a change in his philosophical position. Just how radical was this "turning around" *(Kehre)*, as Heidegger himself describes it, is hard to say. The short, very concentrated and difficult work *Vom Wesen der Wahrheit* ("On the Nature of Truth"), first written in 1930 and subsequently reworked many times before its eventual publication in 1943, reveals some of the changes. They might be summed up by saying that for the later Heidegger, Being takes the place of Nothing. Outwardly, the later works are recognizable both by their distinctive use of language and by a kind of edifying strain: man is called upon to be the shepherd and cultivator of Being. Later on we will say a little more about the philosophy of this period, though without any attempt at a systematic exposition. Indeed, one finds a general reluctance to try to locate the later Heidegger in the context of philosophical thought.[7]

Even as a student Heidegger was recognized as unusually gifted in philosophy, and in the 1920's Husserl was very enthusiastic about his new protégé. So much the greater his disappointment, therefore, when it became apparent that Heidegger was intent on pursuing an independent path, and one that led, in some respects, in a direction diametrically opposite to that which he himself had marked out. *Being and Time*, in fact, established Heidegger as the leading philosopher in the German language as far as fashion and influence were concerned. This influence has been very marked in Continental Europe and South America; in English-speaking countries, on the other hand, it has been practically negligible.[8]

[7]A list of Heidegger's writings in chronological order is printed at the end of this chapter, pp. 262-64.

[8]Among the few works on Heidegger published in English we may mention: Marjorie Grene, *Martin Heidegger* (London: Bowes & Bowes, 1957; New Haven: Yale University Press, 1957); Magda King, *Heidegger's Philosophy: A Guide to His Basic Thought* (New York:

Martin Heidegger

Though Heidegger might appear to be "untranslatable," the postwar influence of Hegel and Kierkegaard on French philosophy led to the study of Heidegger and to the translation of his works. In the 1940's, particularly in France, Heidegger's pronouncements were interpreted as expressions of a basic philosophical position to all intents and purposes the same as that of Sartre. Indeed, Heidegger was jubilantly hailed as a leading "existentialist" and "humanist," an affiliation which he repudiated, however, in a long open letter (1946). Since this letter is one of the more easily understood of his writings, we shall later give a summary of it.

Perhaps it is not hard to understand why Heidegger's writings secure him a following "in his time," why they should contain a general appeal. But caution should be exercised in reading into them anything like the "spirit of the times." The precedents are discouraging. The works of Hegel and Nietzsche were both cited in support of movements afoot in their time, with disastrous results for the interpretation of the philosophical writings of both authors.

Heidegger's main preoccupations are with the cultivation not of man, but of Being. In the terminology of Nietzsche, Heidegger is neither a *jenseits* nor a *diesseits* philosopher. There is something of the *diesseits* in his characterization of man as being-in-the-world, though man is not a thing or substance. And there is a *jenseits* strain in his preoccupation with the absence of something, of God, and of Being, a nothingness which is something other than negation in the usual logical sense. The connection between Heidegger's thought and the characteristic traits of our time, it will be seen, are as difficult to pinpoint as they are tempting to assume.

Macmillan; Oxford: Basil Blackwell, 1964); Thomas Langan, *The Meaning of Heidegger* (New York: Columbia University Press; London: Routledge & Kegan Paul, 1959); George Joseph Seidel, *Martin Heidegger and the Pre-Socratics: An Introduction to his Thought* (Lincoln: University of Nebraska Press, 1964); Laszlo Versényi, *Heidegger, Being and Truth* (New Haven: Yale University Press, 1965).

Heidegger in the Third Reich

It adds nothing to an interpretation of Heidegger's philosophical writings to go into his strange relationship to Hitler's Germany. But if we want to look upon Western philosophers in the light of their worldly wisdom and example to others—a focus which brings its many disappointments—we inevitably find ourselves looking for some explanation of Heidegger's remarkable behavior in 1933-34. The sources, however, are meager and not all easily accessible.

It is clear enough from *Being and Time* that Heidegger was not himself an extreme right-wing Nationalist, and that he had no part in the synthesis of racial mysticism and anti-Semitism that found expression, for example, in the cry for a "German physics." His references to the much molested Albert Einstein's theory of relativity are positive and full of insight. He discusses the crisis of physics and mathematics in the 1920's.

> The real 'movement' of the sciences takes place when their basic concepts undergo a more or less radical revision which is transparent to itself. The level which a science has reached is determined by how far it is *capable* of a crisis of its basic concepts.[9]

These remarks certainly bear no witness to an interest in the cultural conflict between "idealistic Germanic" and "Bolshevist Jewish" science.

As early as the first year after Hitler assumed power (November 12, 1933) the universities found themselves exposed to strong pressures. The new rulers of the country demanded conformity and had enough support to see that no university failed to toe the line. The Rector at Freiburg at that time, the medical scientist Moëllendorf, resigned because he felt unable to co-operate as the political leaders demanded.

[9]*SuZ*, p. 9 (29).

Heidegger was unanimously elected Rector by the teaching staff. This was in April, 1933. Concerning his relationship to the anti-Nazi Moëllendorf, Heidegger said later: "Dr. Moëllendorf was very disturbed about the situation; he hoped that my reputation as a professor would help to preserve the faculty from political enslavement."[10]

What did Heidegger's colleagues expect of him? That he should maintain as inflexible a line as possible in face of the pressure from above, or that by a sufficient degree of outward conformity he might make the authorities rely on him and consequently leave the internal affairs of the university in peace? Or what? What in fact was known of Heidegger's political outlook?

In support of the assumption that he was not a Nazi, or at least was not regarded as one, nor even as having leanings in that direction, one can cite the fact that he sent flowers, openly and officially, as a token of sympathy and condolence to the Jewish Husserl, whose son had just been arrested by the police. In an accompanying letter Frau Heidegger expressed, on behalf of her husband, her dismay and hope that the arrest was only the doing of some junior official.[11] Just the same sort of thing had happened, she pointed out, in the weeks of the revolution in 1918! It can also be said for Heidegger that as soon as he became Rector, he forbade duels, and also nominated deans who were not members of the Nazi party. The indications would seem to be, therefore, that Freiburg University had an anti-Nazi as its administrative head.

Heidegger's speech on his inauguration as Rector in 1933, "Die Selbstbehauptung der deutschen Universität" ("The German University's Self-Affirmation,") commonly regarded

---

[10]Translated from the French, "Deux documents sur Heidegger," *Les Temps modernes,* Nos. 4-6, pp. 713-24 (Paris, 1946); p. 717. The author of this particular document, "Visite à Martin Heidegger," is Alfred de Towarnicki, about whom nothing further is known. The name is not listed in any catalogue of French universities or authors.

[11]The passage from the letter is quoted in "Deux documents sur Heidegger," pp. 717-18.

as notorious for its Nazi leanings, in fact contains very little political material. The core of the speech appears to be Heidegger's own philosophy of the essential, in this case taking the form of a tribute to science and its educative effect upon the people. The speech is at the same time an appeal to science always to be *essential*, which in Heidegger's terms means that science must continually be conscious of what lies at its very basis: the questioning attitude toward existence as a whole.[12] Science, instead of being, as the tendency was (perhaps still is), a mosaic of separate disciplines, will then realize its unified basis and thereby its educational capacity and function. Heidegger's well-known division of student courses into work service, compulsory service, and scientific service is not necessarily a Nazi-inspired idea; it can be seen to stem from analogous ways of thinking in Plato. Thus the threefold division can just as well represent a realization of Heidegger's own "program." It is to be noted that the speech concludes, not with a "Heil Hitler!" but with a word of wisdom from Plato himself: "all great things stand in peril" (τὰ ... μεγάλα πάντα ἐπισφαλή, *The Republic* 497d, 9).[13]

Nevertheless, there are documents which show unmistakably Heidegger's sympathy with "Hitlerism," in particular a speech to the students from about the same time. A few excerpts convey its tone.[14]

[12]The whole of Heidegger's philosophy may be characterized as an attempt to understand what it is to *ask*, rather than as an answer to definite questions.

[13]Heidegger himself later provided this formulation: "Wer gross denkt muss gross irren" ("Whoever thought on a big scale had to err on a big scale"). *Aus der Erfahrung des Denkens* (Pfullingen: G. Neske, 1954), p. 17. Neither this quotation nor that from Plato should be interpreted as having anything to do with Heidegger's political mistakes. How Heidegger himself understands the phenomenon of "standing in peril" or of "going astray" is dealt with at length in, for example, *Vom Wesen der Wahrheit* (henceforth referred to as *WW*) (4th ed.; Frankfurt am Main: V. Klostermann, 1961), pp. 21 ff.

[14]I have tried to preserve the style of the speech with a "literal" translation. Some German writers have severely criticized this style, thinking Heidegger's "violence" to the language as reprehensible as his

German students!
The National Socialist revolution brings complete upheaval to our German life . . . Do not let dogmas and "ideas" be the rules of your being. The Führer himself and alone is the German reality, present and future, and its law. Learn always to know more deeply: from now on every matter requires decision, and every action responsibility. Heil Hitler!

Heidegger joined the Nazi party and subsequently never left it.[15] Commenting on this he has said:

One day the chief administrative officer *(préfet)* arrived at the university offices, followed by two officials of the county administration; he insisted in the name of the minister that I be enrolled in the party. The minister pointed out that my joining would facilitate the university's practical ties with the outside world. After a good deal of thought I declared myself prepared to carry out this formality in the interests of the university, on the absolute condition that neither during my rectorship nor later on should I have any personal connection with the National Socialist Party. I made it clearly understood that I would accept no direction whatsoever, nor any other positions.[16]

No close familiarity with Hitler's Germany is needed to realize the futility of an attempt to lay down such conditions.[17]

behavior as Rector. The speech is taken from K. Hiller, "Dokument über Martin Heidegger," in the same author's *Köpfe und Tröpfe. Profile aus einem Vierteljahrhundert* (Hamburg and Stuttgart: Rowohlts, 1950), p. 71.
[15] It was hardly up to him to bring his resignation into effect, but we know of no document that shows that Heidegger ever tendered his resignation.
[16] "Deux documents sur Heidegger," p. 718.
[17] The critical reader may find the following hypotheses relevant: (1) Heidegger's memory has failed him; (2) He was quite extraordinarily naïve or else uninformed about the German regime; (3) He had a quite unusually optimistic view of the regime's future development

If one's criterion of "Nazism" includes references to the philosophical ideas of Hitler, Goebbels, and other political leaders, or to the doctrines of Rosenberg and other leading ideologists, it is questionable whether Heidegger was at any time a Nazi. But on these terms one could just as well doubt whether prominent personalities among the regime's active supporters were Nazis. By adopting a more politically flavored concept, on the other hand, one might reasonably conclude that during his first months as Rector, Heidegger joined Hitler's regime as an active Nazi.

Of course the official party philosophers, such as Rosenberg, were anathema to Heidegger professionally; to him their philosophizing was altogether on the wrong track. He must have been deeply dismayed at their (partly successful) attempts to curry favor with the students. And yet, direct attack on the party philosophy was unnecessary; in Heidegger's view "it was enough to express the fundamentals of my philosophical viewpoint in order to criticize the superficial and primitive dogmatism in Rosenberg's biologism."[18]

Heidegger's lectures while Rector do not appear to have supported in any way specifically Nazi ideas. In fact, if we are to believe what he himself says, it was just the contrary. He emphasizes that he very soon came into disrepute in Nazi circles, and was later, after having resigned as Rector, subjected to frequent attacks from Nazi quarters, especially Rosenberg's circle. The attacks had already begun at the end of his rectorship, or shortly after.[19]

It was in the beginning of 1934 that Heidegger resigned as Rector, as a result of increasing disagreement with the regime. He says himself that he intended to resign as of the first of January, 1934.[20]

(cf. Frau Heidegger's interpretation of the young Husserl's arrest); (4) He had a high opinion of his (philosophically grounded) personal standing and reputation with the Nazi leadership.

[18]"Deux documents sur Heidegger," p. 720.

[19]See *ibid.*, pp. 719 ff.

[20]*Ibid.*, p. 720.

While Rector, Heidegger had reinstalled two anti-Nazi professors: Moëllendorf, whom he had succeeded as Rector, and the jurist, Wolf. An order was received from Rosenberg's (so-called education) office to revoke the nominations. Heidegger declared himself opposed: "I have nominated them; they come under my responsibility. If you revoke the nominations, I resign." So he resigned.

So goes the version inspired by Heidegger himself. But even if the source is not unbiased, one can hardly doubt that as Rector at Freiburg, Heidegger insisted on going his own way, and that when this proved impossible he submitted his resignation. He had believed that his own path and that of the Nazi chiefs need not cross, but soon—very soon—he realized his mistake.

Heidegger seems at one time to have dreamt that with himself as Rector at Freiburg the spiritual climate of Germany would come to adapt itself to *his* teaching. "The university is the place for spiritual lawgiving," he declared in one lecture.[21] Indeed, he seems, in 1933, to have looked upon Hitler's regime as a potential tool in the hands of true philosophy.[22] Significantly, it didn't occur to him that he would be subordinated to the established Nazi ideologies and to the party bureaucracy. Given a free rein, with himself as spiritual "Führer," and with Hitler following his recommendations, what kind of a Germany might not have been possible? This seems to have been his vision. What in fact, then, did Heidegger actually think of the prospective "German life"?

Since there is so little to go on, the facts here, as elsewhere, are hard to identify. Heidegger's main philosophical works give an exceedingly sketchy base on which to build recommendations, directives, or norms for personal or social life.

---

[21]*Ibid.*, p. 719.

[22]The unreserved tribute, in his rectorial address, to science and a philosophically based attitude of inquiry supports this. Moreover, the impression conveyed by the above-mentioned document in *Les Temps modernes* ("Deux documents sur Heidegger") agrees with the results of the French-appointed commission of inquiry (1945). Cf. p. 185 below.

The methodology in *Sein und Zeit* excludes all directives and evaluation. Conceivably one might conclude from his doctrine of "das Man" that he was opposed to certain things, that he regrets them, but there is certainly nothing here from which one may derive positive norms or directives. Nor does Heidegger's own behavior as a wielder of worldly authority at the University of Freiburg provide us with any material with which to supplement his writings. As with Hegel, Nietzsche, and others, Heidegger's own life is far from providing concrete examples of his abstract thought. Kierkegaard complained about system builders that they inhabited small kennels instead of their own spacious systems. Would he have felt the same about Heidegger? Possibly, but even if so, it is not at all certain that Heidegger would have been offended. One reason for his trying to keep himself in the background may well be that he does not consider himself to have realized his philosophy in life, nor to be in a position to give instructions on how this could, or could not, be done.

In 1945 Heidegger's past was investigated by a specially appointed tribunal. In its conclusion it made a distinction between those who were primarily guilty, the activists, the less responsible, the sympathizers, and the not guilty. Heidegger was placed under the categories of "less responsible" and "sympathizers," and thus avoided losing his professional rights. Nevertheless, a majority of the teaching staff at the University of Freiburg protested against his officially retaining his chair. The matter continued to be disputed until Heidegger reached retirement age in 1959, though during this period he continued to hold regular lectures.

All attempts since the war to get Heidegger to pronounce on his actions during his rectorship have been in vain. On the other hand, there has been no difficulty in getting him to voice his views on Hitler's regime. The following account can be taken as typical of Heidegger's discussions of the Third Reich with sympathetically disposed philosophical journalists in the years after the war.

185

The time has come for us to be indiscreet. We take a glance at politics. What does Heidegger think about the re-education of the young, about his people's responsibility? He freely declares that it will be a difficult and lengthy process to get rid of the effects of the poison, that Hitlerism, in a way, was nothing but the historical explosion of a "structural" sickness in mankind as a whole. But he refuses to accuse the "German," to admit to a kind of collective decline in the German community. The philosopher's only hope is to awaken in his followers, little by little, the true meaning of their freedom.[23]

It is very rare for accounts of Heidegger's philosophy, or discussions of particular points in it, to touch upon the Rector at Freiburg in 1933. In my own view, this is just as it should be, especially as the central point in his philosophy is so remote from the problems confronting man in situations where he must choose and act. An estimate of a philosopher's originality and worth must not necessarily take account of his experience and wisdom (σοφία).

"Being and Time": The phenomenological analysis

The work

Heidegger's main work *Sein und Zeit (Being and Time)* was published in 1927 in the eighth volume of Husserl's phenomenological yearbook *(Jahrbuch für Phänomenologie und phänomenologische Forschung)* and is dedicated to Husserl "in friendship and admiration." Its aim, says the author, is to reawaken an understanding of, and to elucidate the funda-

---

[23]"Deux documents sur Heidegger," p. 715. The quotation is from the first of the two documents, "Entretien avec Martin Heidegger." The interviewer, Maurice de Gandillac, is considered a reserved admirer of Heidegger's philosophy and not uncritical of him personally. He summarizes Heidegger's attitude as "gently evasive" (*"mollement evasive"*).

mental questions about, the meaning of *Being*. In the course of this project, Heidegger has been led to a fundamental interpretation of *Time*, but was not able to include this in the framework of the book. Thus it was an uncompleted work (Part One, A and B) which came out in 1927. For a long time Heidegger hoped to fulfil his plan (Part One, C, and Part Two), but he has now abandoned it. The work as we have it, therefore, is really only a torso.

The separate sciences investigate all things and their relationships, that is to say, all that is to be found. But in so doing they constantly assume that there is no need to explain what it is to *be*. A spurious kind of self-evidence, or obviousness, has led to the ignoring of this latter question's claims to be taken up in all its depth. And although the question of what it is to be was part of the very atmosphere that Plato and Aristotle lived and breathed, since their time it has been lost sight of.

In the resumption of this question we encounter enormous difficulties of a purely linguistic nature, simply because we have no words or grammar with which to set about it. Heidegger, it must be noted, is not himself of the opinion that he has provided a satisfactory solution to the problems which any linguistic presentation of the study of Being must incur. The language with which he has decked out *Being and Time* he himself describes as "hard and unbeautiful." In the following exposition we will make no attempt to improve upon it, even though the effect in ordinary, or fairly ordinary, English words is a little strained, not to say strange, and also, a more serious matter, even though these words are liable to evoke inappropriate associations. However, it would defeat the purposes of an introductory exposition to make all the qualifications necessary to avoid misinterpretations.

Three terms
Remarks on our exposition of Heidegger

An important preliminary, however, is that the reader be willing to absorb certain expressions and distinctions that must at first strike him as in some respects rather peculiar. The three main German expressions are "Seiendes," "Dasein," and "Existenz." With a grasp of the use of these three terms it is relatively simple to expound some of the basic ideas in *Being and Time.* The oddity of Heidegger's use of these expressions is due to the fact that the kind of thinking he wants to awaken in us is alien to all conventional modes of thought. Because he is not simply inducing in us new ways of ordering our old ideas, as, say, in the case of David Hume, Heidegger has to dispense with ordinary usage of language and to introduce altogether new terms and new ways of using old ones,[24] frequently without even a definition. Therefore, if his words and phrases at first take us aback, that would seem a good beginning. Heidegger does not mean them to be familiar.

The multitude of things and relations to be found in the world he refers to as *Seiendes,* which, following the English translation of *Sein und Zeit,* we shall translate as "entities"[25] or, collectively, (the) "what-is" *(Das Seiende).* These terms are straightforward renderings of the Greek ὄν and ὄντα, present participles of εἶναι ("to be"). Among the many different entities we find human beings, except that a human being is not correctly described as *simply* an entity: he is an entity and something besides; he is, one might say, *also* an entity, not *only* an entity. Man's special way of being is referred to as *Dasein,* which can be translated "being there," though here, following convention, we will use the German term. In respect of his Dasein, man is distinguished from mere entities by "standing out" from them, that is by *existing.* Here "exist" is taken in a special sense, in which the original force of the Latin prefix "ex" ("out of") is brought back into play. Thus

---

[24]An interesting study of Heidegger's usage is given by Erasmus Schöfer, *Die Sprache Heideggers* (Pfullingen: G. Neske, 1963).

[25]Other current renderings are "beings," "essents," "existents." For expository and other reasons we have retained the terminology of the Macquarrie and Robinson translation.

"exist" has the sense of "stand out from," as in *ex-*("out of") *sistere* ("to stand, place, set"). Man stands out from entities, he ex-sists. Man's existence is the same as his standing out from entities. The three expressions, "entity," "Dasein," and "existence," must be distinguished from "Being" *(Sein)*. Of this more later.

The following exposition aims at being no more than an introduction to Heidegger's ideas. If it succeeds, the next step must be to read the works themselves. A main function of an introduction, therefore, should be to reduce opposition to the Heideggerian terminology, failing which the original works are almost certain to seem unnecessarily forbidding. In many cases it would only defeat Heidegger's purpose to attempt a translation of his terms into more usual expressions; yet because of his method of constructing words, it does seem feasible to get at the required meanings by dismantling the terms into their components, components which comprise the most familiar and earliest learned parts of everyday language. Heidegger's aim is to achieve a "phenomenological" freedom from presupposition or prejudice, and one way of doing this, he believes, is by attending to the basic meanings, and relations between meanings, of "the most elemental words." He also goes from the words themselves to their roots and stems, and from substantival to verb forms *(Das Wesen zu wesen!)*. "Unheimlich" ("uncanny") is resolved into "un" and "Heim," and Heidegger takes the main import of the term for theory of Being to be the sense of absence from the familiar and comfortable. We shall note too the avoidance of psychological and anthropological terms in favor of expressions of "ways of Being."[26]

The most important requirement for the reader, however, is to remain as open-minded as possible to the terminology,

[26]Examples of this and of distinctions expressed by combined use of Being-words and words that do not suggest Being are: *Freiheit—Freisein, Wahrheit—Wahrsein, Mensch—Dasein, Entdeckung—entdeckend-sein, Entdeckheit—entdeckt-sein, In-der-Welt-sein, Seiendes, In-der-Unwahrheit-sein.*

and to maintain correspondingly as unreflective an attitude as he can—in fact, an attitude usually considered more appropriate for reading poetry. The reader's powers of reflection can then be more effectively employed upon the complicated connections Heidegger invites him to form between the words he has introduced.

Heidegger considers that etymology can help us to approach the most original sense of a word. Not that we should make a cult of words; as he himself says, "we must avoid uninhibited word-mysticism." "Nevertheless," he continues, "the ultimate business of philosophy is to preserve the *force of the most elemental words* in which Dasein expresses itself, and to keep the common understanding from levelling them off to that unintelligibility which functions in turn as a source of pseudo-problems."[27] We note in this passage the typical "Being"-oriented terminology: we read of Dasein rather than man, and to say that it "ex-presses it-self" gives an impression of Dasein's immanence in this Being. A totally different, and misleading, effect would be given by rewriting the passage: "the words in which man expresses the basic features of his existence."

Some of the main Heideggerian word resolutions are: *entdecken* > *ent-decken* ("dis-cover," or "un-cover"), *entsprechen* > *ent-sprechen* ("ac-cord with"), *existieren* > *ex-*[s]*istieren* ("to exist"), *erschliessen* > *er-schliessen* ("dis-close"), *anwesend* > *an-wesend* ("having pre-sence"; Greek: παρουσία), *Verweisung* > *ver-weisung* ("re-buke"), *Umsicht* > *um-sicht* ("circum-spection"), *Dasein* > *da-sein* ("Being-there"), *möglich* > *mögen-lich* ("poss-ible"), *niemand* ("nobody") > *ni-(cht)* ("no") + *Man* = *das Man* ("the 'they' "), *eigentlich* > *eigen* + *lich* ("auth-entic"), *Ekstase* > *ek* + *stasis* ("ec-stasis"), *Besorgen* > *be* + *Sorge* ("con-cern"), *verfallen* > *verfallen* ("de-cline," "fall").

Man is "thrown" into the world; thus it is possible to talk

[27]*SuZ*, p. 220 (262).

of a kind of fall which is a falling away. Generally, with Heidegger, one must first grasp the connections between the component parts of words before understanding the connections between the words themselves.

It is not impossible, perhaps, that some philosopher and philologist might render Heidegger in a style that eliminated its Teutonisms, in the linguistic sense. But clearly such a project would involve such extensive recreation and rethinking that nothing like it can be contemplated here. Thus I trust the reader will exercise his indulgence as he makes his way through the many un-English constructions in the following. He may at least be consoled by the consideration that in keeping fairly close to the original he avoids sources of error that a freer account would inevitably give rise to.

Heidegger changes what logical empiricists call the "logical syntax" of words, and what in Oxford philosophy is referred to as their "grammar." He does this to stress certain important philosophical points. For example, in the crucial section on 'anxiety' there is no indication at all that it is *men* who *are* anxious. Heidegger carries out a "Copernican revolution," or rather, a counter-counter-revolution to the counter-revolution of Kant: man is removed from a position of power which one might have thought was—simply as a matter of syntax or "grammar"—inseparably his. Man *is* not anxious, he doesn't *have* feelings, he doesn't *make use of* language. The expression "be anxious about something" is used, it is true; what is anxious, however, is not man but, surprisingly enough, anxiety. A basic question we will find goes: "what is anxiety anxious about?" If one immediately objects that the only things that can be anxious are living beings, perhaps only human beings, a rejoinder might be that the terms of the descriptions of an analysis of Being do not at all contradict this view; on the contrary, the view itself presupposes these descriptions in the sense that an adequate account of the differences between man and what is not man, between person and what is not person, will have to employ or presuppose the account given by an analysis of Being, and not conversely. It is not the case, as Kierkegaard believed, that an account of anxiety in terms of an analysis of Being must include some reference to something that *is* anxious, that is to man.

> In anxiety—we say—"it is to oneself uncanny" *(ist es einém unheimlich)*. What do this "it" and this "to one-self" mean? We cannot say what it is in the face of which one feels uncanny. One feels it thus as a whole. All things and we ourselves sink into a state of indiffer-ence. Not, however, in the sense of a mere disappearing, but in the moment they are taken away, they *turn to* us.[28]

They turn to *us*. But what does "us" refer to? In order to follow Heidegger we have to exchange our usual psychologi-cal and anthropological concept of man for the ontological concept of ex-sistence, Da-sein. We have to leave our existen-tial perspective in order to take up a categorial one.[29]

The method: phenomenology

Heidegger describes his own method as phenomenological. His aim is a pure description of states of affairs—with no explanations, theories, or hypotheses. The phenomenologist's motto is "to the facts!" What he describes, therefore, must be

---

[28]*WM*, p. 16.

[29]Cf., for example, "Analysis of (everydayness in) life serves . . . the purpose of avoiding the circumstance that interpretations of man's life fall within the scope of anthropological-psychological descriptions of his 'experiences' and 'capacities.' Which is not to assert the "falsity" of anthropological-psychological cognition. But it is a matter of showing that, in spite of its correctness, it does not extend to the problem of the existence of life, which must be constantly kept in view when one asks questions about Being." *Kant und das Problem der Metaphysik* (2d ed.; Frankfurt am Main: V. Klostermann, 1951), pp. 211-12. See the expressions in note 26.

something immediately intuitable for the uninhibited and unprejudiced observer—in a way, not unlike the disclosures of the obvious made by the later Wittgenstein. Consequently, one finds in Heidegger's work no trace of conjecture or hypothesis, no propositions with leads as to how they might be confirmed or disconfirmed by constructing this or that experimental set-up.

To say that Heidegger's method is phenomenological is itself to postulate a certain relationship between his thought and that of Husserl. What are Heidegger's views on Husserl? His acknowledgment of Husserl's contribution to phenomenology is warm and unstinted. Yet Husserl himself considered Heidegger in no way to have continued or developed his own work. A significant factor here is Heidegger's abhorrence of -isms, his eschewing of any sort of system building. What is essential in phenomenology, he says, "does not lie in its actuality as a philosophical 'movement' *(Richtung)*. Higher than actuality stands *possibility*. We can understand phenomenology only by seizing upon it as a possibility."[30] (Note the word "possibility," the ability to *be* something.) Heidegger's view is diametrically opposed to that of Husserl, who envisaged phenomenology as a fundamental science with its own intricate structure of concepts.

After the "turning around" of Heidegger's thought in the early 1930's (at about the same time as Wittgenstein's more radical "turn"), the split between his own and Husserl's thought became clear. Heidegger has himself remarked upon this, for instance declaring that phenomenology for Husserl provided no access to the question of the meaning of Being and consequently that it is condemned to remain one of the movements within traditional metaphysics.[31]

[30]*SuZ*, p. 38 (63). "Possibility" is a translation of *Möglichkeit*. In this passage one should probably keep in mind the *mögen* ("to be able") in *mög(en)lich-keit*. Cf. *Platons Lehre von der Wahrheit. Mit einem Brief über den Humanismus* (henceforth referred to as *P-H)* (2d ed.; Bern: A. Francke, 1954), p. 57.

[31]See *P-H*, p. 87.

From man to Dasein

Heidegger begins his account by declaring that the entity to be analyzed first is ourself *(wir je selbst)*. The Being of this entity, its way of being, is mine *(je meines)*. It cannot be separated from, or thought independently of, the *individual*. "These entities, in their Beings, comport themselves [in understanding] towards their Being. As entities with such Being, they are delivered over to their own Being."[32] This suggests a kind of self-reflection—perhaps one might think here of Kierkegaard's concept of reflection; but as Heidegger develops the notion we shall see that it differs widely from Kierkegaard's.

"This way of characterizing Dasein has a double consequence," Heidegger continues. Note again that he doesn't say "This way of characterizing *man* . . . ." One may, to begin with, insert "man" wherever Heidegger has "Dasein," since this can make it easier to grasp what is meant. On the other hand, it is crucial that one's attention should gradually move away from ordinary concepts of 'man' and of 'man's condition' to man's specific way of Being. The topic is to be Dasein, not mankind.

The two consequences, according to Heidegger, are the following:

1. Man's essence *(Wesen)* lies in his "to be" *(Zu-sein)*, in his "existence." For this latter word to be apt here, we must not take it in the sense of the Latin *"existentia."* In this sense the term applies to tables, trees, houses, as much as to men. But, as we noted earlier, existence, for Heidegger, connotes something essential in the *way* man *is*. Man's, or rather Dasein's, essence is its "how," not its "what."

2. The Being which "is an *issue* for this entity [i.e., man] in its very Being, is in each case mine *(je meines)*." Thus Dasein is never to be understood as an instance or a special case of

---

[32]*SuZ*, pp. 41-42 (67). The two words, "in understanding," are inserted on the basis of the formulations in *SuZ*, pp. 12-13 (32-33).

some kind of entity, as with things that merely occur or "are present-at-hand" *(vorhanden)*. The character of *my* Being *(Jemeinigkeit—Je-mein-ig-keit—*literally "each's mineness") requires use of the personal pronoun: "*I* am," "*You* are." Dasein's characteristic of being mine permits two ways of existing, the authentic and the inauthentic. In the inauthentic I lose or surrender myself, the *mine*ness of *my* personal perspective on everything. (We will come back to this in our examination of "das Man.")

In this characterization of man's form of Being, Heidegger thinks he has managed to transcend the fateful subject-object distinction that has dominated philosophy since Descartes. He points out that Descartes, in his "Cogito ergo sum," refrained from any analysis of the term "sum." He remarks, perhaps a little scathingly, that when it comes to asking what Being is in their discussions on the human subject, the soul, person, and so forth, modern philosophers (including Husserl) show a remarkable modesty or self-sufficiency. It is not a matter of terminological arbitrariness on his own part, says Heidegger, that he avoids such terms as "I" or "the subject," and expressions such as "life" and "man," to designate the entities that we ourselves are.[33]

The above account of Dasein will, so Heidegger leads us to understand, presuppose something fundamental that he calls Dasein's Being-in-the-world *(In-der-Welt-sein)*. Although this is a uniform, undifferentiated phenomenon, and we must conceive it as such, certain features of it can be brought separately into relief.

The phrase "Being-in" in "Being-in-the-world" is not to be taken as analogous to the relationship of the water to a glass when we think of its *being in* the glass. Nothing spatial is intended, nothing like water in the glass or clothes in the cupboard, but something more basic, or original, something closer, in fact, to the relationship intended or implied by such

[33]*Ibid.*, pp. 46-47 (71-72).

expressions as "at home in," "residing at," "familiar with." (The German word "in," Heidegger tells us in his first, and far from last, etymological note, stems from "innan," which is equivalent to the Latin *habitare:* "to reside.")

Heidegger gives as examples of the many different ways of Dasein's "Being-in-the-world"—to be concerned with something, to make something, to use something, to discuss something, and many others.

At this point we can conveniently pause a moment and attempt a phenomenological analysis. Suppose yourself to be in the situation of preparing food, using a whisk. Or better, next time you do something like that, suddenly stop and take stock of the situation. Ask yourself then, what would be the most direct description of what happens *(zu den Sachen!)*. One of the points Heidegger stresses is that the description can hardly convey any report of an "I" confronting an external world and contriving to manipulate it. There is something that cognitively precedes the subject-object distinction. In the situation of my using a whisk, the Heideggerian analysis fastens onto something that cuts across the distinction between me and the world, and it is this feature that is indicated by the expression "being-in-the-world." The ways of "Being-in" which he mentions exemplify a kind of Being which he calls "concern" *(Besorgen)*.[34] Thus one is concerned to achieve something, to complete something, to provide food for oneself. Heidegger's term "Besorgen" does not, however, cover such uses of the English word "concern" as "it concerns the children," "it is a big concern," or "he was concerned at their misfortune." The term "Sorge" (Latin: *cura*) covers all the phenomena of concern in Heidegger's sense; it may be translated as "care." Dasein's essence lies in its existence. Existence, as we noted, is something uniform but nevertheless has a complex structure. Being-in is thus part of this structure of Dasein—without a world we cannot have

[34]*Ibid.*, p. 57 (83).

Being. Under the term "existential" Heidegger includes all structures which are essentially included in Dasein, thus Being-in-the-world. In Dasein, man's Being-in-the-world is occupied with itself, with man's own Being. A stone is indifferent to itself, or rather, the way in which a stone "is" excludes by the same token both its indifference to and its occupation with its own Being. Essentially man's way of Being is precisely that in which he comports *(verhalten)* himself—even though now in one way, now in another—to himself. We shall encounter other existentials: "that we are in a certain state of mind" which can manifest itself in elation, dejection, or indifference; "understanding" in a certain fundamental sense (which can manifest itself in misunderstanding!); and "being authentic or inauthentic" (the latter manifesting itself in fallenness).[35]

In *Being and Time* Heidegger is not trying to develop an epistemology; his field is ontology. But it is clear that the above account provides a characteristic starting point for a determination of the essence of *cognition* as a way of Being within the frame of "Being-in-the-world." Cognition is not, at least from the most fundamental point of view, a subject's cognition of the world, the apprehension of something outside by something inside. Being-in is, as we noted, precisely not Being-inside. And Being-there *(Da-sein)* is, of its own nature, already Being-in-the-world; therefore the classical epistemological problem of the possibility of knowledge and of the subject's ability to apprehend the world as it is in itself, rather than simply as it appears "to me," does not arise. Even to say something about something must primarily be understood as a way of Being. The criterion of "correspondence with reality" cannot itself have any immediate relevance with

[35]Ex-sistence, the essence of Dasein, may be said to be multi-dimensional. It has an authentic (inauthentic) dimension—a degree of falling-away, a dimension of mood or attunement, and dimensions of understanding, misunderstanding, non-understanding, etc. Behind these dimensions nothing lies concealed, in particular no substance, no absolute "I."

regard to the truth of propositions; it cannot belong to a pure phenomenological description of what it is to speak truly rather than falsely.[36]

> When Dasein directs itself towards something and grasps it, it does not somehow first get out of an inner sphere in which it has been proximally encapsulated, but its primary kind of Being is such that it is always 'outside' alongside entities which it encounters and which belong to a world already discovered.[37]

We will briefly discuss the two existentials, "state of mind" and "understanding," before undertaking a rather more detailed examination of "authenticity," "inauthenticity," and others.

Psychologists undertake investigations into the various states of mind that a man can be in. He may be joyful, sad, elated, depressed. Yet even in a state of acute listlessness or indifference he never achieves an empty state of mind; he is always and inescapably in some state of mind (*Befindlichkeit:* whatever state one may find oneself in) or other. Heidegger tries to draw attention here to a primordial, underivative mood (*Stimmung:* "attunement") which enters into the very structure of the entity. This primordial mood must be considered something apart from the particular moods, which are indeed entities in their own right, insofar as they are states in which one finds oneself. One important mode *(Modus)* of state of mind is fear.[38]

As part of the inner structure of the kind of Being called Dasein, we must include *understanding*.[39] For the term "understanding" to be apt, however, we must work our way back

---

[36]This is interpretation. Cf. *SuZ,* pp. 62 (89-90) and 205 (248-49).
[37]*SuZ,* p. 62 (89). The similarity between this starting point for a theory of knowledge and that of the later Wittgenstein is striking. However, the similarity can hardly be determined more fully, unless one could discover, or construct, a suitable common multiple.
[38]See *ibid.,* pp. 134-42 (172-82).
[39]*Ibid.,* pp. 142-53 (182-95).

to something primordial and underivative. Whatever we "see," we see in a context which makes it possible for tables, chairs, cars, bridges, and so on, to be seen as such. This context may be, for example, that of the respective utilities of these objects. Thus they become understood *as* something in a context which already represents understanding. Theoretically, to dispense with understanding would be to be left with a kind of blank gazing; as soon as one postulates the slightest grasp of something *as* something, understanding is presupposed. Thus understanding is an existential; it betokens, originally and inescapably, the kind of Being that belongs to Dasein.

Understanding implies a construing or interpreting. Only through misunderstanding the basic conditions of Being would one try to dispense with this in an account of Dasein. Whatever is grasped in a certain way has already been understood; this applies to mathematics as much as to historical understanding. Mathematics is not a stricter discipline than historiology *(Historie)*, but narrower, "because the existential foundations relevant for it lie within a narrower range."[40] And although the historian is not as independent of the standpoint of the observer as the natural scientist is supposed to be, a recognition of the essential conditions under which interpretation can be performed shows that in both cases the situation is basically the same.[41]

What, more than anything, marks the existential known as "understanding," according to Heidegger, is that it develops itself as a projection *(Entwurf)* in the direction of one among many determinate possibilities. The word "projection" here includes the sense of "project" which is synonymous with "plan" or "design," but the emphasis is on the forward-directedness contained in "project," even the sense of throwing forward of the Latin *proicere (pro:* "forth"; *jacere:* "to

[40]*Ibid.,* p. 153 (195).
[41]*Ibid.,* pp. 152-53 (194-95).

throw"); Existence proceeds through understanding's constant projection of possibilities.

Everydayness, inauthenticity, and "das Man"

The entity which has Dasein and occurs *also* but not *only* as something "present-at-hand" is myself. To say that it is myself is correct, formally, but different kinds of Being are open to me within the frame of Being-in-the-world. The world can dominate me more or less. Dasein, in Heidegger's view, is for the most part, on the average and proximally *(zunächst)*, *absorption* in *(Aufgehen in:* "be taken over by," "be absorbed in"*)* the world. Thus one can ask: "*Who* is it that is Dasein in everydayness?" If there-Being (man) asks himself this, he will perhaps reply: "It is *I myself*."[42] But the more force that is put into this answer, the more misleading it becomes. Is it really me more than you? I can lose myself, but to lose myself in this way is not to vanish as Dasein, or to disappear as an existent altogether; it is to act in a definite manner, to adopt one of many different kinds of Being. A more correct answer must draw on further aspects of Being-in-the-world than those we have already mentioned: namely, Being-with *(Mitsein)* and Being-there-with *(Mitdasein)*.

Within our everyday surroundings we meet others in a context of mutual functions: for example the bookstore owner from whom we bought this book, or the person who lent it to us, or the owner of the field we keep to the edge of because he has "kept it up decently," or the people we work with, and so on.[43] The others are *with* us in our own Being-in-the world; they aren't discovered later in some *abstract* spatial world. Even when we exclaim "They're just standing about with their hands in their pockets!" the kind of Being the others have differs from that of stones found lying about in a

[42]*Ibid.*, pp. 114-15 (150-51).
[43]*Ibid.*, p. 118 (153).

field. "Just standing about" and "being quite alone" are them-selves kinds of Being within the frame of Being-with. "Even Dasein's Being-alone is Being-with in the world. The Other can be *missing* only *in* and *for* a Being-with."[44] Accordingly, our own Dasein is a Being together with others, a Being-with, a *Mitsein* and a *Mitdasein*.

The individual can care more or less for others, for instance, when they are sick. When the degree of "solicitude" *(Fürsorge)* for others becomes very low, Being-with ap-proaches merely being present-at-hand, the mere Being-present-at-hand *(pures Vorhanden sein)* of several subjects, a mere multiplicity of I's. Only "approaches," however, since ontologically "there is an essential distinction between the 'indifferent' way in which [e.g., material] things at random occur together and the way in which entities who are with one another do not 'matter' to one another."[45]

Because Being-in-the-world is Being-with, understanding of one's own Dasein implies an understanding of the Dasein of others. Thus there is no need to postulate a primordial or original empathy which bridges the gap from one self to an-other.[46] The gap does not exist.

With the help of the account of Dasein as Being-with, Heidegger then comes to a very characteristic answer to the

[44]*Ibid.,* p. 120 (156-57).

[45]*Ibid.,* pp. 121-22 (158).

[46]*Ibid.,* p. 124 (161-62). This phenomenological description removes any possibility of meaningfully raising the problem of solipsism, and, as we have mentioned above, the problem of knowledge. The "I" and the "you" are both there together in their Being-in-the-world, and only altogether specially constructed concepts introduced *post festum* can be used to press the claims of such "problems" as "Is there anything other than my own experiences?" "Can I acquire knowledge of a world that is independent of me?" and so on. Heidegger's undermin-ing of these questions is reminiscent of the later Wittgenstein's treat-ment of them, and generally of linguistic philosophy's treatment of the "other minds" problem. The words "I" and "me," in their cognitive use, do not occur originally in such a way as to give rise to any fatal separation between myself and the world, or myself and others. See *SuZ,* p. 205 (249).

question of "who" it *is* that Dasein, proximally and for the most part, is in average everydayness.

Man is concerned with the difference, the distance, between himself and other men. For example: Is the difference to be eliminated? Has one somehow dropped behind the others? Or has one an ascendancy over them which must be preserved? Thus Dasein's possibilities are governed by "the others"; not, however, in the form of specific people; on the contrary, any other individual at all can represent the Others. Generally, in average everydayness, says Heidegger,

> One belongs to the Others oneself and enhances their power. 'The Others' whom one thus designates in order to cover up the fact of one's belonging to them essentially oneself, are those who proximally and for the most part *'are there'* in everyday Being-with-one-another. The "who" is not this one, not that one, not oneself [*man selbst*], not some people [*einige*], and not the sum of them all. The 'who' is the neuter, *the "they"* [*das Man*].[47]

Let us, at this point in the drama, briefly subscribe to the demands of ontological rigor,[48] and quite simply ask ourselves: What has happened? Where has Heidegger led us? The plainest answer might seem to go roughly as follows. Martin Heidegger, after his studious and painstaking apprenticeship with the Master himself (Husserl), has undertaken what was to be, according to his best phenomenological intentions, a maximally prejudice-free and theoretically presuppositionless study of the phenomenon of man, or more accurately, of the kinds of Being which belong to man, and his possession of which distin-

---

[47]*Ibid.*, p. 126 (164).

[48]The reader of Heidegger may frequently find himself impatiently wondering "What it *really* amounts to," as if the account could be "boiled down" to something more accessible to a common understanding. The trouble with this is that our common understanding contains expressions and models (e.g., Cartesian ones) whose hold upon us is just what Heidegger is trying to release.

guishes him from stones on the one hand, and God on the other. Bearing in mind the motto "to the facts," and taking a good hard phenomenological look at man, what does he find? Well, having searched in vain in the current German vocabulary and grammar for expressions capable of describing what he sees, and rather than disappoint with a display of dumb gestures, he exclaims, "das Man!" trusting that this expression will evoke the associations appropriate for the pure description of the kinds of Being characteristic of man in his generality and everydayness.

But back to a more faithful account of the matter! Precisely because one's own Dasein is stamped by that of others, the "dictatorship" of "the Others" comes to be overlooked, the distance dissolves, the difference disappears.

> In this inconspicuousness and unascertainability, the real dictatorship of the "they" is unfolded. We take pleasure and enjoy ourselves as *they* [*man*] take pleasure; we read, see, and judge about literature and art as *they* see and judge; likewise we shrink back from the 'great mass' as *they* shrink back; we find 'shocking' what they find shocking.[49]

The averageness of the "they" is something the "they" is concerned to preserve. It watches out for anything exceptional or importunate; all priorities become "noiselessly suppressed." Everything that is primordial gets "glossed over . . . overnight" as something that has been long familiar. Everything achieved by effort becomes just "something to be manipulated." "Every secret loses its force."[50]

The dictatorship of the "they" does not build upon any special insight on the part of the "they." The dictatorship depends on a listlessness, on a lack of sensitivity in face of differences in level and genuineness. "By publicness every-

---

[49]*SuZ*, pp. 126-27 (164).
[50]*Ibid.*, p. 127 (165).

thing gets obscured, and what has thus been covered up gets passed off as something familiar and accessible to everyone."[51] And that it is admirable for something to be accessible to everyone is taken for granted.

It is the "they" who relieve (*entlasten:* "disburden") Dasein of its Being, reduce the responsibility, and make the everyday easy. Moreover, the individual cannot be said to *lose* his own self; he has yet to find his way to it.[52]

The "they" *(das Man)* is not a particular man, nor mass man, listless or apathetic man, let alone a "universal subject." Neither is it an essence that has lost its human stamp. Stripped of all metaphorical overtones "the 'they' " is a term for an existential; it belongs to Dasein's positive constitution as a primordial phenomenon.[53] But "If Dasein discovers the world in its own way [*eigens*] and brings it close, if it discloses to itself its own authentic Being, then this discovery of the 'world' and this disclosure of Dasein are always accomplished as a clearing-away of concealments and obscurities, as a breaking up of the disguises with which Dasein bars its own way."[54]

If we may draw upon an analogy with Spinoza's *Ethics*, we are not yet at Heidegger's equivalent of the fifth part of the *Ethics*, the doctrine of freedom. We are still in the middle of Part Four, where man's bondage is presented without as yet any hint of possible salvation.

It is Dasein in the dictatorship of the "they" that we have described above. The stress has been on the Being which is characteristic under such dominion. If the emphasis is shifted to another item, *Da*-sein, a phenomenon is uncovered which Heidegger calls Dasein's *Verfall* ("fall") into the world, its restless absorption in the world. By "Verfall" Heidegger comprehends the three items: idle talk *(Gerede)*, curiosity *(Neugier)*, and ambiguity *(Zweideutigkeit)*. Idle talk is speech in which neither speaker nor hearer stands in any

[51]*Ibid.*, p. 127 (165).
[52]*Ibid.*, p. 127 (165).
[53]*Ibid.*, p. 129 (167).
[54]*Ibid.*, p. 129 (167).

primordial or genuine relation to what they are talking about. It leads "publicness" to average understanding. "Idle talk is the possibility of understanding everything without previously making the thing one's own."[55] Constant curiosity is not research-mindedness or wonder, but a seeking for novelty without any genuine desire to understand it. We hurry on, or rather *it* hurries on, and the result is an absent-mindedness and a distraction that consolidates Being-with under the dictatorship of the "they." Such Being-with obscures the difference between genuine and false conversation, understanding and wonderment. The "they" does not know what is what, does not ask after it. Hence ambiguity.

Heidegger stresses that he doesn't mean anything disparaging by the term "Verfall." We are not to suppose that the "fall" of Dasein is in any way regrettable. It goes far too deeply into Dasein for that; it is not something of which, perhaps, "more advanced stages of human culture might be able to rid themselves."[56] The "they" may be thrown into the world more or less, but to be *capable* of falling is a form of Dasein's development, a specific feature of ex-sistence, in fact an existential. Only the "they" *are in a position* to fall.

The illusory understanding of everything, including the most diverse and alien cultures, inevitably leads to belief in a universal synthesis of cultures. But then it becomes indefinite what is to be understood, also what it *is* to understand. "Versatile curiosity," a restless "knowing it all," tranquillizes Dasein, which then, comparing itself with everything, "drifts along towards an alienation [*Entfremdung*]" which obscures another of its capacities, its capacity for authentic Being.[57]

Anxiety and its disclosure of the potentiality for authentic Being

There is a basic state of mind or, to use a less psychologically weighted term, *mood* which contrives to disclose us to our-

[55]*Ibid.*, p. 169 (213).
[56]*Ibid.*, p. 176 (220).
[57]*Ibid.*, p. 178 (222-23).

selves, to authentic Being. This basic mood is anxiety *(Angst)*. Anxiety discloses the freedom to choose and take hold of oneself. Anxiety confronts Dasein with its own freedom *(Freisein:* "Being-free"). Heidegger has a rather peculiar way of putting it: "Anxiety makes manifest in Dasein its *Being towards* its ownmost [*eigensten*] potentiality-for-Being —that is, its *Being-free for* the freedom of choosing itself and taking hold of itself *(die Freiheit des Sich-selbst-wählens und -ergreifens)*."[58]

No doubt it is possible to grasp a good deal of Heidegger's thought without any close study of his many special words and turns of phrase. Yet, to acquire any reasonably penetrating insight into his meaning, attention to his terminology, and, just as important, to the forms of expression he avoids, is essential. It becomes gradually clear that his highly idiosyncratic constructions have an inner regularity and formal consistency, and that this can, in fact, come to help one grasp the ontological project in all its width and depth. For example, in the passage quoted above the "that is" connective introduces a new series of terms which step by step lead us to purely ontological expressions within contexts which one might think ontology had nothing to do with. The odd construction "Being-towards" *(Sein zum)* Heidegger uses later for something central to his complex analysis of death: "Being towards death" *(Sein zum Tode)*.[59]

The essence of anxiety can best be brought out by a comparison with fear. When one is afraid, one fears something specific, but anxiety (of the kind here discussed) is not anxiety about some particular thing, something in the world, some "entity." When I am anxious, or have anxiety, the

[58]*Ibid.*, p. 188 (232).
[59]Two or more linked chains of expressions can be formed which express the ontologizing of the topics:
Mensch > Dasein
Substantialität > Seins als Vorhandensein
Anwesenheit > Sein als Anwesenheit
Eigene möglichkeit > eigenes Seinkönnen

world, indeed, is not relevant at all; it "has the character of completely lacking significance."[60] That which threatens me is so close that "it is oppressive and stifles one's breath, and yet it is nowhere."[61]

What is it about anxiety that makes it capable of leading man to self-understanding? And in the event of its doing so, to what kind of self-understanding does it lead him?

In anxiety all entities sink away into insignificance, into a "nothing and nowhere." The world has nothing more to give one. In anxiety, falling into the world and superficial understanding of oneself from the standpoint of the average are not possible. The natural Being-home in average everydayness is gone. Anxiety "brings [Dasein] back from its absorption in the 'world.' "[62] The basic mood is now one of not belonging at home anywhere or with anyone, of being "not-at-home." Thus anxiety brings uncanniness (*Unheimlichkeit*. Note here that Heidegger identifies *Unheimlichkeit* with *Un-zuhause:* "not-belonging-at-home-ness").

Anxiety causes entities, in their wholeness, to draw back, to slip away. Anxiety lets us hover in ourselves. Behind us there is—nothing. "Anxiety reveals nothingness."[63]

From this characterization of anxiety, or rather, of its func-

---

(Eigentliches Leben) > *eigentliche Existenz* > *eigentliches Sein*
(Subjekt in der Welt) > *In-der-Welt-sein*
Stimmung > *Befindlichkeit*
(Ich) > *Ich-sagen* > *das Seiende als Ich-bin-in-einer-Welt*
(Worum der Mensch sich ängstet) > *Worum die Angst sich abängstet*
The expressions in parentheses are those that one might have expected Heidegger to use, but which he only uses, if at all, in less significant contexts. The terminology of Being leads to complicated expressions: "Das Sein des Daseins besagt: Sich-vorweg-schon-sein-in-(der-Welt-) als Sein-bei (innerweltlich begegnendem Seienden)." The English translation goes: "The Being of Dasein means ahead-of-itself-Being-already-in-(the-world) as Being-alongside (entities encountered within-the-world)." *SuZ*, p. 192 (237).
[60]*Ibid.*, p. 186 (231).
[61]*Ibid.*, p. 186 (231).
[62]*Ibid.*, p. 189 (233).
[63]*WM*, p. 16.

tion, Heidegger proceeds now to take an astonishing step. Because everything that there is, ourselves included, slips away in anxiety, we have nothing to characterize as the object of our anxiety: "All that obtrudes is the world in its world-hood," not that which is within-the-world. So long as the whole thing is fresh in our memory, however, we may say: "it was really *nothing*."[64] But we are in fact giving a truer account than we imagine when we say that it was "*really* nothing." That in the face of which we were anxious was nothingness *(das Nichts)*. And yet it was the world itself—the "most primordial 'something'"—that slipped away into nothing. Thus it was the world-as-such in face of which we were anxious. However, the world, as we have been told, belongs essentially to Dasein's Being as Being-in-the-world. Therefore we can also say: "that in the face of which anxiety is anxious is Being-in-the-world itself."[65]

The falling and the subjection to the "they" can now be characterized as a fleeing from homelessness in anxiety, and as a fleeing into the safety and home-comfort that inauthenticity gives. But the flight cannot succeed altogether.

> Anxiety can arise in the most innocuous situations. Nor does it have any need for darkness, in which it is commonly easier for one to feel uncanny. In the dark there is emphatically 'nothing' to see, though the very world itself is *still* 'there,' and 'there' *more obtrusively*.[66]

Thus we are not completely protected against anxiety, however much we fall into the world. But anxiety, real anxiety, in the context of Being, is a comparatively rare phenomenon. Generally, therefore, the possibility of authentic Being is hidden from man's view.

If we may be allowed a brief "fall" from ontology into philosophy of life, we can draw a conclusion here: through

[64]*SuZ*, p. 187 (231).
[65]*Ibid.*, p. 187 (232).
[66]*Ibid.*, p. 189 (234).

anxiety we attain to a clarity in our own character as human essence. It is not in our power directly to regulate the supply of anxiety, but as Heidegger describes falling and subjection to the "they," the state must allow of a division into degrees such that the possibility of gradual anxiety is not precluded. In becoming free, the possibility of anxiety announcing itself as such increases, but also, its tendency to release the panicky fall back into inauthenticity decreases. In the main work, *Being and Time*, there is, of course, nothing directly stated either for or against such a "conclusion." The work lacks a "Part Five" which would correspond to Spinoza's "gospel" of freedom. In Heidegger's later writings, on the other hand, there are indications of a theory of freedom.

Being-towards-death

In his doctrine of the "they" Heidegger has made clear what Dasein is in its inauthenticity. But anxiety opens the door to an understanding of Dasein in its authenticity. What then does authenticity consist of? Unfortunately, Heidegger's portrayal of authenticity lacks the depth and concrete detail we find in his account of inauthenticity—bondage to the "they." The notion of authenticity, it appears, includes the possibility of wholeness: Dasein can be a whole. But nothing can be whole without finitude, thus there can be no existence without death. "The 'end' of Being-in-the-world is death."[67] Death limits and determines the individual's possible Dasein as a completed whole. Death has retro-active power: without it, there would be no understanding of life.

We cannot experience our own death, but we do experience the deaths of others. Since Dasein is Being-with-one-another, this is enough for drawing up an ontological demarcation of Dasein's wholeness. By the death of others, by the experience of the Other as a lifeless body, "we can experi-

[67]*Ibid.*, p. 234 (276-77).

ence that remarkable phenomenon of Being which may be defined as the change-over of an entity from Dasein's kind of Being (or life) to no-longer-Dasein. The *end* of the entity *qua* Dasein is the *beginning* of the same entity *qua* something present-at-hand."[68] Because even a dead body can be an object for the student of pathological anatomy and thereby an *object* for a science interested in life, it cannot be understood as just any kind of material body. The dead is phenomenologically something un-living; it is not just a material thing, but something that can *be thought* of as having lived.

We can experience the death of others, but not as a transition from Dasein to an "objective" just-present-at-hand-Being. (And yet surely it is precisely this transition which is what is fantastic, ungraspable, essential in *death*.) Death is essentially tied to the individual; it is in each case *my* death. Although others can "die for us," they cannot die our deaths for us. Our deaths cannot be delegated.

Death is unique, too, in that we cannot put it behind us, get it over and done with. It cannot be understood in the same way as a friend's arrival, or a thunderstorm.[69] Furthermore, it releases the individual from all else; with death all his relations with other things vanish.

From the pathological point of view we can learn about the processes of death, but Heidegger's concern is quite different: it is to find a suitable characterization of Dasein insofar as it is a Dasein-which-ends-with-death. Death, in this context, is not chronologically the last occurrence—indeed, it isn't even experienced; it is something about life—from birth on. Dasein is phenomenologically a Dasein-in-relation-to-death, a Being-towards-the-end *(Sein zum Ende)*, or Being-towards-Death *(Sein zum Tode)*. "Death is a way to be, which Dasein takes over as soon as it is. 'As soon as man comes to life, he is at once old enough to die.' "[70]

[68]*Ibid.*, p. 238 (281).
[69]*Ibid.*, p. 250 (294).
[70]*Ibid.*, p. 245 (289). The quotation is from *Der Ackermann aus Böhmen*.

The expression "Being-towards-death" is a perturbing one, and there does seem to be something macabre in characterizing death as a kind of property of our Dasein, as that which makes it a whole. But we must remember that Heidegger is committed by his program to describing the phenomena which occur immediately for the individual. It is only for *others* that one's own death is chronologically established as at the end of life; for oneself this "that-I-shall-die" must be a phenomenon that characterizes one's living, thus as something that comes before chronological death. In a phenomenological account the description in terms of existentials which Heidegger undertakes must precede, or be presupposed by, any other description or explanation of death—whether it be biological, psychological, theological, ethical, metaphysical, or whatever.

Dasein is from the very first moment "thrown into" the possibility of death. The notion can be trivialized, of course: as soon as one is born one may die. But it is only in anxiety that the possibility of death is disclosed to the individual; not in a sickly fear of dying through visualizing one's own death, but in anxiety, or better, openness in the face of one's own potentialities when confronted with something authentic, impassable, or relationless.[71] Since death partly determines what Dasein is, in anxiety it stands out as Dasein's possibility or Being-possible, and therefore as the very possibility of Being-in-the world.

In these and other expressions, the term "possible" is a rendering of Heidegger's "möglich." He plays on the "mögen" *(möglich, mögen-lich)* in the sense of "to be able," "to be in a position to" (cf. *ver-mögen*). "Possibilities" in this terminology refers to capacities for development, for potentialities considered as active things or forces. The possibility of death is Dasein's potentiality for being a whole.

---

[71]"In the face of" must be interpreted in some other way than as "for"; it is not analogous to the "of" in "fear of." Anxiety in the sense intended has no object analogous to that of fear, nor to that of anxiety "on behalf" of someone, or of anxiety "lest" something.

In fleeing from the authentic, in falling, Dasein draws a veil over death. It is "known" as a constantly occurring mishap. Someone or other "dies,"[72] we ourselves for the time being are spared—but then we die also. The most personal death, my own, becomes dissolved in the "they's" death, the death of no one in particular. One evades death, one turns away and hides from it. We are even told not to let ourselves be troubled by the thought of death. *The 'they' does not permit us the courage for anxiety in the face of death . . .* The "they" concerns itself with transforming this anxiety into fear in the face of an oncoming event."[73] Thus fear of death becomes branded as weakness and cowardice. And through the cultivation of a lofty indifference in the face of the fact that one shall die, Dasein is alienated *(entfremdet)* from its ownmost non-relational potentiality-for-Being.[74] We all know we will die; but precisely the fact that this is general knowledge reveals that death is grasped as the death of others, as an occurrence, and that the knowledge in question in no way involves the laying bare of phenomena, in no way involves the truth. It is *das Man*, the "they," who says that we know we shall die. It is idle talk *(Gerede)*.

So much for the inauthentic relationship to death, inauthentic Being-towards-death.

In authentic Being-towards-death the *possibility* of death must be grasped and upheld as such. There cannot, indeed, be any question of realizing death, nor of overcoming it through meditating on death as a fact. In authentic Being-towards-death it has to be kept in mind that the possibility of death is the possibility of the most authentic existence, the possibility of Dasein's being fully itself.

One might perhaps have hoped for a full and clear account of what this implies for men, for their attitudes to *life* and in life. But this would be to introduce other than purely

[72]*SuZ*, p. 252 (296).
[73]*Ibid.*, p. 254 (298).
[74]*Ibid.*, p. 254 (298).

ontological considerations. Heidegger does, however, provide some hints: openness in the face of the possibility of death makes the individual free and prepared to die: "One is liberated from one's lostness in those possibilities which may accidentally thrust themselves upon one."[75] It lays the self's task open to view and shatters all stagnation in a way of existence in which everything is achieved. Death hands over the individual to himself,[76] but in doing so also makes it possible for the individual to understand the "existence-possibilities" of others, to grasp their possibility for authentic existence.[77]

In these concluding remarks on authentic Being-towards-death, Heidegger seems, despite strong indications to the contrary, not actually to question Spinoza's dictum, "A free man thinks of death least of all things; and his wisdom is a meditation not of death but of life."[78] The later Heidegger, as we shall see, dispenses altogether with talk of anxiety and Being-towards-death. "Knowing joy" and "the final joy" take the place of anxiety. "Knowing joy *(Die wissende Heiterkeit)* is a door to the eternal."[79]

"Being and Time": The analysis of Time

A repeated fundamental analysis from the point of view of the phenomenon of time

We have followed Heidegger through his analyses of a series of phenomena belonging to Dasein, the kind of Being peculiar to man. In the case of each of these phenomena Heidegger

[75]*Ibid.*, p. 264 (308).
[76]*Ibid.*, p. 308 (356).
[77]*Ibid.*, p. 264 (308).
[78]Spinoza, *The Ethics*, Part Four, Proposition 67, in the translation by R. H. M. Elwes, *Works of Spinoza* (New York: Dover Publications, Inc., 1951), II, 232.
[79]*Der Feldweg* (2d ed.; Frankfurt am Main: V. Klostermann, 1956), p. 6.

introduced a distinction between what is fundamental to the kind of phenomenon, that is, inseparable and primordially bound to Dasein, and what *can* be and often does vary from one individual to another, as in the case of joy and sorrow, understanding and misunderstanding. The kinds of phenomenon which are bound to Dasein in the former way are "existentials," structural properties of the unity of Dasein.

The existential "state of mind," our being in some mood or other, underlies alternating sorrow and joy. A kind of primordial apprehension of our surroundings underlies both understanding and misunderstanding, and also total lack of understanding.

All this and much more is included in the first main section of *Being and Time*. The second, and last, section of the published work is entitled "Dasein und Zeitlichkeit" ("Dasein and Temporality"). In it, Heidegger goes through the whole series of phenomena once again, but on a deeper plane which takes account of the very meaning or essence of Dasein's way of Being. It is an attempt to understand our way of Being on the basis of that which ultimately makes it possible. Heidegger calls this basic factor "Temporality" *(Zeitlichkeit)*. It has some connection with what the "they" calls "time," and also with what scientists refer to as "time," but it is not at all the same. (However, where there is little danger of misunderstanding we shall prefer the term "time" to "temporality.")

The existential, fundamental analysis of Dasein in the light of Time is a more difficult task than the direct phenomenological analysis we have tried to outline in the foregoing. Since the main essentials of Heidegger's philosophy can be grasped from this latter analysis, the less tenacious reader may, without loss, skip the admittedly very cryptic remarks which follow.

Time as the meaning of Dasein's Being

Heidegger's temporal analysis begins with the question:

"What meaning has Dasein's form of Being?" or: "What is the meaning of care?" "We must take an undistracted look at [Dasein's primordial self-constancy and totality]," says Heidegger, "and understand it existentially if we are to lay bare the ontological meaning of Dasein's Being."[80] What makes this totality possible? The answer must be that Dasein is something that is directed not only to the future (death) but also to the past—as well as encompassing the present. In Dasein, all this is given in one: past, present, and future. But in that case the past must not be defined as something already departed, or the future as something not yet arrived. One must see how, in Dasein's care, the direction is inevitably forward, Dasein is "ahead of itself," but also backward, since Dasein is what it has become. From this primary existence in the future, against the background of Dasein's already having existed in a determinate way in the past, we come to its existence in the present. Future and past constitute, are structural properties of, the present; or: existence in the present is made possible on the basis of a primary existence, or Dasein, in the future and the past. There are three fundamental existentials in Dasein's care-structure which show this: namely understanding, state of mind, and falling.

Understanding is characterized by a forward direction in its projection *(Entwurf)* and is therefore primarily futural *(zukünftig)*. Understanding, on the other hand, always finds itself in a state of mind;[81] it flows from the state of mind which is characterized by its making known to Dasein that this is given and *has* to be, that is, Dasein's facticity *(Faktizität)* or thrownness *(Geworfenheit)* which in relation to all understanding is in the past. The state of mind makes known what Dasein has become as the basis of what it has been. It conveys a message about the "burden" that Dasein at each moment of time *already* has. State of mind is primarily

---

[80]*SuZ*, p. 323 (370).
[81]*Ibid.*, pp. 142-43 (181-82).

in the past. On the basis of the primarily future-oriented projection of understanding, and the primarily past-oriented state of mind, Dasein thus falls into a present "association" with things in the world, the understood. Falling is thus primarily present. Each of the three existentials necessarily implies the other two; or: the future implies the past and present, the past implies the future and present, and the present implies the future and past. Thus Heidegger can say: "The primordial unity of the structure of care lies in temporality."[82] Temporality underlies Dasein's care-structure; it is care's unitary *(einheitlich)* meaning.

This allows Heidegger to answer his own question. It is Temporality that is the meaning of Dasein's kind of Being. Or more summarily: Time is the meaning of Dasein's Being.[83]

Heidegger takes this to be the solution of his first main problem: factual existence's primordial wholeness is to be ontologically understood in terms of its basis, Temporality.[84] And the way is clear to press on toward the solution of the second problem—unsolved in *Being and Time*—of finding the meaning of Being in general.

The temporal character of the individual basic phenomena

The human self—what I am myself—can be understood neither as a kind of substance nor as a kind of subject. Heidegger is far from Descartes' "I think, therefore I am" and the Cartesian epistemological separation of the knowing subject from the object of knowledge. The entity that is

[82]*Ibid.*, p. 327 (375). The original is italicized.
[83]An illustration of the primariness of the future in regard to man's understanding is provided in Heidegger's rectorial address: "All science is committed to the beginning of philosophy (with the Greeks). . . . This beginning still continues. It does not lie behind us as something that has been long ago, it stands before us. The beginning has come into our future. . . ." "Die Selbsthauptung," p. 11. (See note 3 above).
[84]*SuZ*, pp. 436-37 (486-87).

myself has its center in the phenomenon of existence *(ex-sistere,* cf. pp. 188-89, above). I stand out from something; I am self-subsistent *(selbst-ständig),* but, of course, in-the-world *(in-der-Welt).* (Otherwise the "I" would be a substance, an entity on a footing with all other present-at-hand things.) In falling into the "they" I am on the way to becoming something only present at hand. Since ex-sistence and care are structurally identical, what has been said about care's temporality can be transferred to the self.

Temporality underlies the historicality *(Geschichtlichkeit)* of the self and existence.

Existence's temporality encompasses the future, the past, and the present. The present *(Gegen-wart),* the authentic *(eigent-lich),* is not to be confused with the *now (das Jetzt),* in the commonly shared, eternal time of everyday understanding. The real present, the present of existence, Heidegger calls the "moment of vision" *(Augenblick:* "glance of the eye").

> S. Kierkegaard is probably the one who has seen the *existentiell* phenomenon of the moment of vision with the most penetration; but this does not signify that he has been correspondingly successful in Interpreting it existentially. He clings to the ordinary conception of time, and defines the "moment of vision" with the help of "now" and "eternity."[85]

The aptness of this comment cannot be discussed here. It is one of the many places in *Being and Time,* and in Heidegger's later works, where he takes exception to views that don't strike him as ontologically essential. He can, in general, be said to interpret the term "existentialism" in an "existenziell" rather than an "existenzial" direction. The distinction expressed by these two German words can be stated roughly by saying that Heidegger sees existentialism as stressing particular subjective aspects of things, rather than the general ontological

[85]*Ibid.,* p. 338 n. (497).

features of Being as such. Later, we shall have an opportunity to take up Heidegger's reaction to existentialism when we discuss his letter on humanism.

Toward the end of *Being and Time* Heidegger gives an analysis in terms of temporal understanding, of state of mind, falling, idle talk, Being-in-the-world, science (as a way of existence and a mode of Being-in-the-world), space (Dasein's making room for itself), and much else. In this concluding section Heidegger emerges as a systematizer. Here for the first time one can trace the beginnings of the construction of a system which tries to comprise a whole set of approaches to traditional philosophical problems. But not least because of the obscurity of the concept of temporality itself, the whole system is hard to grasp. However, the work is not an attempt to give conclusive results. Even if the style is dogmatic, Heidegger asserts repeatedly that his primary aim is to open and reopen discussion on the fundamental questions which lie behind the prima facie obviousness of everyday life, and, by the same token, behind the conceptual structure of science. He wants to demonstrate the value of asking these questions, their *Frag-würdigkeit*. These analyses are undoubtedly an intensive attempt to find some transition from the conclusion about the meaning of Dasein's Being to the answer to the book's main question about the meaning of Being in general. Characteristically, Heidegger concludes his first main work with a question: "Is time Being itself?" This question is not directly answered in his later philosophy.

Science and nothingness

The objectivity of science

Heidegger's inaugural lecture as professor at the University of Freiburg in 1929 was entitled "What is Metaphysics?" Its importance lies not least in its indication of the place of science in human existence. "Our Dasein—in the community of research workers, teachers, and students—is determined through science," says Heidegger, and so he asks: "What happens to us, essentially, in the core of our Dasein insofar as science has become our passion?"[86] The question is a topical one. "The rooting of the sciences in the basis of their being" has become "extinct."[87] The rebirth will come about when the scientist takes nothingness (*das Nichts*, also sometimes rendered here as "the nothing") seriously.[88] Heidegger elaborates on this startling message. But first we must be clearer what he means by nothingness, or the nothing, and here we are best advised to turn to his remarks on the limits of science.

Common to the most diverse sciences is one thing: "In all sciences we comport ourselves, following their inmost tendency, towards entities *(Seiende)* themselves. Seen from the point of view of the sciences, no field has preference over another, neither nature over history nor vice versa. No one kind of treatment of the objects is superior to the others." "In the sciences there is accomplished—according to this view—a coming-near-to the essentials of all entities."[89]

Anxiety and nothingness

The entity itself is what the scientist pries into, "the thing

[86]*WM*, p. 7.
[87]*Ibid.*, p. 8.
[88]*Ibid.*, p. 25. The first part of the sentence is interpretation.
[89]*Ibid.*, p. 8. The two quotations can be cited in support of a rare tolerance (in choice of topic and method) which is essential for the survival of the "joy" of research. We need to understand widely different studies *qua* studies. Yet the researcher himself usually sets rigorous limits to what is "worth" studying. And in choice of *methods* there is perhaps even less tolerance: induction is scorned, mathematics suspected, botanizing, bird watching, and other delightful aspects of the nature-lover's researches ridiculed as bordering on mere collecting. We often disguise our intolerance by such expressions as "Man is the proper study of man" or in sentiments favoring natural science. All of which betrays little understanding for, or preoccupation with, the fact *that* something is, and with the "miraculous" in every thing in itself.

itself" is given the first and last word. Such an objectivity means a "subjection to entities themselves."[90] But precisely when the scientist really plays his own game, precisely when he ensures his "ownmost," he speaks about something *else*. "Only entities are to be explored and besides that—nothing; entities alone and further—nothing; entities alone and beyond that—nothing."[91] But, asks Heidegger: How about this nothing? *(Wie steht es um das Nichts?)*

So long as it aims at an answer of the type: The nothing *(das Nichts) is* so and so, it goes so and so with *it*, the question is meaningless *(widersinning:* "nonsense"). The nothing just isn't an entity, something that one may come across; it is no kind of object. Any answer that claims to identify or specify the nothing will contain contradictions, and thus the nothing must be excluded from the orbit of the thinkable, which is made up precisely of *possible* objects.[92]

However, there is a basic human mood—a mood of Dasein—which reveals the nothing directly, namely anxiety. Thus revealed, however, the nothing does not appear as something that we can *think*. Because we cannot conceive the nothing as some entity, we should not attempt to formulate propositions about it as an object of thought.

Anxiety, as we mentioned earlier, is a mood that differs essentially from fear; fear is *of* something, but anxiety (in this sense) is in principle not anxiety *about* anything. Indeed it is not even *we* who *have* anxiety.

The further characterization of anxiety and the nothing must be left to Heidegger. We can only mark his words as best we can; "translation" is out of the question.

In anxiety, what-is *(das Seiende)* slips away into the nothing which is, in its essence, opposing, banishing. The nothing's

[90]*WM*, p. 8.
[91]*Ibid.*, p. 9.
[92]*Ibid.*, p. 11. ". . . thought—essentially always thought *of something*." The thinking here is traditional (metaphysical and formal logical) thinking. In order to think nothingness, or, which comes to the same, Being, another way of thinking is required ("Andenken").

essence is making-nothing *(Nichtung)* (alternative expressions: "to nothing," "to not," "to nihilate," "to make nought"), rather than annihilating *(Vernichtung)*, and rather than negating *(Verneinung)*. *The nothing makes itself nothing.* Thus the nothing is the condition of the what-is revealing itself as such, that is, precisely of the *what-is* being and not the nothing.

> In the bright night of nothingness, revealed in anxiety, arises first the primordial openness of things as such: that they are things and not nothing.[93]

This openness alone is what makes it possible for the what-is as a whole—including man—to be revealed to the specifically human kind of Being. *Da-sein* means: the to-be-held-ness into (in) nothing.[94] Thus the nothing doesn't afford us the opposite concept to the what-is; the nothing has no separate existence, it belongs to the essence of Being itself *(zum Wesen des Seins selbst)*.

The primordial anxiety can awaken at any moment in our existence, there is no need of any *unusual* circumstance, anxiety is constantly poised to spring.

Man impinges upon what-is insofar as he holds himself into the nothing. This belongs to the essence of Dasein, and *is itself metaphysics*. Metaphysics then belongs to "human nature," and its basic question—which the nothing itself provokes —goes: How is there anything at all and not rather nothing?

After this account Heidegger returns to his characterization of the role of the scientist.

Wonder and the nothing

What he has just said about anxiety and nothingness, according to Heidegger, allows us to see how our existence has been put into the hands of the *scientist:* Only because the nothing

[93]*WM,* p. 19.
[94]*Ibid.,* p. 19.

discloses itself can the strangeness of entities strike us and awaken *wonder*. From this springs the "why?" and only because this "why" is possible can we ask about reasons. And because we can ask about and give reasons, our existence, our souls, are in the hands of the scientist.[95]

One wonders how all this was understood by the students, teachers, and scientists who were present at this inaugural lecture. Heidegger's words seem capable of giving rise to quite diverse impressions. They may have brought home to his hearers the seriousness of scientific engagement and the absoluteness of its basic demand for objectivity; or they may have suggested the debasement of science when the scientist—through not having relived the mood of anxiety—has no living contrast in himself, between what-is (seen as a whole) and nothing. For only then can what-is generate that deep wonder which anchors science in the essence of man.

One should add that the scientific research to which Heidegger so unreservedly ascribes a central place in human existence is one which is ultimately anchored in philosophy. To chemistry or physics as *isolated* sciences he attaches no such significance. Indeed, in later writings he has spoken of the great danger for man implicit in a science dissociated from philosophy.

It is not only the research scientist who is led on by wonder and amazement; these also direct and set their seal upon the philosopher's—the Heideggerian philosopher's—every step.

Poetry and philosophy, not science, have access to the nothing

When Heidegger introduced his students to metaphysics in the summer semester of 1935, he dwelt at length on the following question, especially on its second half. "Why is there anything at all, rather than nothing?"

[95]*Ibid.*, p. 26.

In this translation it is possible that essential points in the philosophy of nothing get lost; so let us start off with a more faithful rendering: "Why are there entities at all and not rather nothing?" *(Warum ist überhaupt Seiendes und nicht vielmehr Nichts?)*

For an answer, Heidegger gives an example but adds strong qualifications. These should not lead us to suppose, however, that the answer may be false; only that the person giving the "answer" cannot have posed the question in an authentic way. Thus the example can also throw light on the important term "authentic": if a question is not posed authentically its answer cannot be authentic either.

> Anyone for whom the Bible is divine revelation and truth has the answer to the question "Why are there entities and not rather nothing?" even before it is asked: everything that is, except God himself, has been created by Him. God himself, the uncreated creator, "is." One who holds to such faith can in a way participate in the asking of our question, but he cannot really question without ceasing to be a believer and taking all the consequences of such a step. He will only be able to act "as if" . . . .[96]

In asking why a specific entity *is*, some maggot, say, that ruins the grapevines, one's attention immediately transfers to some other entity. One's thinking remains in the circuit of entities. But if one asks about entities *tout court*, contrasted to nothing, the question acquires quite another force and depth. Such force and depth as to transform it into a question about "a ground . . . which will explain the emergence of things as an overcoming of nothingness."[97] Our questioning begins to float in space; it seems to have no firm basis.

---

[96]*Einführung in die Metaphysik* (henceforth referred to as *EM*), p. 5. (2d ed.; Tübingen: Max Niemeyer, 1958). Quotations are taken, with slight alterations, from the English translation (see note 7), Anchor Book edition, p. 6.
[97]*Ibid.*, p. 22 (23).

As we have seen, it is in anxiety and when Dasein is in various other ways appropriately attuned that "the nothing reveals itself."

The question is the basic one of metaphysics and takes us into questions about Being. The metaphysician's themes first define themselves when the basic question is elaborated in sufficient detail.

According to Heidegger's definition, fundamental ontological thought and description differ from scientific thought and description, and it would be unfortunate to make science the measure of the requirements of rigor for all thinking. Phenomenological description and scientific description range over different fields. Phenomenological descriptions rank higher; they belong together with poetry. In both it is, as one says, "as if it was the first time the what-is became expressed and evoked."[98]

A true account of the nothing is not the business of science, but of the (fundamental) phenomenologist and the poet.

Heidegger finds support in a quotation from Hamsun. It is said of the solitary aged August in *The Road Leads On (Men Livet lever):*

> Here [in the high mountains looking out over the sea] he sits between his ears and all he hears is emptiness. An amusing conception indeed. On the sea there were both motion and sound, something for the ear to feed upon, a chorus of waters. Here nothingness meets nothingness and the result is zero, not even a hole. Enough to make one shake one's head, utterly at a loss.[99]

"In principle, nothingness remains inaccessible to science,"[100] says Heidegger, and means here, as in the passages above and

[98]*Ibid.*, p. 20 (22).
[99]Knut Hamsun, *Men Livet lever* (Oslo: Gyldendal, 1933), pp. 274-75. English translation by Eugene Gay-Tifft, *The Road Leads On* (New York: Coward McCann, 1934), p. 508. Quoted (in German) by Heidegger in *EM*, pp. 20-21; p. 22 in the English translation.
[100]*EM*, p. 19 (21).

often elsewhere, the abstract and theoretical sciences. About nothingness phenomenology makes clear, for example, that it reveals itself in anxiety. Phenomenology can also be said to contribute to a *description* of what it is that is then revealed, besides merely associating the word "anxiety" with what is revealed.

Insofar as the nothing is disclosed it is a "phenomenon" in the first of the senses of the word Heidegger has announced he will use in his text. In this sense a phenomenon is something which shows-itself-by-itself. Here, therefore, the phenomenological description (by definition) leads to no abstract or hypothetical scientific theorems.

When Heidegger talks of "logic" and its limits he means to include in it Aristotle's law of contradiction. Heidegger interprets this within the frame of his own philosophy as a proposition about something essential to what-is as such: that "every absence *(Abwesen)* remains alien to a presence *(Anwesen)* because it plucks away presence in its un-essence. It brings capriciousness and thereby destroys the essence of Being."[101] The law of contradiction says about entities as such (what-is): the essence of what-is consists in the continual absence of contradiction. Aristotle, however, according to Heidegger, found it unnecessary to consider further the presuppositions of the law. Heidegger's position is at least intelligible here, on the basis of the foregoing—so we may all draw our own conclusions about it on the basis of our own presuppositions. About nothingness the law of contradiction says nothing. On the contrary, nothingness says something about the law; that is, the phenomenon of nothingness lies at the basis of *there being* anything, of the disclosure of the Being or essence of what-is. Insofar as this is so, the Being or essence of entities, of what-is, implies the phenomenon of nothingness (cf. pp. 220 ff., above). And nothingness makes out for us the individual entities about which the law of

---

[101]*Nietzsche*, I, 602. Cf. the discussion in the following passages.

contradiction in traditional logic is valid. Thus, the mutual implication of Being and nothingness lies at the very foundation of our making out, identifying, what-is and hence of the validity and scope of the law of contradiction. To put it in another way: the condition for one's not being able to say of an entity both that it is and that it is not (in the same respect) is that the Being, or essence of the entity is as well as is not![102]

The philosophy of nothingness and gnosis

In order to appreciate better the force of the Heideggerian terminology we may profitably have recourse to accounts of mythical and quasi-philosophical speculations in which some of the central expressions in "the philosophy of nothingness" occur. Many central expressions in technical philosophical terminology have their origins in pre-philosophical or non-philosophical symbols and ideas, and even if the connections

[102]Although this rendering of Heidegger's assumptions is somewhat free, the reasoning does seem to be tenable. If so, one could allow that Heidegger's later thinking, thought-about-Being, is able to operate in a field where the law of contradiction in a *positive* sense can be dispensed with. But to accept this we must first, of course, accept his assumptions, and accordingly accept that what Heidegger understands as the Being or essence of things is accessible through the experience of the nothing. The following would have to be meaningful statements: "The nothing is (in the same respect and at the same time) not-nothing," "Being (in the same respect and at the same time) is not-Being or nothing," which according to Heidegger is not only possible but correct. If one denies that these statements are meaningful, it is difficult to see how one could hold that there are still areas of thought in which the law of contradiction does not apply. My own view is that the paradoxical character of "Being" and "Nothing" in Heidegger can be resolved without doing violence to anything essential in his position. In accepting "Nothing is, with reference to A, not-nothing" and "Being is, with reference to B, not-Being or nothing," I would try to formulate A and B on the basis of certain points of view according to which Nothing is not-Nothing and Being is not-Being. The law of contradiction would not then be affected.

have, in time, worn thin, the study of them gives access to a kind of insight which can do much to enrich one's understanding of the basic intuitions of contemporary professional philosophy.

"Gnosis" is a label connected with a wealth of mythical, quasi-philosophical speculations and practices which infiltrated into Hellenic culture from the East in the first century of the Christian Era.[103] The concern of gnosticism is primarily with soteriological and eschatological matters. St. John the Evangelist is regarded as being influenced by gnostic ideas. Characteristic of these ideas is a sharp division between God and the world. The world is God's enemy. (In one place the creator is spoken of as a repentant.) The cosmos is the kingdom of darkness, which is itself an active force hostile to light. In the past, the primal, godly man fell and became a slave both in and of the world. In the future, man's authentic soul will rise up and in its ascent move through countless hostile spheres up into the unworldly light.

In Mandaean[104] literature, some of it gnostic, one can find a striking, not to say amazing, wealth of "Heideggerian" words and turns of phrase. We hear for example, of the authentic life living as a stranger in the world which thereby acquires the character of "the alien." Life's way is in the world, through the world, and eventually out of it. Mandaean writings open with the formula: "In the name of the great, first alien life from the light worlds, in (the name of) the sublime, which stands over all created things." The beyond is

---

[103]"Soteriology" is the doctrine of salvation. "Eschatology" is the doctrine of the ultimate things (e.g., death, judgment, state after death). Cf. Hans Jonas, *Gnosis und spätantiker Geist*, Vol. I, *Gnosis* (Göttingen: Vandenhoed & Ruprecht, 1954), p. 5. The following exposition is mainly taken from this work. Jonas plainly knows his Heidegger, but he seems to imbed him in an interpretation of gnostic literature, not so very implausibly perhaps. Cf. Ingvar Horgby, "The Double Awareness in Heidegger and Wittgenstein," *Inquiry*, II (1959), No. 4, 235 ff.

[104]The Mandaeans are an ancient sect, still surviving, of southern Babylonia. Their religion is a form of gnosticism.

not heaven, but something as much beyond heaven as beyond earth, *outside* everything that is. Hence all that is becomes no longer *all*, there is something, life, which sets limits to that which is. In space—a demonic power—the soul is imprisoned and tries to escape. "With no way out [the accursed, unsaved soul] roams around in the labyrinth it has come into, full of pain."[105] "Who has cast me into the world's torment? . . . Why have you made this world?"[106] A transitional symbol here is "being thrown into." "Ptahil [the demiurge] threw the mold, which the other [in life's kingdom] had formed, into the world of darkness."[107] The altogether unmythological concept of 'thrownness' *(Geworfenheit)*, according to Hans Jonas, is a "last, secularised resumption of a theological tradition originating from that epoch."[108]

Being and Time came into existence in the years 1917-27. It is hard to say how deeply Heidegger's own theological career and the exigencies of the time, which were accentuated to an unparalleled degree in Germany, influenced the terminology in his philosophy of nothingness. But however profound the influence, it is already apparent from the main drift of *Being and Time*, and altogether clear from Heidegger's later thinking, that it can provide no more than background illumination to his philosophical intentions. For those who have not undergone a period of study in theology and the history of religion, however, this kind of illumination may be very welcome.

Truth and dis-covery

The concept of truth

In Heidegger's view, since the time of Plato and Aristotle, Western man has stagnated in a misconception of truth, in a

---

[105]Jonas, *Gnosis und spätantiker Geist*, I, 99.
[106]*Ibid.*, p. 102.
[107]*Ibid.*, p. 106.
[108]*Ibid.*, p. 104.

misunderstanding both of truth's essence and of the phenomenon itself. This has not only put philosophers on the wrong track, it has ground such deep ruts into the course of man's history that his very future is at stake.

Truth is said, traditionally, to consist in an agreement between a statement and its object. But what significance have *statements* in this connection, and *in what* does the relationship of agreement *consist?* There are indeed many ways in which one thing can be in agreement or disagreement with another. A necessary condition for following Heidegger here in his search for an answer is to compare his abstract remarks with his own examples. Concentrated absorption is essential if one is to even so much as *raise* the problem of truth which the "correspondence theory" must solve if it is to be tenable. The following is a simplified rendering of one of Heidegger's (few) examples.

With my back turned to the wall I utter the true assertion *(Aussage)*[109] "The picture on the wall is hanging askew." Upon turning round I confirm the assertion. As a true assertion, it has a certain relation to something—but to what? To a psychical representation, an inner mental picture of the picture on the wall? No, to the slanting picture itself. The confirmation of my statement takes place somehow "on" the picture. What was asserted shows itself as it is: the picture is seen to be askew. That, "phenomenologically," is what we find in the confirmation of the truth of the assertion. There is no mental picture in my head which I can then compare with the picture on the wall to establish whether there is a correspondence (in a not at all easily grasped sense of "correspondence"). That the assertion is true means that it *uncovers* the

---

[109]Heidegger gives three senses of "assertion," which together, he says, "encompass the full structure of assertion" (*SuZ*, pp. 154-55 [196-97]). The three senses are 'pointing out' *(Aufziegen)*, 'predicating,' and 'communicating' *(Mitteilung)* or 'speaking forth' *(Heraussage)*. For remarks on the traditional notion of truth, see *SuZ*, pp. 217-18 (259-61).

entity, an occurrence that takes place *at* the entity. The assertion allows the entity to be seen in its uncoveredness. " 'Being-true' ('truth') means Being-uncovering."[110]

The example illustrates, among other things, Heidegger's appeal to our understanding of the phenomenon of recognition showing itself as true. The confirmation "takes place somehow" on "the picture itself." The role of the assertion in this process is thus a comparatively modest one; as a self-sufficient object or entity, an assertion itself is scarcely able to be uncovering, be true. If we are to retain the idea of an assertion's truth, therefore, it will not be in the sense of "assertion" which we find in formal logic.

At this point we must say a little about Heidegger's theory of the origin of the function of the assertion. Originally the assertion has served "the understanding interpretation" *(die verstehende Auslegung)*. If I say: "The hammer is too heavy," traditional logic's analysis of the assertion to the effect that a hammer-thing is attributed a property 'too heavy,' is not the primary one. Preceding it is something that can occur without words: for instance, exchanging one hammer for another which is lighter. Or saying simply: "too heavy." Linguistic articulation, however, is not a general presupposition of understanding interpretation.

A hammer is basically something I do something with, something which I concern myself with in connection with what I am doing. It is only by a very special kind of reflection that we distinguish between 'Hammer without reference to what I need it for' and 'property of being heavy.' Such an analysis results in seeing the hammer *as (als)* an object with a property, and in the construction of assertions which say (in their function of stating) that the object has the property. Heidegger calls this 'as' the assertion's "apophantical 'as' " and opposes it to *the understanding interpretation's 'as,'* which he calls the "existential-hermeneutical 'as' " ("hermeneutical,"

---

[110]*Ibid.*, p. 219 (262).

from the Greek work ἑρμενεία which Heidegger translates as "*Auslegung*," "interpretation").[111] In the understanding interpretation the-too-heavy-hammer appears as a phenomenon, not as an object-plus-property. The function of the assertion, from the ontological point of view, originates in the understanding interpretation, that is in something that fundamentally characterizes Dasein.

If one continues to see the function of the assertion in the light of "the understanding interpretation's 'as,' " it becomes easier to take seriously the conception of the relation between assertion and object which is illustrated in the slanting picture example. It points out the entity (the-crooked-picture-on-the-wall) in its uncoveredness. Even without expressing anything, I myself (as Dasein) could perform the function of uncovering, but the assertion in many cases makes the uncovering easier, and it has, besides, the practical function of announcing the performance.

Heidegger thus identifies what makes an assertion a true assertion with a function, the function of uncovering. " 'Being-true' ('truth') means Being-uncovering." But doesn't this mean that Heidegger in effect abandons the philosophical tradition and makes his own concept of truth? On the contrary, he thinks: the identification implies that we return to an original concept of truth, one which can still be found in Plato and Aristotle. Before letting Heidegger speak in defense of his own view we should mention that the Greek word for "true," ἀληθής, can be considered a translation of ἀ and ληθή, "hidden away," "covered up" (the verbal stem λαθ: to escape notice," "to be concealed"). The prefix "ἀ" is translated as "not" or "un-," whence a possible sense of ἀληθής: "revealed," "un-covered."

> "Being-true" ("truth") means Being-uncovering *(entdeck-end-sein)*. But is not this a highly arbitrary way to define "truth"? By such drastic ways of defining this concept we

[111]*Ibid.*, p. 158 (201).

may succeed in eliminating the idea of agreement [or correspondence] from the conception of truth. Must we not pay for this dubious gain *(Gewinn)* by plunging the 'good' old tradition into nullity? But while our definition is seemingly *arbitrary*, it contains only the *necessary* Interpretation of what was primordially surmised in the *oldest* tradition of ancient philosophy and even understood in a pre-phenomenological manner. If a λόγος (assertion) as ἀπόφανσις is to be true, its Being-true is ἀληθεύειν in the manner of ἀποφαίνεσθαι—of taking entities out of their hiddenness *(Verborgenheit)* and letting them be seen in their unhiddenness (their uncoveredness).[112]

Heidegger assumes that his definition of "Being-true" as "Being-uncovering" renders so adequately the sense of the Greek word traditionally translated as "truth" that he does not hesitate to use his definition in translating from the Greek. In Plato's allegory of the Cave we have read about the man dragged out into the sunlight, whose eyes are so filled with the glare that he is unable "to see a single one of the objects we now call true."[113] But Heidegger does not use this traditional rendering; he says that the man is not able to see "that which is now opened up to him as the uncovered *(Unverborgene)*."[114] Heidegger's definition presents the whole allegory, at least for us, in a new light.

To *be*-uncovering is a kind of Being which is characteristic of Dasein. It depends on a kind of openness which itself forms Dasein's basis and is constituted by "state of mind," "understanding," and "discourse" (cf. p. 198). Heidegger thinks that since Dasein's openness makes possible the phenomenon of

---

[112]*Ibid.*, p. 219 (262). ἀπόφανσις and ἀποφαίνεσθαι have the same root; the first is a substantive which nevertheless expresses a process (something that occurs in time), the second is an infinitive form.

[113]*The Republic*, Book VII, 515-16. Translated by A. D. Lindsay (rev. ed.; London: J. M. Dent & Sons, 1923), pp. 236-37.

[114]*P-H*, p. 13.

uncovering, it is itself the most original, the primordial, truth-phenomenon.[115]

Perhaps we could summarize some of the most important points of Heidegger's theory of truth in the following way.

Traditionally truth is a property of assertions, and what is true is that which corresponds with reality. In order to see the truth-phenomenon correctly, however, we must get away from this idea of correspondence or agreement. This notion is in fact not a primary one at all in the Greek, and consequently also in the Western word for truth, ἀλήθεια. "The 'Being-true' of the λόγος as ἀληθεύειν means that in λέγειν as ἀποφαίνεσθαι the entities *of which* one is talking must be taken out of their hiddenness *(Verborgenheit)*."[116]

True discourse (λόγος) uncovers *(entdeckt)* these entities and thus lets them be seen as something no longer escaping notice (ἀ-λήθης). The word for untrue, false discourse, ψεύδεσθαι, contains the notion of covering over, concealing, hiding from view: "putting something in front of something (in such a way as to let it be seen) and thereby passing it off *as* something which it is *not*."[117]

A true assertion is thus one which lets us see the matter it is about, which thus, so to say, pre-sents the matter for inspection. It is not necessary that the assertion in order to achieve this should have a kind of content which comprehends, or is in agreement with, the matter the assertion brings to light. It is enough to have an "unambiguous relation": to any unambiguous assertion there must correspond a function of discovering a certain discoverable, and conversely.

Therefore, what is primary in ἀλήθεια , thus also in the concept of truth adequately determined, is (1) a *transition* from being covered-up to being uncovered, and (2) the property of immediate accessibility in that which is uncovered. Even Kant's Copernican revolution wasn't so comprehensive

[115]*SuZ,* p. 220 (262-63).
[116]*Ibid.,* p. 33 (56).
[117]*Ibid.,* p. 33 (57).

as to dislodge the correspondence theory, as neo-Kantians have sometimes thought. Heidegger quotes from the *Critique of Pure Reason* something in Kant's characteristic style:

> Truth and illusion *(schein)* are not in the object so far as it is intuited, but in the judgment about it so far as it is thought.[118]

And truth "is in the judgment" in the way that the knowledge it expresses "is in agreement with its object."

Nietzsche also failed to take up the questions which must be raised if the correspondence theory is to be put on trial. In particular, he neglected the question of the essence of truth, an omission "repeated since Plato and Aristotle" and "generally in the whole of the history of Western philosophy."[119]

Sheer sensory perception (αἴσθησις) gives a more original form of truth than assertion. Seeing, for example, always discovers colors, the visual experiences of color are always true. This simple, direct perception, the pure νοεῖν, can *only* discover, it *cannot* cover; it can never be false.[120] (This relation is used by Heidegger in his interpretation of Parmenides. See pp. 255 ff. below.)

To find a truth, in this view, is definitely an act of some kind, but an act that is in a certain sense completely passive or ancillary in its relation to what is: to find a truth means to *come upon* a discourse which quite simply *lets us* see something. "The curtain goes up", and when it has gone up there is nothing more to say.

The analogy to the later Wittgenstein's disclosure of the obvious is striking. The idea is to put oneself into a position where something *shows itself*. All disquieting questions then disappear, there is no further philosophizing to do. Language gives no picture of reality. No purpose is served by duplication.

[118]From *Critique of Pure Reason*, p. 350. Quoted in *ibid.*, p. 215 (258).
[119]*Nietzsche*, I, 511.
[120]*SuZ*, p. 33 (57).

Man, language, and truth

What can uncover? Or, in the terminology of Being: What can *be* uncovering? Only something which has the form of Being which is Da-sein (there-being), being-present, being-in-the-world. Dasein is thus the basis of the phenomenon of truth; it is what makes truth at all possible ontologically.

This puts man in a special position with regard to the truth, for (so far as one knows) only man has Dasein and without Dasein there is no truth. "Dasein expresses itself *(spricht sich aus)*: it expresses *itself* as a Being-towards entities—a Being-towards which uncovers. And in assertion it expresses itself as such about entities which have been uncovered."[121]

In his later writings Heidegger gives language an ever more central place. Language is not to be considered a servant of man, owned by him, his own means of expression; man *serves* language which is itself owned—if it is owned at all—by Being. But more about this later in a rather different connection.

True discourse is that which takes the entities of which one is talking out of their hiddenness. Dasein alone can talk in such a way, and the only entity whose Being is Dasein is man. We must say, therefore, that Newton's law of gravitation *became true* (if it ever has been true) when a certain entity whose kind of Being was Dasein, the flesh-and-blood Isaac Newton said

$$G = k \; \frac{m_1 . m_2}{r^2}$$

(or something similar) and thereby uncovered and laid bare a state of affairs or rather, matter that had hitherto been concealed: namely, that of which one is talking. And when or if

$$G = k \; \frac{m_1 . m_2}{r^2}$$

ceases to be uncovering in this way, the assertion ceases to be true, if, for example, there were no longer any human beings (or none who are interested in gravitation?).

---

[121]*Ibid.*, pp. 223-24 (266).

Another possibility is that

$$G = k \; \frac{m_1 \cdot m_2}{r^2}$$

may become untrue, false. It masquerades as something uncovered, but is only a cover, "putting something in front of something . . . and thereby passing it off as something which it is not."

Do these consequences not follow from Heidegger's account of the relativity or subjectivity of truth? Does it not drive us directly into epistemological idealism—into the making and unmaking of truth by man?

> Newton's laws, the principle of contradiction, any truth whatever—these are true only as long as Dasein *is*. Before there was any Dasein, there was no truth; nor will there be any after Dasein is no more. For in such a case truth as disclosedness, uncovering, and uncoveredness, *cannot* be. Before Newton's laws were discovered, they were . . . neither true nor false. [But this] cannot signify that before him there were no such entities as having been uncovered and pointed out by those laws. Through Newton the laws became true; and with them, entities became accessible in themselves to Dasein . . . .
>
> That there are "eternal truths" will not be adequately proved until someone has succeeded in demonstrating that Dasein has been and will be for all eternity. As long as such a proof is still outstanding, this principle remains a fanciful contention . . . .[122]

To be true is to be uncovering, consequently truth is a kind of Being, a kind of Being which in its essence is "relative" to Dasein. But Dasein cannot, of course, have any influence on how much my assertion uncovers and lays bare the *entity* of which I am talking.

So much for the defense of the uncovering theory of truth.

[122]*Ibid.*, pp. 226-27 (269-70).

Heidegger, however, is seldom content merely to defend a possible or actually made objection.

It is just *because* truth as uncovering is a *Dasein's way of Being* that it cannot be a matter of Dasein's making or unmaking. Truth is not at the discretion of Dasein. Even the universal validity of propositional truth is based solely in the fact that Dasein can uncover entities in themselves and free them.

Uncovering occurs, in other words, "at" that which is uncovered—as in the unveiling of a statue; but while to unveil a particular statue any particular piece of cloth will do, it seems that to uncover a particular entity one needs a definite, specific assertion. It is this that makes it impossible for Dasein to alter the truth at its own discretion. The uncovering "binds" it to every possible assertion: only *one* becomes true and remains true.

But not only does the theory of truth as disclosure give the only possible basis for establishing the universal validity of truth; it also gives the only possible basis for a consistent refutation of scepticism, or rather, for the banishment of scepticism from the orbit of the possible and intelligible. For from the above it follows further that where there is Dasein, there—in principle—there is truth, since the uncovering kind of Being is precisely Dasein's way of Being, and therefore to say "truth cannot be given" amounts to an attempt at suicide, a renunciation of Dasein as one's kind of Being. (But how could one then speak and say that there can be no truth?)

To believe in the possibility of truth is a spurious act of faith, and to postulate truth as a "presupposition" a totally redundant performance.

> *Why must we presuppose that there is truth?* What is 'presupposing'? What do we have in mind with the 'must' and the 'we'? What does it mean to say 'there is truth'? 'We' presuppose truth because 'we', being in the kind of Being which Dasein possesses *are* 'in the truth'.

We do not presuppose it as something 'outside' us and 'above' us, towards which, along with other 'values', we comport ourselves. It is not we who presuppose 'truth'; but it is *'truth'* that makes it at all possible ontologically for us to be able to *be* such that we 'presuppose' anything at all. Truth is what first *makes possible* anything like presupposing.[123]

The "turning around" *(Die Kehre)* in Heidegger's thinking after *Being and Time* is generally assumed to have been first expressed in a specific section (pp. 14-17 of the fourth edition) in the repeatedly revised *(überprüfte)* lecture "On the Nature of Truth" *(Vom Wesen der Wahrheit)*. Heidegger has himself intimated in a note in the second edition of the lecture that the turning point occurs here.[124] The section is headed "On the Essence of Freedom."

Earlier in the lecture Heidegger has repeated the *Being and Time* motif that what underlies the possibility of assertions that conform *(sich richtet)* to the object and hence allow for the possibility of truth as exactitude or correctness *(Richtigkeit)* is that Dasein offers itself freely to be bound by correctness. Not only does such Being-free for the revealing of the open *(das offene)* make truth possible; Heidegger is also able, provisionally, to conclude: "Truth's essence is Freedom."[125]

But now in the section on "The Essence of Freedom" a new key term is introduced, "letting-be": freedom to disclose the truth consists in letting each entity be the entity it is. But not with indifference; on the contrary: "This letting-be, that is freedom, is in itself ex-posure, ex-sisting."[126] Existence has its roots in truth as freedom, and freedom as letting-be.

Man "does not possess the property of Being-free; rather the

[123]*Ibid.*, pp. 227-28 (270).
[124]The note appears in the second edition, 1949.
[125]*WW*, p. 12.
[126]*Ibid.*, p. 15.

contrary: freedom, the ex-sisting un-covering Dasein possesses man."[127]

There is no "beyond" which lights up the world for man. Man's kind of Being *is* enlightening. Man as Dasein, that is insofar as he is present in Being and, conversely, Being is present in him, is the essence which constitutes the difference between something's being brought to the light of day, discovered, and something's being covered up, shrouded in darkness.

Implicit in Heidegger is the rider: and this is, in all eternity, enough! Here, if anywhere, is "the wonder-ful" to be found. Man misunderstands himself when he *seeks* the light, seeks "the meaning of his existence," or "a goal" which will be illuminated for him. Beyond the light-giving function which man, as Dasein, himself is, there is no further source of illumination.

Humanism or watch over Being?

Thought and language

The ("Letter on Humanism") *Brief über den Humanismus* is a reply to the French philosopher Jean Beaufret who had posed a number of questions to Heidegger. Heidegger picked out one of these for special treatment: "How can one restore a meaning to the word 'humanism'?"

The letter was written in 1946 and published together with *Platons Lehre von der Wahrheit* ("Plato's Theory of Truth") in 1947.

It opens with a forthright and concentrated declaration on man, action *qua* ful-fill-ment, and Being, which reminds one of Spinoza's theory on analogous matters: man, action *qua* development to greater per-fection, and substance. But then Heidegger introduces a characteristic strain from quite differ-

---

[127]*Ibid.*, p. 12.

ent spheres of thought: the idea of a kind of direct connection between language and Being, according to which Man is no longer to be thought of as disposing of language as he will, as if it belonged to him as his own most cherished means of expression:

> We are far from considering the essence of action with sufficient power. Action is acknowledged only as it gives rise to some effect. Its reality is judged by its utility. But the essence of action is ful-fillment. To ful-fill means to unfold something in its full essence, to follow something on to its full essence, to bring it forward *(hervorbringen)*. What can be fulfilled is therefore really only that which already is. But that which before all else "is," is Being *(das Sein)*.
>
> Thinking ful-fills Being's relation to man's essence. It does not create or develop this relation. Thinking only shows the relation for Being as it is given to thinking itself by Being. This presenting consists in Being's coming, in thinking, to language *(zur Sprache)*. Language houses Being: Man is the lodger (literally: "lives in the dwelling" [*Behausung*]) of language. Thought and poetry are guardians of the lodging. Their vigil is the fulfillment of Being as something revealed, insofar as through what they say they bring Being to expression and preserve it in language.[128]

Thought's mission is thus neither *technical*, to be a tool for man when he makes things, nor *theoretical*, as in science. Both conceptions betoken a derailment and both have affected the history of mankind since the time of Plato and Aristotle. For one thing, "philosophy" gets into difficulties—it, too, is thinking. But how is it to justify its existence in the face of the sciences?

It holds that this is best brought about when it places

[128]*P-H*, p. 53.

itself on the level of science. This endeavor, however, means to abandon the essence of thought. Philosophy, if it is not a science, is pursued by the fear of losing reputation and validity. . . . "Logic" is the sanction of this interpretation, beginning with the sophist and Plato.[129]

Heidegger, in his later works, tries to get away from any hint of a scientific framework—away also from the expository form of writing exemplified in *Being and Time.* Does this mean that now at last he reveals his true character as a champion of "irrationalism"? Very far from it, replies Heidegger: to set scientific goals for thought is like trying to see how long a fish can live on dry land. Is it irrationalism to bring thought back to its true element?

Heidegger's formulation of the non-scientific nature of thought is radical: he does not use, as one might have expected, *"philosophic* thinking," or *"metaphysical* thinking," but the unqualified expression. Aside from the fact that the label "irrationalism" has a generally negative feel, it appears to be not altogether inappropriate. Heidegger's "thinking" definitely aims at replacing reason; he may not want to make cave-dwellers of us, but the dethronement of reason is implied by the role he gives to his thinking.

What then does Heidegger, in his later philosophy, "philosophy of Being", mean by thinking? We have just quoted one straightforward answer. The question itself is not one that can be answered in terms of a definition: that would be counter to the main trend of his philosophy. But there are some isolated remarks in the letter on humanism which seem better able to throw light on the matter.

> Thought, to put it simply, is the thought of Being. The genitive expresses two things at once. Thought is the thought of Being, insofar as thought, effected by Being, belongs to Being. Thought is, at the same time, the

[129]*Ibid.*, p. 55.

thought of Being insofar as thought, belonging to Being, hearkens to Being.[130]

Thinking is something that cannot occur during the dictatorship of the "they." If man is to approach Being once more—as Plato and Aristotle did—then we must learn to "exist in the nameless":

> Man, before he speaks, must let himself be addressed by Being, thereby running the risk of having not much or seldom anything to say. Only in this way is the word to be given back the preciousness of its essence, and man the lodging for his inhabitance in the truth of Being.[131]

Humanism and the falling of thought

From a perspective of thought-about-Being it is naturally difficult to be concerned about the word "humanism." This, like other -isms, merely testifies to the depth of thought's fallenness, to the preoccupation of philosophy with particular things and their relations rather than with Being itself. When such a word has lost its meaning, why trouble to give it one? The Greeks, after all, managed perfectly well in their great heyday without the *word* "philosophy."

> One doesn't think any more, but one is occupied with "philosophy." In the competitions of such occupations, these present themselves publicly as -isms, and try to surpass one another. The authority of such titles is not accidental. It rests, particularly in modern times, on the peculiar dictatorship of publicness *(Offentlichkeit)*.[132]

Language comes under the dictatorship of publicness,

---

[130]*Ibid.*, pp. 56-57. The English translation is taken from Laszlo Versényi, *Heidegger, Being and Truth* (New Haven: Yale University Press, 1965), p. 112.

[131]*Ibid.*, pp. 60-61.

[132]*Ibid.*, p. 58.

which is another way of describing the subjection to the "they." It is an outcome of this that one tries to use the *word* "humanism" despite the fact that its meaning has been lost.

What is one to mean by the word "humanism"? That man shall not be inhuman but human?

> But in what does man's humanity consist? It lies in his essence. But by what and how is the essence of man determined? Marx demanded that the "human man" should be recognized and acknowledged. He found this man in "society" . . . . Christ regards man's humanity, the *humanitas* of *homo*, from the point of view of the delimitation toward the *Deitas*. He is, according to the history of salvation *(heilsgeschichtlich)*, man as "God's child." . . .[133]

All determinations of man's essence so far proposed commit the mistake of not providing any answer to the question of the truth of Being itself. Neither, therefore, has there been any inquiry into the connection of man's essence to the truth of Being. "Being is still waiting to become worthy of man's thought."[134] As things stand now, conceptions of man's nature are determined by general interpretations of nature, history, the world, the foundation of the world, that is, by "the what-is in its totality," not by the Being of entities. Our own determinations of the concept of man don't look deep enough.

Heidegger's argumentation against versions of humanism as theories of man's essence is clearly based on parts of *Being and Time* which we have discussed earlier. The main point is this, that ontological inquiries go deeper than ontical ones; consequently, that questions about the Being of entities must be presumed adequately answered before one proceeds to ask about individual entities themselves or—as in "metaphysics"—

[133]*Ibid.*, p. 61.
[134]*Ibid.*, p. 65.

about all entities or the what-is in its totality. This basic view-point is then applied to the question "What is man?" and the result, naturally, is that one must distinguish between those answers that place man among entities and those that elucidate the features of man's kind of Being, that is, which clarify man's—an entity's—Being. The first kind of answer presupposes an answer to the second.

More concretely: all determinations of man as a living essence, as a rational animal, as soul, or as any other thing *within* the frame of categories of entities, presuppose that one already knows what it implies to refer to something as a living essence, a rational animal, and so on.

Heidegger refers to page 42 in *Sein und Zeit:* "The essence of Dasein lies in its existence,"[135] but adds (with a view to, among other things, Sartre's existentialism) that the word "existence" does not stand here for "existentia" in opposition to essence *(essentia).* His revised (1946) formulation goes:

> That which man is, that which in terms of traditional metaphysics is the essence of man, lies in his ex-sistence *(Eksistenz).*[136]

Heidegger on Sartre
Existence and ex-sistence

In looking for the most clearly formulated account of "ex-sistence" we must turn once again to "What is Metaphysics?" Heidegger goes back to the elements, "ek" ("out of") and "stasis" *(stare:* "to stand"). Ex-sistence is Dasein's standing-out-of in the truth of Being, the latter being again traced back to un-hiddenness, dis-closed-ness, the illumination of Being *(Lichtung des Seins).*[137]

---

[135]*Being and Time,* p. 67.
[136]*P-H,* p. 68.
[137]*Ibid.,* pp. 70-71. In the "letter" Heidegger uses fewer newly coined expressions than later; nevertheless, he says about Dasein: "Es west im Wurf des Seins als des schickend Geschicklichen." Cf. also p. 173.

From these remarks the differences between Heidegger's and Sartre's intentions are not hard to pinpoint.

> Sartre . . . formulates the principle of existentialism as: Existence precedes essence. He takes "existentia" and "essentia" in the metaphysical sense, which from the time of Plato has implied: Essentia precedes existentia. Sartre turns this statement around. But a metaphysical statement's contrary remains metaphysical. Apparently in this statement he sticks to metaphysics and forgets the truth of Being.[138]

The term "existentialism" is an apt one with regard to Sartre's central statement that existence is prior to essence, but this statement has not the slightest thing in common with the statement quoted above from *Being and Time*. If in our subjection to the "they," we wish to bestow an -ism on Heidegger, it must be "ex-sistentialism." Even this will only cover his doctrine of the character of Dasein, not his philosophy of Being in general. As for the relation between existence and essence, that is something which *Being and Time*, according to the work's program, is unable to throw any light on: the relation is one *within* the world of entities, while the program of ontology is devoted to the deeper question of the Being of entities.

Here we could interpolate that it may well be that *Being and Time*, not only programmatically but also in fact, has managed to stay within the strict bounds of ontology. Heidegger's later writings, however, contain a doctrine of man and a declaration for man which have not a few traits in common with those of Sartre. The latter's 'l'existence,' indeed, has certain features in common with Heidegger's 'Dasein,' and it too is to some extent distinguished from 'existentia' within what Heidegger calls the meta-physical tradition. One can therefore say with some justice that though

[138]*Ibid.*, p. 72.

Heidegger, in his remarks on Sartre, points to something central in which Sartre's views and his own intentions in *Being and Time* differ, he pays no attention to obvious points of similarity.

Entities can open themselves for man precisely because man ex-sists and is not something that simply occurs along with other things. In the light of Being the entity appears as an entity. Man is that which watches over Being's open-ness, its un-concealed-ness, and consequently its truth. As ex-sisting, Man is Being's shepherd.[139] The falling away discussed in *Being and Time* consists in Being's truth being forgotten under the pressure of entities.

Homelessness and alienation
Marxism

The homelessness which stamps man in modern times is due to his trying to be at home exclusively among entities, and it results in a concern for them and their utility. "Homelessness becomes a destiny of the world."

> What Marx, in an essential and significant sense, recognized from Hegel as the alienation of man has its roots in the homelessness of modern man. This in turn is called forth by the mission *(Geschick)* of Being as it occurs in the form of metaphysics, as well as being reinforced and at the same time covered up by its homelessness. Because Marx, in experiencing alienation, is grasping an essential dimension of history, the Marxist view of history surpasses every other historiography. And due to the fact that neither Husserl nor, as far as I see, Sartre has recognized the essential importance of the historicality of Being, neither Phenomenology nor Existentialism bears on the dimension within which a fruitful discussion with Marxism is alone possible.[140]

[139]*Ibid.*, p. 75.
[140]*Ibid.*, p. 87.

This glance at Being's relation to time as history ("the history of Being") must have interested many of Heidegger's readers, not least Sartre, for whom Marxism has played an especially important role. (Interestingly, the remark on Sartre contains a qualification, a confession of uncertainty—a rare phenomenon in Heidegger's writings.)

The elimination of the world's needs through thought-about-Being

The last parts of the sixty-seven page "letter" have the character of a passionate defense of the position that thought-about-Being and man's vigil must have priority as the aim of the future: "What is needed in the present distress of the world is this: less philosophy, more attention to thought; less literature, more concern with the letters."[141]

Since the defense sets thought-about-Being up against other things, it has a concretizing effect, which is one good reason for "translating" some of Heidegger's formulations in the following passage, either in free quotation or in brief summary.

If someone speaks against "humanism," one understands him to be defending brutishness and barbarity.

If "logic" is opposed, one thinks arbitrariness is being put in its stead.

If one speaks against "values," there is horror and alarm at a philosophy that dares to bring everything into disrepute: "culture," "art," "science," "human values," "God."

But can it not be seen "that just by characterizing something as 'value,' that which is thus valued is deprived of its worth?"[142] The valued object becomes debased; it is a mere object of man's value judgments. "Value-thinking is . . . the greatest conceivable blasphemy in the face of Being."

To speak against (what is called) "humanism," against "logic," or "values," is not to speak in favor of the opposite, but for something more original, basic—something which

[141]*Ibid.*, p. 119.
[142]*Ibid.*, p. 99.

man must open himself to before he can give a permanent meaning to the words "humanism," "logic," and "value." The way to this is shown by the thinking which inquires after the truth of Being and which determines man's essence on the basis of his special relation to Being.

Speaking against what is called "humanism" *can* turn out to be speaking *for* humanism, if the word is interpreted as having a more basic sense than it has in metaphysics and its other uses. Man's essence depends on ex-sistence, his task is that of a servant, to stand guard over Being's open-ness. So the concept of humanism must be determined in such a way that it will not "depend on man as such." A remarkable humanism! Should we call "humanism" a humanism which is directed against all "humanisms" hitherto so-called? Or should we not rather make open opposition to "humanism" and take the risk of causing offense?

But what about ethics and morality? Aren't we led in an a-human humanism to ethical "nihilism"? Where lies the way from fundamental ontology to ethics?

> The wish for a moral theory craves the more ardently for fulfilment the more the overt perplexity of man, no less than the covert, rises beyond measurable proportions. All care must be devoted to the binding (of man) to moral theory, in which technological man, delivered up to mass-being as he is, can be brought to a dependability that is only possible through a correspondingly technical collection and ordering of his plans and actions as a whole.[143]

Such forceful utterances are scarcely designed to encourage the inquirer to repeat his expressions of concern for ethics. But one can certainly approach the same topic indirectly. One can ask: Does thought-about-Being offer a purely theoretical presentation of Being and of man, or are there practical consequences to be drawn from it as well? The

[143]*Ibid.*, pp. 104-5.

answer is that this thinking is neither theoretical nor practical; it precedes the drawing of the distinction. It is, insofar as it *is*, thinking to call Being to mind and nothing more than that. Such thinking has no result, no effect. It fills its own essence insofar as it is.[144]

And yet, in the end Heidegger says things that do seem to be aimed at satisfying a need for ethics—though a need ontologically purified and diverted. But before citing these thoughts it may be in place to remind ourselves here that thinking can bring something to fulfilment (cf. pp. 239 ff., above), and that this is some kind of result or effect, even if not strictly so in Heidegger's terminology; 'result' and 'effect,' in his view, are to be determined within the frame of what-is. If something gives rise to something, in the shape of an entity or a change in an entity, it is difficult not to regard this something itself as an entity. But thought-about-Being is not an entity, for which very reason it can have no result or effect.

Back then to the possibility of ethics:

> Only insofar as man, ex-sisting in the truth of Being, belongs to this [Being] may the assignment of those directives which are to be law and rule for man *(die Zuweisung derjenigen Weisungen)* come from Being itself. "To assign" in Greek is νέμειν. Νόμος means not only law, but more originally the assignment contained *(geborgen)* in the mission of Being. This alone enables man to accommodate himself *(verfügen)* to Being. Such a conformation alone is able to support *(tragen)* and attack. Otherwise every law is but a product of the human intellect. More important than any setting up of rules is man's finding a halt *(Aufenthalt)* in the truth of Being.[145]

The extending of man, in Heidegger's philosophical sys-

[144]*Ibid.,* p. 111.
[145]*Ibid.,* pp. 114-15.

tem, to the outer edge of what-is is carried out with a clear awareness of the consequences; it also provides a key to one of Heidegger's strangest scruples. In the main he has ignored objections to his philosophy, but the charge of anthropocentricism has provoked a rejoinder, albeit in a footnote.[146]

Man at the center! Indeed, he says, man certainly comes into the center as a problem, but precisely because he is pushed out, not only from the center and to the periphery of what-is, but right out into nothingness. In fact, Heidegger offers us an "anthropocentrism" which lays stress *exclusively* on showing that Dasein's essence stands out from everything, is ec-static—consequently, ec-centric in the highest degree![147]

In his later works Heidegger has unequivocally stated that men face a crisis, that something fearful has happened and something decisive is imminent. The crisis is not only cultural, ethical, social. It goes much deeper, so deep indeed that it involves man's very essence. Some change must be effected, *from the basis up*, and whether it takes decades or centuries is a matter of minor importance.

Heidegger declines to be called a cultural pessimist: to think that the crisis went no deeper than culture! Spengler's *Der Untergang des Abendlandes 1918-22* contained violent warnings and prophecies which German students duly took to heart; but they were trifling compared with the words of doom Heidegger imparted to his students in 1935:

> The spiritual decline of the earth is so far advanced that the nations are in danger of losing the last bit of spiritual energy that makes it possible to see the decline (taken in

---

[146]*Vom Wesen des Grundes* (4th ed.; Frankfurt am Main: V. Klostermann, 1955), p. 42.

[147]Axiologically and metaphysically Heidegger's counterargument seems convincing; but does it hold epistemologically? Although Heidegger does not provide anthropocentric expressions in the case of the exact sciences, one wonders whether those he does provide can be combined with his general doctrine of existentials.

relation to the history of "Being"), and to appraise it as such.[148]

In a lecture on technology he warns against seeing "something natural" in it. The truth about modern technology is that it gives us a new understanding of what the essence of entities consists in. For Plato an entity's essence was its idea, that which was permanent in it, and which could also be seen by man.

If technology's way of understanding the essence of things displaces others, man will no longer meet himself in truth. Perhaps the artist can come in here to help us, and Heidegger quotes Hölderlin. ". . . poetically man resides on this earth."[149]

In a lecture on "the thing" *(das Ding)* Heidegger declares that the *influence* of modern science in Europe is toward an annihilation of the fully human and meaningful understanding of things, or rather, toward the prevention of the appearance of the essence of things.

> The thinghood of things remains covered up, forgotten. The essence of things never appears, that is, never comes into language.[150]

Heidegger is not afraid to illustrate his statement with a concrete example. He gives a comprehensive analysis of the essence of a jug, of what is juggish about the jug. If the jug is empty its emptiness is something other than a hollow space

---

[148]*EM*, p. 29 (p. 31 in the English translation). My general impression of what Heidegger stands for at his best suggests that it is unwise to quote from *EM*. It gives every indication of having been written in a fever which is altogether out of tune with the serene mood of *Sein und Zeit*, the work in which the ontologist par excellence speaks. Besides, it looks as if Heidegger in *EM* goes out of his way to *defend* one of the more dubious parts of his philosophy: the doctrine of the nothing.

[149]*Vorträge und Aufsätze* (henceforth referred to as *VA*) (Pfullingen: G. Neske, 1954), p. 43.

[150]*Ibid.*, p. 168.

filled with air. The jug encloses something, something can be held in it, and the jug keeps what is held in it. If there is wine in it, then there is a drink in it, not something in a fluid state, as the physicist would describe it. *One* pours the wine, *it* is not poured, and so on. The contrast between the description of a jug's essence and the scientifically influenced description reminds one of the contrast between a description of what a thing means and implies for a man who is open to all possible experiences associated with the thing, including those which have roots thousands of years ago, and the wretchedly meager and banal description one gets from popularized science. To follow Heidegger's philosophical intentions more closely, then, one must avoid (1) the distinction between a thing as such and man's "concerned, care-ful" association with it, and (2) essential descriptions of things in the form of descriptions of human *experiences* of the thing ("psychologizing").

Science and technology may have overcome all distances, but things have come no nearer to us. Being is no closer. Everything is equally far from us, equally near, in fact without distance.

The horrifying thing is not the latest doomsday weapon, but the fact that nothing any more is near to us, that things no longer appear for us, essentially, in their illuminating fulness.

Heidegger and his predecessors

Heraclitus and Parmenides

Like Wittgenstein and many other thinkers in our century, Heidegger turned against the greater part of traditional philosophy. But unlike Wittgenstein, he has involved himself deeply with a long line of central thinkers down through the centuries, in such an original way, too, and with such generally interesting results that traces will remain whatever the fate of the complex program of thought-about-Being. Heidegger thinks he has overcome metaphysics, and since metaphysics is, in his view, the core of the philosophical tradition, he thinks he has overcome philosophy. The metaphysical tradition is concerned with questions about what-is within the frame of what-is. Its answers are given in the form of idealism, materialism, spiritualism, (in)determinism, and so on. But these do not reach down to the fundamental questions about the Being of what-is, or meaning generally. Heidegger calls his efforts an attempt at thought-about-Being. He is not a philosopher or a metaphysician, but a thinker.

But is he not an ontologist? Is it not precisely Being that he is trying to talk about? In a wide sense, yes, but the distinction between asking about what-is and the Being of what-is is such an important one for Heidegger that he feels he must reject the title "ontologist" as not appropriate. In *Being and Time* he introduces what he calls "fundamental ontology," not as a part of ontology, but as saying something more profound, something pre-ontological. Where ontology classifies different kinds of entities—living essences and lifeless ones, psychic and material, causes and effects, necessary and contingent, subjects and objects, and so on,—fundamental ontology corresponds to the antecedent question of "what we really mean by the expression 'Being.' "[151]

A statement of the kind "All that is falls into two main classes, that which has extension in space and that which has not" presupposes that it is already clear what is meant by the expression "all that is." Fundamental ontology is led in its research to concentrate attention first of all on the question of what Dasein consists in. (We tried to explain earlier how Heidegger comes to give priority to this—cf. pages 188 ff.) If this is clarified, the question of the meaning of Being at all and in general must then be tackled directly. This, as we noted, is not done in *Being and Time*, but Heidegger's later

[151]*SuZ*, p. 11 (31).

works give contributions to an answer, even though in a style quite different from that of the main work.

Heidegger's opposition to traditional philosophy is due to his conviction that already with Plato and Aristotle the falling-away had begun. Before these, in the beginning of the great period of Greek philosophy, thinkers had been occupied with the same question that Heidegger has tackled—though less aware than he of its peculiarities. The two major names here are Heraclitus and Parmenides.

Two works on Heraclitus have come from Heidegger's hand, one concentrating on the interpretation of the expression "λόγος" in fragment B50, and the other on "ἀλήθεια" in fragment 16.

> The history of art speaks about the language of forms. Once, however, in the beginning of occidental thought, the essence of language flashed up *(blitzte)* in the light of Being. Once, when Heraclitus thought λόγος to be the guiding word for thought about the Being of entities. The flash, however, at once died out. Nobody perceived its beam and the proximity of what it illuminated.
>
> Heraclitus is called the dark one *(Der Dunkle)*. But really he is the bright one. For he says what is illuminating.

(Heidegger conceives of any expression of something as liberating it, illuminating it, as if to bring it into the light was to set it free. "The free is the field of the uncovered."[152])

These words form a transition to one of Heidegger's main topics already discussed: the true as the un-covered, the come-to-view, the unveiled. "Truth," "ἀ-λήθεια", means etymologically "un-coveredness," "come-to-view-ness." By translating "ἀλήθεια" as "truth," something which in man's pre-philosophical state was self-evident is lost.[153]

[152]*VA*, p. 229.
[153]*Ibid.*, p. 258.

What does the bringing of something from coveredness ("untruth") or concealedness to un-coveredness consist in? How can such a thing happen?

Heidegger thinks that Heraclitus has posed this fundamental question in fragment 16—which in rank and scope thus becomes the first.[154]

Heidegger recognizes in Parmenides the thinker who first made the simple apprehension (νοεῖν) of there being something present (cf. p. 234, above) as a clue in interpreting Being. Heidegger, predictably, bases his article on Parmenides on the provocative fragment "For thinking (νοεῖν) and Being are the same." This Heidegger construes as: "Being is that which shows itself in the pure apprehension which belongs to beholding, and only by such seeing is Being discovered."[155]

This thesis, he adds, has remained the foundation of Western philosophy. In it, Parmenides was the first to discover the Being of entities and to "identify" this with an observational understanding of Being.

The relation to Heidegger's thoughts on "Being" is as yet ambiguous. P a r m e n i d e s also said, "For Being *is*" (ἔστίν γὰρ εἶναι). *Is* Being? "If the 'is' is said about Being without further interpretation, then Being is too easily perceived as an 'entity.' "[156] But perhaps, in a genuine sense, it is *only* Being which is, and never the what-is. Parmenides' thought is today still unthought. "Here may be measured how it is with the development of philosophy. Insofar as it pays attention to its essence it does not develop at all."[157]

Plato and Aristotle

Heidegger believes that it is with Plato that the falling-away

[154]Fragment 16 goes: "How can one hide oneself from that which never goes down?"
[155]*SuZ*, p. 171 (215).
[156]*P-H*, p. 80.
[157]*Ibid.*, p. 81..

in philosophy first begins even if the deepest pre-philosophical insights were still living in his time. In *Platons Lehre von der Wahrheit*, Heidegger gives a detailed interpretation of the allegory of the Cave in *The Republic*, Book 7. The main point, as one would expect, is that the cave is what hides, or covers, and that he who is able to free himself from the chains in the cave sees things in their uncoveredness, as they are. In other words: all steps in the allegory concern truth, ἀ-λήθεια. For the Greeks this was self-evident because their word for truth means, quite literally, un-coveredness.

With Plato the question of the Being or meaning of entities was still a living one, and Heidegger uses as a motto in *Being and Time* a quotation from the dialogue *The Sophist:*

> For manifestly you have long been aware of what you mean when you use the expression "being". We, however, who used to think we understood it, have now become perplexed.[158]

Although the question was one that held the interest of Plato and Aristotle, after them it died away. As for Aristotle, he it was who instituted the tradition according to which "Being" is seen as the widest and most general concept. But this tradition has not made the concept of Being any less obscure.

Nietzsche

In 1961 Heidegger released for publication a collection of lectures and papers on Nietzsche written between 1936 and 1946. The title is simply *Nietzsche*, but Heidegger opens the foreword of this more than one-thousand-page work by informing his reader that the thinker's name stands here, not for Nietzsche himself but for the subject matter of his thought. We may well understand why Heidegger should feel it neces-

[158]*SuZ*, p. 1 (19).

sary to follow in the tracks of Nietzsche. For Nietzsche has given an answer to the question, "In what does the Being of entities consist?" Or so at least Heidegger assumes, construing Nietzsche's determination of the "will to power" as "the innermost essence of Being" as saying that "the will to power is the fundamental character of entities as such."[159] The structural basis of Nietzsche's metaphysics is the concealed unity of basic philosophical theses. Heidegger quotes, approvingly it seems, Nietzsche's prophetic words in 1881/82: "The time is coming when the struggle for mastery of the world will be waged—it will be waged in the name of *basic philosophical doctrines*."[160] Thus Nietzsche's thinking is revealed as the consequence and fulfilment of the whole Western metaphysical tradition. Although we cannot go further into the matter here[161] Nietzsche becomes, much more profoundly than Husserl, Heidegger's real philosophical predecessor. Heidegger characterizes metaphysics as "anthropomorphy —the shaping and viewing of the world in accordance with man's image."[162] Nietzsche's metaphysics, understood as will to power, is the epitome of metaphysics, and it is this that Heidegger wants to overcome with his thinking-about-Being.

Attempt at an over-all view

The above exposition has been aimed at guiding the reader into some of the central areas in Heidegger's world of thought. For someone convinced not only that he understands Heidegger's ontology as a systematic construction but also

---

[159]*Nietzsche*, II, 264. This was written in 1940. On page 260 it is determined as "das Wort für das Sein des Seienden als solchen, die essentia des Seienden".

[160]*Ibid.*, 261.

[161]An instructive analysis of Heidegger's relation to the philosophical tradition appears in Walter Schulz's article, "Über den philosophiegeschichtlichen Ort Martin Heideggers," *Philosophische Rundschau*, I (1953/54), Nos. 2/3, 4.

[162]*Nietzsche*, II, 127.

that this ontology is both original and tenable, the next step will be to try to make a more thorough systematization of the various points, a task that requires a fuller working out of the fundamental theses. The above account assumes no such conviction, and it has avoided any attempt at a predominantly ontological exposition with its inevitable increase in technical terminology.

As far as the ontological system in *Being and Time* is concerned, the stress has been on clarifying its ontological *intention*. Heidegger attempts a new beginning in philosophy, starting from a new concept, or rather, a new intuition of essence. One could hardly expect this new intuition to be presented in a few concise statements, except to an audience with an unusually high degree of philosophical literacy. But Heidegger's terminology provides a useful means of access. The expressions he chooses are intended to stop us in our (well worn) tracks, and by constant attention to the differences between them and more usual terminology we begin to see which way we must look in order to have a view of the Heideggerian landscape. Generally speaking, one can have a *kind* of view of man, the world, or our cosmic situation, and so forth, which is more or less clear, but in which not every single detail is clear. To achieve more than this with Heidegger one must try to follow his own path to *Being and Time*. This means a renewed study of Husserl, Plato, Aristotle, and other philosophers whom Heidegger specifically refers to. To read these anew does not, of course, guarantee an understanding, but there is no doubt that it is a necessary condition.

One very potent source of interest in a philosopher is the feeling that what he says is directly relevant to one's own personal situation, as if the significance of his words was their significance for oneself, here and now. But Heidegger's thought is not oriented toward the here and now of individual men's lives; his intention has not been to make an individual man's life more meaningful *for him*, by bringing out what is essential for *him*, for *others*, or for everyone. Essence and

Being are central in Heidegger's message, but the expressions do not take the form "essential for—" or "Being for—." Clearly the existential, subjective experience of meaning and significance is not inessential for an understanding of his thought, but in his view, ordinary situations of meaning and significance are without ontological depth. Heidegger is not concerned with existential meaningfulness, but with Dasein's *existensiale* "meaning" *(Sinn)*. He is not concerned, in the usual humanistic way, with man, his life, his existence, but with Being, language, and Dasein's relation to Being. Humanism repels him. God and the absolutes are indeed absent, but it is fatal to assume that one can cultivate man, the human, as a suitable replacement, or indeed to believe that we have the right at all to focus on our needs for meaning and aims in life.

In giving an account of Heidegger's thoughts, one is frequently tempted to use un-Heideggerian expressions and concepts which seem to make Heidegger's opinions more intelligible. But one could not do so without incorporating Heidegger into a kind of philosophy of life, according to which his "ideas" would be interpreted as direct contributions to, say, "phenomenological" linguistics, psychology, social anthropology, and other disciplines. Heidegger makes it quite plain, however, that he is *not* trying to contribute to these. And whether or not his influence and meaning in terms of the history of ideas lie in his "anthropocentricism," his own intention is strictly ontological. Thus even if his project could never be fulfilled or may have gone onto the wrong track, an account of his work can have only one aim: to try to convey the thinker's basic intention—cost what it may.

Heidegger has been asked what is the ultimate source (*Weisung:* "instruction," "directive") of his philosophy, of the insights that have guided it. The question, however, is not one that can be answered independently of the philosophy itself. In replying, Heidegger counters with another question: What ultimate authority did Plato have to think of Being as idea?

There is some justification for complaining that Heidegger does not introduce his new words or new meanings of words by clarifying their relation to older words, for example through definitions. But since he is concerned with the deepest foundations of all thinking we can hardly expect a definition in itself, without further ado, to convey the new content of such expressions as "Being" or "Essence." The indirect approach, on the other hand, has advantages. Traditional philosophy covers such wide-ranging problems as the question of man's nature, of science, of the "I" and the outside world, of the possibility of knowledge, and so on. By heeding the words and formulations Heidegger uses in discussing these topics, it is clear that the difference between his and other contemporary philosophers' terminology is a systematic one. One sees how Heidegger ontologizes the terminology and how certain expressions which are central in Descartes and Husserl are not used at all, even where it would seem most natural to employ them.

As a rule Heidegger tries to convey the meaning of a new expression through characteristic *uses* of the expression in question. One has to take a "jump" into his terminology, or rather, a series of jumps. If this doesn't lead to experiences of understanding, the exercise has been unsuccessful; if it does, all we can say is that it may have been successful. Equally, it may have led to misunderstandings, but as Heidegger emphasizes, misunderstanding is an important kind of understanding. Continued reading of Heidegger, further jumps, may bring better understanding. The mark of success will in the last instance be consistency: if one gets a sense of a work's structural whole on the basis of more than one interpretation of its basic words and formulations, one must select an interpretation which gives a consistent meaning to the work as a whole, allowing of course that the author has been consistent in *his* own interpretation.

These remarks apply to Heidegger's writings before the "turning around." After this Heidegger states clearly and plainly that his philosophy has no kind of scientific pretension and that it comes nearer to, though without actually becoming, poetry.[163]

It is often said, and not least among philosophers who have a high regard for Heidegger, that it is difficult to see how there could be any continuation or development of his philosophy; insofar as it has any potential, it has already realized it. Heidegger's influence is of another kind: the study of his philosophy has philosophical effects, it liberates thoughts. There is no continuity, however, between these and Heidegger's own intentions. In Sartre, for example, we find ontological aims partly, or altogether, abandoned. And in psychology and psychiatry inspired by Heidegger, the strict ontological viewpoint is deliberately dropped. But Heidegger has had no intention of contributing to psychology; indeed, he sees himself as a more consistent opponent of "psychologism" than Husserl himself. His doctrine of man tries to be as independent of (empirical) anthropology and psychology as formal logic is of (empirical) doctrines about human thought processes.

Heidegger's work has great importance as an invitation to dialogue, to conversation, with the old Greeks, especially the pre-Socratics, but naturally most of all with Plato and Aristotle. Heidegger attaches to the pre-Socratics a significance and a wealth of insight which it is impossible to put objectively to the test. Here, as with Kierkegaard, one is witness to a systematically constructed belief in a golden age. Whether or not, or to whatever extent, painstaking research can transform it into historical insight, it has its own stimulating effects.

Here we find what is perhaps Heidegger's main strength, whatever the criticisms by coming generations: his continual pointing inwards and backwards, his attempts to pose questions in depth, to pursue his inquiry one pace behind what are

[163]*Unterwegs zur Sprache*, p. 173.

reckoned the fundamental questions. He tries to cast ultimate positions adrift, to make them problematical without setting himself firmly in a new position. We may well ask ourselves whether this is not something which we must constantly try to do, and in ever new ways—repetitions of old attempts can dull the edge of our sensibilities; when the astounding is duly accepted as such, it has to be recaptured in new surroundings, or given a new form. Heidegger has not succumbed to the systematizer's chief enemy: the elimination of the value of a question, in Heidegger's sense of the "frag-würdige," by its very solution.

Bibliography of Heidegger's Work in Chronological Order

"Neuere Forschungen über Logik," *Literarische Rundschau für das katolische Deutschland*, Vol. 38 (Freiburg im Breisgau, 1912), pp. 465 ff., 565 ff.

Die Lehre vom Urteil im Psychologismus. Ein Kritischpositiver Beitrag zur Logik (Leipzig: J. A. Barth, 1914).

Die Kategorien und Bedeutungslehre des Duns Scotus (Tübingen: J. C. B. Mohr, 1916).

"Der Zeitbegriff in der Geschichtswissenschaft," *Zeitschrift für Philosophie und philosophische Kritik*, Vol. 161 (Leipzig, 1961), pp. 173-88.

Sein und Zeit, I. First published in *Jahrbuch für Philosophie und phänomenologische Forschung* (Halle an der Saale: Max Niemeyer, 1927).

"Besprechung von: E. Cassirer: *Philosophie der symbolischen Formen*. 2. Teil: Das mythische Denken" (Berlin: Bruno Cassirer, 1925), printed in *Deutsche Literaturzeitung für Kritik der internationalen Wissenschaft*. N. S., Vol. 5 (Berlin, 1928), pp. 1000-12.

"*Vom Wesen des Grundes*," in *Festschrift für Edmund Husserl* (Halle an der Saale: Max Niemeyer, 1929; 3d ed., Frankfurt am Main: V. Klostermann, 1949).

Kant und das Problem der Metaphysik (Bonn: F. Cohen, 1929; 2d ed., Frankfurt am Main: V. Klostermann, 1951). English translation by James S. Churchill, *Kant and the Problem of Metaphysics* (Bloomington: Indiana University Press, 1962).

Was ist Metaphysik? (Bonn: F. Cohen, 1929; 6th ed., Frankfurt am Main: V. Klostermann, 1951).

Die Selbsthauptung der deutschen Universität (Breslau: Verlag Wilh. Gottl. Korn, 1933).

Heidegger and his predecessors

Vom Wesen der Wahrheit (Frankfurt am Main: V. Klostermann, 1943).

Erläuterungen zu Hölderlin's Dichtung (Frankfurt am Main: V. Klostermann, 1944; enlarged ed., 1950, 1951).

Platons Lehre von der Wahrheit. Mit einem Brief über den Humanismus (Bern: A. Francke, 1947).

Holzwege (Frankfurt am Main: V. Klostermann, 1950).

Der Feldweg (Frankfurt am Main: V. Klostermann, 1953).

Einführung in die Metaphysik (Tübingen: Max Niemeyer, 1953). English translation by Ralph Manheim, *An Introduction to Metaphysics* (New Haven: Yale University Press, 1959; New York: Doubleday & Co., Anchor Books, 1961).

Aus der Erfahrung des Denkens (Pfullingen: G. Neske, 1954).

Was heisst Denken? (Tübingen: Max Niemeyer, 1954).

Vorträge und Aufsätze (Pfullingen: G. Neske, 1954). English translation forthcoming, *Lectures and Addresses* (New York: Harper & Row).

Was ist das—die Philosophie? (Pfullingen: G. Neske, 1956). English translation by William Kluback and Jean T. Wilde, *What is Philosophy?* (London: Vision Press, 1956).

Zur Seinsfrage (Frankfurt am Main: V. Klostermann, 1956). English translation by William Kluback and Jean T. Wilde, *The Question of Being* (London: Vision Press, 1958).

Der Satz vom Grund (Pfullingen: G. Neske, 1957).

Identität und Differenz (Pfullingen: G. Neske, 1957).

Hebel—der Hausfreund (Pfullingen: G. Neske, 1957).

"Grundsätze des Denkens," *Jahrbuch für Psychologie und Psychoterapie*, Vol. 6 (Freiburg and Munich, 1958), pp. 33-41.

"Vom Wesen und Begriff der φύσις," *Aristoteles Physik*, Vol. 1. In *Il Pensiero*, III (Milan-Varese, 1958), 129-56, 265-89.

"Antrittsrede vor der Heidelberger Akademie der Wissenschaften," *Wissenschaft und Weltbild*, Vol. 12 (Vienna, 1959), pp. 610 ff.

Gelassenheit (Pfullingen: G. Neske, 1959). English translation by John M. Anderson and E. Hans Freund, *Discourse on Thinking* (New York: Harper & Row, 1966).

Unterwegs zur Sprache (Pfullingen: G. Neske, 1959).

"Aufzeichnungen aus der Werkstatt," *Neue Züricher Zeitung*, Sept. 27, 1959, p. 5.

"Hegel und die Griechen," *Die Gegenwart der Griechen im neueren Denken* (Festschrift for H. G. Gadamer) (Tübingen: Max Niemeyer, 1960), pp. 43-57.

"Hölderlin's Erde und Himmel," *Hölderlin Jahrbuch*, 1958 and 1960 (Tübingen, 1960), pp. 17-39.

"Sprache und Heimat," *Hebbel Jahrbuch* (1960), pp. 27-50.

Nietzsche, Vol. I (Pfullingen: G. Neske, 1961). English translation forthcoming (New York: Harper & Row).

Nietzsche, Vol. II (Pfullingen: G. Neske, 1962). English translation forthcoming (New York: Harper & Row).

Die Frage nach dem Ding. Zu Kants Lehre von den transzendentaler Grundsätzen (Tübingen: Max Niemeyer, 1962).

Kants These über das Sein (Frankfurt: V. Klostermann, 1962).

This list is mostly taken from *Zeitschrift für philosophische Forschung*, Vol. 11 (1957), pp. 402 ff. Heidegger's reviews of books and his lesser articles are also listed there, together with a comprehensive bibliography of his work up to 1955.

Jean-Paul Sartre

Life

Jean-Paul Sartre was born in Paris on June 21, 1905, and is thus roughly fifteen years younger than our three previous philosophers. Though French born, Sartre's early intellectual contact was with German, more specifically Protestant, thinking. His father—a marine officer—died when Sartre was only two years old, and the child was taken into the care and keeping of his maternal grandfather, a professor of German and a native of Alsace-Lorraine. Sartre's grandfather, a close relative of Albert Schweitzer of Lambaréné, was a Calvinist. He has been described as "no ordinary father figure, but the personification of a distant and exalted Authority, almost, one might say, the God-figure."[1]

When Sartre was eleven his mother married again—once more a marine engineer—and they moved to the small port of La Rochelle. After about two years at a local school, Sartre was sent to Paris to continue his studies. In 1924, at nineteen, he was accepted as a student at the renowned École Normale

[1] The quotation is from the opening page of a short but excellent book in the series "Writers and Critics": Maurice Cranston, *Sartre* (Edinburgh and London: Scott & Boyd, 1962). I have taken some of the biographical material from this book, which also contains an admirable bibliography (pp. 115-18).

Supérieure, where he received his education in philosophy. In the 1930's he taught philosophy at various schools in the provinces, for some time in Le Havre which provided the model for "Bouville" in his first and generally regarded best novel, *La Nausée*. While a student, Sartre met Simone de Beauvoir and the two became life partners, sharing the same preoccupations and interests. She too taught philosophy in the 1930's. In her autobiography we catch a glimpse of Sartre's personality, not least of his capacity for reflection and of his tendency to systematize. We begin to understand the part played by systematization in his two main philosophical works.

Sartre's first major work in philosophy, *L'Etre et le néant (Being and Nothingness)*, was first published in 1945, but he had been working on it since the early thirties. He himself has pointed out this fact in reply to those who suggested that the work was an expression of war and crisis. "My book *L'Etre et le néant* . . . was the outcome of research undertaken since 1930. I read Husserl, Scheler, Heidegger, and Jaspers for the first time in 1933 during a one-year stay at the Maison française de Berlin."[2] Hegel, Husserl, and Heidegger are the three thinkers to whom Sartre owes most, a fact he makes no attempt to conceal and which does nothing to detract from the originality of his main work, every page of which bears the imprint of its author's highly personal thought and style.

Although Sartre had begun to contribute to literary journals before he was twenty, it was not until 1936 when he was thirty-one, that his first book, *L'Imagination*, *(The Imagination)*[3] was published. The title of the book is perhaps mislead-

---

[2]*Critique de la raison dialectique* (Paris: Gallimard, 1960), I, 34. The work will be referred to henceforth as *CRD*. Quotations are in the present translator's version by kind permission of Alfred A. Knopf, Inc. (New York) and Methuen and Co., Ltd. (London), publishers of the English translation of this part of *CRD*, under the title, *Search for a Method*.

[3]*L'Imagination* (Paris: Presses Universitaires de France, 1936). English translation by Forrest Williams, *The Imagination* (Ann Arbor: The University of Michigan Press, 1962).

ing; it is not an account of a concept of imagination, but rather a criticism of the accounts of mental images, or more generally of the activity of producing mental images, given by Descartes, Hume, Leibniz, and other leading philosophers and philosopher psychologists. Already in this, his first book, Sartre gives evidence of his deep preoccupation with a peculiar feature of man—his living, whether he wants to or not, in a world which in a certain sense simply does not exist, a world, too, which is itself full of negations, things determined by their absence, copies of things, a world characterized by its own incompleteness or constant disappearance.

For Sartre, Husserl's phenomenology was a turning point in the history of psychology. To simplify, what Sartre admired so much in Husserl in the 1930's could be summarized as follows: Husserl pointed out that psychology, like physics, is concerned with what *really* exists, in the sense of factual existence. This "attitude naturelle" leads the psychologist in describing imaginary, hence unreal, objects, always to address himself to the question of *how* they come into existence, in terms of the person's, the subject's, own activity. There is a tendency to fix everything in the natural world. But in the phenomenological reduction, or *epoché*, the natural world is put "in parentheses": one concerns oneself not with factual existence at all, but with the intentional objects of consciousness. These might be things of the same order as natural objects, an-apple-on-the-table, or an-apple-as-a-(memory) image, or they might be essences, that is to say whatever, in the case of a type of object, is a necessary and sufficient condition of there being an object of precisely that type. Such "intentional" essences are described through a kind of intuition, referred to as the phenomenological intuition of essences, and not through introspection and induction as in naturalistic psychology.

In accordance with this view, Sartre sought an answer to the question: What is an image? What is the image's essential structure grasped by a reflective intuition? The question doesn't make investigation into the natural psychology of image-experiences superfluous, nor does it mean that the laws of their occurrence in men's consciousnesses are redundant. But before any such investigation can take place, according to Sartre, there must be an intuition of *what* the experiment is to investigate, thus an intuition of a kind of intentional object, the "image" which then becomes an object of investigation. There could be nothing that any experimenter ultimately grasped as a possible essence of "the image," unless it was precisely an *intended* essence. The main point is that naturalistic investigations into the conditions for producing images and for variations in the internal properties of images (e.g., sharpness or richness in color) in terms of (external) stimuli are unintelligible unless one has *beforehand* a grasp of what an image *is*. There are no centaurs in the physical world, and yet the centaur is not an *imagined* synthesis of man and animal. What we immediately understand as the content of an image of a centaur is neither something physical nor something imagined, but plainly and simply a centaur. Sartre concludes his own very sketchy account in *The Imagination* by saying that an image is a kind of consciousness, imaging-consciousness. The image is not essentially *in* consciousness, nor is it something mental.

In 1940 came a contribution to phenomenological psychology which Sartre had already announced in 1936, *L'Imaginaire: psychologie phénoménologique de l'imagination (The Psychology of Imagination)*. The link between the topic of this work and Sartre's own system is clear. *L'Imaginaire* provided a training ground for Sartre's own powers of imagining. Here he cultivated the psychological virtuosity and analytical penetration that he needed for his account in *Being and Nothingness* of the distinctive property of consciousness, its being and nothingness. The capacity to imagine, to present to oneself that which is not real, Sartre concluded, is not a contingent *character* of consciousness; far from being a mere adjunct to consciousness, it is consciousness itself "insofar as it realizes its freedom."[4] Consciousness is continually transcending the real, the actual. When I am waiting for my friend Pierre to arrive on the 7.35 p.m. train—we will encounter his absence in all its fullness in *Being and Nothingness*, (see below, p. 300)—my actions have a meaning which presupposes something that has not yet occurred, namely Pierre's arrival. This "event" "is" a kind of absence, a nothing. Whenever we act, consciousness itself is something that constantly releases itself from the actual. It is outside the actual, or in process of going beyond it. Whence a second aspect of consciousness, also one that has to do with "nothing": consciousness makes itself into a nothing in relation to the content of consciousness.

The approach to Sartre's philosophy, viewed as a genuine philosophical system, is by way of phenomenological psychology; there is little to be gained by trying to interpret it as an expression of "our times," "modern man," "*angst* and disintegration," "alienation," and so on. An essential part of phenomenological psychology is its criticism of what it regards as the "illusion of immanence"—the view that the image I have of Pierre's arrival, when I think of this expected event, is "within" my consciousness. The assumption that images are things inside one, mental objects either in one's head or in consciousness, is a common-sense one, in Sartre's view. It is in an ordinary unreflective frame of mind that we talk of "the image of Pierre." However, it would be more accurate to speak of "consciousness of Pierre-in-image" or imaging-consciousness of Pierre."[5] Imaging-consciousness is consciousness of the object Pierre, not consciousness of a picture in consciousness which serves to represent the real Pierre. In criticizing Hume's notion of 'ideas' as objects in, or compris-

---

[4] *L'Imaginaire: psychologie phénoménologique de l'imagination* (29th ed.; Paris: Gallimard, 1948), p. 236. English translation by Bernard Frechtman, *The Psychology of Imagination* (London: Rider, 1949; New York: Philosophical Library, 1949).
[5] *Ibid.*, p. 17.

ing, consciousness, Sartre is taking issue with a fundamental assumption in Anglo-Saxon common-sense philosophy.

Sartre's own account of mental images has much in common with other rejections, in both philosophy and psychology, of the kind of "duplication of entities" we get when we feel we must distinguish between a tree-in-consciousness and a tree-in-the-garden—hence outside consciousness. Here one is reminded very strongly of Gilbert Ryle's version, which we have already mentioned (see p. 158, above).

In an essay entitled *La Transcendence de l'égo: esquisse d'une description phénoménologique* ("The Transcendence of the Ego: A Sketch of a Phenomenological Description"), published in 1936-37, Sartre raised the question of whether, if one neutralizes the natural attitude by *epoché* and confines oneself strictly to what is given, that is, to intentional objects, there is an "I" to be located behind consciousness. Suppose I intend a centaur, are there two things presented, an intentional centaur and an "I" that intends it? Or can there be an imaging-consciousness of a centaur *without* any reference to an "I" to whom the consciousness belongs? To this all-important question Husserl had answered no, but Sartre's answer was that there can be such a consciousness.

This answer paved the way for Sartre's own species of phenomenological analysis as we find it in *Being and Nothingness*. The basic axiom in this main work may be put in the form of the statement that "there are only phenomena." Since the transcendental "I" postulated by Husserl cannot be understood as being one among all other phenomena, Sartre concludes that it does not exist. In our normal unreflective, or rather pre-reflective, involvement in things, there is no "I" that forms part of the structure in our experiences.

In 1938 Sartre delivered the manuscript of a novel which he had entitled *Melancholia* to the well-known publisher Gaston Gallimard, who proposed the alternative title *La Nausée*. Under this latter title the novel marked Sartre's breakthrough as a writer. The following year he published his *Esquisse d'une théorie des émotions*[6] *(Sketch for a Theory of the Emotions)*, and in 1940, *L'Imaginaire*, which we have already referred to.

Until World War II politics were not of direct concern to Sartre. His war experience changed this. Due to poor eyesight he served as a non-combatant with the meteorological service. In June, 1940, he was taken prisoner by the advancing Germans. Captivity revealed to him, he believes, the true nature of freedom—and also the possibilities of the theater as a means of influencing people. At Christmas-time his first short piece was staged, with his fellow prisoners as actors.[7] In 1941 Sartre was repatriated for "health reasons," and in Paris during the four years of occupation he became intensely active in politics and writing. *Les Mouches* was performed as early as 1943 and aroused enormous enthusiasm. Sartre was active in the resistance movement, working with, among others, the phenomenologist and psychologist Maurice Merleau-Ponty. By the time of the liberation, in 1944, Sartre had become a central figure in the cultural life of Paris and the word he used to describe his philosophy, "existentialism," the main cultural slogan of the day.

In 1943 he had published the seven hundred and twenty-two-page *Being and Nothingness*. Despite its tendency to obscurity, the work was widely read and even more widely admired. Even its characteristic German—or more precisely, Hegelian—stamp told in its favor, proof that here too the French could outdo the Germans—in that field, moreover, where the latter had always been acknowledged masters: more or less unintelligible, speculative metaphysics and system building.

[6]*Esquisse d'une théorie des émotions* (Paris: Hermann, 1939). English translations: (1) *Outline of a Theory of the Emotions,* trans. Bernard Frechtman (New York: Philosophical Library, 1948); (2) *Sketch for a Theory of the Emotions,* trans. Philip Mairet (London: Methuen, 1962).
[7]See Philip Thody, *Jean Paul Sartre: A Literary . and Political Study* (London: Hamish Hamilton, 1960; New York: The Macmillan Co., 1961).

Although *Being and Nothingness* was not an easy book to grasp, the connection between its words and what Sartre had to say both in the political and the literary sphere seemed altogether obvious. Each aspect of Sartre's many-sided activity seemed to be supported by all the others.

In his well-known tribute to freedom in 1944, the tie between politics and philosophy comes out clearly.

> We were never more free than under the Nazi Occupation. We had lost all our rights, beginning with the right to speak. We were insulted daily and had to bear those insults in silence. On one pretext or another—as workers, Jews, political prisoners—Frenchmen were deported. . . . And because of all this we were free. . . . Every instant we lived to the full the meaning of that banal little phrase "All men are mortal." The choice that each of us made of his life and his being was a genuine choice because it was made in the presence of death; because it could always have been expressed in the form "Rather death than. . . ."[8]

In the years after liberation the political situation in France became more complex, the relation between thought, involvement, and action less transparent. Perhaps the basic mood of *Being and Nothingness* is more clearly perceptible to a reader during an occupation than in a "cold war." In an occupied country the directions in which authentic choice lies can be expressed quite simply by a constantly repeated "No!"

In *Being and Nothingness* we find the expected academic glance at past philosophers, but the work acquires a charm of its own from the way in which Sartre's past and present literary colleagues are quite naturally included in his round of calls. As part of the order of the day we find visits to Balzac. Cézanne, Dostoevsky, Faulkner (his account of the triumph

<hr/>

[8]*Situations* (Paris: Gallimard, 1949), III, 11-12.

and freedom of those to whom violence is done, e.g., in *Light in August*), Flaubert (his fate in the hands of the psychologizing biographer), Gide (treated as a colleague even in abstract discussion), Joyce, Kafka (*The Trial:* to be human is always to be on trial), Lawrence, Malraux, Mauriac, Poe, Proust (in the guise of, among other things, an intellectualistic psychologist!), Rilke, Sophocles, and many others.

Of the more important philosophical figures of the past, four are present throughout the work: first and foremost Descartes (Sartre looks for a new point of departure, a new *cogito*), and Hegel, but also Kant, implicitly present, or felt as a shadow, and—remarkably enough—Spinoza. Marx has only a very modest place, he is *not quite* banished.[9] With Husserl and Heidegger, however, Sartre involves himself in a technical philosophical discussion, in which Husserl most frequently comes off worst: Sartre is looking for an essentially different concept of *phenomenon* to form the basis of his whole *Essai d'ontologie phénoménologique*.

The enormous popularity enjoyed by Sartre at the end of the war must not, of course, be taken as proof of a general grasp and acceptance of his tidings—rather the reverse. The history of philosophy does nothing to bolster one's expectations of a correlation between being popular and being understood. In the following exposition we shall try both to represent Sartre and to interpret him, but always keeping to his own ways of expressing himself, however strong the temptation to resort to speculative paraphrase.

There are tempting speculations to make, too, about Sartre and "the times," "modern man," and so on, but it is difficult to see what basis there can be for venturing any such views. We may quote one bold author who says that to "understand Jean-Paul Sartre is to understand something important about the present time. As philosopher, as politician, and as novelist,

[9]For political references in the work, see Thody, *Jean Paul Sartre*.

Sartre is profoundly and self-consciously contemporary; he has the style of the age."[10]

In matters of ethics, naturally, Sartre is far from being alone in his views. His ideas on the subject have something in common with those of a number of writers and thinkers, also often classed as "modern." R.-M. Albérès points to a common motif in the moral view of Sartre, Bernanos, Camus, and Greene: they "isolate the human being from the life of the cosmos," and declare him the disposer of his own dignity and salvation "insofar as he pronounces his responsibility."[11]

In Sartre's philosophy, a man is to be judged for his actions alone; his intentions don't count. No excuse can be made by appealing to the complexity of things, or to lack of opportunity to demonstrate one's "real" self. Sartre's own moral and political antipathy to the bourgeois, and his belief in a kind of communism as the only hope in combatting it, had also, therefore, to be expressed in action. For an author this involved constantly taking a public lead on matters of controversy. Sartre's emphasis on political actions and on results in preference to sentiments has brought him very close to the political program of communism. He describes himself as a Marxist, but not a dialectical materialist, nor yet a communist. There are cogent ethical and philosophical grounds for this. He has been violently, often personally attacked, by writers of the French Communist party. Dialectical materialism—the party's philosophy—stands in decisive opposition to Sartre's position in *Being and Nothingness*, and in a rather more qualified opposition to the position he takes in his second main work, *Critique de la raison dialectique* ("Critique of Dialectical Reason"), published in 1960.[12]

---

[10]Iris Murdoch, *Sartre: Romantic Rationalist* (Cambridge: Bowes & Bowes, 1953; New Haven: Yale University Press, 1953).

[11]R.-M. Albérès, *Jean-Paul Sartre* (Paris: Éditions Universitaires, 1954), pp. 138-39.

[12]Cf. the article on materialism and revolution in *Les Temps modernes*, June and July, 1946, and the section "Question de methode"

It is often said that Sartre attempted to create his own revolutionary party but failed because only intellectuals joined it, and none of the proletariat whom the revolution was to benefit.[13] This is perhaps not altogether true: in 1948, Sartre joined with other outstanding left-wing socialists to set up the *Rassemblement Démocratique Révolutionnaire* ("Revolutionary Democratic Assembly"). The aim, as Sartre saw it, was to bring together those who were oriented to the Left but held differing political opinions on details, in order to give strength to what he considered a less authoritarian and doctrinaire revolutionary political program than that of the Communist party.[14]

It was an especially important consideration for him that the Communist party did not allow free discussion of all crucial political issues; Sartre has always been a bold and uncompromising champion of debate. Sales of the new organization's publications, however, were slight, and internal discord soon led to its complete dissolution. Following this far from encouraging episode, Sartre came out in stronger support of the actual policies put into effect by the communists, though still without being a party member. Indeed, he has gone on record as saying that it is only through the Communist party that the workers can exist as a class; without it there would be simply a mass of underprivileged persons.

(pp. 15-32) in *CRD*. Sartre's political views and activity are well presented from a sober, Anglo-Saxon, non-socialistic point of view in Thody, *Jean-Paul Sartre*. Accounts from socialistic viewpoints bear more strongly the stamp of their authors' commitment. The most violent attacks and bitter accounts come from communists. (In the literary and moral field we can mention Mauriac's characterization of Sartre as an excrementalist.)

[13]Albérès writes that it was when Sartre was "rejected" by communism that he, together with David Rousset and Gérard Rosenthal, founded this independent party. *Jean-Paul Sartre*, p. 34.

[14]For its aims, see *Entretiens sur la politique* (Paris: Gallimard, 1949), a discussion between Sartre, David Rousset, and Gérard Rosenthal, published by them conjointly.

In the 1950's Sartre undertook a revision of Marxism, and in 1960 he published the first part of a large work in which he sought to adapt existentialism to a Marxist framework, *Critique de la raison dialectique*.

The title suggests something of a parallel with Kant's *Critique of Pure Reason*. The word "dialectical" has an important function in the work and can only be made more precise within a framework of Hegelian thinking. As a rough indication, one could say that a relation between two items *A* and *B* is dialectical if *A* and *B* are distinct but such that *A* cannot be determined without *B*, nor *B* without *A*. Though *A* and *B* are distinct, they can neither be thought nor can they exist in isolation. "Dialectic" alludes to the development and changing of items which stand in a dialectical relation to one another. The word "dialectical" might therefore be reasonably paraphrased "transcending change," though the word "change" here must not be associated with the *thing* itself that changes. The relation between intention and action exemplifies a dialectic in this way, insofar as a particular action can only be determined with reference to an intention, thus to something which *may* be realized in the future, and the intention can only be determined with reference to the action. The two items cannot be delimited or identified in isolation, but mutually determine one another. Gradually, as the action proceeds, the determination of the intention becomes modified, which again alters the determination of the action. There can be no strict "identity with itself," therefore, in the case of action or of intention. This absence of self-identity characterizes all steps in dialectical relations, thus in all "dialectics" as Sartre uses the word. Sartre tries to elucidate man's relation to state and society from the standpoint that all these relations are dialectical.

Existentialism, says Sartre in the Preface to his new work, must find its place within the framework of Marxist philosophy, "because—as will be seen later—I consider Marxism to be the unsurpassable (*indépassable*) philosophy of our time, and because I look upon the ideology of existence [a new name for his earlier "existentialism"] and its 'comprehensive' method as an enclave within Marxism itself which at the same time embraces and rejects it."[15]

In any one period there is one and only one living philosophy. It should present itself, like a mirror, or a vision of the world, as "the summing up of contemporary knowledge."[16] Existentialism has existed only as a "parasite" upon the living philosophy of the time, namely, the true Hegelian Marxism, and will (in Sartre's new work) be integrated into it. Kierkegaard and what he stood for hardly count any more, except insofar as Kierkegaard is inseparable, philosophically, from Hegel.

Sartre criticizes contemporary Marxists (in the Communist party) for having lost sight of Marx's recognition of the peculiarity of human existence. Furthermore, they look upon Marxism as though it were already a science, and not, as it yet is, simply a set of statements about which way to go.

> . . . we reproach contemporary Marxism for arbitrarily casting aside all the concrete conditions of human life and for preserving nothing from the totality of history but the abstract skeleton of universality. The result is its total loss of the sense of what man is: it has nothing with which to cover up this lack but the absurd psychology of Pavlov.[17]

What we should do, however, is not reject Marxism, but "recapture man in the heart of Marxism."[18]

Sartre introduces a concept of alienation closely akin to that of Marx, but with features that preserve its continuity with *Being and Nothingness*. My own action is alienated if its

---

[15]*CRD*, pp. 9-10.
[16]"la totalisation du Savoir contemporain." *Ibid.*, p. 15.
[17]*Ibid.*, p. 58.
[18]"à l'intérieur du marxisme." *Ibid.*, p. 59. The whole chapter from which we have quoted is a reply to the eminent Hungarian Marxist Gyorgy Lukacz's penetrating criticism of Sartre in his book *Existentialisme et Marxisme* (Paris: Éditions Nagel, 1961).

effect is as though it were the act of another person, or of "the others." In the case of such an action, I become as though I were the others, and no one is himself. Through subjection to public opinion a man behaves otherwise than would be natural for him; he acts *as the others*, and each one of the others does the same.

Under capitalism, the materials that go into producing things function as means of alienation between men. The effects spread to all walks of life and to all creative activity. The main cause of their extensiveness is that men still live in a world of scarcity, a world of things of which there is an insufficiency. "In a milieu of scarcity all the structures in a society depend on its means of production."[19]

In his attempt to incorporate his existentialism into a new Marxist synthesis, Sartre has put emphasis on man as a member of society, a member of a class, a representative of an epoch, in short, on collectivity. But his "message" to individuals concerning fundamental choice is hardly less impressive. Witness to this is his intense interest in the author Jean Genet who early in his life *chose* to be a thief and who, according to his diary, also goes in wholeheartedly for other kinds of asocial courses of action. The concluding passage from Sartre's book on Genet shows the philosophical background for Sartre's palpable interest:

> Genet is we. That is why we must read him. To be sure, he wants to impute to us mistakes that we have not committed, that we have not even dreamed of committing. But what does that matter? Wait a bit until you are accused: the techniques have been perfected, you will make a full confession. *Therefore*, you will be guilty. At that point you will have only to choose: you will be Bukharin or Genet. Bukharin or our will *to be together* carried to the point of martyrdom; Genet or our solitude carried to the point of Passion.

[19]*CRD*, pp. 224-25 n.

If we maintain the hope and firm intention of escaping this alternative, if there is still time to reconcile, with a final effort, the object and the subject, we must, be it only once and in the realm of the imaginary, achieve this latent solitude which corrodes our acts and thoughts. We spent our time fleeing from the objective into the subjective and from the subjective into objectivity. This game of hide-and-seek will end only when we have the courage to go to the limits of ourselves in both directions at once.[20] At the present time, we must bring to light the subject, the guilty one, that monstrous and wretched bug which we are likely to become at any moment. Genet holds the mirror up to us: we must look at it and see ourselves.[21]

Existentialism as a philosophical system

Basic positions
The theory of the phenomenon

Sartre's book *Being and Nothingness* is divided into six sections. It opens with an Introduction in which the author introduces most of his key terms and discusses his method. Then follow four parts, the first about "nothingness," nihilation, negation, and bad faith, the second about consciousness and its being-for-itself. The third takes up being-for-others, or my self looked at by others. This part deals with community, love and hate, and many other things. Part Four consists of a detailed development of the theory of consciousness as a theory of freedom. The Conclusion, the

[20]Does Sartre here seem to suggest that man is perhaps not an entirely useless passion? That he pursues something which, one day, if he has courage enough to penetrate to his own depths, may be realized? Sartre's remarks here may be compared with what he says in *L'Être et le néant* (e.g., p. 138 n.) about a kind of *en-soi-pour-soi*.

[21]J.-P. Sartre, *Saint Genet: Actor and Martyr*, translated from the French by Bernard Frechtman (New York: George Braziller, Inc., 1963). Reprinted with the permission of the publishers. Copyright © 1963 by George Braziller, Inc. and copyright © 1952 by Librairie Gallimard.

sixth section of the book, includes a short discussion of the possibility of an ethics based on the preceding account. In order to come to the *central philosophical foundation* of Sartre's ambitious and many-sided philosophy, we will give a fairly detailed account of the Introduction and Part One.

Some familiarity with Heidegger's *Sein und Zeit (Being and Time)* makes the study of Sartre very much more simple: one notes how Sartre deepens, perhaps partly changes, a number of Heidegger's concepts and viewpoints. Many terms are in effect direct translations of Heidegger's into French. However, no really fruitful introduction can be effected by trying to make the similarities and differences explicit. One inevitably comes up against considerable purely philosophical difficulties, and besides, the project presupposes some common framework in which both Heidegger's and Sartre's philosophies can be accommodated.

Another aid to study, and source of added motivation too, is to revive in oneself an appreciation of the difficulties that Descartes and later philosophers sought to overcome in explaining the relation between mind or consciousness and matter, between soul and body, thought and extension. In addition, one should recall the persistent problems of epistemological scepticism and subjectivism. How does the knowing subject *get out* to the objects of knowledge? One need only remind oneself of the well-known difficulties arising from the subjectivity of sense-qualities, for example Kant's thing-in-itself, and from the fact that one can have no direct experience of the consciousnesses of other people.

Sartre, like Heidegger, is trying to find new paths through, and perchance out of, this wilderness, and he is not to be easily daunted by what he encounters on the way. Like Carnap and Wittgenstein, Heidegger and Sartre are convinced that there is something fundamentally wrong with the traditional Cartesian point of departure and the opposition between realism and idealism, dogmatism and scepticism.

Naturally, Sartre has learned not only from contemporary

philosophers; in *Being and Nothingness* the craftsman's as well as the professional philosopher's touch is clearly Hegelian. The prospect of comprehending everything within Being and Nothing, and thus of making these the framework of a philosophical system, is one that the great German master himself held out. Sartre translates the passage where Hegel expressly says so, putting it in italics: *"there is nothing in heaven or in earth which does not contain in itself being and nothingness (Sein und Nichts)."*[22]

Sartre attempts to exploit Hegel's world of ideas as well as his terminology but often finds himself forced to be critical as much of the thoughts as of the concepts. Man, says Sartre, is a useless passion, and it may be that the same applies to his own passion for Hegel, insofar, at least, as the end product, the system intended and in many respects realized in Sartre's main work, differs essentially from Hegel's, and indeed is hardly compatible with it. But to business! The following is an account of what Sartre has to say about "the phenomenon," including some account of his basic position concerning the relation between phenomena and consciousness.

"Modern thought has realized considerable progress by reducing the existent to the series of appearances which manifest it."[23] The reduction of the existent to the series of its manifestations has freed us from the distinction between the

[22]G. W. F. Hegel, *Wissenschaft der Logik* (Der Philosophischen Bibliothek, Vol. 56 [Leipzig: Felix Meiner, 1934]), p. 69 (Book I, sec. I, chap. 1, Part C): "Wenn das Resultat, dass Sein und Nichts dasselbe ist, für sich auffällt oder paradox scheint, so ist hierauf nicht weiter zu achten. . . . Es wäre nicht schwer, diese Einheit von Sein und Nichts in jedem Beispiele, in *jedem* Wirklichen oder Gedanken aufzuzeigen. Es muss dasselbe, was oben von der Unmittelbarkeit und Vermittlung, (welche letztere eine Beziehung aufeinander, damit *Negation* enthält), vom *Sein* und Nichts gesagt werden, dass es nirgend im Himmel und auf Erden Etwas gebe, was nicht beides, Sein und Nichts, in sich enthielte."

[23]*L'Etre et le néant: essai d'ontologie phénoménologique* (Paris: Gallimard, 1943), p. 11. English translation by Hazel Barnes, *Being and Nothingness* (New York: Philosophical Library, 1956; London: Methuen, 1957), p. xlv. Henceforth the work will be referred to as

exterior and interior of things, the shell and the kernel, between that which is superficially accessible in a thing and the
thing's inside, its mysterious, timeless or unalterable nature.
That inner nature or reality which people have thought they
could in some way dimly perceive, or divine, but which is not
revealed to the light of day, quite simply doesn't exist. Thus
it would be inappropriate even to say that we should *give up*
our search into the inner nature of things. The very distinction between that which appears and the real, or between that
which *appears to be* and that which is "is no longer entitled
to any legal status within philosophy."[24]

These are the statements with which the work opens and
they indicate immediately the metaphysical and phenomenological tradition in which Sartre places himself. It is this
Franco-German metaphysical tradition that Sartre comes to
identify as modern thought. It is striking how it differs from
other candidates, particularly the British tradition in philosophy. In the latter tradition, philosophical doubt, through
Hume and others, has put all ontology and metaphysics in
question, but has left common sense undisturbed. In the Franco-
German tradition, however, it is precisely common sense that
has been gnawed away by doubt, while the ontological and
phenomenological mode of thought remains more or less intact.

According to Sartre all manifestations of the existent stand
on an equal footing.[25] He provides two examples by way of
illustration, some of the few in the work which he draws
from the exact natural sciences: 'Force' in mechanics is no
longer some strange unknown which lies concealed behind
changes in speed or direction; it is the sum total of these very
changes and is thus just as manifest as they are. Similarly with
an electric current, which is only the sum total of such elec-

---

EN, the page references to the English edition being given in parentheses. When the English translation has been slightly altered, the
reference is italicized.
[24]*EN*, p. 11 (xlv).
[25]*Ibid.*, p.11 (xlv).

trical phenomena as the alterations in the needle of a galvanometer. Behind the perceptible changes there is nothing, so electricity is not something over and above them. However, the series of manifestations is not a finite one; in principle it is infinite, the phenomena are inexhaustible.[26]

Having dispensed with the inner, we cannot continue talking of an "outer," since this can only be defined in relation to something "inner." What we are left with is what appears, hence the phenomenon, as we find it, says Sartre, "for example in the 'phenomenology' of Husserl and Heidegger."[27]

At the same time and "by the same stroke" we get rid of the duality of potency and act, possibility and actuality, potentiality and fulfilment. The act becomes everything. "We shall refuse, for example, to understand by 'genius'—in the sense in which we say that Proust 'had genius' or that he 'was' a genius—a particular capacity to produce certain works, which was not exhausted exactly in producing them. The genius of Proust is neither the work considered in isolation nor the subjective ability to produce it; it is the work considered as the totality of the manifestations of the person."[28] So long as the person is still productive his genius undergoes change, insofar as any addition to the collection of its manifestations means a change in the collection's identity.

---

[26]*Ibid.*, p. 12 (xlvii). The examples from physics bring to mind the "empirio-critic" Ernst Mach's interpretation of physical phenomena, but Sartre has almost certainly been more influenced by Pierre Duhem and Henri Poincaré, both important French philosophers of science. The examples are interesting in that with Sartre they occur in a setting of phenomenological ontology. Mach, Poincaré, and Duhem incorporate them into, respectively, empiricist, Kantian, and neo-Thomist philosophy. In his discussion with Naville in *L'Existentialisme est un humanisme*, Sartre also embarks upon theory of science and adopts a markedly anticausal position. "Naville: ' . . . you will admit that the sciences employ the notion of causality?' Sartre: 'Absolutely not. The sciences are abstract, they study the variations in abstract factors and not real "causality." ' " (Paris: Éditions Nagel, 1946), pp. 139-40.

[27]Cf. *EN*, p. 12 (xlvi).

[28]*Ibid.*, p. 12 (xlvi).

If we carry the dictum "the act is everything" over into the field of morals, we get a denial of the view that people can behave badly but really, inwardly, be morally good, or conversely, that good behavior is compatible with a, more or less, bad moral character. One cannot excuse oneself by pleading a lack of opportunity to show one's true mettle, give one's moral dispositions free rein, put them to the test, and so on. What a man has to offer is no more and no less than what he does offer, in whatever situation he happens to be placed. This is merely a variation on the theme of the exhaustiveness of the phenomenal, a theme that does away with anything that cannot appear to somebody. The existentialist slogan "Existence precedes essence" can be applied in a variety of contexts, among them the one we are discussing: "Man is nothing else but that which he makes of himself."[29] His essence is what he makes of himself, and what he makes of himself is no more than the sum total of his past, his biography, in fact.

The view of oneself, things, the world, and one's actions which underlies the above theses concerning phenomenon and act very largely determines the whole of Sartre's philosophy, and every new element introduced into the design has to be seen in the light of these theses.[30]

---

[29] *L'Existentialisme est un humanisme* (Paris: Éditions Nagel, 1946), p. 22. English translations: (1) *Existentialism*, trans. Bernard Frechtman (New York: Philosophical Library, 1947); (2) *Existentialism and Humanism*, trans. Philip Mairet (London: Methuen, 1948). Mairet's translation is reprinted as "Existentialism is a Humanism" in Walter Kaufmann, *Existentialism from Dostoevsky to Sartre* (New York: The World Publishing Co., Meridian Books, 1956). The quoted passage is from p. 291 of this edition.

[30] A technically more penetrating account of Sartre's theory of the phenomenon must embrace many questions, among the more important of which is the following.

Exactly what concepts does Sartre mean to express by "appear" and "appear to"? One reason the question is central is that Sartre also introduces here concepts of 'being,' 'law,' and 'synthesis' which seem to run counter to his so-called anti-essentialism. According to (what Sartre understands as) modern thought, something that exists can still

A phenomenon, as a matter of definition, *is* as it appears; it is identical with its appearance. Thus if we were to consider Aristotle's and Heidegger's question about what it is to *be*, the answer in the light of the theory of the phenomenon should perhaps be that "the being of appearances is their ap-

---

be said to have an *essence*, but in a special sense: namely, as the synthesis of, or law for, its successive manifestations. The essence of the thing "is" thus the appearance of the law; it "is" the synthesis of its manifestations. Because the synthesis itself is something that appears, it can be grasped in intuition. Things thus manifest their essence. This explains, according to Sartre, the possibility of an intuition of essences, Husserl's *Wesensschau*. Among the terms Sartre uses for that which binds the series of manifestations together into a thing (an "entity," in Heidegger's sense) are "reason," "synthesis," "synthetic unity," "law which rules." But he himself sees a fundamental difficulty in this view of manifestations and essence.

The individual manifestations form endless series. (Electrical phenomena will continue, the series of different manifestations has no end, even though certain things recur.) Man grasps only a finite number of links in the series; he must therefore, so to speak, bring things to a conclusion. He sees the same thing in different manifestations. Proust's work as a whole, although it is already concluded, provides a basis for endless different interpretations and various analyses of aspects. In this sense his work is inexhaustible. In this way the essence of any existent can only manifest itself completely in an infinite series of individual manifestations.

Accordingly, an intuition cannot grasp an essence with one or any finite number of dated intuitions of the essence's manifestations. The relation between manifestation and essence is taken up again by Sartre in a later section, where he introduces a new way of describing it. One can distinguish between a thing's color, its smell, and so forth, and always on the basis of these properties determine some essence to which they stand in a relation analogous to that between sign and signified. Thus various groups of manifestations (color, smell; color, shape, weight, etc.) correspond to distinct signs (e.g., "dog" and "chien") which have the same sense, when the groups are manifestations of the same thing.

I have hesitated to incorporate these remarks in the text, not only because of their technical implications, but because it is doubtful whether the considerations are essential for a deep and genuine understanding of Sartre's basic view of existence. In his second major philosophical work, *Critique de la raison dialectique*, Sartre seems to attribute to things, states, and epochs a far-reaching inner firmness and solidity. His rejection of the *inner* nature of things should be understood primarily as a rejection of certain metaphysical positions, not of

pearing." In other words, being amounts to that which is as it appears. However, Sartre does not take this answer to be fully in accord with Berkeley's principle "Esse est percipi" ("to be is to be perceived"). The concept of *percipi* implies the concept of *percipiens*, someone who perceives, a perceiving essence, whether human or divine. The fact that Sartre does not wholly subscribe to Berkeley's principle is because he thinks to do so would entail commitment also to Berkeley's metaphysics and theology.

And yet it is clear that even if *everything that is* exists in the way that the phenomenon exists, and phenomena are things which appear, it is implied that there is something to which the phenomenon appears, and this "something" cannot itself be a phenomenon.

The word "something" is put in quotation marks because what it refers to must have a quite special character, as Sartre says, "a peculiar existence," indeed so special that it would be incorrect to refer to it by substantival or pronominal expressions like "something" or "this," since these normally refer to physical objects or at least to phenomena. One important feature of this "something" that is not a thing is that "it" *reveals itself as consciousness*. For Sartre, consciousness is "that to which appearances appear," or "that for which whatever appears are appearances." The word "consciousness" in this context must not, of course, be given a sense according to

---

the "realism" that common sense seems to imply (e.g., the realism that is implicit in the belief that a house can be moved somewhere else, rebuilt, refurbished, etc., and still be the same, largely independent of how it appears to individual people at particular times).

Our conclusion can be put thus: Sartre opens his work with an implicit statement which, reasonably interpreted, does not fit into his system as a whole: namely, the statement that existing things can (and must) be reducible to "a series of appearances which lay bare the existing thing."

Sartre does not attempt, in the spirit of Plato, to "save the appearances" by introducing hypotheses about ideas, nor does he introduce Kantian "Dinge an sich" as a limiting concept. The appearances do not need to be saved, nor is there anything that could save them.

which consciousness is ascribed the character of some kind of *thing*.

The relation between the philosophical term "consciousness" (in Sartre's sense) and the concept of a knowing subject in modern theories of knowledge is complex. Consciousness is, for Sartre, something "transparent," in that it is nothing substantially additional to the phenomenon which is *for* consciousness. The "knowing subject," on the other hand, is usually conceived as something existing independently of the objects it apprehends; the possibility remains open that there are objects which cannot appear to a subject, or subjects which apprehend no objects. This, in Sartre's view, is true of Berkeley's knowing subject. As we shall see, it is important for the whole of Sartre's philosophy that consciousness is indissolubly tied to the phenomenon, yet without being entirely absorbed in it. Consciousness "exists," and what consciousness is "of" also "exists," but the word "exists" is used in these cases to denote two essentially different kinds of existence, or existences that differ essentially in status. In fact, to be a phenomenon and to be consciousness are so different that it could only be according to an extremely abstract concept of existence (as, for example, in formal logic) that both were said to exist in the *same* sense.

Sartre manages to retain Husserl's principle that consciousness is always consciousness *of* something. Insofar as something appears to consciousness, there is a consciousness of that thing. If nothing appears—as, presumably, in death—then there is no longer any consciousness. So much follows from the concept itself. Sartre is also able to follow Husserl (and the neo-realists) in their criticism of the usage according to which we say that something is *in* consciousness, as though when, say, we see a tree, there is a picture, a kind of copy of the tree, in our consciousness. Nothing at all, not images, thoughts or feelings, can, in Sartre's view, be in one's consciousness. Consciousness has nothing whatsoever in common with a container. Whatever the relationship of consciousness to the objects at which it is directed, it is not such that the latter are outside the former. "A table is not *in* consciousness —not even in the capacity of a representation. A table is *in* space, beside the window, *etc.*"[31]

When a thing appears to consciousness there is something consciousness knows about that thing, namely that it appears. But the phenomenon that appears is not something about which one has any knowledge in a more qualified sense of the term. Knowledge in this more qualified sense implies a kind of consciousness about that which appears which presupposes reflection. When consciousness is not reflective as in knowing-consciousness, Sartre calls it "pre-reflective." The concept of pre-reflective consciousness is important since it contains an implicit rebuttal of Descartes and "rationalism."

However, the concept of knowing-consciousness must be handled with some caution. If knowledge implies consciousness of itself, and this consciousness must itself be a kind of knowing-consciousness, it might seem that we were forced to assume the existence of an infinite series of knowings, of knowledge that one knows that one knows, and so on. What is needed is some principle which enables us to avoid this assumption. The word "of" in "consciousness of" must denote an immediate relationship, not a relation between a piece of knowledge (or a process of knowing) and that which knowledge is knowledge of. In Sartre's view this is completely borne out by phenomenological intuition. In knowing-consciousness there is something which appears, namely knowledge, as a pre-reflective object of consciousness.

In ordinary perception it is difficult to come upon anything immediate: "If I count the cigarettes which are in that case, I have the impression of disclosing an objective property of this collection of cigarettes: *they are a dozen.*"[32] But I need have no knowing-consciousness concerning the fact that I am counting. I count pre-reflectively, yet consciously. On being

[31]*EN*, p. 17 (li).
[32]*Ibid.*, p. 19 (liii).

asked what I am doing, I "reflect" on what I am doing, set myself, as it were, outside what I am doing. I get knowledge *about* the circumstance that I am counting. It is true that when I am counting pre-reflectively I can be said to be conscious of counting, but in order to avoid confusing this "of" with the "of" in "knowledge of" something, it is better to avoid this form of expression: instead of a pre-reflective consciousness of counting, we should talk rather about a counting-consciousness. This latter formulation also reminds us that we never have consciousness except as *x*-consciousness, that is consciousness of something or other: counting-consciousness, twelve-cigarette-consciousness, pleasure-consciousness, and so on.

Between pleasure and consciousness of this pleasure there is no boundary to be drawn. But just for this reason pleasure cannot be defined as an *experience* of or in consciousness. *Definiens* and *definiendum* are here identical. A definition in this form only acquires meaning if one employs literary concepts of consciousness, according to which we say that pleasure is in consciousness whereas, say, the sun in which we take pleasure is outside consciousness.

On this point, as in most others where Sartre's pronouncements on consciousness seem startling or dubious, a return to the theory of the phenomenon can clarify matters: everything that exists is a phenomenon, something that appears. But implicit in the concept of phenomenon is the notion that phenomena appear *to* something, and the word "consciousness" is itself the term denoting this to-relation. What has to be grasped is that the second something in "something appears to something" is not anything that exists in the same way, or the same sense of "exists," as a phenomenon exists when, by abstraction, it is thought in isolation from that to which it stands in the relation of appearing-to.

In other words, consciousness must in no way be thought of as an additional phenomenon to all the others. Because the to-relation is implicit in the concept of phenomenon, Sartre is able to deny the existence of phenomena other than in relation to consciousness: without phenomena there is no consciousness, without consciousness there are no phenomena. To put it more awkwardly, though from a philosophical point of view more perspicuously: there can be nothing that appears without there being something that it appears to, and there can be nothing that is appeared to without there being something that appears to it. This way of putting it impresses upon us that Sartre's point of departure is not phenomenon *and* consciousness, but something—as an object of phenomenological analysis—having two poles: the phenomenon pole and the consciousness pole. Although attention can be focused on one or the other pole, this in no way implies that there are two entities. Sartre's terminology makes it easy to overlook this, especially if one isn't conversant with Hegelian dialectic.

From the above it should be evident that if consciousness, in these terms, lends itself to a non-contradictory determination, it is only by a hair's breadth. (The reader may note here that to be on the safe side we do not refer to Sartre's *concept* of consciousness, since this would imply unreserved acknowledgment that the determination of Sartre's use of the term "consciousness" does not include contradictory assertions, or else that there can be an account of what it is to be a concept in which the law of contradiction is given a specifically Hegelian status.)

In allowing ourselves to speak of there *being* phenomena and of there *being* consciousness, we have to be clear that the word "being" implies something quite different in each case. On the other hand, Sartre uses "being" or "to be" as such very general terms that it is possible to say, in his terminology, that phenomena and consciousness exemplify different *ways* of being. The being of the phenomenon he calls *being-in-itself*, and the being of consciousness he calls *being-for-itself*.[33]

---

[33]"*l'être-en-soi*" and "*l'être-pour-soi*." Sartre's use of the word "being" (etc.) and of combined words in which "being" is one of the compo-

Sartre's account of being-in-itself is vivid. This kind of being, he says, *is* what it is, something opaque, solid *(massif)*, neither active nor passive, and without relation to itself; it is not created, bears no mark of a god's having brought it into being, but neither does it create itself; it is something which in itself cannot be attributed to or derived from something other than itself. Everything existing in-itself is "contingent"; necessity can be defined only in relation to ideal entities, not to existents. It simply is, and therefore can be neither possible nor impossible.[34]

This is the account of the in-itself expressly subscribed to by Sartre in his existentialist system. The difficulties the would-be interpreter encounters in assessing the system's conclusiveness and freedom from contradiction are daunting enough; they are unnecessarily compounded by trying—as is often done—to incorporate into the system the words used by Roquentin in *La Nausée*, to describe "existence": "gluey," "sickly," "visceral," and so on. These terms are coined not for a philosophical treatment of the in-itself, but for a literary treatment of the subject of existence. Sartre refers to them in *Being and Nothingness* as anthropomorphic.

The main stress in the philosophical characterization of the in-itself is on its superfluousness. The in-itself is *de trop:* it cannot be derived from anything, either from another being, or from a possibility, or from a necessary law. Sartre adds: "Uncreated, without reason for being, without any connection with another being, being-in-itself is *de trop* for eternity."[35] This statement might seem once again to invite the

---

nents is complex enough, and certainly important enough, to deserve a doctoral dissertation. When, for instance, Sartre says consciousness "is not," or "is a nothing," one may take this as an abbreviated form of "does not exemplify the way of being that is being-in-itself," and when he says consciousness "is," one may substitute "exemplifies the way of being that is being-for-itself." Such short cuts to understanding, however, evade the question of what different meanings the term "is" may have for Sartre.

[34]*EN*, pp. 30-34 (lxii-lxvii).
[35]*Ibid.*, p. 34 (lxvi).

question of whether Roquentin's celebrated glossary of dyslogistic terms has any place in Sartre's system. Can they not be treated as terms on a par with *"de trop* for eternity" as philosophically apt characterizations of phenomena or of being-in-itself? The answer must surely be in the negative. For one thing, it is clear that Sartre undertakes to distinguish between 'phenomenon' and 'being'—a complete section in the exposition of the theory of the phenomenon is devoted to the distinction.[36] And for another, Sartre also distinguishes between things-in-themselves *seen from the points of view, respectively, of the presence and absence of bad faith.* When Roquentin eventually seems to throw himself into a project—the writing of a novel—the trees smile and mean something. But even before this happened he may have been just as unable to see things-in-themselves, that is, unrelated to human purposes, and so on, because he had a purpose then, too, insofar as he sought to take flight in self-deception.

That this is indeed the case is confirmed by, for example, a passage in *Being and Nothingness* in which Sartre poses precisely the question of what a boulder is when it will neither be moved away nor climbed upon, but simply *is* where it lies. The answer is not in Roquentin's vein.

> A particular rock, which manifests a profound resistance if I wish to displace it, will be on the contrary a valuable aid if I want to climb upon it in order to look over the countryside. In itself—if one can even imagine what the rock can be in itself—it is neutral, that is, it waits to be illuminated by an end in order to manifest itself as adverse or helpful.[37]

Admittedly Sartre is here discussing the necessity of there being things capable of offering resistance if there is to be freedom, but in doing so he employs an ontologically relevant concept of "brute things" (*choses brutes*), which he identifies

[36]*Ibid.*, pp. 14-16 (xlviii-1).
[37]*Ibid.*, p. 562 (482).

with Heidegger's *factum brutum*. Brute things are neutral, clearly not importunate and disgusting. The rock or boulder does not become soft by being seen as a neutral thing-in-itself.[38]

And yet, it is not unthinkable that Sartre should say that if the rock were to be removed from the context of its utility and adaptability to personal ends, it would acquire the Roquentinian properties. Perhaps we should express the matter thus: the sticky sweetness of things is nauseating for a given individual only on the basis of the choice he has made, and particularly on the basis of his fundamental projects (*projets fondamentaux*) and *original* choice (*choix original*). These projects can be revealed by a person's taste for things, including food: "I can love slimy contacts, have a horror of holes, *etc.* That does not mean that for me the slimy, the greasy, a hole, *etc.* have lost their general ontological meaning [it is horrible in itself for a consciousness to *become slimy*] but on the contrary that *because* of this meaning, I determine myself in this or that manner in relation to them."[39] Every taste that appears does so not as an absurd datum, but as an evident value. It isn't a matter, for example, of the slimy being a symbol for "the possibility that the in-itself might absorb the for-itself."[40]

So much, then, for the in-itself. Let us go on to the for-itself. Sartre's account of being-for-itself in Part Two of *Being and Nothingness* constitutes one of the work's most original sections. The extremely substantial and condensed Introduction concludes with the "provisional" characterization of being-in-itself which we have just outlined. Between this and the account of being-for-itself Sartre has inserted a sec-

---

[38]"Brute things" in their neutrality must not be confused with "things-in-themselves" unrelated to consciousness. According to Sartre's theory of the phenomenon there is no such thing: without a phenomenon, no consciousness; without a consciousness, no phenomenon.

[39]*EN*, p. 706 (614). The passage in brackets is interpolated from p. 702 (610).

[40]*Ibid.*, p. 702 (609).

tion, Part One, with the title, "The Problem of Nothingness" ("Le problème du néant"). This comprises two chapters, entitled "The Origin of Negation" and "Bad Faith" ("La mauvaise foi"). The first of these, of considerable length, is broadly conceived and develops certain purely philosophical considerations; the second, somewhat shorter, concerns a matter of more general human interest, though the treatment of it tends to leave the reader with the feeling that he is groping with something quite unfamiliar to him.

Applied phenomenology: absence and disappearance
Introduction

Phenomena—that which appears—have no interior; there is nothing inside or behind them that constitutes what is properly real about them. They lack, according to the terms of Sartre's theory of the phenomenon, the solid or substantial character which we generally ascribe to them and which makes us secure in our confidence in them. If in trying to characterize whatever appears to consciousness we do all we can to suppress any inclination to believe in the "internal" solidity and substantialness of things, we find that a great number of the descriptive terms we need are negative terms, saying what is not. The impression conveyed, in thus withholding one's prejudices about solidity and endurance, is one of absences, of lacks, holes, pauses, hiatuses, silences, emptinesses, and omissions.

By lengthening or shortening a pause in a piece of music, that is by altering the length of time in which no sound occurs, we change the sounds, the phenomena, which the pause encompasses. In characterizing absence generally we are accustomed to resort to psychological expressions. But phenomenologically there is no basic reason for this, no reason why, in this particular case, we should describe tone-filled time intervals in musical, non-psychological terms, while absences of tone are described in psychological terms of "experiences" such as "expectancy," "feeling of tension," and so on. Purely as a phenomenon—that is, as something appearing to consciousness—absence has just as positive a stamp as presence. If one talks of *experiences* of things absent, consistency in usage requires one to talk also of experiences of things present. Presence has no claim to be regarded as distinctive in this regard, as if it could put in a personal appearance, while absence can only appear, as it were, by proxy in the form of an experience relating to what might have been present. In point of fact, phenomenologically the terminology of "experiences" is best avoided, since it is either redundant or inappropriate, the former if it signifies simply that something is experienced, the latter if it is supposed to refer to a psychological occurrence distinct from the thing experienced. If one wants a qualifying word here the better choice would be "phenomenon." Thus one can talk of "absence-phenomenon," "presence-phenomenon," "nothing-phenomenon," "nihilation-phenomenon," and the like. Corresponding to this, one also has the "consciousness" terminology and talks in terms of "absence-consciousness," "presence-consciousness," and so on.

Sartre's account of negatively defined "things" can easily appear paradoxical if one forgets that he is describing phenomena, what appears to a consciousness. Criticism of detail is of course in order and can be set about without preliminary. However, any basic criticism would have to be directed at the ontology upon which the descriptions are based, and unless one keeps this ontology in view criticism can easily degenerate into barren polemics. Thus, for example, in criticizing a statement like "Absence or nothingness are things which appear when . . ." one must first distinguish between the philosophical position upon which the acceptability of such statements depends and the phenomenological descriptions which emerge from applying the basic distinctions to the phenomena. As a description, the above statement could be formulated more explicitly according to its implicit ontological framework as "The absence-phenomenon or nothing-phenomenon are things which appear when. . . ."

Sartre, accordingly, opens *Being and Nothingness* with a discussion of his ontological presuppositions, partly under the rubric of "the progress of modern thought." Here basic criticism is in order. But on another fundamental point it is less clear that objections are warranted. If one accedes to the, in part at least, very explicitly presented phenomenological ontology, it is, if anything, reassuring rather than otherwise to find negative entities being given such a distinguished status in the work as a whole.

Hegel's theory of nothingness and negation has generally been found unpalatable. However, in the hands of Heidegger and Sartre, this theory has undergone some change, a deflection toward the phenomenological which presents the points in a new light and calls for renewed consideration and appraisal.

A good number of absence-phenomena can only be adequately described by using "activity" words, verbs or participles that, roughly speaking, connote negative processes, for example that something occurs which brings about a disappearance, makes into nothing, takes something away, uncovers, introduces hiatuses, holes, and other forms of conspicuous absence. In such cases absence can hardly be treated as anything beyond the relevant process of disappearance or removal. (A disappearing act is completed as soon as the object in question has duly and effectively disappeared.)

To take a familiar, trivial example: I am awakened in my hotel by the thud of a shoe which my neighbor is putting outside his door to be polished. A vivid, almost painful expectation of the thud of shoe number two fills my consciousness (not in Sartre's technical sense of "consciousness"). My "mental set" is fully oriented to the thought of a second thud, less obtrusive than the first, to be followed shortly thereafter by the resumption of sleep. But what if my neighbor puts the second shoe down less clumsily, makes no noise? What if he has already done so? Or is one-legged? Then is the time to set about a phenomenological analysis of the absence of thud number two. What features does it present? In my own case this absence is full of events: I "hear" thud number two over and over again, but as a series of unreal thuds to which the expected thud, if it came, would not belong. One could describe this by saying that along with each imagined thud there goes something that can be best described as a "No!"—a refusal to accept the "thud" as the one anticipated: it is "pushed aside," "suppressed," it "can happen again." It just isn't *the* thud: "away with it!" This is but a small part of what occurs; perhaps a good way of describing the phenomenon as a whole would be to say that it has the character of "being made nothing of", as a phenomenon it has the character, one might say, of being discounted. In the following sections we will use as a technical term the word "nihilation" (rather than "annihilation" which, as a word already in use, has associations that are not always appropriate).

At a more elevated plane a corresponding analysis can be carried out with the characterizing of various types of pauses, or decreases in tempo, in a piece of music. Here accounts in terms of "absences of notes" serve particularly aptly to cover the very dramatic "nihilation" phenomena to be found in musical compositions.

Although Sartre's own examples are clear enough, they are often so infused with theoretical considerations as to make any straightforward formulations of them difficult, if not impossible.

"Le néant" (the nihilated) and "néantisation" (nihilation)

Non-being, says Sartre, is always within the bounds of human expectation. From his examples we can begin to understand what he means here by "non-being." When I expect to find 1500 francs in my wallet, it may be that I find only 1300. If one discounts expectation, all that could be said would be that either there are 1500 francs in the wallet or there are 1300; it could not be said that there were "only 1300." In fact, expectation introduces two new phenomena: "only 1300" and "not 1500." The expression "only 1300" is used to refer to a phenomenon of a negative kind: we imply by it a reference to the missing, therefore non-existing, 200 francs. "It is because a physicist *expects* a certain verification of his hypothesis that nature can tell him no. It would be in vain to deny that negation appears on the original basis of a relation of man to the world. The world does not disclose its non-beings to one who has not first posited them as possibilities."[41] But the non-being is not thus reduced to the status of so-called subjective entities. What happens is understood on each occasion as the realization of one of many possibilities.

In order to press home the essential human element in all negation, Sartre does not balk at expressing himself paradoxically; in fact he seems to make a point of doing so.

A volcanic eruption or an earthquake alters the landscape. Where once stood a village, now there is lava, or piles of debris. Something other than what was there has now taken its place. The earthquake as something which is in-itself cannot *destroy* anything. It is only for human beings that there is "no longer" a village, and therefore only for something that understands absence can the concept of destruction be constituted. "It is necessary then to recognize that destruction is an essentially human thing and that *it is man* who destroys his cities through the agency of earthquakes or directly, who destroys his ships through the agency of cyclones or directly."[42]

This example is illuminating in the exceptional clarity with which it exhibits Sartre's predilection for the startling and paradoxical. Although the point of this paradox is fairly evident, it is often difficult to see whether there is anything

---

[41]*Ibid.*, p. 41 (7).

[42]*Ibid.*, p. 43 (9). Sometimes Sartre seems to be a slave to his own complicated terminology. Questions are "solved" which can hardly be considered meaningful except on the basis of a prior evaluation of the terminology's possibilities. Consciousness is constantly nihilating the

basically unparadoxical in the meaning that Sartre expresses in paradoxical terms.

There is some obscurity in the present case. What basis is there for distinguishing "destruction" from the more neutral expression "change," or "something other than what was"? Surely the sentence "Where there was a village, now there is something else" is also one with a human stamp? For even the language of the physicist is human in the sense of the theory of the phenomenon as expounded by Sartre. Moreover, once one tries to distinguish between what is conditioned by human thought and what isn't, one soon gets involved in the difficult notion of a thing-in-itself. If man destroys with the help of earthquakes, then why should we not say equally that it is man who alters or maintains the warmth of the sun with atomic power, and indeed that his hand is evident in all things? And it seems, furthermore, that if anything should not be concerned with all things, that thing would be man, too, since "not being concerned with"—something negative— also bears the stamp of the human.

If Sartre's remarks on earthquakes are carried to their logical conclusion they amount to no more than an empty refer-

---

past, according to Sartre, therefore there is a gap between the present, hence also consciousness, and the past; they become separated for all time. But why can the gap between consciousness in the present and the past not be eliminated? After all, the incredible has often been achieved in respect to overcoming the apparently impossible. The answer, according to Sartre, is that in this case there is something absolutely insurmountable separating the parties, namely *nothing:* "This nothing is absolutely impassable *(infranchissable)*, just because it is nothing; for in every obstacle to be cleared there is something positive which gives itself as about to be cleared. The prior consciousness is always *there* (though with the modification of "pastness"). It constantly maintains a relation of interpretation with the present consciousness, but on the basis of this existential relation it is put out of the game, out of the circuit, between parentheses—exactly as in the eyes of one practicing the phenomenological *epoché*, the world is both within him and outside of him." *(EN,* pp. 64-65 [28].) It would be interesting to see an analysis of the problem in the spirit of Carnap or Wittgenstein.

ence to man, a variation on the Protagorean theme of "Man is the measure of all things."[43]

So much, then, for non-being. More important for an understanding of Sartre's doctrine of man is a grasp of his concept of *le néant*, or 'nothingness.' *Le néant* is a more basic concept than negation. The latter, as a rule, Sartre reserves for statements expressing denials: "It is not snowing" as opposed to "It is snowing." Nihilation (*néantisation*) as a function or activity of consciousness, on the other hand, is presupposed by negation, according to Sartre. Logicians are therefore on the wrong track when they try to test the theory of nihilation by reducing it to negation. Naturally it cannot be done. But the fact that it cannot be done throws no discredit on the nihilation theory.

Sartre's actual phenomenological analysis offers the best introduction to his idiosyncratic terminology, not least in the case of the nihilation terminology.[44] Sartre's description of Pierre's absence in the café—which we have mentioned before—goes straight to the point and clears away much of the mystical obscurity that seems to go with the terminology.

> I have an appointment with Pierre at four o'clock. I arrive at the café a quarter of an hour late. Pierre is

[43]We should note that Sartre qualifies his remarks: "*In a sense*, certainly, man is the only being by whom a destruction can be accomplished." (*EN*, p. 42 [8, my italics].)

[44]'Nihilation terminology' is here used as a common name for the following terms:

nier	deny
négativité	negativity
négation	negation
négatité	*négatité*
non-être	non-being
rien	nothing
négatif	negative
le néant	nothingness
néantisation	nihilation
néantir	nihilate

Négatité and the two last expressions were coined by Sartre himself.

always punctual. Will he have waited for me? I look at the room, the customers, and I say, "He is not here." Is there an intuition of Pierre's absence, or does negation indeed enter in only with judgment? At first sight it seems absurd to speak here of intuition, since to be exact there could not be an intuition of *nothing* and it is the absence of Pierre that is this nothing. Popular consciousness, however, bears witness to this intuition. Do we not say, for example, "I suddenly saw that he was not there." . . . It would seem that we have found fullness everywhere. But we must observe that perception always implies the building up of a form upon a background. No object or group of objects is expressly designed to be organized into form or background: it all depends on how I direct my attention. When I go into this café to look for Pierre, there occurs a synthetic organization of all the objects in the café into background against which Pierre is given as about to appear. The organization of the café into background is a preliminary nihilation (*néantisation*). Each element in the room, a person, a table, a seat, tries to isolate itself and to bring itself into relief against the background formed by all the other objects, then falls back into the non-differentiation of this background and dissolves into it. For the background is that which is seen only incidentally, which is given only marginal attention. . . . This nihilation is actually apparent to my intuition; I witness the successive disappearance of all the objects before my eyes, particularly the faces, which hold my attention for a moment (Is that Pierre?) then immediately disintegrate just because they are not Pierre's face.[45]

---

[45]*EN*, pp. 44-45 (*9-10*). The translation in this and the three succeeding quotations is that of Mrs. John North in Mary Warnock's *The Philosophy of Sartre* (London: Hutchinson University Library, 1965), except that Barnes's "nihilation" is retained in preference to Mrs. North's "nihilization."

"We must observe that perception always implies the building up of a form upon a background. . . ." More generally, Sartre might have said: Remember, I am submitting results based on the ontology of the phenomenology of perception. Often enough Sartre's theory of nihilation-consciousness and other central points is recounted, considered, and criticized, without being thrown into relief against *its* background, without being seen as the kind of theory it is.

Sartre assumes that the reader is willing to carry out experiments in the psychology of perception himself and to cast his results in an ontological mold. In order for the examples to be intelligible, one must undertake to observe and recapture the experiences described. But something more is required: one must look for a basis in one's own experience for the distinctions implied by the nihilation terms Sartre uses. He himself erects a huge philosophical superstructure over these terms, and his presentation of it is bound to be more or less meaningless if one hasn't acquired such a basis oneself. It is natural in reading Sartre, therefore, to go back from time to time to the phenomenon theory and to the examples—particularly, perhaps, to Pierre's absence!

The intuitions "Pierre is present" and "Pierre is absent" both have a positive content. The latter does not consist in a kind of absence of the former; the intuition of absence is not an intuition of nothing, but of something. In describing this something Sartre leans heavily on a conceptual apparatus analogous to, but far from identical with, that of Gestalt theory. The café and everything in it appears as a background in an elementary and simple way once Pierre appears. "To appear as a background" is a distinctive way of appearing. Sartre here can only appeal to self-observation. What happens to enable the background features to appear as such Sartre describes as a disappearance (*évanouissement*). Not total disappearance—no more than any object can be subjected to if it is still to "appear" in the background, without having first been in the foreground. If Pierre does not appear, then the café and everything in it appears as background, but not in the same elementary, simple way. Pierre's absence

> fixes the café in its state of evanescence; the entire café remains *as background* and continues to appear as an undifferentiated whole to the marginal attention which is all I give it. It slips further away and continues its process of nihilation. Only it changes into a background in the interests of a *particular* form; it carries this form everywhere just before it, it holds it out to me everywhere: and this form which constantly creeps between my eyes and the real solid objects in the café is a continual process of disappearance. Pierre standing out as nothing against the background formed by the nothingness of the café.[46]

All the time that we are—concentratedly—looking for Pierre in the café, the objects and faces are subjected to a nihilating. When we are satisfied that Pierre is not there, the objects and faces continue to be nihilated; for we look at the café as the café in which Pierre is not to be found. Only when we give up the search and say to ourselves, "Oh, well, I'll call him later," does the café itself get a chance to become foreground rather than background. "Yes, Yes—a glass of beer, thanks."

Sartre's terminology is open to criticism. In a number of quite important points, the nihilation terminology might appear to be not the best choice. As we shall see, there seem to be preferable ways of expressing what Sartre calls consciousness's "nihilating of the past" (cf. pp. 305 ff., below). It is possible, however, that in his phenomenologizing of Hegel's system, Sartre has thought it both fruitful and instructive, for those conversant with Hegel, to retain the latter's *Nichts*-terminology.

But to return to Sartre's own account. When we realize

[46]*Ibid.,* p. 45 *(10).*

that Pierre is not in the café and we are still occupied with
the thought of his not being there, what happens is that Pierre
is

> standing out as nothing (*le néant*) against the back-
> ground formed by the nothingness of the café. So that
> what is apparent to the intuition is a fluttering movement
> of non-existence, the non-existence of the background
> whose nihilation calls for and demands the appearance of
> the form and the form itself—a non-existence gliding like
> no-thing over the surface of the background. The basis of
> the judgment 'Pierre isn't here' is therefore formed by
> the intuitive apprehension of a twofold nothingness.
> . . .[47]

It is intuitions such as this that bring out non-being. A
normal negation, which only has a meaning as a thought or
meaning content, does not have this function. A jokingly
uttered "Wellington isn't in the café, neither is Paul Valéry,
etc." are examples of negation that lack reference to an intuition. They are "pure abstractions, nothing more than applications of the principle of negation, devoid of reference, and
they do not succeed in establishing a *real* connexion between
this café, Wellington, or Valéry."[48] It is non-being which
conditions and maintains negation (or the negative judgment), not the other way round.

In affirming that it is the negative judgment which is conditioned and maintained by non-being, Sartre is opposing,
among others, those who take the nihilation terminology simply to be based on a misapprehension and misuse of negative
judgments, that is, judgments in which the terms "not" and
"nothing" have a special logical function. It is only a misunderstanding, in this view, to think that these basically logical
notions can be thought to provide a foundation for ontological
speculations *à la* Heidegger and Sartre.

[47]*Ibid.*, p. 45 (*10*).
[48]*Ibid.*, p. 45 (*10*).

But once one accepts Sartre's view of the matter, and unless one simplifies it unduly, linguistic and logical criticisms of this kind are not at all easy to press home.

Man, consciousness, freedom, and nihilation

In Part One of *Being and Nothingness* Sartre tries briefly to make it clear why descriptions of nihilation and negative entities (*négatités*, a word coined by Sartre) must be undertaken with such care.

As pointed out, it is man who introduces non-being, implants it right "in the heart of being."[49] Before man appears on the scenes, being-in-itself is completely "opaque." The supreme creator of non-being is consciousness, and one of the most consequential and significant acts of consciousness is its nihilation of its own past: "consciousness continually experiences itself (*se vit elle-même*) as the nihilation of its past being."[50]

Consciousness "is" not its own past; on the contrary it is something that has itself an affect on what is past. Thus consciousness escapes all the stability which could make it into an essence and which could give it a nature. As Hegel said, "Wesen ist was gewesen ist" ("Essence is what has been"). Consciousness, as Sartre puts it, "is always something other than what can be *said* of it."[51]

Consciousness makes it possible for man—who is indeed more than just pure consciousness—to take a negating attitude not only to things outside him, but also toward himself, his own states, feelings, images and all his "psychical content." To this content belong also, of course, a person's motives. Insofar as these are taken up as objects for consciousness, they too are "outside" it, or more correctly, consciousness sets them at a distance. "I am condemned to exist forever beyond

[49]*Ibid.*, p. 57 (21).
[50]*Ibid.*, p. 65 (28).
[51]*Ibid.*, p. 515 (439).

my essence, beyond the causes and motives of my act. I am condemned to be free."[52]

To clarify this and to illustrate the conclusion he draws, Sartre has recourse again to Pierre's absence.

> . . . in order to be established or realized, [Pierre's absence] requires a negative moment by which consciousness in the absence of all prior determination, constitutes itself as negation. If in terms of my perceptions of the room, I conceive of the former inhabitant who is no longer in the room, I am of necessity forced to produce an act of thought which no prior state can determine nor motivate, in short to effect in myself a break with being. And in so far as I continually use *négatités* to isolate and determine existents—*i.e.*, to think them—the succession of my "states of consciousness" is a perpetual separation of effect from cause, since every nihilating process must derive its source only from itself. Inasmuch as my present state would be a prolongation of my prior state, every opening by which negation could slip through would be completely blocked. Every psychic process of nihilation implies then a cleavage between the immediate psychic past and the present. This cleavage is precisely nothingness.[53]

As for man's "nihilation" of his own past, including all his states of mind up to the present moment, one can get a living impression of this without any recourse to phenomenological descriptions of absence and disappearance. Experiences of "going further," "pushing aside," "writing off as *passé*," "putting at a distance," suffice to lend meaning to theses about consciousness being constantly "outside," "apart from," "beyond," all states which have already been grasped as such. Suppose I suddenly have the urge, say, to open the window, but stop myself just as I am on the point of getting up to do

[52]*Ibid.*, p. 515 (439).
[53]*Ibid.*, p. 64 (27).

so; the thought of others who might not want to have the window open, or of how difficult it is to get such a window open, has interrupted the pattern and changed it.

First "I am" in a to-open-the-window state of preparedness, but then "I am" a disposer of this state of preparedness. The latter belongs then to my past; it is already part of my biography. As such it can be made an object of reflection, just as the window itself. Consciousness is already far away. The nihilation terminology suits the picture here when one considers that every time consciousness leaves something, it is doing something positive, pushing the thing away from it, diminishing itself—nihilating the thing *qua* element of itself.

Things have causes and effects; but however closely these causes and effects attend upon that which consciousness has set itself at a distance from, they cannot reach consciousness itself.

In consciousness, therefore, man sets himself outside the network of causal dependences in the world, by the same token as he sets himself outside the things in the world. Consciousness "breaks" the causal chain in a very special sense, and it achieves this only because it itself *is* not something, not something substantial, not something which can be held fast as a link in a chain. Man, says Sartre, separates out a nothingness, or more correctly, something nihilated, which isolates him from all else, and Descartes, in keeping with the Stoics, gave this nothingness a name: *freedom*.

About "freedom" in this sense, Sartre is able on the basis of the foregoing and without further ado to establish that it is not something which only visits man on rare occasions: "there is no difference between the being of man and his *being-free (être-libre)*."[54] Indeed, far from being a rare visitor. freedom is billeted on man for life; man is "constrained to be free."

When in self-reflection I apprehend my own freedom, when I realize that consciousness is not determined by the

[54]*Ibid.*, p. 61 (25).

past because the past is constantly "nihilated," and in this way grasp my total separation from the world and with it the impossibility of excusing my choices, there occurs *anguish*. "In each instance of reflection anguish is born as a structure of the reflective consciousness in so far as the latter considers consciousness as an object of reflection."[55] Theoretically speaking, in the face of anguish I should be able to adopt various attitudes, but the immediate and most natural behavior when confronted with anguish is flight. I flee from the responsibility of choice and escape it by depicting myself as a *thing*, determined by my past. "Psychological determinism, before being a theoretical conception, is first an attitude of excuse, or if you prefer, the basis of all attitudes of excuse."[56]

Can one deceive oneself?

The naïveté and vanity of human beings, perhaps more often their sheer mendacity, seems to emerge most clearly in the characters in Sartre's plays and novels. Even in his portrayals of heroes he makes it quite transparent that the person in question has failed to understand the most important thing of all, freedom. All choices that are authentically human "are" choices of freedom as such. Mathieu in *La Mort dans l'âme (Iron in the Soul)* dies the death of a hero. "Bullets were whining round him free in the air. 'The world is going up in smoke and me with it. . . .' Mathieu went on firing. He fired. He was cleansed. He was all-powerful; he was free."[57] The contrast between Mathieu's practice and what Sartre preaches

---

[55]*Ibid.*, p. 78 (40). "Anguish" is the term used in the English translation of *L'Être et le néant*, and it has been retained here despite the fact that "anxiety" was used earlier to render Heidegger's parallel concept of *angst*. The difference in terminology is in some ways quite suitable.

[56]*Ibid.*, p. 78 (40).

[57]*La Mort dans l'âme* (Paris: Gallimard, 1949), p. 193. English translation by Gerard Hopkins, *Iron in the Soul* (London: Hamish Hamilton, 1950); American title, *Troubled Sleep* (New York: Alfred A. Knopf, 1951).

with regard, among other things, to choice of freedom for freedom's sake has been remarked upon by many,[58] and quite obviously Mathieu is not to be taken as a model for human conduct.

One is tempted to ask whether there is any character at all in Sartre's literary works who avoids self-deception and whose actions are guided by the principle of freedom. Such a person's freedom of choice would have to be shown in his consciousness of his unlimited responsibility, and by his own guilt and anguish. But how could such things be exhibited, how recognized by others? By a gloomy, melancholic nature, careworn and anxious? Or by calm confidence, as in the case of Hoederer in *Les Mains sales (Dirty Hands)*? Can one surmount one's anguish once one has experience of full freedom and responsibility?

It seems that none of Sartre's literary *personae* are to be considered models. Not one of them measures up to being a hero according to the standards laid down in Sartre's philosophy; not one of them, therefore, exemplifies the conduct required of the would-be existentialist in Sartre's sense.

There are many ways in which a man may adopt a negative attitude. A person may make himself into a permanent negation: Scheler's "Der Mensch der Argenis" ("the man of resentment"). Irony is another variation: "In irony a man annihilates (*anéantit*) what he posits within one and the same act; he leads us to believe in order not to be believed; he affirms to deny and denies to affirm; he creates a positive object but it has no being other than its nothingness."[59]

And yet there is one attitude to which Sartre devotes particular attention and for which he has a special name, "la mauvaise foi"; we might call it bad faith, false faith, or self-deception. "If bad faith is possible, it is because it is an immediate permanent threat to every project of the human

---

[58]Cf. Thody, *Jean-Paul Sartre*, p. 58; and Cranston, *Sartre*, p. 73.
[59]*EN*, p. 85 (47).

being; it is because consciousness conceals in its being (*être*, here near to *essence*) a permanent risk of bad faith."[60]

In all but one crucial detail Sartre's concept of bad faith is correlative to the more usual, contrary notion of good faith. To do something in good faith usually means to do it with sincerity, genuinely and without concealed or ulterior motives. By "bad faith," however, Sartre means not simply the contrary concept; bad faith occurs when one is insincere to *oneself*, not (just) to others.

It is very difficult to give a short account of Sartre's notion of bad faith or self-deception which is also an adequate one. It is true that Sartre himself gives a brief account of the notion in his short polemical work, *L'Existentialisme est un humanisme*, but the presentation he offers there is extremely simplified and imprecise from a philosophical point of view. Indeed, as it is discussed in this latter work the topic seems barely recognizable as the one introduced in *Being and Nothingness*.

It has to be said that even in the main work Sartre's account of bad faith, in the light of the theory of the phenomenon and of the distinction between the in-itself and the for-itself, is less than successful. It would, of course, have been too much to expect the analysis to lead to positive results in the reader's own struggles against self-deception, as if a brief encounter with the arguments was all that was required to strengthen his good intention to avoid deceiving himself. But an analysis that ends with more paradoxes than it began with can hardly be counted a success. In the end the reader is left with the impression that he has been in neither good nor bad faith, and that in any case it is absurd to try to avoid deceiving oneself. Should the inconceivable occur and he succeed in avoiding self-deception, he would find himself, or rather others would find him, transformed into something like a stone.

So at least one might reasonably conclude. But there is

[60]*Ibid.*, p. 111 (70).

another way of looking at it, and one which suggests itself to the philosopher concerned with such questions as freedom of the will, the relationship of consciousness to the body, reflective consciousness, and so on. These and other matters prove extremely resistant to accounts which assume man to be something so simply and sufficiently substantial (materially or spiritually) as to be able to function as a fully fledged link in a causal chain. Sartre here tries his hand with a concept of consciousness in which consciousness is altogether incompatible with what exists in any substantial sense. Consciousness is nothing, but at the same time it is not *no* thing. The attempt to strike a balance between "not being something" in every sense of the expression, on the one hand, and in almost every sense of the expression, on the other, must inevitably lead to highly singular and paradoxical sounding statements, to say the least. Here we should bear in mind that the theory of the phenomenon and the distinction between the in-itself and the for-itself forms the philosophical foundation for the individual phenomenological analyses that Sartre undertakes. As with other philosophers, the criterion of a true and adequate account of a complicated phenomenon will be that the phenomenon can be adapted to the philosophical framework without any undue force. It may be that the framework or basis strikes the outsider as involving peculiar, even paradoxical, positions, but however this may be, in the testing of the philosophical system itself any explanation that stands in agreement with these positions must be considered successful. From his scrutiny of what it is to be in good or bad faith Sartre emerges with theses that are, at least partially, in clear accord with his basic philosophical positions.

As for the question of the truth or falsity of the conclusions taken individually, it seems clear that much depends on the tenability of the phenomenological analysis in regard to the so-called *négatités*, those mined from the rich vein of Pierre's absence, and many others. But the value of Sartre's analysis of self-deception hardly lies in the conclusions them-

311

selves, supposing one can even make these out, so much as in the host of subtle phenomenological observations he makes.[61] In the following discussion we will confine ourselves to outlining some of the main points in Sartre's presentation.

Bad faith has, like lying, the function of "hiding a displeasing truth or presenting as truth a pleasing untruth (*erreur*) . . . [But] what makes all the difference is the fact that in bad faith it is from myself that I am hiding the truth."[62] Here the deceived and the deceiver are the same, and yet different, since it is not the deceived who is deceiving nor the deceiver who becomes deceived. For relatively unphilosophical minds this paradox may seem neither particularly interesting nor intractable. Something in me deceives something else in me; or so many would resolve it; after all, the personality is a very complex thing. But for a philosophical mind, sensitive to paradoxes, the matter looks quite different.

Consciousness is consciousness *of* something. If I were able "*un*consciously" to hide something from myself, the "I" who could do this would have to be conceived as analogous to dispositions, instincts, and other things which are-in-themselves. Such hiding cannot be seen from the point of view of consciousness, but only from outside, by a scientist, a Sigmund Freud for instance—and is therefore of no interest for the phenomenologist. In the following, however, we will only discuss what *appears* to (appears-to) a consciousness, phenomena; in self-deception the deceiver and the deceived must both appear as phenomena for a consciousness.

What one does not know, one cannot hide away. Consequently, in order to conceal some truth from myself, it must be something I know. If I *succeed* in hiding a truth I know, my consciousness changes and I take a step in the direction of good faith, for then in all candor I believe in the opposite of what is true, or else no longer recognize what the matter is

[61]See, for example, the analysis of a woman's first assignation with a (particular) man. *EN*, pp. 94-95 (55-56).
[62]*Ibid.*, p. 87 (*49*).

312

about. However, if I do not succeed in hiding the truth, but carry on as if I had succeeded, I become a cynic. But then in no circumstances do I ever, in this way, enter upon a stable state of "being in bad faith." (Concerning the possibility of unstable—metastable—states we shall hear something later.) Either I do not succeed at all in deceiving myself, or I "deceive myself" so fundamentally that the term "deception" no longer applies.

As for good faith, a distinction has to be made between *finding oneself* in good faith and trying to *come into* a state of good faith. Not to try to deceive myself (for example, not to try to believe that I am brave when I am in fact cowardly) means to try to be something which actually exists, with all its effects and causes, accordingly as something in-itself. As a property, courage has in fact palpable effects, and causal psychoanalysis can disclose some of its causes. But on the other hand, it is impossible for me to become something in-itself. I can never become brave in this sense (without loss of freedom). As soon as courage becomes an object for me I am myself beyond it. If I save someone from drowning then I do it as a "play actor." And cowardice, too, is already part of the past when it is taken up as an object. I *am* not a coward, I *was* one. One seeks in vain to attain to a stable state—whether of false or good faith.

But then what is implied by the notion of my already being in good faith? It seems that I must either be acting pre-reflectively on the basis of some conviction or else be posing to myself the question: "Am I in good faith?" and answering affirmatively. But how is the latter possible? If I do answer affirmatively, and my eyes are opened to the possibility of the opposite, I am no longer in good faith, but have a former state of belief as an object of consciousness. What is needed now is a change of consciousness back from questioning and over once again to the possibility of good faith.

But there is more to be said than this: here we have a new point of departure for an interpretation based on the fundamental philosophical position. At this point it may be as well to leaven our rather abstract discussion with an example or two.

Let us consider [the] waiter in the café. His movement is quick and forward, a little too precise, a little too rapid. He comes toward the customers with a step a little too quick. He bends forward a little too eagerly; his voice, his eyes express an interest a little too solicitous for the order of the customer . . . he gives himself the quickness and pitiless rapidity of things . . . he is playing *at being* a waiter . . . [he] . . . plays with his position (*condition*) in life in order to *realize* it . . .

A grocer who indulges in day-dreams is offensive to the customer because he is no longer wholly a grocer. Courtesy requires him to contain himself within his function as a grocer, like the soldier at attention who makes himself into a soldier-thing, by his direct but unseeing gaze which is no longer even intended to see. . . . We take ample precautions to confine a man to what he is; it is as if we lived in continual fear that he would get out, overflow, and suddenly elude his position. But at the same time the fact is that the waiter cannot be a waiter from within and immediately, as an inkwell *is* an inkwell, or a tumbler a tumbler.

[If I am the waiter in question] what . . . I attempt to realize, is a being-in-itself of the café waiter, as if it were not just I that gave my duties and the rights of my position their value and urgency, as if it were not my free choice to get up each morning at five o'clock or to remain in bed, at the risk of being fired. As if from the very fact that I sustain this role in existence I did not transcend it on every side, as if I did not constitute myself as one *beyond* my position. . . . But if I am one [a waiter], this cannot be in the mode of being-in-itself. I am a waiter in the mode of *being what I am not*. . . .

Perpetually absent to my body, to my acts, I am despite myself that "divine absence" of which Valéry speaks. . . . On all sides I escape being and yet—I am.[63]

It is important to remember that all mental life and every mental state once it has become object of memory and hence objectified are included in what is beyond consciousness. Such items come into the same category as tables and chairs, things which are in-themselves, though with an important proviso: my consciousness is bound in some way or other to *my* past, not to the pasts of others. If, up to this moment, *A* has been a diplomat and *B* a waiter, there is no question of *A* taking over where *B*'s consciousness stops, or vice versa. But whatever the nature of the relation between a given consciousness and the past states that are objects for "it," the past itself has no power to determine anything; the role of the past, in a way, is to present the items to judgment.

To resume the question of bad faith: as soon as it is clear to me that I am on the point of concealing the unpleasant truth from myself, the project collapses. Consequently, I can never find myself in a *state* of bad faith. On the other hand, bad faith can certainly have the kind of being which consists of being *on the point* of disappearing—indeed, there can be a continual "vacillation" between good faith and cynicism; bad faith is "metastable" (Sartre's word).[64] Since this vacillation can be *constant*, it is possible for it to form an enduring and normal aspect of life. In fact, many people live in this way.

> . . . the first act of bad faith is to flee what it can not flee, to flee what it is. The very project of flight reveals to bad faith an inner disintegration in the heart of being, and it is this disintegration which bad faith wishes to be. . . . Good faith seeks to flee the inner disintegration of

[63]*Ibid.*, pp. 98-100 (59-60). The translation in the second and third paragraphs is from Warnock, *The Philosophy of Sartre* (see p. 58).
[64]*Ibid.*, p. 88 (50).

315

my being in the direction of the in-itself which it should be and is not. Bad faith seeks to flee the in-itself by means of the inner disintegration of my being.[65]

Bad faith is a threat to being human and this is possible because consciousness, which although not the whole man is nevertheless his core, is at the same time in its essence (*être*) what it is not and not what it is. With this conclusion we come back to our starting point: all things are phenomena—that which *appears to*—but what is appeared to is not some new phenomenon in addition to the others. Phenomena appear to men, but only to that in men which is their momentary core, namely consciousness, which is just another word for the for-something character possessed by phenomena. Consciousness is consciousness of, and is therefore not that of which it *is* conscious, that is, not that which is in the sense of the phenomenon-in-itself, of what is to be found, the factual.

Man is more than his own consciousness, and therefore in his mental life he can comport himself in different ways toward "having" consciousness. Hence good and bad faith, authenticity and inauthenticity, and whatever else plays a part in man's own consciousness, in his for-itself.

Sartre repeatedly uses the form of expression:

(1) Consciousness is what it is not, and is not what it is.

This calls for comment, and the following are some considerations concerning the relation of the expression to the so-called laws of reasoning.

In the common philosophical tradition we hear of three principles or laws—of identity, contradiction, and excluded middle. Although the names and certain standard formulations recur often in the literature, what they say or express often varies from one philosopher to another. Little thought has been taken of the semantical variations; consequently it is not surprising that we find the expression "law of identity" in one philosopher referring to an absolutely unbreakable principle with universal application, and in another expressing a claim of considerably more modest proportions.

Among the linguistic forms associated with the designation "law of identity" we find, for example, "$A = A$," "A is identical with itself." From this it is only a short distance to

(2) A is what it is and is not what it is not.

If we substitute for "A" in (2) the expression "consciousness" we get

(3) Consciousness is what it is and is not what it is not.

Many philosophers appeal to the properties of a given expression itself, without reference to its content or meaning, in deciding whether or not it infringes the laws referred to above. According to such criteria it would be an infringement of the law of contradiction to assert (1) and (2), or (1) and (3), conjunctively. Or more strictly, by inserting "and" between expressions (1) and (2), and between (1) and (3), we would produce a contradiction. It is on this basis that (1) is said to infringe the law of identity. This is then construed according to whether or not the law of identity is taken to be absolutely valid: in the former case what Sartre says about consciousness is false or meaningless; in the latter it may be accepted that there is at least one case of something falling outside the law's validity or area of application, and that consciousness is perhaps that thing.

In the Hegelian tradition, and more particularly in Marxist philosophy, the "law of identity" is referred to in such a way, and the most common expressions for it so used, that it can scarcely be doubted that the law's scope and validity is not thought to be absolute. It is precisely this tradition that Sartre appears to follow, and since he too seems to take properties of expressions rather than semantical or ontological features as criteria for deciding whether or not something infringes the "laws," it would be entirely consistent of him to affirm that

(1) infringes the law of identity. Consciousness would be something to which the law of identity is not applicable.

Suppose, however, that we adopt semantic criteria instead. The claim that there is an infringement of the law would then clearly presuppose that in all its four occurrences the term "is" has an identical meaning. This can be assumed also for the four occurrences of "is" in (3). But now if we go back to the phenomenological descriptions of consciousness, that is, to the descriptions of being-for-itself, it seems to be difficult to combine these with what (1) might be thought to express, taking "is" to mean the same in all its four occurrences. It is not impossible to produce expressions related to (1) in which "is" can mean the same in each of its four occurrences, but such expressions are not such as necessarily break the law of identity: "Consciousness is, as for-itself, that which it is not as in-itself, and is not, as for-itself, what it is as in-itself." "*Consciousness* (of) my cowardice *is* consciousness (of) this cowardice which it is not, and consciousness (of) my cowardice is *not* the cowardice which it is (of)." The word "of" (*de*), following Sartre's rule, is put in parentheses as a reminder that it does not connect two things which can be separated: no consciousness except consciousness *of* some phenomenon, and no phenomenon except for a consciousness. Since for logical thinking semantic concepts of the law of identity are the most important, our conclusion is that Sartre does not in fact say anything about consciousness which requires us to assume that such laws have an exception.

Sartre's philosophy of *le néant* has been exposed to a criticism parallel to Rudolf Carnap's indignant protest against Heidegger's philosophy of *das Nichts*. Characteristically the critic's appeal in this case is not to our scientific sensibilities and the logical calculus of predicates but to that much respected tribunal in British philosophy, *Alice through the Looking Glass*. A. J. Ayer writes:

> . . . Sartre's reasoning on the subject of *le néant* seems to me exactly on a par with that of the King in 'Alice

through the Looking-glass'. 'I see nobody on the road,' said Alice. 'I only wish I had such eyes,' remarked the King. 'To be able to see Nobody! And at that distance too!' And again, if I remember rightly: 'Nobody passed me on the road'. 'He cannot have done that, or he would have been here first.' In these cases the fallacy is easy enough to detect, but although Sartre's reasoning is less engagingly naïve, I do not think that it is any better. The point is that words like 'nothing' and 'nobody' are not used as the names of something insubstantial and mysterious; they are not used to *name* anything at all. To say that two objects are separated by nothing is to say that they are *not* separated; and that is all that it amounts to. What Sartre does, however, is to say that, being separated by Nothing, the objects are both united and divided. There is a thread between them; only, it is a very peculiar thread, both invisible and intangible.[66]

Staking everything, as he appears to, on the assumption that information about the use of certain words can suffice to topple philosophical systems in ruins, Ayer's criticism is certainly bold, and puts one in mind of the rather surprising fragility of the walls of Jericho. Ayer hardly intends merely to give an account of how the word "nothing" *happens* to be used, since he recognizes that at least Sartre uses it in some other way. Accordingly he must have in mind, though without saying so, some basic rule or norm, such that any infringment of it automatically leads to nonsense. But, without here going into what those rules might be, it is as well to recall that philosophers since the time of Heraclitus have, to some extent, taken a delight in unusual uses of words, and that not

---

[66]A. J. Ayer, "Novelist-Philosophers: V—Jean-Paul Sartre," *Horizon*, XII, No. 67 (July, 1945), 18-19. In my brief comment on the quotation I have disregarded the fact that Ayer's description of what Sartre does is not sufficiently exact. Even if "object" is taken in a very wide sense, it is hardly apt, for example, to describe consciousness as a kind of relation between two objects.

infrequently the unusual has come to be accepted as idiomatic and everyday. A critical evaluation of Sartre's nihilation terminology and of his philosophy of nothingness calls for something more fundamental than the considerations invoked, not all of them explicitly, by Ayer. Perhaps a possible point of departure is an examination of the terminology of phenomenological description and its relation to other descriptions.[67]

Myself as an object for others

Every human being has the kind of existence Sartre calls for-itself; all things that the individual human comes in contact with are phenomena for his consciousness, and among these are included other human beings. These, like everything else, can only appear as phenomena, and not of course as different

[67]Thus one could revert again to Pierre's absence, and to an examination of the relation between sentences in the descriptions of this absence (as an object) and system sentences of the type "Consciousness can break the causal chain because it *is* nothing." Absence, etc., are *objects* for phenomenological description. But they are not objects in the thing- and process-world in reference to which it makes sense to say that they are causes or effects. Therefore such objects can neither break nor comply with causal laws. They cannot occur as links in causal chains.

It is reasonable to assume from Sartre's theory of the phenomenon that the same must apply to "consciousness." The theory implies that consciousness does not, strictly, follow causal laws, but that neither does it break them. To say "consciousness can break the causal chain because it *is* nothing" would seem, in that case, to be an unhappy or incautious formulation for a philosophical systematizer to have chosen. However, it cannot be assumed that Sartre would accept that some of his paradoxical formulations are philosophically unfortunate, since he may well interpret them in ways which are reasonable in a Hegelian, though probably not in any other, environment. Possibly one could, on the basis of the theory of the phenomenon as Sartre himself formulates its main outlines, reconstruct the plot of *Being and Nothingness* without paradoxical expressions or distinctively Hegelian turns of phrase. In my view, this would mean an essential strengthening of the system—of its claim to validity. But of course this view implies a philosophical position in opposition to at least certain aspects of the Hegelian style and way of thought.

consciousnesses. Or to be more exact: Pierre sees other men as phenomena, therefore as things that appear *for* something, namely Pierre's consciousness. Their consciousnesses, their "real" for-themselves relationships and therewith the phenomena that are for these consciousnesses, all lie outside the range of what Pierre can possibly come in contact with. It looks as if solipsism is lurking round the corner. How does Sartre escape the fatal assumption of a cleavage between each individual human being and between each individual human being's world? By pointing out that such a cleavage does not correspond to a phenomenologically tenable account of our immediate experiences of others—of others, that is, not as bodies, but as persons in a common world.

Sartre's answer to any possible charge of solipsism is provided in a more penetrating account of the others' share in the development of my own concept of myself.

> I have just made an awkward or vulgar gesture. This gesture clings to me; I neither judge it nor blame it. I simply live it. I realize it in the mode of for-itself. But now suddenly I raise my head. Somebody was there and has seen me. Suddenly I realize the vulgarity of my gesture, and I am ashamed. It is certain that my shame is not reflective, for the presence of another in my consciousness, even as a catalyst, is incompatible with the reflective attitude; in the field of my reflection I can never meet with anything but the consciousness which is mine. But the Other is the indispensable mediator between myself and me. I am ashamed of myself *as I appear* to the Other.

> By the mere appearance of the Other, I am put in the position of passing judgment on myself as on an object, for it is as an object that I appear to the Other. . . . Shame is an immediate shudder which runs through me from head to foot without any discursive preparation. . . . The very notion of *vulgarity* implies an inter-monad relation. Nobody can be vulgar all alone!

Thus the Other has not only revealed to me what I was; he has established me in a new type of being which can support new qualifications. . . . Thus shame is shame *of oneself before the Other;* these two structures are inseparable.[68]

The relation between being a human being and being-in-itself is thus less simple than we have been assuming. There is a phenomenologically quite primordial and specific relation between myself and others. It is not a relation directly between individual consciousnesses, but one in which an object, the body, is a necessary intermediate link. I appear as an object, in-itself, for the Other, and *with the other's help* I see myself as an object in the world—defenselessly exposed to the other's look.

> Pure shame is not a feeling of being this or that guilty object but in general of being *an* object; that is, of *recognizing myself* in this degraded, fixed, and dependent being which I am for the Other. Shame is the feeling of an *original fall,* not because of the fact that I may have committed this or that particular fault but simply that I have "fallen" into the world in the midst of things and that I need the mediation of the Other in order to be what I am.
>
> Modesty and in particular the fear of being surprised in the state of nakedness are only a symbolic specification of original shame; the body symbolizes here our defenseless state as objects. To put on clothes is to hide one's object-state; it is to claim the right of seeing without being seen; that is, to be pure subject. This is why the Biblical symbol of the fall after the original sin is the fact that Adam and Eve "know they are naked."[69]

From this quotation we can see why Sartre's essay in phenomenological ontology came to be a work of seven hundred

[68]*EN*, pp. 275-77 (221-22).
[69]*Ibid.,* p. 349 (288-89).

and twenty-two densely packed pages. The highly abstract and general themes are illuminated by examples and applications; these are clarified in turn; and then often, to conclude, we are given a kind of clarificatory psychology which Sartre calls "existential psychoanalysis" and which has come to be known also as "Sartrian psychoanalysis." Sartre is himself fully aware that the hypotheses contained in it go beyond the scope of phenomenological description of one's own experiences. Characteristically, however, and in clear opposition to Heidegger, Sartre is not at all concerned with making a sharp division where psychoanalysis takes over from description in terms of phenomenological ontology.

Sartre develops his original theory of man's being-for-others with great care. Of the topics which he here introduces to philosophy we must mention at least "the look" (*le regard*) and its philosophical implications. This Sartre explains and interprets in a lively examination covering fifty-eight pages.

Heidegger understands the specific feature of human existence to be a kind of standing out from the world, an ek-stasis, ex-sistence. Sartre reckons with a threefold ek-stasis, the first being fulfilled with pre-reflective consciousness of things, the second with reflective consciousness, as in knowledge, and the third in man's ek-stasis as an object for another. In this latter case I "stand out from" myself insofar as I see myself as object for another.

Existentialist psychoanalysis, as Sartre pictures it, tries to grasp, against the widest possible background, a human being's choice, especially and in the last instance his *original* choice (*le choix original*). Man's reflection is permeated by an intense light, though what it illuminates is not necessarily expressible in conceptual terms. Existential analysis is there to offer assistance. However, because what has to be clearly determined is a person's conscious choice, the whole apparatus of Freudian psychoanalysis with its causal methods and hypotheses about the unconscious has to be discarded. Sartrian psychoanalysis is in principle concerned only with series of intentions, motives, or conscious decisions to do this or that, not with states and causal chains, whether these be psychical or physiological. This is one respect in which Sartrian psychoanalysis differs essentially from that of Freud. Another difference, it might be pointed out, is that Freud's ideas have now been tested and modified in the course of some generations, while Sartre's form of analysis—though it has been by no means without influence in psychotherapy and psychiatry —is in essential respects an as yet untried project. As Sartre himself admits, his psychoanalysis "has not yet found its Freud."[70]

Sartre's psychoanalysis has a certain structural similarity with Freud's: both include a theory of symbols and a procedure for reducing the derivative to the primitive. Both, too, are "depth" psychologies. The differences within these similarities can be seen, for example, in the different symbolic value each attaches to the child's predilection for holes. Both accept the child's inability to resist the temptation to put his finger in holes, or even himself if the hole is large enough. Psychoanalysts tend to explain this in sexual terms. But Sartre sees in the hole "the empty image of [one] self."[71] Though consciousness is outside everything, as a nothing, it nevertheless tries to become something in-itself. Holes provide (symbolically) the opportunity to fulfil this wish: I have only to put myself in a hole in order to exist in a world which positively makes room for me! Adults are constantly striving to complete things, to fulfil plans or themselves, to fill in gaps, round things off, and so on; that is, they try to constitute or bring about a completeness (a completeness which is strictly the prerogative of a deity). The task of existential psychoanalysis is to reduce the activities of children and adults to their bases in ontology. Not, of course, that analysis itself becomes ontology. Nevertheless, it is based in ontology. "What ontology can teach psychoanalysis is first of all the

[70]*Ibid.*, p. 663 (575).
[71]*Ibid.*, p. 705 (613).

true origin of the meanings of things and their *true* relation to human reality."[72]

A comparison between Freud's, Heidegger's, and Sartre's statements about the significance of individual things and relations conveys clearly both the wealth of, and the interconnections of, their different meanings. Among the features shared by Freudian and Sartrian analysis, for example, is the liability of the results of the analysis to prove offensive to the person analyzed. According to Freud, marked generosity can often be reduced to certain anal-erotic attitudes. Sartre represents generosity as a form of destruction: consciousness keeps itself apart from things, it nihilates them; to give them away is a derivative way of maintaining this separation.[73] They are no longer mine, yet they *were* mine. They persist in a kind of "honorary" existence, *res emeritae*. But the destructive urge underlying generosity is nothing but an urge to possess. To give is to enjoy, to appropriate and consume the object that is given, thus to possess it in an especially intimate, even though short-lived way.[74]

Love and hate

Being and Nothingness offers many surprises, something that cannot always be said of rigorously systematic philosophical works. For reasons not difficult to understand, Sartre's theory concerning the various specific attitudes that two consciousnesses can adopt toward one another has caused something of a stir.

My freedom (in the sense intended by Sartre in *Being and Nothingness*) is not restricted by things whose being is in-themselves. Under the other's gaze, however, I am reduced to an object; I acquire properties, a nature, and thus I am de-

[72]*Ibid.*, p. 694 (603).
[73]*Ibid.*, p. 684 (594). The next two sentences are a rather free rendering of Sartre.
[74]See *ibid.*, p. 684 (594).

prived of my freedom, from the point of view of the other. Correspondingly, the other's freedom is taken away when he becomes an object for me under my gaze. Certainly, one consciousness tries to communicate directly with other consciousnesses, but this, as we have noted, is impossible. It is impossible because of the nihilating role of consciousness. "The Other is on principle inapprehensible; he flees me when I seek him and possesses me when I flee him."[75] Contact between consciousnesses can only be effected through the mediation of the body which has the requisite being-in-itself. Hence the need for bodily union in default of the communion of consciousnesses.

It is true, of course, that the other exists for me independently of any such contact: in the case of shame, and many other experiences, the other is constituted for me as a center of subjectivity distinct from myself, as another for-itself, while I am constituted for myself by my being-for-others. But in the case of experiences like these, there can be absolutely no contact between two consciousnesses, since the other sees me as an *object*, while I see myself as an object for the other as *subject*. It is never possible for the other and myself to see one another as subjects; the one necessarily degrades the other by his look. Harmonious co-existence, therefore, cannot be an original relationship. Because of their basic structure, consciousnesses are originally in conflict: it is a case of either me or you. "The essence of the relations between consciousnesses is not the *Mitsein;* it is conflict."[76]

Love as a fundamental relation must therefore be studied as a kind of conflict. Those in love seek to be united on the level of consciousness, seek accordingly to come into contact with one another as subjects, as free essences on an equal footing with one another. But contact at this highest level is excluded on principle. Contact here can only take the form of a kind

[75]*Ibid.*, p. 479 (408).

[76]*Ibid.*, p. 502 (429). "Mitsein" is Heidegger's expression in *Sein und Zeit* (cf. pp. 200 ff., above).

of possession, and it is possible only for *objects* to be possessed, not subjects. The consequences are catastrophic. If I put myself, as an object, into the power of the other, I am choosing masochism. This implies an abandonment of consciousness and cannot succeed as a state. To choose, on the other hand, to try to rule the other by treating him as a thing, is to choose the way of the sadist. But this leads nowhere either. "Love," says Sartre, "is a contradictory effort."[77] As a fundamental mode of being-for-others, love contains in its being-for-others "the seed of its own destruction."[78] Thus our respect for the other's freedom is "an empty word."[79]

If one objects that this does not agree with the facts, that empirical investigation will show otherwise, Sartre can reply that he is only concerned with basic attitudes. As to what can happen in actual situations, in which the interplay of many forces has to be taken into account, that is not for him to describe. As in the case of Hobbes he can take his point of departure, conceptually and systematically, in a *bellum omnium contra omnes* without precluding the possibility of a state of relative harmony.

Since the ideal of love cannot be realized at the highest level, it is natural to try to resolve the conflict with the other by destroying him, liquidating his for-itself, killing him. This is the way of hate. But hate, too, is unable to fulfil its purpose:

> . . . hate too is in turn a failure. Its initial project is to suppress other consciousnesses. But even if it succeeded in this—i.e., if it could at this moment abolish the Other —it could not bring it about that the Other had not been. Better yet, if the abolition of the Other is to be lived as the triumph of hate, it implies the explicit recognition that the Other *has existed* . . . He who has once been for-

[77] *EN*, p. 444 (376).
[78] *Ibid.*, p. 445 (377).
[79] *Ibid.*, p. 480 (409).

others is contaminated in his being for the rest of his days even if the Other should be entirely suppressed; he will never cease to apprehend his dimension of being-for-others as a permanent possibility of his being. . . . After the failure of [hate's] attempt nothing remains for the for-itself except to re-enter the circle and allow itself to be indefinitely tossed from one to the other of the two fundamental attitudes (love and hate).[80]

It has perhaps occurred to Sartre that this conclusion about the more intimate relationships between human beings should not be his final word, and that the reader should have some small straw to clutch at. At any rate, the following footnote is appended to the above passage:

These considerations do not rule out the possibility of an ethics of deliverance and salvation. But this can be achieved only after a radical conversion which we can not discuss here.[81]

Is "here" in this chapter, or in this work? As we shall see, Sartre later on in the work does point to a resort for men if they radically relinquish the spirit of seriousness (*esprit de sérieux*) and also change in other ways. But he provides no prescription for a morality of redemption and salvation by way of conversion. And he promises only a morality, not salvation or redemption as a condition to be achieved.

Possibly in the footnote Sartre is thinking of a later work intimated in the last sentence of *Being and Nothingness*. However, it is difficult to identify anything he has written later with such a work. The conclusion must be, therefore, quite speculatively, that Sartre has either not wanted to, or found himself unable to, complete *Being and Nothingness* in a positive direction.

[80]*Ibid.*, pp. 483-84 (412).
[81]*Ibid.*, p. 484 (412).

Freedom and responsibility

The intensity of Sartre's style and his choice of terminology make it difficult for the reader not to wonder at the end of each section: "What does he want of me now? What is he aiming at?"

In the section on the close and basic relationship between consciousnesses he is mainly a killjoy: you must not believe that everything is set fair for a heavenly or comfortable togetherness. On the contrary: abjure instantly all such optimism and faith. Then you will at least have some foundation for a positive contribution—and just how necessary that is you shall see!

In the short section on "freedom and responsibility" the message is clear and there can be no mistaking the main features of the trail Sartre blazes for us. The word "responsibility" he takes in a sense he describes as ordinary (*banal*): "consciousness (of) being the incontestable author of an event or of an object."[82] In order to grasp Sartre's theory of responsibility it is perhaps a good thing to bear in mind that the expression "to be responsible for . . ." is normally used to refer to more special relationships. If we interpret "responsibility" in this way wherever it occurs in Sartre's text the positions arrived at are certainly peculiar. However, it may be that Sartre means us to interpret it in both ways, both in the more usual narrow sense and in the extremely general sense he himself defines:

> In this sense the responsibility of the for-itself is overwhelming since he is the one by whom it happens that *there is* a world; since he is also the one who makes himself be, then whatever may be the situation in which he finds himself, the for-itself must wholly assume this situation with its peculiar coefficient of adversity, even

[82]*Ibid.*, p. 639 (553).

though it be insupportable. He must assume the situation with the proud consciousness of being its author . . .[83]

Is it not a little drastic to let the for-itself be author of the world? Not if "world" is taken in the technical sense which it has in the theory of the phenomenon, and "author" is given an abstract meaning. Phenomena are what appear *for;* the sum total of things is the world; the "world" is therefore not something defined independently of the for-itself; everything in it has a relation to the for-itself. Since there is no other real world, no occult world behind what appears for the for-itself, there is nothing more than what appears for the for-itself. Thus the latter is a necessary condition of the existence of the world.

Consciousness is a necessary condition of *all* that appears-for, thus for all that is in-itself. But the converse is also true: there are only phenomena and, as far as I can see from the formulation of the theory of the phenomenon at the beginning of *Being and Nothingness,* the relationships of the *pour-soi* and the *en-soi* are exactly parallel. If, therefore, the for-itself's relation to the in-itself is interpreted as being that of a necessary condition, one cannot object to an interpretation of the in-itself's relation to the for-itself according to which the relation is of exactly the same character. Consequently there is as good reason for saying "the world is a necessary condition of consciousness" as for saying "consciousness is a necessary condition of the world."

But then the term "author" becomes somewhat artificial, and it seems that if Sartre is to save his thesis, interpreted in this way, another criterion must be found, stronger than "necessary condition" and definitely favoring the for-itself in relation to the in-itself. On the other hand, there are other

---

[83]*Ibid.,* p. 639 (553-54). The English translator prefers the personal pronoun here on the grounds that the for-itself is being described in concrete personal terms rather than as a metaphysical entity. The French "il" can of course be translated "he" or "it."

possible interpretations. For instance an interpretation of the for-itself as a kind of *causa sui* could be based on the passage quoted above about the for-itself being "that which makes himself be." Certainly Sartre doesn't give this status to the in-itself, and this might indicate a difference in ontological status. Some have been led by this to classify Sartre as an idealist, a title he himself will not accept. (The distinction between realism and idealism is, in any case, hardly one that Sartre would acknowledge, and he could point to his theory of the phenomenon in support of this.)[84]

Sartre has described his existentialism as "just" an attempt at a consistently thought-out atheism. It might be a reasonable assumption, therefore, that Sartre has looked for something to take over the various functions that have been attributed to God. And it does indeed look as though Sartre thought it necessary to preserve the functions that would have been God's if He had not been absent. Thus Sartre says unequivocally that insofar as God has been dispensed with, we must look for something else capable of creating or discovering values. Here consciousness takes over the role of God. In addition, God has also borne full responsibility for *everything*, as the author of all things, including the cruel, the insane, and the senseless. If something is to take over this responsibility, again it must be consciousness. Sartre's extreme thesis concerning responsibility would perhaps have been more intelligible if one of its explicit premises had been the need to maintain the office of God without its occupant. At least it seems clear that if anything can succeed God, consciousness is the only serious candidate. And if one accepts the idea that a replacement is necessary, what Sartre says about our extensive responsibility becomes rather more intelligible.

---

[84]Jean Wahl, *Petite histoire de l'Existentialisme* (Paris: Éditions Nagel, 1954). English translation by Forrest Williams and Stanley Maron, *A Short History of Existentialism* (New York: Philosophical Library, 1949).

Whoever has responsibility cannot reasonably complain about what he has been responsible for.

> It is therefore senseless to think of complaining since nothing foreign has decided what we feel, what we live, or what we are. Furthermore this absolute responsibility is not resignation; it is simply the logical requirement of the consequences of our freedom. . . . The most terrible situations of war, the worst tortures do not create a non-human state of things; there is no non-human situation. It is only through fear, flight, and recourse to magical types of conduct that I shall *decide* on the non-human, but this decision is human, and I shall carry the entire responsibility for it. . . . If I am mobilized in a war, this war is *my* war; it is in my image and I deserve it. I deserve it first because I could always get out of it by suicide or by desertion; these ultimate possibles are those which must always be present for us when there is a question of facing (*d'envisager*) a situation. . . . Therefore we must agree with the statement by J. Romains, "In war there are no innocent victims."[85]

This quotation may form the basis of a variety of speculations about Sartre's ethical standpoint in regard to the unconditional rejection of torture. (During the Algerian war Sartre came out strongly against torture, but this fact is of no exegetical value.) One interpretation in accordance with the text would be: In themselves, without relation to a man's basic norms or "basic projects," ethical judgments have no meaning. But man's freedom is such as to countenance diametrically opposed basic norms. Whatever attitude I have to torture or the horrors of war must therefore be understood as originating in some freely chosen basic norm. The attitude I have delimits or defines war *ethically* for me; it is in *this sense* that I have chosen it and it is for war thus delimited that

[85]*EN*, pp. 639-40 (554).

I am responsible. This kind of interpretation makes Sartre's denial that there are non-human situations less of a defense of neutrality and passivity than an appeal to each of us to realize the scope of our responsibility—whatever our ethical standpoint.

But what can I do about the fact that I happen to live in these cruel times? Suppose I had been born in another, less cruel time; would I then have had less responsibility? If so, what kind of responsibility is it that depends on such accidental facts as when I was born?

Sartre's answer to these supposed objections is in line with the "anti-substantial" movement which he takes to be characteristic of modern thought.

> . . . each person is an absolute upsurge at an absolute date and is perfectly unthinkable at another date. It is therefore a waste of time to ask what I should have been if this war had not broken out, for I have chosen myself as one of the possible meanings of the epoch which imperceptibly led to war. I am not distinct from this same epoch; I could not be transported to another epoch without contradiction.[86]

This passage allows us to bridge the gap to Sartre's Marxist inspired and politico-reformist activism, as we see it in his declaration of intent in *Les Temps modernes*, for example.

> Since the writer has no means of evading himself, we would that he directly embraced his own times; it is his unique opportunity (*sa chance unique*), one that is made for him as he is made for it. One regrets Balzac's indifference before the days of '48, Flaubert's fearful lack of comprehension in the face of the Commune; one is regretful *for them:* there is something there that they have missed forever. We want to miss nothing of our time: perhaps there are more beautiful times, but [this one] is

[86]*Ibid.*, p. 640 (555).

ours; we have only *this* life to live, in the middle of *this* war, or perhaps *this* revolution.[87]

The discussion of our total responsibility ends with a conclusion in which Sartre very clearly brings out the connections between the many parts of his system, and which also calls to mind a parallel aspect of Heidegger's philosophy, his theory of uncovering and of *angst* (cf. pages 205 ff., above).

> The one who realizes in anguish his condition as *being* thrown into a responsibility which extends to his very abandonment has no longer either remorse or regret or excuse; he is no longer anything but a freedom which perfectly reveals itself and whose being resides in this very revelation. But as we pointed out at the beginning of this work, most of the time we flee anguish in bad faith.[88]

What if we manage to refrain from flight? Can we then "live" the freedom that we "are"? Can a practical morality emerge for one who manages to seek freedom for freedom's sake? Sartre suggests, in conclusion, that this and other questions fall outside the framework of his essay in phenomenological ontology, and he says he will devote a future work to them. Thus he lets *Being and Nothingness* refer beyond itself as if the very negativeness of the portrayal has prevented him from arriving at anything positive. And indeed, the wealth, vividness, and penetration of Sartre's observations of and on the unfreedom, anonymity, self-deception, and god-forsakenness of what he takes to be normal life have made it out of place to offer even so much as a tentative "Yes, but so what?"

Man's desire to be

"Man is the desire to be."[89] There is something which man

[87]*Situations* (Paris: Gallimard, 1948), II, 12-13.
[88]*EN*, p. 642 (556).
[89]*Ibid.*, p. 652 (565).

lacks and his lack of which constitutes, or makes intelligible, this fundamental desire of his. "The for-itself is the being which is to itself its own lack of being."[90]

This much we are told, then, of the *original choice*—the project which gives the direction for a person's whole life insofar as it is conscious and consists of standpoints, evaluations, acts: it is the project *to be*. Since the point is one that almost inevitably invites misunderstanding, we shall elaborate a little.

We are told that a man sets himself the original project as something temporarily prior to (not just as epistemologically *a priori*) the particular empirical wishes, needs, feelings, and so on. The desire to be exists and manifests itself only in and through jealousy, greed, love of art, cowardice, courage, that is, in everything that can set its stamp on a man, and can only set its stamp on particular men in particular situations.

However, every for-itself is always *existing* in its own (quite peculiar) way. Whatever this general lack may be, therefore, it cannot be characterized as an altogether general lack of being, in all the senses of the word; it must be some general lack of a definite kind of being: namely, of *being-in-itself*. As mentioned earlier, in every for-itself there is imbedded a desire to be a for-itself-in-itself (*pour-soi-en-soi*), that is, an essence-in-itself (*être-en-soi*), an in-itself-for-itself (*en-soi-pour-soi*). This, then, is a desire to attain to an *ideal*, to a consciousness which would provide the foundation of its own being-in-itself, by means of its pure consciousness of itself. "It is this ideal which can be called God."[91]

Sartre's justification for employing a term with such a long and distinctive history may be that in his view men have in fact often intended such an ideal, however much the properties and functions they have attributed to their gods seem at first glance essentially to differ from those of a consciousness that constitutes its own being.

[90]*Ibid.*, p. 652 (565).
[91]*Ibid.*, p. 653 (566).

But at least Sartre's concept of God is not altogether divorced from the tradition, for his thought here is not so very remote from that of Spinoza. For Spinoza, God is being-in-itself, that is something that both exists and is to be understood through itself and nothing else; and God can also be said to have ideas—all true ideas "are in God."

The being of man is desire, and this desire can only be satisfied by an increasing approximation to God, that is, by man's unfolding himself in such a way that his action can come to be understood in terms of himself and hence of God. Then man approaches precisely that form of being in which he is pure consciousness (of ideas) and yet also has being-in-itself.

For Sartre, God "represents the permanent limit in terms of which man makes known to himself what he is. To be man means to reach toward being God. Or if you prefer, man fundamentally is the desire to be God."[92]

But this, for Sartre, in no way diminishes man's freedom. It is true that man cannot do otherwise than want to be God, but that is a matter of definition, of what it is to be a man. Man cannot as such choose not to be man. Moreover, divine being is the ultimate meaning of his *wanting*, not the actual content of his particular wishes. Man's wishes have to do with choices in concrete situations, and in these there are in principle no limits to our freedom of choice.

What then has a phenomenological ontology given to man?

[Ontology] has merely enabled us to determine the ultimate ends of human reality, its fundamental possibilities, and the value which haunts it. Each human reality is at the same time a direct project to metamorphose its own For-itself into an In-itself-For-itself and a project of the appropriation of the world as a totality of being-in-itself, in the form of a fundamental quality. Every human reality is a passion in that it projects losing itself so as to

[92]*Ibid.*, pp. 653-54 (566).

found being and by the same stroke to constitute the In-
itself which escapes contingency by being its own foundation, the *Ens causa sui*, which religions call God. Thus
the passion of man is the reverse of that of Christ, for
man loses himself as man in order that God may be born.
But the idea of God is contradictory and we lose ourselves in vain. Man is a useless passion.[93]

With these words Sartre concludes the last part of his
work.

"La Nausée"

Sartre published his first novel, *La Nausée*, five years before
L'Etre et le néant. It should not be regarded as a psychological
and artistic amplification of the philosophy of the main
work.[94] Much misunderstanding of existentialism as a philosophical position is due to Sartre's literary works being taken
as philosophical source books without reference to the content of the main work.

Now that we have examined some of the essential topics in
the latter work we are in a better position to place *La Nausée*
in relation to Sartre's philosophy. The novel can perhaps be
seen to provide illustrations of a number of philosophical
points in *Being and Nothingness*, among them the following
five:

(1) Freedom is not disengagement, non-involvement, or
freedom from restrictions. Freedom leads to dejection
(Sartre, as we noted earlier, originally entitled the work

---

[93]*Ibid.*, p. 708 (615).

[94]According to Hazel E. Barnes in the introduction to her translation
of *L'Etre et le néant*, "one might truthfully say that the only full
exposition of *La Nausée*'s meaning would be the total volume of *Being
and Nothingness*" (p. xvi). But it would perhaps be more apt to say
that there was a certain disillusioned "attitude to life among the
between-wars intellectuals which Sartre gives us an extreme analysis
of." Hans Aaraas, "Jean Paul Sartre," *Vestens tenkere* (Oslo: Asche-
houg, 1962), III, 290.

Melancholia). Roquentin is free from restriction, without work or family. He can go where he wants, all "possibilities" are open; but he is not involved, he is uncommitted, his actions are arbitrary, "actes gratuits" in Gide's sense.

(2) In the uncommitted, entirely disinterested state, when disgust is at a maximum, there occur the psychological conditions for seeing things with their relationships to man at a minimum, without their aims, functions, shapes, and so on. They are seen then as what they "are in themselves," a limiting concept which, however, has only a remote resemblance to Kant's thing-in-itself. Nor are they to be confused with the "in-itself" in *Being and Nothingness*, where it is said that phenomena (with their human references) have being-in-themselves.

(3) In themselves, then, things seem not only *de trop*, superfluous, but swollen, soft, or slimy, bloated, dull, amorphous, naked, inert. Man, too, seems to be equally superfluous. Roquentin appears to himself "flabby, torpid, full of half-digested food." The whole world becomes a swollen, soft, bloated being, lacking any reason for its existence—it becomes the *nauseating* and *absurd*. This nausea, it will be noted, is not the same as the anguish spoken of in the main work.

(4) The world in itself, or rather, as looked at by one who flees from his for-itself, lacks necessity, purpose, value. Everything is contingent, accidental, haphazard. "My tongue may turn into a centipede," a realization that plunges one into a "horrible ecstasy."[95]

---

[95]This (point 4), Maurice Cranston thinks betrays Sartre's special philosophical and religious background *(Sartre,* pp. 16-17). "Some people may well find themselves wondering here: just what is all this fuss about? After all, Roquentin's dramatic discovery that the world is contingent is one that could have been made by any reader of David Hume in the eighteenth century or after. . . . the laws of science—or of nature—are not iron laws. The future is not bound to be like the past. . . . there is no necessary link between causes and effects. . . . In all this, one may feel, there is no cause for excitement even, let alone

It seems that a number of commentators have misinterpreted Sartre's concept of a world-in-itself as a form of 'thing in itself' concept. Accordingly they take Sartre's account of the world-in-itself to be intended as a description of the world as it *really* is. But for Sartre descriptions from uncommitment have no greater cognitive weight than descriptions from commitment.

When things finally smile, "mean" something, Roquentin does not reject this meaning—the text in *La Nausée* gives no hint of such a rejection.

Even if Roquentin could be said to reject meaningfulness "in and behind" things, it is difficult to infer from this any conclusion about Sartre's own views. The theory of the phenomenon aims to show how meaningfulness is something that belongs to phenomena and thereby to things, and that a "thing-in-itself" cannot be found. The "meaninglessness" of things for the uncommitted person is, phenomenologically, a kind of meaningfulness, and Sartre's atheism is, philosophically, more a phenomenological absolutism than a denial of meaning in things.

(5) As something in itself, the world is there for man to do what he will with it: man is free to create his own life, his norms, his possessions, to pick and choose, to become involved. In exchange, he is responsible for all of this, guilty of what he makes of it and of himself. Roquentin sees a possibility in writing a novel. Yet his rather commonplace reflections about this resemble more an anxious patient's hopes about some new possibilities of therapy than man's experiences in the—almost divine—creative choice of himself and his life hinted at in *Being and Nothingness*.

Much of the confusion about Sartre's existentialism can be

'horrible ecstasy'. . . . And yet to raise this objection is perhaps to speak too hastily in the language of common sense, or empiricism, or of the Enlightenment. The language and the spirit of existentialism belong to another, and altogether more emotional order, to Romanticism, and indeed, historically, to religion."

traced to the use of the word "existence" in *La Nausée*.[96] By interpreting the word as a synonym of "in-itself" one attributes to Sartre a depressing view of the world, to say the least. Philosophically it is more reasonable, however, to interpret it in the direction of man's *existence when he flees from his freedom*. The terms "existence" and "existing things" in *La Nausée* express more of a limiting concept, things in themselves, *experienced in a distinctive state*, a state of uncommitment. The root of the chestnut tree which for Roquentin (before he suspects the possibility of salvation) is dissolved in a shapeless, meaningless mass, is as a phenomenon a succession of appearances whose synthetic unity constitutes the thing, a collection of appearances *for*. But a man can, like Roquentin, flee from the for-relation, and even if the flight cannot succeed, it has far-reaching effects on how the fleeing person experiences the world.

Sartre's vindication of existentialism

"L'Existentialisme est un humanisme": the character of the work

The most familiar and widely read of Sartre's works is the lecture, *L'Existentialisme est un humanisme* ("Existentialism is

[96]Cranston (*ibid.*, p. 111) comments impressively on Sartre's "religious sensibility," but does him an injustice by going on to identify Sartre's feeling for outside nature with Roquentin's experiences of it. "It is a religious sensibility which shrinks from the external world, and perceives it, as Sartre does, as entirely viscous, sticky, messy, sweetish, nauseating. The humanistic sensibility rejoices in nature; but Sartre sees natural objects as "vague," "soft," "flabby," "creamy," "thick," "tepid," "dull," "sickly," and "obscene." It is true that according to *Being and Nothingness* outside objects have the kind of being he calls in-itself—everything has it, except consciousness, but it is surely unwise to identify the in-itself with Roquentin's "l'existence"; and even if it was wise, one could conclude little from this about Sartre's own feeling for outside nature. On this topic one can consult Simone de Beauvoir's diary notes which record their many expeditions together in walking-boots with packs on their backs. (Cf. Cranston, *Sartre*, p. 12.)

a Humanism")[97], published in 1946. Those who delight in philosophy as the intellectually clear expression of total views must, not without a certain regret, acknowledge that the philosophy of *Being and Nothingness* is not continuously developed in its author's later theoretical writings. The 1946 lecture does not elaborate on the earlier work, nor is it any kind of abridged or popularized version. It is, according to its express purpose, a defense of existentialism aimed at a wide public for whom "existentialism" during the later years of the war had become a household word, for some of praise, for others of condemnation. The essay is a passionate "witness" as its language reveals.

Its definitions do not define so much as coerce and cajole: ". . . existentialism, in our sense of the word, is a doctrine that [renders] human life possible; a doctrine, also, which affirms that every truth and every action imply both an environment and a human subjectivity."[98] Ambiguities and complications are not discussed; the whole of existentialism appears as terribly simple—a matter of anguish and abandonment.

> As you will soon see, it is very simple. First, what do we mean by anguish. The existentialist frankly states that man is anguish *(l'homme est angoisse)*. His meaning is as follows—When a man commits himself to anything, fully realizing that he is not only choosing what he will be, but is thereby at the same time a legislator deciding for the whole of mankind—in such a moment a man cannot escape from the sense of complete and profound responsibility. There are many, indeed, who show no such anxiety. But we affirm that they are merely disguising their anguish or are in flight from it. . . . But in truth, one

---

[97]*L'Existentialisme est un humanisme*, henceforth referred to as *EH*. See note 29 above for details and translations. Page references to Mairet's translation in Kaufmann, *Existentialism from Dostoevsky to Sartre*, are given in parentheses. When the English translation has been slightly altered, the reference is italicized.
[98]*EH*, p. 12 (*288*).

ought always to ask oneself what would happen if everyone did as one is doing; nor can one escape from that
disturbing thought except by a kind of self-deception.[99]

In *Being and Nothingness* the being-terminology is based
upon technical philosophical usage; in the lecture, without
reference to the doctrines of phenomenon and consciousness,
the expression "man is anguish" is philosophically extremely
indefinite. And where in the investigation has the normative
element come in? From the first principles or in the course of
some anti-Humean argumentation? On the basis of *Being and
Nothingness* we can safely answer that Sartre takes the
normative to come in right from the start; it is based on a
phenomenological analysis of consciousness. With every genuine choice a value is constituted, and thereby also the normative. On the other hand, *Being and Nothingness* offers no
further account of how a choice which I make can be pre-
scriptive in respect of *another* person's actions.

In a discussion with Naville (published as an appendix to
the lecture), Sartre provides another—again only apparently
simple—explanation of what anguish "is":

> In fact, anguish is, in my view, the total absence of justifi-
> cation [in one's choice] together with responsibility in
> respect of everything.[100]

The anguish in question is not one that only philosophers can
have:

> It is anguish pure and simple, of the kind well known to
> all those who have borne responsibilities. When, for in-
> stance, a military leader takes upon himself the responsi-
> bility for an attack . . . he chooses to do it and at bottom
> he alone chooses. No doubt he acts under a higher com-
> mand, but its orders, which are more general, require

[99]*Ibid.*, pp. 27-28 (*292*). Mairet has "man is in anguish."
[100]*Ibid.*, p. 100.

interpretation by him and upon that interpretation depends the life of ten, fourteen or twenty men. In making the decision, he cannot but feel a certain anguish.[101]

God's absence

Sartre's system is atheistic; not only does a personal God have no place in it, but even the more or less philosophical gods, like Spinoza's Substance, are deliberately excluded. And yet, as we noted, many of the *functions* attributed to gods and divine agencies in non-atheistic systems are retained; it is as though Sartre dismissed all thoughts of gods yet wanted to assign their functions to something else. Since he undertakes no criticism of these functions, perhaps "atheistic" is, after all, hardly the best designation. Sartre's system, like Heidegger's, is *modeled* on systems which include divine entities, with substantial, autonomous being.

It has often been alleged that Sartre is deeply engaged morally and religiously, that God's *absence* is a terrible problem for him. It is tempting to quote one of the characters in his play *Le Diable et le bon Dieu (The Devil and the Good Lord)* which seems to express an awesome absence. (We recall the awesome expression of a more modest absence in the case of Pierre and the café.)

> I demanded a sign, I sent messages to Heaven, no reply. Heaven ignored my very name. Each minute I wondered what I could *be* in the eyes of God. Now I know the answer: nothing. God does not see me, God does not hear me, God does not know me. You see this emptiness over our heads? That is God. You see this gap in the door? It is God. You see that hole in the ground? That is God again. Silence is God. Absence is God. God is the loneliness of man. There was no one but myself; I alone decided on Evil; and I alone invented Good. It was I who cheated,

---

[101]*Ibid.*, p. 32 (293-94).

I who worked miracles, I who accused myself today, I alone who can absolve myself; I, man. If God exists, man is nothing. . . .[102]

In "Existentialism is a Humanism" the spotlight is turned not only on anguish, but also on abandonment, Heidegger's *Verlassenheit*.

And when we speak of "abandonment" . . . we only mean to say that God does not exist, and that it is necessary to draw the consequences of his absence right to the end. The existentialist is strongly opposed to a certain type of secular moralism which seeks to suppress God at the least possible expense. . . . [It] is, I believe, the purport of all that we in France call radicalism [that] nothing will be changed if God does not exist; we shall rediscover the same norms of honesty, progress and humanity. . . . The existentialist, on the contrary, finds it extremely awkward [*gênant*] that God does not exist, for there disappears with Him all possibility of finding values in an intelligible heaven. There can no longer be any good *a priori*, since there is no infinite and perfect consciousness to think it. It is nowhere written that "the good" exists, that one must be honest or must not lie, since we are now upon the plane where there are only men. Dostoevsky once wrote "If God did not exist, everything would be permitted"; and that, for existentialism, is the starting point.[103]

In *Being and Nothingness* we find premises from which we may conclude that the possibility of something good *a priori* and of a world of values disappears once God, or more

[102]*Le Diable et le bon Dieu* (Paris: Gallimard, 1951). English translation by Kitty Black, *Lucifer and the Lord* (London: Hamish Hamilton, 1953); American title, *The Devil and the Good Lord* (New York: Alfred A. Knopf, 1960).

[103]*EH*, pp. 33-36 (*294-95*). Mairet translates "gênant" by "embarrassing."

generally, something substantial, does not exist. The theory of the phenomenon provides the necessary basis. Nothing exists substantially; consequently nothing has value.

Here the theory counters the view that it is an objective fact, for example, that man should be honest and not lie. If, like Nietzsche, one has seen through "the illusion of worlds to come" the question arises: must there be something that can take over the function which the illusion fulfilled? Sartre answers here, as did Nietzsche, in the affirmative: "if I have excluded God the Father, there must be somebody to invent values."[104]

But is it not a little forced to talk of the *inventing* of values? No! For "to say that we invent values means neither more nor less than this; that there is no sense in life *a priori*."[105] The implication here is that meaning is given to life and that a thing is given value by the individual *a posteriori*, by his acts of choice in concrete situations. He who chooses can be said to "invent values."

If there was a God who created man and gave him a specific nature, he would also have created a specific scale of values for man. Man's essence would then precede his existence. The relation between essence and existence would be as in the manufacture of paper knives. First one draws a picture of the knife and determines how it is to be made. In such a case the aim is clarified beforehand: in short, the knife's essence precedes its existence. Here the slogan "Essence precedes existence" acquires a straightforward meaning on the analogy of plans preceding products.[106]

---

[104]*Ibid.*, p. 89 (309).

[105]*Ibid.*, p. 89 (309).

[106]See *ibid.*, pp. 17-19 (289-90). But is this straightforward meaning adequate philosophically? Can it be used to clarify what is implied by "existentialism" when it is said to affirm that existence precedes essence? Surely not. That essence is no kind of schema or plan that precedes existence may be readily admitted, but we are not told what it is instead. Is existence to be understood by the analogy of a knife whose manufacture was not in accordance with a predetermined plan,

The existentialist, according to Sartre, finds much to regret in God's non-existence. For if God did exist, then it would be possible to *find* values in an intelligible heaven. Accordingly, it would be a positive achievement according to Sartre if one *found*, say, the value "sincerity" in such a heaven. However, it is hard to see just how such a discovery would adapt itself to phenomenological description and how it would compete with any sincerity-consciousness which may already have constituted itself in the lucky finder. Later on in "Existentialism is a Humanism" Sartre's words suggest that the difficulties which God's existence would spare him are not among the most critical that face him: "Even if God existed that would make no difference."[107] Man's problems lie elsewhere: not in finding God, but in finding himself.

The individual's responsibility—choosing for all mankind

Sartre endorses the statement that "everything is permitted," but according to his philosophy of freedom he cannot adopt the most reasonable interpretation of the expression—namely, that everything is permitted *from an ethical point of view.* For in order to perform even a single action with moral relevance there must be a choice. Before the choice is made it is neither the case that anything is permitted, ethically, nor that it is not permitted: the category of the ethical is simply not yet constituted.

In Sartre's view, choice implies an ontological and phenomenologically founded responsibility to all mankind and an anguish consequent upon this.[108] The responsibility is present for a man in whatever state he imagines himself.

---

a product without a blueprint, something that manufactures itself, or chooses itself as a knife just as it becomes a knife—or what? On this point, as with most others, the popularizations in *EH* confuse rather than clarify.

[107]*Ibid.*, p. 95 (311).

[108]Although Sartre himself does not say so, a consequence seems to be that responsibility for a man's death implies greater anguish than

Far from excusing passions and actions brought about by passion, the existentialist believes that man is responsible for absolutely all his actions and for the passions as well. In his actions man chooses himself ("this is what I want to be"), and even if there are factors which man cannot change, his attitude to those factors, his approval or disapproval, is something that is in his power. Man cannot excuse himself; even if the passions can make man a slave in an external sense, this need not affect his view of this fact, his attitude toward it.

To understand the main function or aim of Sartre's anti-essentialism it is perhaps right to stress the ethical rather than the ontological aspect. In making his choice an individual creates his norms, and a genuine choice of a pattern of action occurs in the performance of actions (insofar as the action is physically possible). If one is called to account, therefore, only one's actions are taken into the reckoning. Here we see Sartre's opposition to those ethical and psychological positions which appear to undermine the authority of an activistic morality of this kind. Such positions seek to soften the judgment by allowing the person to be characterized by properties independent of his actions, even of everything he says or does at all.

Sartre counters such views with his "anti-essentialism": man has no essence to draw on as a source of excuses for what he has done or not done. Sartre's theory of the phenomenon may indeed be mainly aimed at laying bare men's false excuses, and at proclaiming the extent of their responsibility as far greater than it is usually supposed. This is also one of the themes in the play *Huis clos*. The main character, Garcin, tries to make excuses for being a cowardly deserter;

---

responsibility for rescuing him from death (even if he wants to die). It seems after all, then, that he does assume a yardstick according to which to contribute to a man's death is more serious than, say, to ruffle his hair, and to contribute to *saving* a man from death cannot weigh heavily on one or increase one's anguish. The ontological phenomenological foundation for degrees of anguish is not made clear.

life gave him no opportunity to show the courage which was always really his. Sartre ridicules any such "essentialism" in the service of bad faith.[109]

Just how, then, do values arise? What Sartre says suggests that the fact that something acquires value for a particular person in a particular situation cannot be divorced from the fact that this something is chosen by that person in that situation. "To choose between this or that is at the same time to affirm the value of that which is chosen."[110] Thus it is analytically true that we always choose the good and reject the evil.

[109]Essentialism and anti-essentialism were natural topics of ethical discussion in occupied countries during the war. Then the tendency was toward anti-essentialism. A person was stamped as a hero, crook, traitor, patriot, etc., without much respect for the context, the man's former actions and life, etc. Since the war the tendency has perhaps gone in the opposite direction. Possibly Sartre's plays from the occupation period should be seen against the background of the actual discussions in France at that time.

[110]EH, p. 25 (291-92). Given certain reasonable additional premises, the next sentence can be derived from the one quoted. Sartre seems by his "for" to draw conclusions in the opposite way. The quoted sentence continues: "for we are unable ever to choose the worse. What we choose is always the better." Sartre here comes very close to Protagoras. The criticism this became subject to on the part of Plato and later philosophers again becomes relevant. The quoted sentence nevertheless concludes with "and nothing can be better for us unless it is better for all." If Peter chooses monogamy and rejects polygamy, monogamy is good for him. If it is good for him, it is good for everyone, consequently also for Paul. If Paul chooses polygamy and rejects monogamy, polygamy is good for him. Monogamy and polygamy then acquire both properties for Peter and for Paul. It would lead us too far afield to attempt an interpretation of Sartre that would avoid such a conclusion. One possibility, however, is to let Peter's and Paul's choices be bound by definition to their respective life situations. Then the value statements will also be bound to the situations. And because the situations differ, there will be no inconsistency between Peter's and Paul's choices. There are, however, at least two objections to such an interpretation: Sartre's own examples (e.g., a choice of monogamy) suggest that the choice is not relative to situations in such a way that two persons cannot be (or that it is exceedingly unlikely that they should be) in the same situation. Secondly, the appeal to responsibility will be reduced: if I can assume that my choice situations are specific to me, or that it is

Man cannot *excuse* himself through being determined by his past, his surroundings, his inheritance, his passions. Sartre stresses this less encouraging aspect of his indeterminism. He says less about its encouraging side: that man has it in himself to hold everything at a distance and to determine new choices, make "new projects," or "a clean new start." Nothing is so terrible that it can bind one's future, that one's past can brand or stamp one permanently. It is no accident that Sartre mentions Descartes *and* the Stoics when referring to the background of his concept of freedom.

Sartre's lecture can be interpreted unphilosophically as a gospel. It is in the nature of man, of his consciousness, to be, in the last instance, "outside" everything that has ever happened to him, all his past, all his affiliations and associations with other men, and his personal achievements.[111] Man's free-

---

exceedingly unlikely that another person will enter into the same situation, the choice as a choice "for all mankind" becomes theoretical and blurred.

The difficult, general pronouncements on pp. 25-26 (291-92) in *EH* can be interpreted in another way if stress is laid on the examples given on pp. 26-27 (292-93). Seen in this context the formulation "nothing can be better for us [me?] unless it is better for all" (p. 25 [292]) is to be interpreted: Nothing can be good for me unless at the same time I *postulate* it as (existing) value for all.

[111]In the face of all eventualities affecting the person, especially in the case of accident, pain, financial ruin, etc., one can distinguish between two basic attitudes, one consisting in "not letting oneself be put out, imposed upon, got the better of," etc., and the other in "giving up," "going to pieces," "losing one's grip," "no longer being oneself," and so on. In especially distressing circumstances, such as loss of one's nearest, complete financial ruin, torture, chronic disability and sickness, impossible family or sexual relationships, a collapse is to be expected. It is abnormal, perhaps even a little unpleasant or offensive, if there isn't at least some temporary breakdown when one suffers a mental or bodily catastrophe. The urge to "become as a child" is in place here. One may think, for example, of the children playing among the ruins of Berlin in 1945, hungry and homeless, but reacting little to the despair and suffering of their, in many cases, bereaved, parents, although of course the children did not set themselves "outside" this suffering or the circumstances that occasioned it; they were simply not affected by the circumstances in the same way.

dom implies that in the last instance he can free himself from all this and project himself into new situations with new ties, aims, and norms, if necessary, or with a total disregard of the external situation in all its catastrophic state. There is no need, however, for the cultivation of insensitivity; the overcoming of the external situation does not necessarily imply that one is "remote" in the everyday or psychological sense. Ontological remoteness, being-for-itself with its threefold ekstasis, is enough.

Many conclude from the fact that, according to "existentialism," there are no norms which, antecedent to man's action and choices, can stipulate which of them are right or wrong, that therefore man must act arbitrarily, contingently, capriciously, haphazardly. No, says Sartre, the one does not follow from the other; and he invites us to compare this with how men judge the artist and his work. There is no aesthetic moral to be found, and

> . . . does anyone reproach an artist, when he paints a picture, for not following rules established *a priori*? Does one ever ask what is the picture that he ought to paint? As everyone knows, there is no pre-defined picture for him to make: the artist applies himself to the composition of a picture, and the picture that ought to be made is precisely that which he will have made. . . . there are values which will appear in due course in the coherence of the picture, in the relation between the will to create and the finished work. No one can tell what the painting of tomorrow will be like; one cannot judge a painting until it is done. What has that to do with morality? We are in the same creative situation. We never speak of a work of art as irresponsible. . . . There is this in common between art and morality, that in both we have to do with creation and invention. We cannot decide *a priori* what it is that should be done.[112]

[112]*EH*, pp. 76-77 (305-6).

One may reasonably object that insofar as anything is called a creation and a discovery, it is contrasted with many other things that are made but do not involve creation and discovery. Sartre has norms for what *can* be art and what *can* be morally right, but it seems that ultimately the conditions which must obtain for positive decisions are not themselves of an aesthetic or moral kind. In *Being and Nothingness* there is an attempt to show phenomenologically that man cannot, as such, escape his "freedom," thus not consciously choose or reject it.

All sincere choices have the same value

There is something that men are "condemned" to want to realize. Here Sartre comes very close to giving what is traditionally referred to as a description of man's nature, of man's essence "prior to his existence," and also of categorical, *a priori*, even if "formal," values and norms. Sincerity, consistency, "to want altogether and not piecemeal and partially," "not to evade the issue," suggest something very like an absolute yardstick. From this point of view Sartre appears as an "essentialist," as one who assumes that man has certain properties which are timeless and constitute his essence. Sartre not only ascribes to men an altogether original, specific, *a priori*, inescapable freedom, but postulates norms in terms of which this freedom must be defended and given expression to in humanity. Hence the pronouncements about conscious choice, sincerity, authenticity, about a positive ethical value being attached only to ethical, that is sincere, *action*. Man tries to be like the God who has vanished, but in vain. (Could one really expect otherwise?) Sartre is a pronounced upholder of essentialism, or a pronounced critic of "it," depending on how certain extremely flexible words are interpreted.[113]

---

[113]Sartre touches on this theme in "Présentations des temps modernes," *Situations* (II, 22): "For us, what men have in common is not a nature, it is a metaphysical condition: and through that we under-

Sartre aptly terms his existentialism, "humanism," or "theory of freedom," a "pre-commitment" (*pré-engagement*) —thus still a commitment, yet something more than a doctrine; namely, "a project which is unspecified."[114] But to give the nuances their proper stress let Sartre himself speak:

> . . . whenever a man chooses his purpose and his commitment in all clearness and in all sincerity, whatever that purpose may be, it is impossible for him to prefer another. It is true in the sense that we do not believe in progress. Progress implies amelioration; but man is always the same, facing a situation which is always changing, and choice remains always a choice in the situation. The moral problem has not changed since the time when it was a choice between slavery and anti-slavery—from the time of the war of Secession, for example, until the present moment when one chooses between the M.R.P. [*Mouvement Republicain Populaire*] and the Communists.[115]

How far will Sartre go in acquiescing in actions so long as they are sincerely meant and imply a choice of freedom for freedom's sake? When it comes to murder, torture, and the like, can Sartre have recourse to a safety valve, for doubtful cases, by asking: *Can* the action be genuinely intended, or is the essence of this action such that it implies bad faith? Theo-

---

stand the collection of constraints which limit them *a priori*, the necessity of being born and of dying, of being *finite*, and of existing in the world in the midst of other men." If Sartre is to be termed an "anti-essentialist," the term must be given some special, more or less unusual sense. Moreover, "le néant" and "consciousness," which are introduced as *almost* nothing, in the system gradually acquire quite a number of properties.

The most penetrating criticism of Sartre from a professional philosopher, in this and other connections, is perhaps that of Régis Jolivet in the notes to his study of Sartre's main work: R. Jolivet, *Les Doctrines existentialistes de Kierkegaard à J. P. Sartre* (Abbaye Saint-Wandrille: Éditions de Fontenelle, 1948).

[114] Discussion with Naville, *EH*, p. 107.

[115] *Ibid.*, p. 79 (306-7).

retically, Sartre is free to exclude on psychological phenomenological grounds what he abhors on the basis of his
own morality. There have been attempts, by looking into
Sartre's plays, to arrive at a kind of answer here, but in vain,
it seems to me. It is at least clear, however, from his ethico-
political pronouncements that he is not a supporter of an
ethics of non-violence.

The choices man makes are equivalent (equal in value) so
long as freedom is the aim.[116] "One can choose anything, but
only if it is upon the plane of free commitment."[117] But the
conditions for reaching this level are very rigorous—so rigorous that the result in practice can be a far narrower moral
doctrine than one that assumes the opposite principle: that
two opposed moralities are *never* equivalent.

There are, in other words, limits to the freedom of movement one has as a freedom-seeking man. The limits proceed
from Sartre's own, not arbitrary, "definition" of man's basic
situation. Perhaps this definition implies no value judgments
or judgments about what is *in fact* true and right, but it sets
limits no less effectively for that.

> . . . One can judge, first—and perhaps this is not a
> judgment of value, but it is a logical judgment—that in
> certain cases choice is founded upon an error, and in
> others upon the truth. One can judge a man by saying
> that he deceives himself. Since we have defined the situa-
> tion of man as one of free choice, without excuse and
> without help, any man who takes refuge behind the
> excuse of his passions, or by inventing some deterministic
> doctrine, is a self-deceiver. One may object: "But why
> should he not choose to deceive himself?" I reply that it
> is not for me to judge him morally, but I define his self-
> deception as an error. Here one cannot avoid pronounc-
> ing a judgment of truth. The self-deception is evidently a

[116]See *ibid.*, p. 88 (309).
[117]*Ibid.*, p. 88 (309).

falsehood, because it is a dissimulation of man's complete liberty of commitment . . . [and] the attitude of strict consistency alone is that of good faith.[118]

Sartre concludes his apologia by stressing that his view of man, his existentialism and humanism, provides grounds not for despair, but for optimism.

[Existentialism's] intention is not in the least that of plunging men into despair. And if by despair one means —as the Christians do—any attitude of unbelief, the despair of the existentialists is something different. Existentialism is not atheist in the sense that it would exhaust itself in demonstrations of the non-existence of God. It declares, rather, that even if God existed that would make no difference from its point of view. Not that we believe God does exist, but we think that the real problem is not that of His existence; what man needs is to find himself again and to understand that nothing can save him from himself, not even a valid proof of the existence of God. In this sense existentialism is optimistic. It is a doctrine of action, and it is only by self-deception, by confusing their own despair with ours that Christians can describe us as without hope.[119]

One's own freedom presupposes that of others

Although Sartre concludes his defense by emphasizing that existentialism provides no basis for despair, the lecture's rhetorical highpoint is perhaps the declaration of freedom, one's own and others':

. . . When once a man has seen that values depend upon himself, in that state of forsakenness he can will only one thing, and that is freedom as the foundation of all values.

[118]*Ibid.*, pp. 81-82 (307).
[119]*Ibid.*, p. 95 (310-11).

. . . [That] simply means that the actions of men of good faith have, as their ultimate significance, the quest of freedom itself as such. . . . And in . . . willing freedom, we discover that it depends entirely upon the freedom of others and that the freedom of others depends upon our own . . . but as soon as there is a commitment, I am obliged to will the liberty of others at the same time as my own. I cannot make liberty my aim unless I make that of others equally my aim. . . . Thus, although the content of morality is variable, a certain form of this morality is universal.[120]

If one interprets Sartre's sentences rhetorically (in Aristotle's sense) and so accepts his defense of existentialism as undisguised preaching, the piece must be reckoned an essential aid to interpreting what Sartre's philosophy at the end of the 1940's assumed in practice. It is of course true that the attempt to be philosophically consistent and to build on a small number of basic insights cramps the philosopher's imagination and many-sidedness, and through "Existentialism is a Humanism" we may see a little more clearly where Sartre stands when the flow of his energies is no longer constrained by the iron hand of consistency and systematic rigor.

The systematic works and the apologia. Do they agree with one another?

Even if the sentences in "Existentialism is a Humanism" can be interpreted in many directions, it is doubtful whether its standpoints are compatible with those expressed in *Being and*

[120]*Ibid.*, pp. 82-85 (307-8). It would be no easy matter for Sartre to give this strongly appealing theory of freedom a philosophical form within the frame of phenomenological ontology. But this doesn't mean that nothing at all in the quoted expressions could be salvaged. There is something of Kant in them; indeed Sartre refers to him, though with reservations: "[Kant] thinks that the formal and the universal suffice for the constitution of a morality. We think, on the contrary, that principles that are too abstract break down when we come to the defining action." (*Ibid.*, p. 85 [308]). Sartre mentions exam-

Nothingness. This is true not least of the doctrine that one's freedom presupposes that of others. The relation between the individual for-itself and others, as it is drawn in the main work, allows no basis for such a doctrine. As a whole, the latter work is far more negative in its conclusions. A friend and colleague of Sartre, Francis Jeanson, writes that Sartre is not content with the apologetics in "Existentialism is a Humanism," that it presupposes the development of an existentialist ethics which, far from being put into effect, has not even been shown to be possible. The famous footnote in *Being and Nothingness* (cf. page 328, above) envisages an ethics that, in the event, was never to be realized, and which, according to Jeanson, would imply a transition from the main work's "individualistic" viewpoint to a "collectivistic" one.[121] Jeanson points to a development in Sartre's thought toward a rejection of existentialism as a basis for a philosophical system and toward a more serious preoccupation with Marxism. This interpretation is confirmed by a study of the plan of Sartre's second main work, *Critique de la raison dialectique.* It looks, therefore, as though the 1946 apologia has been left suspended in the air: it can rest on neither of the main works.

An addendum is required to the above account of the relationship between *Being and Nothingness* and the apologia. If the theses of the former work are to be applied to Sartre himself, it is clear that he, too, as for-itself, must come to make his own choice of himself, just as others must, and furthermore that there is no reason why his choice should follow theirs. There is nothing in *Being and Nothingness* that debars a closer specification of norms and an understanding of reality in the direction illustrated by "Existentialism is a Hu-

---

ples from "life" where many details and factors complicate the issue. But it is extremely improbable that Kant actually meant that moral casuistry, i.e., decisions in particular situations, can be derived from abstract principles. There can hardly be more than apparent disagreement on this point between Kant and Sartre.

[121]Francis Jeanson, *Le Problème moral et la pensée de Sartre* (Paris: Myrthe, 1947), p. 13.

manism." In other words, Sartre is, in his own terms, fully entitled to declare that *his* freedom, *his* basic project, implies the freedom of others, and that he doesn't need to ground this choice in the common basis for all kinds of choice which he has presented in *Being and Nothingness*. This would mean a discontinuity in Sartre's total system: at some point or other, we should have to say, he abandons his discussion of man's general condition, the basic condition of all mankind, and goes over to state what look to the outsider like a set of postulates, but which are really the expressions of his own personal norms and projects. It would be unreasonable, of course, for these to be expressed in the "choice" terminology.

We are brought back once again to the question of whether Sartre has a philosophical system. Is Sartre in any strict sense a philosophical systematizer? In fact, can he be said to be at home in the field of professional philosophy at all? Or even in philosophy in a wider sense?

The philosophers of whom it can be most justifiably said, and in the best sense, that they *have* a system are those who, in one or more works, provide a rounded-off, systematic, logically worked-out presentation of their views on all essential philosophical questions. Perhaps the philosopher who especially qualifies is the one who builds up his system in pyramid form: starting out with a set of principles—basic statements and norms—from which the rest are derived by methods which are duly explained. We can think here of Hobbes and Spinoza, or Descartes and Hegel, or Kant and Bentham, or back to Aristotle and Epicurus. With all of these the system is very largely and in a certain sense all-embracing. Underlying the explicit principles there seem to be ways of grasping "God, the world, man, and his (mis)fortunes" (Spinoza's title on the first edition of the *Ethics*). In order to make good their claim to be basic and original these ways of grasping must also have the character of being intuitive, even visionary.

Sartre undoubtedly attempts a pyramidal structure in his

main work. The theory of the phenomenon and the basic statements about the for-itself provide the principles: from these he tries to derive the remainder, except, of course, for the illustrations and empirical applications—the main example of the latter being existential psychoanalysis.

In one important respect Sartre certainly exhibits the system-maker's style to a quite remarkable degree: the words that occur in the formulation of the principles are used in the most extensive way possible in the theses presented. The frequency with which *être* and other grammatical forms of this verb occur is overwhelming, and the same applies to the *néant* terminology based on the principles of his theory of consciousness. Furthermore, underlying the deliberate, solid, and tightly constructed system one seems to detect intense visions or intuitions precisely of "God, the world, man, and his *mis*fortunes." So that even if the work does boil over with imaginative examples, and important points are conveyed in so many different ways, some more literary than philosophical, and despite the fact that the tenor, even in the most abstract sections, is persuasive and declamatory, the main impression of a philosophical systematizer at work remains.

If there are doubts and reservations, these must relate to the content rather than the style, the failure of the formulation of the principles to provoke in the reader confirmatory intuitions, and the apparent arbitrariness or unverifiability of many of the derivations, due in the main to the use of terms of vague or dubious content. With regard to the nihilation terminology, for example, there is no reason to object to it so long as it is used in phenomenological descriptions in Sartre's attempts to convey what he "sees"; on the contrary, some exceptionally rich material of undoubted philosophical relevance is here brought to light. It is when the terms are given parts to play in the system, in theses and definitions, that difficulties of principle are introduced. Finally, there must be considerable doubt about the tenability of some parts of the system, for instance the general theses concerning the basic attitudes between persons (not only between abstract consciousnesses).[122] Much of what Sartre says about love, hate, and community has a strongly subjective stamp—in the sense that it bears indelibly the mark of one man's experience of the world.

Sartre's vindication of existentialism ends, as we mentioned earlier, by stressing that existentialism takes its point of departure in an original despair, but that the despair is conquered when man finds his role as the author of values. Here the connection with the main work is clear: there are values, but man is the being, the only being, through which they can exist. Before men realize this, their "being-determined" attempts to create a synthesis of for-itself and in-itself are marked by self-deception and can only result in the nihilistic view that all actions are of equal value. When Sartre's second main work is completed, it may be possible to say with more justification whether he has managed to show a way out of self-deception and despair, and not simply assured us that there is one.[123]

---

[122]I have only resisted the strong temptation to insert "it seems to me" in this paragraph because I would have had to have done so in every other sentence.

[123]Since the above was written, Sartre has published an autobiographical work, *Les Mots* (Paris: Gallimard, 1964); English translation by Bernard Frechtman, *The Words* (New York: George Braziller, Inc., 1964). For anyone interested in Sartre the man, the book contains much new material. Philosophically, however, there is little or nothing new. The work does advance—one might say—a hypothesis about the genesis of certain points of view ("my grandfather had brought me up in the retrospective illusion," etc.), but no arguments for or against the view. Sartre writes that for almost ten years he has been a man who "wakes, recovered from a long, bitter-sweet madness, a man who does not turn back to and recall his old ways without laughing . . ." (p. 211). If an Aristotle, Hobbes, or Spinoza had expressed such a judgment on their earlier work, one would perhaps have been more eager to tackle the question of what intuitions and arguments could have contributed to such a change of view. Jean-Paul Sartre's violent reactions, his artistic bent, his restlessness with regard to himself, may well have brought about a change of position without his having given it philosophical expression.

Index

Index

362

1970